Frontiers in Sociology and Social Research

Volume 4

Frontiers of Sociology and Sociological Research is a cutting-edge social science book series focusing on new directions in sociological and broader social science research. These new directions could be novel theoretical paradigms, innovative methodologies, and/or substantive findings that exemplify and anticipate trends in subfields. The series is predicated on the observation that any field of knowledge in contemporary times is a dynamic rapidly changing body of perspectives and understanding that continuously builds upon the foundation of extant scholarship. The series encourages manuscript submissions from both new and established scholars of sociology, anthropology, social policy, and other allied disciplines.

More information about this series at http://www.springer.com/series/8690

Philip S. Brenner
Editor

Understanding Survey Methodology

Sociological Theory and Applications

 Springer

Editor
Philip S. Brenner
Department of Sociology
University of Massachusetts Boston
Boston, MA, USA

ISSN 2523-3424   ISSN 2523-3432 (electronic)
Frontiers in Sociology and Social Research
ISBN 978-3-030-47255-9   ISBN 978-3-030-47256-6 (eBook)
https://doi.org/10.1007/978-3-030-47256-6

© Springer Nature Switzerland AG 2020, corrected publication 2021
This work is subject to copyright. All rights are reserved by the Publisher, whether the whole or part of the material is concerned, specifically the rights of translation, reprinting, reuse of illustrations, recitation, broadcasting, reproduction on microfilms or in any other physical way, and transmission or information storage and retrieval, electronic adaptation, computer software, or by similar or dissimilar methodology now known or hereafter developed.
The use of general descriptive names, registered names, trademarks, service marks, etc. in this publication does not imply, even in the absence of a specific statement, that such names are exempt from the relevant protective laws and regulations and therefore free for general use.
The publisher, the authors, and the editors are safe to assume that the advice and information in this book are believed to be true and accurate at the date of publication. Neither the publisher nor the authors or the editors give a warranty, expressed or implied, with respect to the material contained herein or for any errors or omissions that may have been made. The publisher remains neutral with regard to jurisdictional claims in published maps and institutional affiliations.

This Springer imprint is published by the registered company Springer Nature Switzerland AG.
The registered company address is: Gewerbestrasse 11, 6330 Cham, Switzerland

For John, Mentor and Friend

Contents

1 **Why Survey Methodology Needs Sociology and Why Sociology Needs Survey Methodology**.............................. 1
Philip S. Brenner

Part I Sociological Theory and Survey Methodology

2 **Towards Survey Response Rate Theories That No Longer Pass Each Other Like Strangers in the Night**.................... 15
Don A. Dillman

3 **Advancing Theories of Socially Desirable Responding: How Identity Processes Influence Answers to "Sensitive Questions"**.... 45
Philip S. Brenner

4 **Culture and Response Behavior: An Overview of Cultural Mechanisms Explaining Survey Error**...................... 67
Henning Silber and Timothy P. Johnson

5 **Translating Lessons from Status Characteristics and Expectation States Theory to Survey Methods**......................... 87
Bianca Manago

Part II Applications

6 **Stigma and the Meaning of Social Desirability: Concealed Islamophobia in the Netherlands**......................... 115
Mathew J. Creighton

7 **Is Not Knowing the Same as Being Incorrect? An Examination of 'Don't Know' Responses to Questions about Immigrant Population Size**... 143
Daniel Herda

8	Power, Culture and Item Nonresponse in Social Surveys	169
	Katharina M. Meitinger and Timothy P. Johnson	
9	The Measurement of Sexual Attraction and Gender Expression: Cognitive Interviews with Queer Women	193
	Dana Garbarski and Dana LaVergne	
10	How Do Interviewers and Respondents Navigate Sexual Identity Questions in a CATI Survey?	219
	Jerry Timbrook, Jolene D. Smyth, and Kristen Olson	
11	Male/Female Is Not Enough: Adding Measures of Masculinity and Femininity to General Population Surveys	247
	Jolene D. Smyth and Kristen Olson	
12	Correlates of Differences in Interactional Patterns among Black and White Respondents	277
	Jennifer Dykema, Dana Garbarski, Nora Cate Schaeffer, Isabel Anadon, and Dorothy Farrar Edwards	
13	Theories of Public Opinion Change Versus Stability and their Implications for Null Findings	305
	Kevin H. Wozniak, Kevin M. Drakulich, and Brian R. Calfano	
14	Conclusions and Future Directions for Understanding Survey Methodology	325
	Philip S. Brenner	

Correction to: Power, Culture and Item Nonresponse in Social Surveys C1
Katharina M. Meitinger and Timothy P. Johnson

Index 335

Contributors

Isabel Anadon Department of Sociology, University of Wisconsin-Madison, Madison, WI, USA

Philip S. Brenner Department of Sociology, Senior Research Fellow, Center for Survey Research, University of Massachusetts Boston, Boston, MA, USA

Brian Calfano Department of Political Science, University of Cincinnati, Cincinnati, OH, USA

Mathew J. Creighton School of Sociology, UCD Geary Institute for Public Policy, University College Dublin, Dublin, Ireland

Don A. Dillman Department of Sociology, Washington State University, Pullman, WA, USA

The Social and Economic Sciences Research Center, Washington State University, Pullman, WA, USA

Kevin Drakulich School of Criminology and Criminal Justice, Northeastern University, Boston, MA, USA

Jennifer Dykema University of Wisconsin Survey Center, University of Wisconsin-Madison, Madison, WI, USA

Dorothy Farrar Edwards Department of Kinesiology, University of Wisconsin-Madison, Madison, WI, USA

Dana Garbarski Department of Sociology, Loyola University Chicago, Chicago, IL, USA

Daniel Herda Department of Sociology, Merrimack College, North Andover, MA, USA

Timothy P. Johnson Department of Public Administration, University of Illinois at Chicago, Chicago, IL, USA

Dana LaVergne Department of Sociology, Loyola University Chicago, Chicago, IL, USA

Bianca Manago Department of Sociology, Vanderbilt University, Nashville, TN, USA

Katharina M. Meitinger Department of Methodology and Statistics, University of Utrecht, Utrecht, Netherlands

Kristen Olson Leland J. and Dorothy H. Olson Professor and Vice Chair, Department of Sociology, University of Nebraska-Lincoln, Lincoln, NE, USA

Nora Cate Schaeffer Sewell Bascom Professor of Sociology, Department of Sociology, Faculty Director, University of Wisconsin Survey Center, Madison, WI, USA
University of Wisconsin-Madison, Madison, WI, USA

Henning Silber Department of Survey Design and Methodology, GESIS–Leibniz Institute for the Social Sciences, Mannheim, Germany

Jolene D. Smyth Department of Sociology, Director, Bureau of Sociological Research, University of Nebraska-Lincoln, Lincoln, NE, USA

Jerry Timbrook Department of Sociology, University of Nebraska-Lincoln, Lincoln, NE, USA

Kevin H. Wozniak Department of Sociology, University of Massachusetts Boston, Boston, MA, USA

Chapter 1
Why Survey Methodology Needs Sociology and Why Sociology Needs Survey Methodology

Introduction to Understanding Survey Methodology: Sociological Theory and Applications

Philip S. Brenner

The connections between survey methodology and sociology, as well as the other social sciences, extend back for nearly a century, long before the products of survey research became a ubiquitous presence in our daily lives and before survey methodology was an academic discipline in its own right. The first generation of survey methodologists earned doctorates in cognate academic disciplines, coming to the field from psychology, sociology, political science, and statistics. Moreover, because of the relative newness of the field and the limited number of doctoral programs in survey methodology, many in subsequent generations of survey methodologists completed doctoral training in other disciplines as well.

Of these connections, the links between sociology and survey methodology are especially consequential and worth further discussion. Sociologists were among the first academics to adopt survey research methods and were among the first wave of survey methodologists. Sociologists, such as Paul Lazarsfeld and Samuel Stouffer, were influential among the scientists developing the burgeoning discipline and both were early presidents of the American Association for Public Opinion Research (AAPOR), the leading association of survey researchers and methodologists. Moreover, over a third of AAPOR presidents have been sociologists—earning a PhD in the field or joining the faculty of a sociology department.[1]

Today, sociology and survey methodology are neighboring and complementary academic disciplines. Sociology is the study of human society, and sociologists investigate every nook and cranny of it. Sociological research pursues multitudinous

---

[1]Author's own calculation. See https://www.aapor.org/About-Us/Leadership/Past-Presidents.aspx for a list of past presidents.

P. S. Brenner (✉)
Department of Sociology, Center for Survey Research, University of Massachusetts Boston, Boston, MA, USA
e-mail: philip.brenner@umb.edu

© Springer Nature Switzerland AG 2020
P. S. Brenner (ed.), *Understanding Survey Methodology*, Frontiers in Sociology and Social Research 4, https://doi.org/10.1007/978-3-030-47256-6_1

subfields and interests, such as race and ethnicity, gender and sexuality, class and inequality, religion and secularism, and many more. Some sociologists focus on the micro-level, attempting to understand how societal-level phenomena and forces influence the individual, and vice versa. Others focus on the macro-level as they struggle to understand how social forces shaped our past, influence our present, and will transform our future. Spanning these pursuits and levels of analysis, sociologists share an interest in that which shapes and is shaped by society.

Survey research is one set of research methods used by sociologists and other social scientists to investigate social phenomena and understand society. Survey methodology, however, is more than just the practice of doing surveys. It is an academic discipline dedicated to the study of surveys as tools for understanding society (Groves et al. 2009). Survey methodologists focus primarily on the multiple sources of error that can affect survey estimates. This focus, called the "total survey error" (TSE) approach, orients survey methodologists' attentions to the sources and effects of non-sampling errors: measurement, nonresponse, coverage, processing, and adjustment errors (Andersen et al. 1979; Groves 1989; Weisberg 2005). Most of the research in the field investigates the ramifications of these errors and how to correct or avoid them.

Although sociologists were well-represented among the earliest survey researchers and methodologists, psychological theories have been more influential in the development of survey methodology as an academic discipline. In the early years of the discipline's formation, the predominant psychological approach in survey research was oriented toward social psychology. The past four decades, however, saw survey methodology take a cognitive turn along with much of the field of psychology. This Kuhnian shift, named the Cognitive Aspects of Survey Methodology (CASM), reoriented research in the field to the ways in which interviewers, respondents, and question authors contribute error, intentionally and unintentionally, at each stage of the survey response process: comprehension of the survey question, recollection of relevant information, estimation and judgment, and reporting an answer (National Research Council 1984; Tourangeau et al. 2000; Turner and Martin 1984a, b).

CASM has undoubtedly lead to important improvements in survey measurement by identifying and understanding the heuristics that respondents use to comprehend and answer questions, especially when they introduce errors (Schwarz et al. 1985, 1991; Tourangeau et al. 2004, 2007). By understanding these cognitive processes, survey researchers can write questions that sidestep heuristics and avoid these sources of error.

However, many of the stages of the question answering process are also strongly influenced by the social and interactional features of the data collection procedure. By focusing so fixedly on cognitive processes, the social and interactional aspects of survey methodology have been (with notable exceptions) under-investigated and under-theorized. A revitalized research program linking survey methodology with sociological theory is promising, given sociology's rich theoretical foundation and extensive body of research. In turn, survey methodology has more to offer sociology, and social science more generally, than the improvement of survey practice and data quality gained by learning about the *proximate* causes of survey errors in order to estimate, correct, or avoid them. Such a simple contractual relationship obscures the past and potential depth of the relationship between these two fields. Although the improvement of surveys is clearly important, the promise of survey methodology as a social science is the opportunity to learn about human behavior that is afforded by the investigation of survey errors.

Howard Schuman strongly argued for this approach to survey methodology in his call to investigate of survey artifacts: the systematic errors or biases that pull a survey estimate unidirectionally away from its true value, typically caused by characteristics of the study design, or the actions, purposeful or unintentional, of interviewers or respondents. Schuman argued that survey artifacts are not simply errors to be corrected but social phenomena in their own right that provide a window into human nature and behavior: "The basic point I will take is simple: artifacts are in the mind of the beholder. Barring one or two exceptions, the problems that occur in surveys are opportunities for understanding once we take them seriously as facts of life." (Schuman 1982, p. 23). Thus, by investigating the *distal* social sources of survey errors, survey methodologists peer through that window and fulfill their potential as social scientists.

Thus, this volume proposes a revitalization of a sociological approaches to survey methodology by ambitiously applying sociological theory to understand aspects of survey methodology.[2] Current strengths of sociological and interactional theory suggest a number of other areas ripe for the attention of sociologists (and other social scientists with interests in sociological and interactional theories) interested in survey measurement. This approach compliments, and at points challenges, the dominant cognitive paradigm applied by survey methodologists.

The first four chapters focus on direct connections between sociological theories and their applications in survey research.[3] In Chap. 2, Don Dillman (Washington State University) assesses the current state of theory and research on survey nonresponse, laying out a plan for future research and theory-building. He first reviews the current best practices for encouraging survey response and reducing nonresponse, such as using multiple modes of contact, reducing the burden of the response task by constraining the length of the survey, and providing survey incentives with the request for participation. He then uses this review to assess the primary competing theories used to understand and explain nonresponse, including cognitive dissonance theory, reasoned action and planned behavior theory, influence

---

[2] We use the term "sociological theory" broadly. This includes sociological social psychology, theories of neighboring disciplines adopted by sociologists, and those of neighboring disciplines with sociological roots or interests.

[3] This volume was organized in a way that separated the more theoretical chapters from those that applied theory, and organized the applied chapters by substantive topics. However, alternative organizations of this volume could have matched theoretical pieces with relevant applications, or grouped chapters by their methodological interests (e.g., unit or item nonresponse, social desirability) or their theoretical perspectives (e.g., symbolic interactionism, gender theory).

and pre-suasion theories, leverage salience and benefit-cost theories, and social exchange theory.

Dillman's review underscores the need to move past idiosyncratic, post-hoc, and just-so theories of nonresponse designed to explain the phenomenon in narrowly circumscribed conditions or adaptations of general theories that fail to effectively and completely explain the phenomenon of nonresponse across surveys. Rather, Dillman argues that what the field needs is a comprehensive explanation of the phenomenon that is clear in its purpose and grounded in both current research and social theory relevant across social science disciplines. Only with a good footing on a solid theoretical foundation can substantial process be made to comprehensively understand the survey nonresponse and the action needed to address it.

In Chap. 3, Philip Brenner (University of Massachusetts Boston) applies the sociological paradigm of symbolic interactionism and identity theory to understand social desirability bias. He first reviews conventional understandings of "sensitive questions" that treat socially desirable responding to sensitive questions as impression management problems. These understandings focus on impression management as a personality construct that drives socially desirable responding. The chapter critiques this approach by arguing that it lacks explanatory power because it fails to appreciate how social interaction functions in general and more specifically in the context in which survey measurement occurs.

Brenner then turns his attention to identity theory, arguing that it provides a more complete explanation of socially desirable responding by integrating the social context of measurement into its understanding. Rather than wholesale misreporting on every question linked social norms, as should be expected by theories focused on socially desirable responding as a personality construct, respondents misreport in line with important self-views. Only with a more comprehensive understanding of the individual respondent, how they see themselves and what they value, can we understand when and where to expect this measurement artifact and, with additional research, what we can do about it.

In Chap. 4, Henning Silber (GESIS, Leibniz Institute for the Social Sciences) and Timothy Johnson (University of Illinois at Chicago) discuss the application of macro-level theories of cultural difference and change to the total survey error framework. In our increasingly globalized world, they argue that it is crucial that we understand differences between communities and societies and how these differences can influence data collection and survey errors. Their chapter focuses on three orientations to understanding cultural difference which represent collections or amalgamations of theories—cultural orientations in its six dimensions (individualism/collectivism, power distance, uncertainty avoidance, masculinity/femininity, long-term/short-term, and indulgence/restraint), the three-dimension universal values orientation (embeddedness/autonomy, mastery/harmony, and hierarchy/egalitarianism), and national values framework which includes modernization theory (survival/self-expression) and secularization thesis (traditional/secular-rational) arms.

Silber and Johnson then discuss each theoretical approach in terms of its application to the sources of survey error, primarily various forms of measurement and nonresponse errors. While the cultural orientations framework has been most frequently and successfully applied, each shows potential for understanding cross-cultural similarities and differences. As cross-cultural work continues to expand beyond advanced, post-industrialized democracies, much work is left to be done to understand the potential sources of survey errors and differences in them between cultures.

In Chap. 5, Bianca Manago (Vanderbilt University) introduces status characteristics and expectation states theory, a theoretical paradigm that attempts to explain behavior between two or more individuals in interactional groups. The theory focuses on the influence of status characteristics, such as race and gender, on behavior in novel interactional contexts; that is, interactions between people who do not know each other occurring in situations lacking a clear hierarchy outside of their everyday life, such as between jurists as they deliberate a case to which they have been assigned. The theory has been primarily tested and applied in laboratory settings, putting research participants in novel situations, manipulating status characteristics, and measuring their influence on behavior.

Although it has not been previously applied by survey methodologists, Manago argues that status characteristics and expectation states theory may be useful for framing our understandings of interaction in various relevant situations, such as survey interviews, cognitive testing, focus groups, and other types of novel interactional contexts. Of particular interest, the theory may be useful in understanding the distal causes of interviewer effects and other interactional effects that arise in survey measurement and a number of techniques used by survey methodologists during questionnaire design and evaluation.

The remaining chapters apply sociological theory, broadly defined, to survey methodological problems. These chapters present cutting-edge, original research that applies the "sociological imagination" to substantive concerns important to sociologists, survey methodologists, and social scientists more generally, including those interested in a variety of topics, such as health, immigration, race/ethnicity, gender and sexuality, policing, and public opinion.[4]

The first set of applications chapters use cross-cultural data sources to investigate two methodological topics, social desirability and item nonresponse, in the context of substantive topics related to culture and immigration. In Chap. 6, Mathew Creighton (University College Dublin) uses survey experiments conducted in the Netherlands to investigate measurement bias in reports of a set of stigmatized attitudes: anti-immigrant and anti-Muslim sentiment. Creighton compares direct

---

[4] I make distinctions between "subjective" and "methodological" topics here only because they are commonly understood in the social sciences. However, I wholeheartedly reject the division of topics and research into "substantive" and "methodological" areas. Such distinctions are typically used to distinguish topics of "scientific" interest from more "technical" ones; the latter being seen as less consequential than the former. Survey methodology is indeed an -*ology*, and a substantive topic in its own right. There, I use these terms not to distinguish between these types of topics but to argue that by bringing them together on equal footing, we can better understand both: the concepts and their measurement.

reports from a standard survey question on a conventional web questionnaire to masked reports from a list experiment question on a web survey to understand the potential for and sources of error. He applies symbolic interactionist theory on stigma to critique and refine the conventional survey methodological view on stigma as a source of measurement bias.

His experiment finds that respondents to the conventional web survey question were more supportive of immigration than those from the list experiment question. He finds some variation by education in responses on the conventional web survey question as respondents with higher education over-report their tolerance for Muslim immigrants, although respondents at all levels of schooling significantly mask their opposition to immigration. Creighton notes that the list experiment is not used as a criterion measure to zero in on the true value of anti-immigrant or anti-Muslim attitudes. Rather, he argues that anonymity and the different measurement procedure provides an alternate context that alters the way respondents answer.

In Chap. 7, Daniel Herda (Merrimack College) also investigates the social sources of error in measures of anti-immigrant sentiment. Where his previous research (Herda 2010), and that of other scholars, has focused on the social sources and meaning of population size innumeracy—that is, the reasons that some survey respondents think a minority or immigrant population is larger than it actually is—Herda now turns his attention to the social sources of item nonresponse on answers to survey questions that ask respondents to estimate the size of immigrant populations. Where previous work linked positive bias in respondents' estimates of immigrant population size to anti-immigrant sentiment, he now investigates anti-immigrant sentiment as a potential cause of item nonresponse—specifically "don't know" answers.

Analyzing European Social Survey data from 14 European countries, Herda finds that rates of "don't know" responses were lowest in Western and Northern Europe and highest in Eastern and Southern Europe. Across countries, "don't know" responses were related to anti-immigrant sentiment. Moreover, he finds that best practices for handling missing data like these, multiple imputation, may exacerbate total survey error. Rather, Herda concludes, "don't know" responses should be retained and analyzed as a substantive response to this factual question. In his conclusion, we see additional evidence for the need to understand the distal, social sources of survey errors.

In Chap. 8, Katharina Meitinger (University of Utrecht) and Timothy Johnson (University of Illinois at Chicago) continue the conversation on item nonresponse, investigating this relatively under-researched and under-theorized form of nonresponse, in contrast with the extensive research investigating unit nonresponse. Their chapter also takes a cross-national perspective, analyzing International Social Survey Program data from 35 countries spanning North and South America, Europe, Africa, Asia, and Oceania. Meitinger and Johnson estimate the relationship between the propensity for item nonresponse with a series of key sociological constructs, including the status characteristics of the respondent (e.g., class, racial, ethnic, language minority status) as well as cultural constructs reflecting those discussed by Silber and Johnson (Chap. 4), as such power and marginalization, diversity, and culture.

Their findings demonstrate that inequality may be an important cause of item nonresponse as many individual level status characteristics were found to be associated with that outcome. Being a woman, less educated, a member of a minority group, or feeling powerless or marginalized are each associated with increased item nonresponse. These findings underline the need to understand perspectives on survey participation and differences in these perspectives between social groups with a particular focus on the marginalized groups in each society.

The next set of application chapters engage multiple methods—cognitive interviewing, behavior coding of telephone interviews, and survey experiments—to improve our understandings of the concepts of sexual identity/sexual orientation and gender identity and their measurement. Moreover, these chapters bring together survey methodology and sociological theory, including grounded theory and gender theory, to address their substantive topic and improve the state-of-the-art of its measurement.

In Chap. 9, Dana Garbarski and Dana LaVergne (Loyola University Chicago) apply grounded theory—an inductive approach that builds theory in an iterative process during qualitative data collection (Glaser and Strauss 1967)—to the question design and evaluation stage of the survey process. Their focus is the improvement of the conceptualization and measurement of sexual orientation/sexual identity and gender identity (SOGI). They extend research on SOGI measurement by assessing measures of an additional dimension of each: gender expression and sexual attraction.

Garbarski and LaVergne tested six gender expression measures (essentially, how others view one's gender in terms of outward appearance) and sexual attraction measures (the gender/s of people to whom one is attracted) with a convenience sample of self-identified queer women, a population for whom these questions address topics of higher salience when compared the general public. They focused their attention on assessing the ability of these survey questions to validly measure their constructs. Garbarski and LaVergne conclude with a set of suggestions that will allow future surveys to improve the measurement of these concepts.

In Chap. 10, Jerry Timbrook, Jolene Smyth, and Kristen Olson (University of Nebraska, Lincoln) investigate interactional sources of error in measures of sexual identity in telephone interviews. They use behavior coding—a technique that applies quantitative descriptors to the interaction between interviewer and respondent—to investigate interviewer and respondent behavior and interactional difficulties between them, and what these problems tell us about the concept of sexual identity and our measures of it.

They code interactional problems in numerous ways for both respondents and interviewers. Coding schemes noted when respondents expressed confusion or commented that they found the question intrusive (e.g., topic was too personal) or objectionable (e.g., noting a religious belief). They coded interviewer action indicating discomfort with the question, such as apologizing or blaming the researcher, offering "don't know" as an explicit option, or accepting an unacceptable answer.

Also coded were interviewers who altered the question to improve the interaction and make it easier for respondents to answer the question. Relatively few respondents expressed an objection to the sexual identity question or refused to answer it but some interviewers themselves demonstrated discomfort with the question. More frequently, respondents expressed problems understanding the question given its syntactic and definitional difficulties. Interviewers acknowledged these problems and attempted to overcome them by enumerating responses to make it easier for respondents to understand options and provide an adequate answer.

In Chap. 11, Jolene Smyth and Kristen Olson (University of Nebraska, Lincoln) use gender theory—understanding gender as social construction and performance—to evaluate survey measures of gender identity in comparison with conventional binary measures of sex. Their measures of gender identity ask respondents to place themselves on a scale from completely masculine to completely feminine along with their assessment of society's ideal man and ideal woman.

Assessing reliability by comparing gender identity measures with conventional binary measures of sex, Smyth and Olson find that the latter is a signifiant predictor of the former, explaining over three-quarters of its variance. Notably, women are influenced by question order within this battery, shifting their self-ratings a couple of points toward the masculine side of the scale if they rate society's ideal first. In contrast, men are not influenced by question order. This finding in particular illustrates the importance of bringing sociological theory to survey methodological work, and vice versa.

Predictive validity is also assessed, comparing reported gender identity to sexual orientation and commonly gendered household tasks (e.g., housekeeping, which is commonly thought to be feminine compared to household repairs commonly thought to be masculine). These findings add to the growing evidence that measures of gender identity (and sexual orientation) increase the explanatory power of measures of sex and should be added to our standard list of demographic questions routinely asked on surveys. Moreover, Smyth and Olson's application of gender theory gives insight into conventional measures and a path forward that improves measurement validity.

In the last set of applications chapters, two papers examine substantive topics related to race as they examine the measurement of attitudes toward two important public institutions: medicine and law enforcement. In Chap. 12, Jen Dykema, Nora Cate Schaeffer, Isabel Anadon, Dorothy Farrar Edwards (University of Wisconsin, Madison) and Dana Garbarski (Loyola University Chicago) examine differences between Black and White respondents as they answer questions about trust in medical research. This chapter presents findings from an interaction analysis of interviews from a telephone survey with quota samples of White and Black residents of the state of Wisconsin. Respondents were asked a series of questions, some of which specifically mentioned race, regarding their trust in medical research and their views on medical researchers, and their likelihood of participating in medical research and their concerns about doing so. Transcripts were created and used to identify detailed interactional information about the interview, such as conversational turns and tokens such as "um" and "ah."

Five interactional indicators of poorer data quality are used as outcomes, including problems emerging during the respondent's first turn at talk (failing to provide an acceptable answer, requesting the question be re-read or clarified, an affective element or token) and a long question-answer sequence (turns in excess of the paradigmatic sequence question-answer-acknowledgment). Differences emerge between White and Black respondents in the presence of these interactional indictors for the medical research questions. White respondents demonstrated more interactional problems in general than Black respondents on trust in medical research questions that had a race focus, but not those without a race focus. Differences in response behaviors reflect cultural differences between respondents that influence how they interpret and answer the questions and interact with interviewers while doing so.

In Chap. 13, Kevin Wozniak (University of Massachusetts Boston), Kevin Drakulich (Northeastern University), and Brian Calfano (University of Cincinnati) probe the substantive value of null findings. In so doing, they examine the differences between survey methodologists' and other social scientists' differing approaches to survey artifacts. Survey methodologists investigate the proximate causes of survey artifacts, such as context or question order effects, with the aim of correcting for them or avoiding them in the future. Public opinion researchers, including sociologists and political scientists, often take a different perspective, intentionally introducing "artifacts," such as including a block of text or an image in a survey, to understand its influence on public opinion and attitude change. This approach, called framing or priming effects, is a common tool in public opinion research to understand attitudinal change.

But where the lack of a survey artifact typically requires little attention from survey methodologists, a failed intentional artifact, such as a framing experiment, is met with frustration and hand-wringing for the social scientist engaged in research on attitudes and change. It is here that Wozniak, Drakulich, and Calfano focus their attention, investigating the failure of a framing experiment and the nature of attitudinal stability and strength. Their survey experiment randomly assigned respondents to one of four conditions varying the framing of the policing debate after incidents of police brutality against Black Americans. Faced with the lack of a significant effect, they focus their attention on attitude change and stability, explaining the lack of change on the strength of the attitude. Only with a better understanding of attitude strength can we effectively test and advance theory.

Conclusion

Paul Lazarsfeld opened his presidential address to the American Association for Public Opinion Research by noting that some academics (sociologists among them, one assumes) view survey research as shallow. "Those of us who work at universities, however, often have to meet the criticism that technical excellence and usefulness are not enough. The significance of our work is doubted [and some academics believe that] our work does not contribute enough to general theoretical matters." (1950–1, p. 617). But, he argued, survey methodology has the potential to contribute to our understanding of human behavior, much like its kindred disciplines in the social sciences: "Public opinion research can do the same for the larger community if it becomes more aware of its potentialities and more eager to develop them." Lazarsfeld gave a similar message to sociologists in his presidential address to the American Sociological Association. He commented on the benefit to sociological theory from of the study of (survey) methodology: "Such induced sensitivity to methodology can be fruitful for general sociological analysis in areas far afield from what we think of as empirical studies." (1962, p. 757).

In sum, these two fields can greatly benefit from each other. Survey methodology offers sociology rigorous measurement of social phenomena but also contributes mechanisms to test, extend, and develop theory. And sociology strengthens survey methodology by contributing theoretical breadth and depth, helping survey methodologists to understand the social phenomena they encounter inside and outside of the survey interview. It is my hope that the following chapters will intrigue and challenge readers, and motivate them to consider the ways that they can bring sociological theory to their survey methodological work or bring survey methodological artifacts to their empirical work testing of sociological theory.

References

Andersen, R., Kasper, J. D., & Frankel, M. R. (1979). *Total survey error*. San Francisco: Jossey-Bass Publishers.
Glaser, B. G., & Strauss, A. L. (1967). *The discovery of grounded theory: Strategies for qualitative research*. Chicago: Aldine.
Groves, R. M. (1989). *Survey errors and survey costs*. New York: Wiley.
Groves, R. M., Fowler, F. J., Jr., Couper, M. P., Lepkowski, J. M., Singer, E., & Tourangeau, R. (2009). *Survey methodology*. New York: Wiley.
Herda, D. (2010). "How many immigrants?" Foreign born population innumeracy in Europe. *Public Opinion Quarterly, 74*(4), 674–695.
Lazarsfeld, P. F. (1950–1). The obligations of the 1950 pollster to the 1984 historian. *Public Opinion Quartery, 14*(4), 617–638.
Lazarsfeld, P. F. (1962). The sociology of empirical social research. *American Sociological Review, 27*(6), 757–767.
National Research Council. (1984). Cognitive aspects of survey methodology: Building a bridge between disciplines. In T. B. Jabine (Ed.), *Report of the advanced research seminar on cognitive aspects of survey methodology*. Washington, DC: National Academies Press.
Schuman, H. (1982). Artifacts are in the mind of the beholder. *The American Sociologist, 17*(1), 21–28.
Schwarz, N., Hippler, H. J., Deutsch, B., & Strack, F. (1985). Response scales: Effects of category range on reported behavior and comparative judgments. *Public Opinion Quarterly, 49*(3), 388–395.

Schwarz, N., Knäuper, B., Hippler, H. J., Noelle-Neumann, E., & Clark, L. (1991). Rating scales numeric values may change the meaning of scale labels. *Public Opinion Quarterly, 55*(4), 570–582.

Tourangeau, R., Rips, L. J., & Rasinski, K. (2000). *The psychology of survey response*. New York: Cambridge University Press.

Tourangeau, R., Couper, M. P., & Conrad, F. (2004). Spacing, position, and order interpretive heuristics for visual features of survey questions. *Public Opinion Quarterly, 68*(3), 368–393.

Tourangeau, R., Couper, M. P., & Conrad, F. (2007). Color, labels, and interpretive heuristics for response scales. *Public Opinion Quarterly, 71*(1), 91–112.

Turner, C., & Martin, E. (1984a). *Surveying subjective phenomena* (Vol. 1). Russell Sage Foundation.

Turner, C., & Martin, E. (1984b). *Surveying subjective phenomena* (Vol. 2). Russell Sage Foundation.

Weisberg, H. F. (2005). *The total survey error approach: A guide to the new science of survey research*. Chicago: University of Chicago Press.

Part I
Sociological Theory and Survey Methodology

Chapter 2
Towards Survey Response Rate Theories That No Longer Pass Each Other Like Strangers in the Night

Don A. Dillman

For many decades survey methodologists have struggled with the challenge of how to improve survey response rates. The literature is filled with admonitions for how to increase the proportion of sampled individuals who answer survey requests. Examples include more contacts, token cash incentives sent with the survey request, promised payments to those who respond, shorter questionnaires, personalization, special contacts, and sponsorship, to mention a few (e.g. Dillman 2000). However, none of these techniques, when used alone, assures the achievement of high response rates to a particular survey. Understanding how multiple techniques interact to increase or decrease response rates is a strongly desired goal for improving response rates.

Many attempts have been made to develop theories about what causes people to respond or not respond to surveys. Some theories, and the research that encourages their use, have focused on only one or a few techniques. Yet, response rates are in virtually all instances the result of combining many discrete elements into a data collection strategy. Some theories of respondent behavior are used only as a frame of reference for proposing and justifying a particular action aimed at improving response. They are seldom utilized to provide a comprehensive approach to data collection, with the goal of improving response rates to the extent possible.

In addition, various theoretical efforts have for the most part remained uninformed by other theoretical efforts, ignoring each other except with a gratuitous mention of their existence. My purpose in this paper is to provide an overview of frequently mentioned survey response theories and propose further development of theories that will better explain how high survey response rates can be achieved.

Despite the well- intentioned efforts of surveyors to improve survey response rates, current results have reached all-time lows, especially for the telephone

---

D. A. Dillman (✉)
Department of Sociology and the Social and Economic Sciences Research Center, Washington State University, Pullman, WA, USA
e-mail: dillman@wsu.edu

(Dutwin and Lavrakas 2012). Recently, The Pew Research Center reported their RDD telephone survey results had declined from 9% to 6% and they were ending their reliance on such surveys (Kennedy and Hartwig 2019). We are also encountering many social and technological changes that have survey response rate implications. Among them:

- The way most surveys get done has shifted from face-to-face, telephone and mail, to the internet, and now to devices with advanced software capabilities.
- Sources of sample contact lists have changed, with people protecting contact information and selectively releasing access to people and organizations that might want to contact them.
- Society has changed socially, with behavioral norms becoming more heterogeneous.
- Electronic access is increasingly required for obtaining information and services.
- Survey requests, especially electronic ones, are more likely to be viewed with justified fears, that range from delivering malware to freely giving collected data to others.
- The risk of identity theft produces additional fears on the part of potential respondents.

The adjustments being made by surveyors to this new reality have been piecemeal at best. When survey sponsors are asked to explain how they will produce a satisfactory response rate, the most frequent response is to look at specific features of potential survey designs. An example, might be deciding to pay a large post-incentive, perhaps as much as 40, 60, a hundred dollars or more, depending upon the importance of the survey and availability of financial resources. Another frequent decision is to use special contact methods such as federal express or in-person contact to deliver a survey request. In addition, these efforts are often undertaken while ignoring many other causes of improved survey response, such as multiple contacts and the sequential offering of different modes of response.

A tendency also exists for some survey designers to justify their inability to get high response rates as an unnecessary extravagance, sometimes citing for support of this approach a meta-analysis showed nonresponse error (the difference between respondents and non-respondents in ways relevant to the study) is not much different when response rates are low than when they are high (Groves 2006; Groves and Peytcheva 2008). This meta-analysis was for surveys published in the 1980s and 90s that were focused on health issues, and the range of response rates was from about 15% to 70%. These surveys were implemented in most cases before intensive use of the internet and mixed-mode designs were commonly used. The results seem limited and out-of-date.

The perspective provided by such meta-analyses is useful. However, an unintended practical effect is that survey sponsors often make minimal efforts to encourage high response rates choosing instead to draw very large samples, and doing little to encourage response. Examples including using only one contact and ignoring the use of known influencers of response such as cash incentives sent with the request and the use of multiple modes for contacting respondents (Dillman

2017). In addition, the expected response rate standard for evaluating government survey requests provided by the U.S. Office of Management and Budget, remains at 80%.

Focusing on improving response rates needs to be related both to achieving higher response rates and lowering nonresponse error (Williams and Brick 2018). The current interest in adaptive design whereby under-responding types of sample members are especially appealed to in follow-up contacts suggests a way of improving both response rates and nonresponse error. In addition, contacting fewer individuals to obtain acceptable responses may have significant cost benefits as well as potentially reducing the number of requests to participate in different surveys received by members of certain populations. In this paper my focus is on developing better theories to guide survey designs in ways that will improve response rates, while recognizing the need to achieve response from all types of individuals who are asked to answer a particular survey.

What Is a Theory?

Writers define theory in different ways, and theoretical efforts are often quite abstract. In my view a theory consists of an interconnected set of assumptions and propositions about why something does or does not happen.

My focus here is to identify and use theories and the constructs derived from them to explain the response rates for specified survey populations. I seek to develop useful explanations of survey response that will enable researchers to develop and test hypotheses about the survey sample impact of specific data collection strategies. Although individuals may respond to surveys for different reasons, my theoretical interest is in explaining the response rate for the group being surveyed I also aim to connect the theoretical with the practical, learning how to combine response-inducing techniques in ways that will produce response rates that are significantly higher than those now being achieved.

Factors that Influence Survey Response Rates

It is clear from decades of research that many different factors have been found to push response rates either up or down. It is also evident that factors once thought to be effective for improving response rates are less effective than they were in the past (e.g. callbacks on RDD surveys). In addition, some factors now available (mixed-mode designs) that can be used to improve response rates were not generally available and practical for use until this century.

A theory that endeavors to predict and explain the extent to which members of a drawn sample of households or individuals will respond to survey requests cannot ignore known relationships between survey design factors with the potential to influence response. Thus, it is important to identify in an organized way those factors and how they have been shown to influence survey response rates. Doing so provides information critical to evaluating the effectiveness of alternative theories of survey response.

Identified below are seven categories of potential influences on survey response rate. Some of these potential influences on response to surveys are well established in the research literature. Others are new, and reflect the dramatic changes now occurring in how most surveys get done, or surveyors would like for them to be done. These considerations, each of which is discussed only briefly because of length limitations for this chapter, provide a framework of observations that grounds my evaluation of current theories of survey response. Additional background on these observations with more extensive literature references is provided in Dillman et al. (2014).

1. Using multiple modes of survey contact and response improves response rates.

Until near the end of the twentieth of the century, most surveys used a single mode of data collection, usually by face-to-face interviews, by mail, or by telephone. The lack of information technology support until the late 1990s made it difficult to mix modes and coordinate their implementation (Dillman 2000). In addition, factors found effective for improving response to certain survey modes (training of interviewers) often had little or no relevance to surveys conducted by self-administered modes such as the mail or internet.

Thus, one of the dramatic changes of the last 20 years in survey design that must be considered as an important determinant of response rates is the use of *multiple survey modes* to enhance response rates. The use of more than one mode is also encouraged by the desire to reduce costs as well as counter falling response rates.

Some individuals may prefer responding by certain survey modes instead of others. Thus, offering *multiple response modes*, has been shown to improve response as well as improve representation of populations in which some individuals are unable or unwilling to respond over the internet (Smyth et al. 2010; Messer and Dillman 2011). Although these effects may be modest, they cannot be ignored.

In addition, *multiple contact modes*, can also be used to further improve response rates. For example, following a postal request for the recipient to provide an internet response with a quick email that provides an electronic link (a procedure known as email augmentation) to ease the task of responding, has been shown to dramatically improve internet and overall response rates (Millar and Dillman 2011; Millar 2013; Dillman et al. 2016). Although contact information for multiple modes is often not available as a means of reaching respondents, for example, address-based household samples from the U.S. Postal Service, in other cases (e.g. client, student, employee lists) such information may often be obtained.

Another way that multiple contact modes can improve response rates is that increasingly people are more reachable by certain modes than they are by others. Thus, sending postal, email and telephone contacts to the same person, make it possible to connect with people who ignore or are unable to access contact efforts from other modes of delivery. In this way, surveyors may reduce survey coverage error.

Some individuals may also prefer responding by certain survey modes instead of others (Olson et al. 2012). Thus, offering multiple response modes, has been shown to improve response. Offering multiple response modes provides the opportunity to reduce nonresponse error in populations such as the general public in which some individuals are unable or unwilling to respond over the internet (Smyth et al. 2010; Messer and Dillman 2011).

In today's survey world the use of multiple survey modes provides a mostly unprecedented opportunity for improving response rates. It is unlikely that these considerations can be ignored by any theory aimed at providing explanations, as well as, by inference, guidelines for improving response rates to high levels. However, because of the recent development of multiple-mode possibilities for contact and response, and how they can be combined most effectively, most of the current survey response theories have not yet incorporated them.

With few exceptions, we cannot maximize survey response rates by conducting surveys that rely on single survey modes. Thus, the use of multiple contact and response modes is essential for developing a useful theory of response rates in the early part of the twenty-first century.

2. **Sponsorship by a survey organization with known legitimacy that is trusted by potential respondents improves response rates.**

A consistent finding of response rate research conducted in the twentieth century is that *government sponsored surveys* usually obtained higher response rates than did surveys sponsored by others (Heberlein and Baumgartner 1978). Although response rates have declined in recent years to most non-mandatory, government surveys (e.g. Brick and Williams 2012) response rates for government sponsored surveys remain much higher than for private sector and university sponsored surveys.

Government is considered by large portions of the population to have a legitimate right as well as need to conduct surveys on certain topics. For example, government sponsored surveys in the United States are used to establish social security payment amounts and to direct the expenditure of many types of government funding efforts (National Research Council 2014).

The introduction of surveying over the Internet has also introduced new concerns associated with sponsorship, including whether a survey sponsor is known or unknown to the sampled households or individuals. In addition, the ease by which nearly anyone can conduct electronic surveys means that survey requests are now more likely to be received from organizations that people know nothing about.

When some people are asked to respond over the internet to an email request, they fear that clicking on an electronic link to provide survey answers will result in receiving a computer virus or other type of malware. In addition, internet surveying has increased fears that survey data may be kept and used for unauthorized purposes such as marketing or being connected to other data in ways unknown to the respondent, and unrevealed by the surveyor.

Thus, *trust of survey sponsorship*, and how that is communicated to potential respondents, has emerged as a more important issue than was typical in earlier times. Individuals contacted by unknown household callers in the previous century, were likely to give interviewers the benefit of their doubt and agree to be surveyed. For a time, those norms tended to prevail for telephone surveys as well. This lack of trust is now backed my fear of significant negative consequences associated with providing a survey response.

Survey sponsors may be able to create or increase trust through the communications they send to people asked to complete surveys, for example through a postal contact that provides information for contacting the survey sponsor (Dillman et al. 2014). In addition, the survey sponsors may offer inducements, ranging from explanations of how survey results will make a difference to sending incentives that may improve trust of the survey sponsor. Thus, the cooperation effects of sponsorship by a known entity and trust in the sponsor has consequences on response rates that cannot be ignored by a theory of survey response.

3. **Creating smaller less onerous survey response tasks will improve survey response rates.**

The *technology* associated with providing responses in a particular mode may independently affect whether people are willing to undertake the task of responding. Some, though not all, people object to being interviewed by the telephone. More importantly as a barrier to response, people are increasingly unlikely to answer ringing phones, because the first six digits of the identified source of call are often spoofed, making it appear to recipients that it is coming from the same geographic area in which the respondent is thought to live. Also, social norms have changed so that it is both desirable and practical not to answer a ringing phone, but instead wait to see if the caller leaves a message. In addition, some people still do not have *internet access*, now required for responding to some surveys. Or, they may have access, but be uncomfortable answering surveys using that technology.

Also, some internet surveyors construct surveys so that *all questions must be answered*. The requirement is enforced by not allowing the next question to appear until an answer has been provided to the current one.

Long surveys produce cut-offs and lower response rates (e.g. Dillman et al. 2014). The negative effect of *survey length* is especially evident in telephone surveys. Some organizations refuse to do telephone surveys that exceed a certain length. For example, in the 1990s the Gallup Organization set as a standard only doing telephone surveys that would require no more than 18 min to complete. Recent interaction with an internet only surveyor revealed advice to all surveyors to keep their internet survey under nine minutes.

Postal mail research has shown that number of pages affects completion rates (Dillman 2000). However, the effects of length are less noticeable for in-person surveys. This, often leads surveyors to conclude that adding a few, or even many, questions to a survey that is already 30 min long is unlikely to affect response rates. However, termination to phone, internet, and mail surveys, where a refusal can happen without having to ask or tell the interviewer to stop, is likely.

The nature of the response task for completing a survey varies greatly. Some survey topics involve asking questions that are *interesting to respondents*. Others are on topics for which few if any people have any interest. Adding interesting questions and ordering the questions in particular ways has often been used to increase the likelihood that people will start as well as finish answering the survey.

Sometimes surveys contain *difficult to answer questions* that some respondents find impossible to answer. In addition, surveys often include questions that respondents *object to answering*. Thus, it is not surprising that questions get skipped or people stop responding mid-way through a survey.

Often surveys are created on the basis of whatever questions the study sponsors want to ask, leaving it to those that implement the survey to figure out how to get a response. Increasingly, the lack of sensitivity to the nature of the response task is becoming a barrier to obtaining higher response rates.

In sum, there are several aspects of the survey task that make it onerous, and that influence whether people will respond to a survey. The technology expectations, survey length, the questionnaire topic, and the specific survey questions, may each *make a difference*. It is essential that theories of survey response aimed at explaining response rates take these issues into account.

4. **Providing incentives with the request for a response appropriate to sponsorship and task will improve response rates.**

Many different studies have shown that *incentives usually improve response rates* for most surveys (Singer and Ye 2013). Incentives may be monetary or material. Cash is often used when incentives are small, but may be paid by check or some other means when large. Monetary incentives may also be direct, as when cash is sent to a person, or indirect, when in the form of a gift certificate for purchases at a specific company. Material incentives are wide-ranging and often imaginative. They may be chosen more for getting an envelope opened (a refrigerator magnet or thumb drive that make the mailing envelope appear unusual) or a new consumer product that might be inexpensive but valued because of its unusual nature.

Research has also shown that the most powerful effects of small incentives occurs if they are *monetary payments provided with the survey request*. Providing small payments afterwards to respondents or, saying that a donation to a charity will be made for completed questionnaires, may have a small positive effect. In addition, payments afterwards that are quite large are likely to increase response rates, and offers of payments for responding by a particular mode (e.g. internet instead of phone), has been effective in some implementations. Also, prepayment may be combined with offers of post payments. In short there are many different ways of offering incentives, and they are undoubtedly one of the most powerful means of improving response for many, though not all, surveys.

Culturally, the use of incentives seems inappropriate in mandatory surveys, such as the U.S. Decennial Census. The fact that incentives are provided, would seem to suggest that response is not mandatory. However, surveys are increasingly be used in voluntary surveys as a means of getting, holding and capturing attention to the survey process. A comprehensive theory of response rates must deal with not only incentives as having powerful potential for improving response rates, but when and how to use incentives in appropriate ways.

5. **Multiple carefully timed requests for providing answers to surveys that are made through all available channels of communication will improve response rates.**

Asking people to respond to a survey usually involves multiple requests. In fact, one of the early meta analyses of factors influencing response to mail surveys revealed that *number of contacts* was most important (Scott 1961). The same applies to other modes of surveying and traditionally many contacts were used for in-person and telephone surveys, including refusal conversions. In additional *pre-notices* were often added to both mail and telephone to encourage responses.

Deciding what to say to potential respondents has been done differently across modes. When interviewing was the dominant way of conducting surveys, formulating the response request was often left mostly in the hands of interviewers. Certain standards might be set by the survey sponsor for how interviewers were allowed to approach potential respondents. However, it was usually left up to the interviewer to decide how best to achieve respondent rapport, decide what to say when, and how to interject comments that would support the interviewing process by leading to interview completions. It is not surprising that some individuals had greater success than others, and the skills needed for completing interviews depended in part upon mannerisms, voice characteristics, personalities, and other issues that are difficult if not impossible to teach to some prospective interviewers.

Over time it became easier for people to refuse interviews, both in-person and over the phone. Whereas strong norms of politeness with strangers existed in the mid-twentieth century, such norms are now relaxed, and the large numbers of telephone calls for donations, surveys and marketing have increased the likelihood that people will terminate all calls without hearing an explanation of what the request is about. In addition, callbacks from the same number may be blocked, or simply ignored. Thus, whereas at one time, a telephone interviewer could make call backs with success that is now less feasible. Increasingly, the telephone interviewer may have only a few seconds, on a one-time basis, to appeal for a response.

The shift towards self-administration, and mixing of survey contact and response modes provides a quite different set of communication possibilities. Although the ability to provide impromptu, targeted answers to questions from people unwilling to respond, an opportunity now exists for using a *planned set of 4–5 or even more communications*. The communication of the request to respond no longer needs to occur in a frenzied few seconds that is often punctuated with a click to terminate the call.

It seems reasonable that multiple communications need to have the content structured so that they don't simply replicate one another, with each appearing the same as the one that preceded it. Later communications can be structured to appeal to types of people who did not respond well to earlier communications, thus attempting to reduce nonresponse error. However, minimal research has been done on this topic.

The *timing of contacts* is also important. Email augmentation, discussed earlier, a timed email contact that provides electronic links to the survey, thus making it easier to respond, can have a dramatic positive effect on responses received over the internet. Sometimes a quick postcard reminder is intended to encourage respondents to open a previously received request to respond by mail, before the normal household garbage cycle takes over. The effectiveness of a postcard follow-up of this nature depends greatly on timing, because it cannot be effective if the questionnaire has already been discarded.

Decisions also need to be made on when to send or announce incentives. Incentives are typically enclosed with the first survey request, where their effectiveness may get amplified by follow-up mailings. In addition, details such as attaching enclosed cash incentives to the cover letter is seen as a way of getting more attention from the recipient to understand the survey request.

Specialized delivery systems for survey requests, for example sending a third or fourth mailing my Federal Express, has repeatedly been shown to be helpful for improving response. Delaying its use until a third or fourth contact reduces costs, but also helps underscore the importance of the survey and the recipient's response to it by providing a contrasting source of communication.

Some surveyors spend a great amount of front-end planning on how requests to respond will be structured; others spend almost none, choosing instead to take a wait-and-see attitude, adjusting their plans on the basis of early responses costs considerations. However, there can be little doubt that such things as deciding the number of contacts, how they are timed, how they are delivered, and what each contains, affects response for most surveys. The ability of different modes of contact to reach different members of the survey sample and reinforce requests by other modes is also an important issue that needs to be considered by response rate theories.

6. **Shaping the content and display of each request for a survey response in ways that adds value to that request plus all other requests will improve response rates.**

Our shift towards greater use of self-administration means attempts to persuade people to respond to surveys have to incorporate what used to be assigned to the verbal protocol of interviewers, but now needs to be written. In addition, there is much that surveyors are required or feel obligated to say to potential respondents in the various contacts—why a survey is being done, how the recipient of the request was selected, who is sponsoring the survey and how the survey results will be used.

Explanations are also needed on whether and how *confidentiality* is protected and how or whether respondents receive *remuneration*, and *how to access the internet* if needed. This means that URL and access code information must be available. In addition, information needs to be provided on how to get additional information about the survey. Information about *Institutional Review Board (IRB) approval* may need to be provided with contact information for that office. And, government sponsored surveys may be required to provide information on *Office of Management and Budget approval* and contact information for that office. If incentives are used to encourage response an explanation of that may also need to be provide. In short, a tremendous amount of potential content is competing for limited space in each survey request (Schreiner 2019).

Communication occurs in many places. In mail contact s it occurs through size and kind of envelopes, stationery and prose in cover letters, and from inside the questions themselves. In internet surveys it occurs in emails, introductory survey material, how URLs are provided, and requirements for asking certain questions. The opportunity to communicate information that will improve response is to some extent wasted in many surveys. Sometimes surveyors try to force everything potential respondents might like to see into one request, where the respondent can see everything at once. That information may then be repeated nearly verbatim in follow-up requests that all appear to be the same. Such repetition is probably not desirable.

Developing communications with sampled individuals when multiple attempts can be made to encourage response involves a number of decisions. What mode will be used for each contact? For postal contacts what kind of envelopes, postcards or other packaging will be used? For internet surveys, what kind of introductory screens will precede the actual survey questions? And, will motivation information be included on some of the pages?

It would also seem that the separate messages need to consider what communication elements need to be *withheld from a particular contact* in order to place greater emphasis on other topics. Self- administration and mixed-mode surveying effectively convey survey requests in different ways and times in the implementation process. However, knowing what to communicate and when to do it is one of the most under-researched areas of response rate research. Many studies have focused on small changes in wording, and only limited studies have been for testing communication content across contacts for total impact. Despite the lack of research and guidance for how to build communication efforts across contacts, it seems likely that some sets of coordinated messages will be more effective than others, and therefore needed to be considered in response rate theories (Schreiner 2019).

7. **Shaping specific features of survey design to known attributes of those receiving requests to responds, will improve response rates.**

Considerable past research has focused on how *personal characteristics* affects who responds and does not respond to survey requests. This research has shown that many demographic characteristics affect response rates (e.g. Dillman et al. 2014). Age is among them, with young people generally less likely to respond to surveys that are older ones. Education is also an important factor found to affect response and affects people's ability and willingness to respond to certain modes. Use of the internet to collect survey responses has now introduced computer literacy as a factor that influences whether people will respond to surveys conducted by that mode.

Research has also shown that people who have less education, less income and are older do not have internet access to the extent that other people do. Thus, access by that mode is limited in ways that does not typically exist for mail or telephone.

Another personal attribute that influences response is particular attitudes people hold, including predispositions to answer surveys. Some studies have also found that people involved in community activities are more likely to respond to surveys. Past behaviors, e.g. the extent to which people have responded to previous surveys may also be an important contributor to response. A great deal of research has focused on psychological attitudes and beliefs that are theorized to be important influences on response, as discussed in the next section.

Most attributes of potential respondents are techniques that cannot be manipulated for improving response rates, in the same way that for example, number of contacts and the use of incentives can. Yet, they remain important influences on response rates. Understanding those influences may be important for identifying individuals with whom special additional efforts must be made if satisfactory response rates are to be achieved. Thus, they cannot be ignored in theories about how to achieve high response rates.

Connections Among Influence Factors in Survey Designs

Table 2.1 summarizes the seven factors identified here as likely to influence survey response rates. It also provides examples of more specific variables that may channel each type of influence.

Consideration of these potential influencers of response suggests that a theory that ignores any of these broad categories is likely to ignore survey design features that could improve response rates. It also suggests that research is needed for understanding how the individual factors may interact with others in order to improve response rates to the extent possible. To illustrate, some survey designers unintentionally end up with low response rates by ignoring various influence variables.

For example, consider *Hypothetical Design A*, for a government- sponsored study of a sample of individuals for whom postal and email addresses are available. The survey contains 150 items and will take on average 30 min to complete. The designer decides to conduct the survey only through email contacts, which makes it impossible to provide even modest incentives with the request because of the inability to deliver them in a practical way. The survey is implemented by a contractor, who decides to send only one email request to respond. In it the contractor's organization is identified as conducting the survey, and only mentions government sponsorship in a later paragraph of the email. In addition to avoid item nonresponse, answers are required for every question. This survey design seems likely to get a low response, but could do much better.

Table 2.1 Categories of response rate influences with examples of each

Types of known influencers of response rates	Selected examples
1. Using *multiple modes* of survey contact and response improves response rates.	Contact mode(s) Response mode(s) Mode augmentation
2. *Sponsorship* by a survey organization with known legitimacy and is trusted by potential respondents improves response rates.	Government, university, or private sector Known vs. unknown sponsor Trust that request is legitimate Trust in confidentiality and protection of data
3. *Creating smaller less onerous survey response tasks* will improve survey response rates.	Length Mandatory or voluntary Interest vs. uninteresting topic Will results be useful Technology requirements Unanswerable questions Are responses required for all items
4. *Providing incentives* with the request for a response appropriate to sponsorship and task will improve response rates.	Presence or absence Type of incentive; money or material Pre vs. post incentives, or combined
5. *Multiple carefully timed requests* to respond made through all available channels of communication will improve response rates	Number of response requests Timing of response requests Interview vs. self-administered Special contact methods When incentives are sent
6. *Shaping the content and display of each request* for a survey response in ways that add value to that request plus all other requests will improve response rates.	Visual vs. aural Placement; e.g. envelopes, interviewer protocol, inside questionnaire How incentive presented
7. *Shaping specific features* of survey design to known attributes of those receiving requests to responds, will improve response rates.	Education Political identification Gender Occupation

Hypothetical Design B for the same government survey uses knowledge of influencers from the various categories to improve response. A redesigned implementation plan might begin with an attempt to negotiate a shorter questionnaire in order to avoid cut-offs and improve overall response rates (**3 Response task**). In addition, since postal addresses are available the sponsor can begin the data collection with a postal contact to request an internet response (**1 Survey mode**) and send an enclosed incentive (**4 Incentives; 5 Structure of request**) to increase the internet response rate. Sending this contact in a large envelope will increase the likelihood of the request being opened, and attaching the cash incentive to the cover letter will increase the likelihood of it being seen (**5 Communication content**). In addition, prominently identifying the study sponsor as the government (**2 sponsorship**) instead of the contractor will further increase respondent receptivity to responding. Sending a quick email follow-up known as email augmentation (**1 survey modes**

and 5 structure of response request) will increase internet response rates further. A third follow-up that encloses a paper questionnaire (**1 survey modes**) will improve response rate from older, less educated, lower income people (**7 attributes of potential respondents**) who are unable or less willing to respond over the internet.

There can be little doubt that Design B will improve response over Design A. To do that it combines influencers from all seven of the identified categories. This example suggests that focusing on only one or two of the categories of influencers will not raise response rates to the extent possible.

It is also important to realize that not all influence factors or categories will improve response rates for every individual in a survey population. Virtually all surveys have a few individuals who respond quickly without incentives, follow-ups or deep thought. Doing so is more a reflex action than a deliberative process of deciding whether to respond or not respond. In addition, not all influence categories or factors within them are relevant to getting respondent from a particular individual. Our goal is to improve overall *response rates of the group being surveyed*, which is likely to bring all factors into consideration to some degree, making them relevant to a theory of response rates.

Review of Existing Response Rate Theories

Based upon the above conceptual framework, and multiple observations that support the importance of each category of factors posited to influence response, several issues seem important for inclusion in a theory of the causes of high response rates.

First, a theory needs to have breadth, rather than focusing on only one or two potential influences on response. Otherwise, it is likely to fall short of explaining final response rates.

Second a useful response theory needs to connect its theoretical propositions about factors that explain response rates to specific characteristics of survey design. That is, a useful theory needs to make explicit connections to the array of specific design characteristics identified earlier in this chapter. This means that a useful theory needs to address factors that are structural in nature—survey topic, length, and sponsorship, which are not normally factors that survey designers consider routinely open to manipulation as a means of increasing response rates. That theory also needs to take into account factors that are routinely manipulated, such as incentives and how they are delivered, number of contacts and survey mode. A theory cannot be so vague as to argue that only individual predispositions or attitudes towards being surveyed can influence response, nor can it argue that only length of survey will predict the final response rate.

Third, a useful theory needs to consider how individual influencers of response from the seven categories interact with each other, reinforcing other positive influences or countering negative ones. A theory that focuses on only one potential influence on response is unlikely to explain the achievement of high response rates or very low ones. In addition, it would also be helpful for a theory to connect with broader theories of how humans behave and the reasons for particular behaviors.

Florian Keusch (2015) has provided an excellent analysis of how theories about human behavior have been applied to understanding why people do or do not participate in *web* surveys, discussing the strengths and limitations of multiple theories. That analysis is supported by a very detailed summary of the extensive literature on the individual effectiveness of various techniques for encouraging response. It provides excellent insights into the strengths and limitations of various theories for explaining response rates, most of which are discussed below. However, his paper is also limited by its focus solely on web surveys.

My purpose in this paper is broader. My goal is to evaluate theories on the basis of the guidance they might provide for achieving high response rates. This will require in most instances the use of multiple modes of contact and/or response. Thus, we need to get beyond relying on single mode studies. I am also looking for theoretical insight into how to connect other design elements with the use of multiple modes, in an effort to achieve high response rates. I also seek to get beyond the piecemeal strategy that has tended to evaluate response inducing techniques individually, rather than in the context of how they connect with other techniques.

Cognitive Dissonance Theory

One of the earliest theories of human behavior used to explain responding to surveys was Leon Festinger's theory of cognitive dissonance (1957). The theory suggests that people attempt to achieve consistency or cognitive consonance. Thus, if responding to a survey is consonant with how a person sees him or herself, they are more likely to respond.

This theory posits that characteristics of the potential respondent (category 7) predicts response behavior, but has not been explicitly linked to other categories of potential responses. In addition, Festinger's book makes no reference to surveys. At best it only explains one aspect of why a person may respond to surveys, and even that seems not to have been carefully tested. Yet, it makes the useful point that preexisting psychological states are likely to influence behavior.

Although cognitive dissonance may explain an important aspect of why people respond or don't respond to a survey request, it has not been connected to the development of specific actions that when taken together will improve or decrease survey response rates. Convincing people in a survey sample to respond requires more than asking everyone to act consistently with what they have done in the past. Thus, it's not been used in a meaningful way to specify manipulations of most of the seven categories of response factors described earlier in this chapter.

Reasoned Action and Planned Behavior Theory

The Theory of reasoned action and planned behavior (Fishbein and Ajzen 1980) proposes that attitudes will explain behavior to the extent that those perceptions predict behavioral intentions. Thus, like cognitive dissonance theory it focuses on attributes of the survey request recipient. The linkage between attitudes and behavior is said to hold when the decision to take a specific action such as responding to a survey, is under the control of the respondent.

If a person has a positive view of a particular survey then they are more likely to respond to that survey. In support of that Hox et al. (1996), has found that one's internal expectation of responding is positively correlated (.24) to whether they actually respond, as noted by Jans and Levenstein (2015, p. 15). These authors also note that "... this correlation leaves one wondering what other possible predictors of nonresponse are missing."

This theory focuses specific on preexisting beliefs and attitudes of the potential respondent and brings the effects of subjective norms that encourage or discourage response into consideration. These beliefs could stem from various characteristics associated with a survey, for example topic and length. Such a connection has not been explicitly made when applying this theory to survey response research. In addition, structural aspects of survey design such as number of contacts that almost always affects response rates, seem somewhat distant from this theory. Instead if focuses only on whether internal social psychological attributes of the person asked to respond to a survey are positive or negative towards the survey.

A further theoretical development that seems consistent with this approach is what Gloria Origgi (2018) describes as our transition from an information society to a reputational society. She argues that the more information that circulates the more we have to rely on others to evaluate it. When social media dominates are daily existence as they do today, and the volume of information we must digest multiplies, we may rely increasingly on how requests to behave in a particular way are viewed by a source that has a positive reputation from the potential survey respondent.

Adult-to-Adult Communication Theory

Another intriguing, although quite limited, approach to theory was developed by Comley (2006). Based upon his experiences he proposed that an adult-to-adult communication style, as opposed to communication with potential respondents as if they were children, would improve response. Thus, the focus is on communications with respondents, avoiding demeaning statements such as "you must respond to this request today" that sometimes work their way into response requests.

The strength of this theory is its focus on how communication requests might influence response, but it does not provide test data to show its effectiveness. In addition, the sole focus on communications ignores the other categories of influences discussed earlier in this paper. The value of this theory is that it shifts attention from general attitudes that recipients of survey requests might have to how communications with those individuals might effectively be constructed. This approach to communication is not included in most other theories discussed here.

Gamification Theory

Another communication-focused theory was developed by Puleston (2012). It involves trying to make surveys fun for respondents to complete. A goal is to make surveys appear like games, and perhaps award badges or points for respondent efforts.

Efforts to gamify surveys appears to be an attempt to relate surveys more effectively to younger recipients of survey requests, who have experienced, and learned to appreciate, games on computers. Use of the gamification approach is also limited by its singular focus on communications, rather than connecting to other potential influences on response rates.

This approach is also singularly focused as is the adult-to-adult style communication approach favored by Comley (2006). It has been argued that gamification will increase consumer engagement and enjoyment of completing surveys (Bailey et al. 2015). However, it has not been found to improve survey response rates among children, a group where it seems likely to be most effective (Mavletova 2015). An unknown aspect of the gamification process is the potential consequences of turning a serious request for information (e.g. into a request for family expenditures or census questions to obtain demographic information) is whether it encourages people to provide misleading answers as sometimes happens when in a gaming role where strategic decisions are an inherent part of trying to win.

Influence Theory

A social psychologist, Herbert Kelman (1953) provided an early conceptualization of three factors that influence the resolution of conflict being felt by an individual, and might be applied to understanding why a person considers and then decides to do or not respond to a survey request from another person. Three decades later, Robert Cialdini (1984) examined multiple ways of influencing people's behavior in various situations. He specified six principles that people regularly use to decide whether to comply with requests for other individuals, as follows:

Reciprocation When someone does something helpful to another person, there exists a tendency to reciprocate. This perspective helps explain the likelihood that response rates to surveys are increased, sometimes dramatically, by enclosing a small cash incentive with the survey request. The sponsor has "given" something to the recipient of the request, thus motivating the individual to respond. The desire to reciprocate underlies much of the research that has been done on incentives.

Consistency What one does in a given situation, is likely to be similar to what the same person has done in the past. In the absence of a previous behavior like the one a person is asked to do they may simply act in concordance with a preexisting belief. In this respect similarity exists with Festinger's theory of cognitive dissonance.

Social Validation People may also use a generalized referent, deciding to do something on the basis of what they believe another person in their current situation would do. Thus, evidence that others, and perhaps lots of others have done a particular action, will encourage people to respond positive to a request to do the same.

Authority People are more likely to respond to requests when asked by someone who has authority over them. A survey example is surveys of employees by the organization where they are employed. The U.S. Decennial Census is required by our Constitution and people are required by law to respond. This requirement helps explain the very high response rate obtained every 10 years when it is implemented.

Scarcity Cialdini also proposes that people are more likely to take an action if they are told that the opportunity to do so is scare, either because few people are being asked to do so, or because the opportunity is available for only a limited time.

Liking Yet another, factor that influences people to respond to requests, is because they simply like to do the task they are asked to perform. It is also apparent from past research that some people enjoy answering surveys, while others do not.

Cialdini's work focuses heavily on communications. Importantly, he identifies multiple dimensions of communication that may be relevant to convincing people to take a particular action. It is wide-ranging and suggests that people are motivated by multiple psychological characteristics in deciding to take a particular action. It also makes virtually no reference to survey examples or formal experimentation with surveys. In addition, little attention is paid to how the use of each of the concepts might be combined to provide a more powerful influence on human behavior.

Several years later an explicit effort was made to apply these survey heuristics to understanding the decision to participate in a survey (Groves et al. 1992). In addition to examining the use of these heuristics for creating survey response appeals, the implications of helping tendencies and opinion change actions were also examined.

This analysis focused almost entirely upon improving response to interviews. Thus, the examples and implications focused mostly upon how interviewer behaviors could be modified to use the heuristics in appropriate ways and times. They appropriately note that, "In mailed self-administered surveys the influences of the interviewer on the actions of the sample persons are not present." (p. 490).

From the standpoint of being a complete theory of response rates applicable to twenty-first century surveys, it does not, nor could it because of the time period, deal with internet issues and the huge trend away from interviews to self-administration that now dominate survey methodology. Also, it focuses on people's thoughts and beliefs without making connections to specific design decisions for the other six categories of influences discussed earlier in this paper. However, it laid the groundwork for later work by Cialdini (2016) and Groves and his colleagues (2000) that went in somewhat different directions.

Pre-suasion Theory

In 2016 Cialdini published a book titled, **Pre-suasion (2016).** This work was foreshadowed by a conclusion drawn from the Groves et al. work (1992, p. 490). "We might also deduce that the initial tactics of interviewers upon contacting a sample household would concentrate on maintaining contact or rapport building rather than on seeking compliance."

Cialdini describes in detail how a researcher might take action to build personal trust in order to create a privileged moment for asking the person to comply with a request. He also describes further steps to relate on a more personal level with the potential respondent, including creating a mystery in order to lengthen the interaction process. No specific attention is paid to survey design implications.

A mail survey response study that built respondent messages and the questionnaire in accordance with pre-suasion concepts, produced a response rate about one-third lower than the control group that built around a design based upon social exchange theory concepts (Greenberg and Dillman 2017). However, further research using a different population, survey topic, and operationalization of the pre-suasion concepts is needed. My conclusion on Cialdini's work is that the concepts seem quite relevant, but the connection to the seven categories of survey influence (beyond individual attitudes and beliefs) has not yet been made. The lack of application to self-administered and particularly internet data collection methods is especially concerning.

Leverage Saliency Theory

Leverage-Saliency Theory (Groves et al. 2000) builds upon the heuristic concepts introduced by Groves et al. (1992) and response framework ideas developed earlier by Groves and Couper (1998). The basic idea underlying leverage-saliency is that some survey attributes are likely to have positive effects on response while others have negative effects. In addition, individual recipients of survey requests are likely to be motivated to respond or not respond by different attributes. By determining which attributes are more important to a given individual, the survey designer can influence response by making the positive ones more visible, thus leveraging those in a way that increases the likelihood that individuals will respond to the survey request. The authors note that the achieved influence of a particular feature (of the survey) is a function of how important it is to the potential respondent as a positive or negative influence and how salient it becomes to the sample person when requested to respond to the survey.

In support of this theory they report results from an experiment in a mail follow-up survey to a face-to-face survey that had determined the extent of community involvement survey of the interviewed respondents in the first survey effort. Sending the request without an incentive resulted in 21% of the low involvement individuals responding, compared with 50% of the high involvement respondents. However, enclosing a $5 cash incentive to low involvement respondents resulted in 63% response rate compared to 66% who responded from the high involvement group. Thus, the incentive was far more important as a motivation for low involvement individuals to respond than it was for high involvement individuals. In the authors' words, "Leverage-saliency theory suggests that a single survey design attribute will have different "leverages" on the cooperation decision for different persons ... the activation of the potential leverage depends on whether the attribute was made salient to the sample person during the survey request." (pp. 306–307).

A significant contribution of leverage-saliency theory is to show that people with certain attributes are more likely to be influenced by certain survey design characteristics than are others. In the above case, it was obvious the incentive was effective in raising response rates *more* for the low involvement community involvement groups (from 21% to 63%) than the high involvement group (from 50% to 66%). However, from the standpoint of practical survey design, one would be ill-advised to remove use of the incentive from either group! Doing so would have resulted in achieving a response rate 16 points lower (50%) from the high community involvement group than that achieved by applying the incentive only to the low involvement group (63%). Knowledge of what causes response does not in this case support a change in survey design features.

Another concern associated with applying this theory is it assumes that one is able to determine whether particular survey attributes are salient to particular individuals so that a particular attribute can be applied (or leveraged) to those individuals for whom it is salient. That was accomplished in the above survey by conducting a prior interview to determine community involvement. A prior contact to identify specific characteristics of individuals is not typically possible in most surveys.

Although the experiment was applied to a mail follow-up survey the authors' primary interest as expressed in this article and the work with Cialdini (Groves et al. 1992) was to apply it to interview surveys. Surveyors were advised to find from initial reasons for refusals potential ways to tailor arguments to future contact with those individuals. It is now more difficult that in the past to apply this theory as individuals are increasingly unlikely to answer follow-up phone calls and engage in depth with an unknown caller, in either initial or follow-up calls. One attempt to test the ability to use information in initial telephone refusals found no difference in final response rates between an attempt to formulate tailored follow-up letters to individuals who refused the initial request, and a control group with a more generic request (Olson et al. 2011). I know of no other experimental tests that have been done.

Another challenge of applying leverage-saliency theory is the tendency to limit one's focus to one or two design features, thus drawing attention away from trying to understand how to design all of the visible aspects of how to design a particular survey. For example, if certain individuals are not influenced to respond by incentives, that does not mean they will fail to be uninfluenced by more contacts, the content of cover letters, the form of the request to respond, the mode choices offered, and whether respondents are able to understand and answer the questions.

Thus, leverage-saliency theory as currently developed and tested seems limited in its ability to inform us on comprehensive sets of design features that are likely to maximize response from the group being surveyed. By way of analogy, when one decides to buy a car, some may prioritize the size of the engine, others by fuel mileage, some by comfort features and others by color. The challenge of achieving the highest level of sales to potential customers is bringing all of those parts together. Leverage-saliency theory does not yet provide this kind of detail.

Benefit-Cost Theory

Singer (2011) who contributed the development of leverage-saliency theory later proposed a more general theory of survey of participation. In it she argues that people participate in a survey when, in their judgment, the benefits of doing so outweighs the costs. The theory is general in the sense that it proposes that in any situation where a decision is required, people choose to act when, in their subjective calculus, the benefits of doing so outweigh the costs, much like has been traditionally argued with social exchange theory. In addition, she notes that such a decision may be carefully reasoned, or quickly made with the help of heuristics.

Singer supported the proposed theory by discussing previous research on how individuals view confidentiality and risk. One of her conclusions is the perception of benefits, rather than the perception of risk or harm is the most significant in determining whether someone decides to participate in a survey.

Benefit-cost theory is described by Singer as resembling leverage-saliency theory, but, exhibiting significant differences as well. She concludes that that improved benefits are more important than reducing costs when asking people to complete a survey. She also notes that leverage-saliency research has emphasized the role of the interviewer in making some factors salient to the respondent. This suggests that the efforts to identify and address reasons for refusals might more profitably address benefits to be derived from completing the survey, instead of trying to reduce perceived costs, i.e. reasons for refusing to respond earlier over the telephone as explored by Olson et al. (2011).

Singer's theory is insightful with regard to the relative import of benefits vs. costs, especially in emphasizing surveys to think in terms of benefit-cost balances rather than either of them alone. However, it ignores trust considerations and does not focus specifically on implementation details for designing and Implementing surveys in order to achieve high response rates. Thus, it does not deal specifically with several of the influence categories outlined in Table 2.1.

Social-Exchange Theory

Social exchange theory, has similarities to the theory presented by Singer (2011). It was first applied to the design of surveys by Dillman (1978), and has been refined significantly in later editions of that book, most recently in Dillman et al. (2014).

It applies a general model for understanding how people behave in their interactions with others developed by Blau (1964), Homans (1961) and others. Specifically, it posits that people are more likely to comply with a request from someone else if they believe and *trust* that the *benefits* for complying with that request will eventually exceed the *costs* of complying. The rewards may be for personal benefit or the benefit of larger groups (community, society) with which they identify (Dillman et al. 2014). In addition, the ratio of specific benefits to specific costs is considered key to achieving high response rates.

The expected weighing of anticipated costs and benefits associated with responding results in this model sometimes being viewed as a rational behavior approach to surveying. However, nonrational considerations may also influence those evaluations and trust in the eventual outcome. This effect may occur through the application of heuristics and rules of thumb, which have little to do with an explicit consideration of how expected benefits outweigh costs of responding to a survey request. Reducing the decision to respond to a survey in its entirety to an explicit benefit/cost calculus, as emphasized by Singer (2011) seems likely to miss the reasons that some people decide to answer or not answer a survey.

A major difference between a social exchange approach and Singer's benefit-cost theory is the addition of trust as a key element of convincing people to respond to surveys, which her approach does not mention. In the social exchange context, trust is linked to benefits both as a long-term consideration and as occurring when the act of responding occurs. Trust is increasingly difficult to achieve in our electronic age, thus enhancing its importance in the social exchange formulation as described in its' most recent version (Dillman et al. 2014).

The social exchange survey response framework differs from most of the other theories described here by being tied directly to the many decisions that must be made when developing a survey design, providing specific guidance for designing features of the data collection process. Unlike leverage-saliency theory, it does not try to identify which factors are most salient to particular individuals, and then target communications in different ways to different people. Instead, as discussed by Dillman et al. (2014) it relies upon shaping procedures and messages to vary across multiple contacts in an attempt to reach and obtain responses from individuals in later contacts who were less likely to respond to early contacts. Thus, when contrasted with leverage-saliency theory it is not focused on trying to obtain data from potential respondents in order to formulate individualized appeals that are made later in the data collection process.

Ships That Pass Silently in the Night

The theoretical perspectives outlined here have for the most part been developed independently of one another, often by researchers who were simply trying to get perspective on what might be meaningfully applied in some way to improve response to surveys. In addition, some of the theoretical efforts have barely mentioned surveys in their creation and application, while others have gone into much greater detail and used them as guidance for developing detailed design and contact strategies. Many of the theoretical perspectives are social psychological in nature, emphasizing those constructs as influences on behavior, without linking them to the structural features such as sponsorship, number and timing of contacts which have known impacts on response rates. Thus, most of the seven categories of influences identified earlier in this chapter are simply ignored.

In addition, the theories have been developed for different purposes. Some theories, for example cognitive dissonance, reasoned action and planned behavior have been focused far more on trying to understand the natural and underlying causes of survey nonresponse, than on a specific evaluation of how specific actions are likely to improve response rates. Other theories, e.g. gamification, and adult-to-adult communication are singularly focused on steps that if used are expected to improve response rates.

The expressed purposes of theories are also quite different. For example, development of the leverage-saliency theory was explicitly focused on identifying factors that will influence specific individuals to complete surveys and using that information in follow-up communications to convert earlier refusals. The social exchange perspective encourages forming a comprehensive implementation system of many elements. Through multiple contacts and adjustments in appeals it seeks to appeal to and encourage response from all types of respondents.

In addition, most of the theories were developed and applied to evaluating survey strategies before the shift towards the internet and the increasing problems of conducting interview surveys that have produced precipitous declines in response rates to such surveys.

It is also apparent that we are now in an era in which mixed-mode surveys are dominant. The use of multiple contact and/or response modes is now one of the most powerful ways of influencing response. This issue alone, suggests the need to rethink and rebuild theories that will hopefully show how to obtain consistently high response rates for surveys.

The strengths and limitations of the various theories have seldom been compared. In many respects, they are theories that exist, some for many years, but are much like strangers who silently pass by one another in the night, while ignoring potential connections with other theories.

Where Do We Go from Here?

Most of the past theorizing is not very helpful in predicting response rates, because authors have not gone from their theory to articulating exactly what steps they would take to create survey designs that improve response rates. I believe the reason they haven't done this is that one cannot move from emphasizing just one or two abstract ideas to a complete design, and we must do that if we are going to make progress.

However, it would be a mistake to conclude that any of the theories presented here are completely irrelevant to explaining how the decision to respond or not respond to a survey gets made and implemented. Preformed attitudes and behavior heuristics undoubtedly influence response decisions of some people. In addition, specific features of a survey design also get evaluated by potential respondents. Thus, it seems important that various theories be brought together rather than discarded as unimportant.

There is no shortage of studies that have experimented with how specific design features affect response rates. However, most such studies are fairly limited in scope, focusing on one, two or a few design features. In the reporting of experiments, theoretical reasons for testing a particular design feature have also been mostly ignored. Where theory is mentioned it is generally provided as general background and only loosely connected to what the author proposes for investigation. Expressed another way, the conceptualization of tests often focuses on concepts like those summarized in Table 2.1, covering literature on the particular concept under investigation, but not linking their use to other concepts.

There are many reasons for this state of affairs. Research aimed at improving survey response rates is mostly driven by the practical needs of particular surveys. For example, surveyors often declare that they cannot use incentives, the survey questions proposed by the sponsor cannot be changed and/or the letter of request must come from a particular office. And, even though postal, telephone, and email contact information might be available, the current tendency is to use only email because it is cheapest. Efforts to improve theories and the use of theories needs to consider the following possibilities.

A Clear Definition of Theoretical Purpose Is Needed

Most of the theoretical efforts to date, have focused on only one or two ideas. The testing of those ideas has concentrated on whether there is evidence that they can make a difference. I find it difficult to argue that the original Cialdini concepts—reciprocation, scarcity, social validation, authority and reciprocation—are inappropriate or irrelevant. Similarly, the psychological concepts underlying cognitive dissonance and planned behavior and leverage-saliency also seem helpful. However, they remain quite unconnected to how one builds a comprehensive design of specific elements that when brought together will affect response rates. This gap needs to be closed if we are to get beyond researchers accepting these frames of reference, but leaving it up to practitioners to figure out how these concepts might be applied or operationalized into specific attributes of the data collection designs.

The focus of some theories, e.g. leverage-saliency, is less on achieving high response rates than it is in identifying the extent to which the influence of specific design considerations varies across people. In contrast, the focus in this paper, is on the need to explain as completely as possible how to create specific data collections procedures that will produce high response rates. I am also concerned with doing this in a way that effectively reduces nonresponse error by motivating all types of people in survey samples to respond. It is important to know what design attributes have greater effects on the individual decision to respond or not respond, but that is not sufficient for knowing the specific design needed to achieve high response rates from a specific population.

Theories Must Take into Account Potential Influences Not Considered in Past Theories

Today's surveys are increasingly mixed-mode, and self-administered. Telephone and in particular RDD surveys are running up against cultural changes that make voice conversations with strangers more difficult to achieve and less effective when they do occur. Theories that focus only on interviews are less helpful than in the past.

Contact information for individuals is more difficult to get than in the past, and individuals may essentially be outside the possibility of contact by certain modes, and contact information by all modes is less accessible than in the past. The shift away from interviews to self-administration and the increased likelihood of making multiple contacts, often by different modes, with multiple kinds of appeals introduces possibilities for influencing response in ways that did not exist until the early years of twenty-first century.

The world has also changed with respect to costs of privacy and confidentiality, described as less important than benefits by Singer (2011). The increased dependence by most people on the internet makes the collection, retention and later use of personal data more of a threat to people than in the past. This change also increases the need for creating trust.

Most older theories have been silent on the synergistic use of multiple contact and response modes for improving response, making them less helpful than they might be in making design decisions that will improve response rates. In the twentieth century, number of contacts, and incentives such as token amounts of cash with the request were generally identified as the two most powerful influences on response rates. Both remain helpful, but the mixed-mode context facilitates maintaining enhancing their use and effectiveness. An example is the email augmentation of postal contacts that improves the likelihood of web responses. In addition, the sending of incentives with a postal contact is also a heavy contributor to overall response rates and paves the way for effective follow-up contacts.

We are now entering the smartphone era of people having a mechanism for receiving requests and responding to surveys less than an arm's length away at nearly all times of day and night. Learning how to design surveys for smartphone surveys is in its early phases. Living in the twenty-first century requires that we come to grips with many new survey design considerations that influence response rates significantly, with more change to come, which good theory cannot ignore.

Explicit Connections Need to Be Made Between Known Influences on Response Rates and General Theories of Response

Theories are often expressed abstractly. One of the motivations for abstractness is to achieve a wide breadth of application. Most of the theories applied to improving response rates have not made specific connections between the theoretical concepts of interest and the large body of information available from experiments of how specific techniques influence response. Theories that do not connect in explicit ways with the seven types of influences outlined in this paper seem likely to be incomplete and less effective than desired.

In addition, one needs to recognize that in many respects obtaining survey responses involves attempting to create an effective conversation with potential respondents—first gaining their attention, engaging them in a "conversation" or exchange aimed at creating a collaborative outcome, and convincing them to share desired information in response to specific questions. In contrast to an active exchange sometimes achieved in interview situations, the underlying communication efforts are asynchronous in a self-administration environment. The factors affecting the response outcome involves connecting with the potential respondent's predispositions while attempting to tap into preexisting positive response inclinations and overcome negative ones.

In addition, this process involves multiple contacts that introduce new information without knowing how earlier messages might have been perceived by the potential respondent. Theory that guides this process of attempting to turn request recipients into respondents includes defining steps to take, putting those steps in order, and building meaningful connectivity across them. A useful theory for guiding development of this process cannot deal just with whether people see the survey request as cognitively consonant with previous behaviors, or only whether the person holds attitudes consistent with being a survey respondent. Neither can a theory focus just on the size of a monetary incentive, how an envelope looks, or how many contacts should be made. A good theory needs to deal with many potential influences discussed in this chapter simultaneously and in mutually supportive ways.

Theories Need to Be Multi-disciplinary

Some of our theorizing to date has been focused mostly on concepts from a single discipline. For example, Festinger and Cialdini, have focused on psychological influences that are applied quite generally to human behavior. Other theorizing, such as social exchange, has been social-psychological in nature, attempting to link people's social tendencies with psychological inclinations. The works on leverage-saliency, benefit-cost, and social exchange have all involved concepts drawn from sociology.

Theories of what to communicate when and how in order to influence response has been mostly ignored, but clearly needs to be incorporated into response rate theories. How to organize messages across multiple contacts seems especially important, for example deciding what goes into an initial contact, when and how follow-up communications occur by various modes has not been well research with regard to designing the survey implementation process. This seems especially important in light of both the possibility and necessity of multiple communications in order to achieve high response rates. Shifting from interviews to self-administration requires consideration of multiple planned contacts with potential respondents that was thought of much differently during the interview era.

Perhaps the major change affecting surveying is advancements in technology, including the rise of the internet and the many devices for connecting with it that might be used for survey contact and response. For individuals that has involved cultural adaptations as we learn how to cope, with the rapid changes occurring around us on what is normative and effective.

It is not clear how we can best do that. However, when looking at the many documented influences on response rates that have occurred in the past and are now emerging, a great deal of creativity will be needed in thinking about theoretical breadth.

Testing Comprehensive Designs

Another challenge faced by response rate researchers is that the approach to research needs to conform to general testing principles. Scientists like myself have been trained to only make one specific change at a time for experiments, so that the results will be interpretable in a causal framework.

If survey response rates are to be significantly improved, we need to simultaneously work from the other end, i.e. conceptually organized data collection strategies that involve many considerations. It is equally useful to develop, based upon theory, comprehensive designs that specify multiple influence factors, and to do that from different perspectives. Such comprehensive designs can be tested against one another. If one of those designs produces much higher response rates than another, we will not know exactly what caused the improvement, but can then design subtraction research that helps unravel the contributions of each component. This approach seems more promising than trying to inch forward one small change at a time as is now done for many survey response investigations.

One attempt to develop and compare comprehensive designs was the attempt to test pre-suasion theory against a social exchange-based design. The persuasion theory, as operationalized in the test by Greenberg and Dillman (2017) produced a lower response rate than did the social exchange approach. However, this was only one test, on a difficult to survey population (low income and education) and was done for a mail-only survey. Operationalizing the two approaches in different ways with regard to specific elements may have produced different results. Yet, it is a beginning of comparing comprehensive design, and tests like this seem a good place to begin our quest for better response rate theories.

Conclusion

Despite the frequent mention of theory as a basis for explaining why people do or do not answer surveys, the theories have for the most part not been effective in improving response rates. In addition, these theories have not in a practical manner engaged one other in an attempt to build and test comprehensive designs that flow from different perspectives of human behavior. They have for the most part ignored one another.

I believe we can do better, and hope this paper will stimulate others to contemplate better theorizing about response rates, and undertake empirical research to improve response rates. Perhaps this work will result in developing connections among existing theories, and perhaps it will reveal shortcomings that make currently used theories inappropriate.

At the beginning of this century admonitions were frequently offered that survey response rates had irreversibly declined. Subsequent research suggests that is an overstatement. As surveyors have learned to use multiple contact and response modes in supportive ways, and have developed ways to shift designs from predominately interviews to mostly self-administration, a more favorable situation has evolved. High response rate national censuses have been conducted in Australia, Japan, Estonia, and Canada, with much less reliance on interviews than in the past. A series of web-push surveys have shown that on a variety of topics, web-push methods that include incentives with the survey request have produced response from nearly half of the households asked to participate. It now seems plausible that reasonably high response rates can be obtained from lengthy (30 min) surveys (Dillman 2017). The main finding from recent research is that surveyors need to think differently about survey design than was done in the late twentieth century.

As these changes in survey methods, and factors that could significantly improve response rates, were occurring, response rate theories used by some to guide designs were not particularly helpful. Now seems an appropriate time for updating and rethinking theories so that they can provide more effective guidance for the design of future surveys that will produce acceptable response rates and representation of the survey populations.

Acknowledgements Support for writing this paper was provided by the Social and Economic Sciences Research Center (SESRC) in the Washington State University Office of Research at Washington State University (WSU), and the WSU College of Agriculture Human and Natural Resources (CAHNRS) under USDA Hatch Project 410 and by the USDA Multistate Research Coordinating Committee and Information Exchange Group, WERA 1010: Improving Data Quality from Sample Surveys to foster Agricultural, Community and Development in Rural America. The opinions expressed in this paper are my own, but I wish to acknowledge with thanks the helpful reviews and suggestions received from Glenn Israel, Virginia Lesser, Kenneth Wallen and other members of the WERA 1010 Committee.

References

Bailey, P., Pritchard, G., & Kemohan, H. (2015). Gamification in market research: Increasing enjoyment, participant engagement and richness of data, but what of data validity? *International Journal of Market Research, 57*(1), 17–28.

Blau, P. (1964). *Exchange and power in social life*. New York: Wiley.

Brick, M. M., & Williams, D. (2012). Explaining rising nonresponse rates in cross-sectional surveys. *The Annals of the American Academy of Political and Social Science, 645*, 36–59.

Cialdini, R. (1984). *Influence: The new psychology of modern persuasion*. New York: Quill.

Cialdini, R. (2016). *Pre-Susasion: A revolutionary way to influence and persuade*. New York: Simon and Schuster.

Comley, P. (2006). The games we play: A psychoanalysis of the relationship between panel owners and panel participants. In *Proceedings from the ESOMAR world research conference. Panel research 2006* (Vol. 317, pp. 123–132). Amsterdam: ESOMAR.

Dillman, D. A. (1978). *Mail and telephone surveys: The total design method*. New York, NY: Wiley.

Dillman, D. A. (2000). *Mail and internet surveys: The tailored design method* (2nd ed.). New York, NY: Wiley.

Dillman, D. A. (2017). The promise and challenge of pushing respondents to the web in mixed-mode surveys. *Survey Methodology, Statistics Canada, 43*(1), 3–30.

Dillman, D. A., Smyth, J. D., & Christian, L. M. (2014). *Internet, phone, mail and mixed-mode surveys; The tailored design method* (4th ed.). Hoboken, NJ: Wiley.

Dillman, D. A., Hao, F., & Millar, M. M. (2016). Improving the effectiveness of online data collection by mixing survey modes, Chapter 13. In N. Fielding, R. M. Lee, & G. Blank (Eds.), *The Sage handbook of online research methods* (2nd ed.). London: Sage.

Dutwin, D., & Lavrakas, P. (2012). Trends in telephone outcomes, 2008-2015. *Survey Practice, 9*(3). https://doi.org/10.29115/SP-2016-0017.

Festinger, L. (1957). *A theory of cognitive dissonance*. Stanford, CA: Stanford University Press.

Fishbein, M., & Ajzen, I. (1980). *Predicting and changing behavior: The reasoned action approach*. New York: Taylor and Francis.

Greenberg, P., & Dillman, D. A. (2017). *Mail communications and survey response: A test of social exchange vs. pre-suasion theory for improving response rates and data quality*. Paper presented at American Association for Public Opinion Research Annual Conference, New Orleans, LA, May 18th.

Groves, R. M. (2006). Nonresponse rates and nonresponse bias in household surveys. *Public Opinion Quarterly, 70*(5), 646–675.

Groves, R. M., & Couper, M. P. (1998). *Nonresponse in household interview surveys.* New York, NY: Wiley.

Groves, R. M., & Peytcheva, E. (2008). The impact of nonresponse rates on nonresponse bias. *Public Opinion Quarterly, 72*(2), 167–189.

Groves, R. M., Cialdini, R. B., & Couper, M. P. (1992). Understanding the decision to participate in a survey. *Public Opinion Quarterly, 56,* 475–495.

Groves, R. M., Singer, E., & Corning, A. (2000). Leverage-saliency theory of survey participation. *Public Opinion Quarterly, 64,* 299–308.

Heberlein, T. A., & Baumgartner, R. (1978). Factors affecting response rates to mailed questionnaires: A quantitative analysis of the published literature. *American Sociological Review, 43,* 447–462.

Homans, G. (1961). *Social behavior: Its elementary forms.* New York, NY: Harcourt, Brace and World.

Hox, J., De Leeuw, E., & Vorst, H. (1996). A reasoned action explanation for survey nonresponse. In S. Laaksonen (Ed.), *International perspectives on nonresponse* (pp. 101–110). Helsinki: Statistics Finland.

Jans, M., & Levenstein, R. (2015). Rethinking leverage-salience theory and causes of survey nonresponse: Integrating emotion, mood, and affect into theory of nonresponse.

Kelman, H. C. (1953). Compliance, identification and internalization: Three processes of attitude change. *Human Relations, 6,* 185–214.

Kennedy, C., & Hartwig, H. *Response rates in telephone surveys have resumed their decline.* Pew Research Center. Accessed March 30, 2019., from https://www.pewresearch.org/fact-tank/2019/02/27/response-rates-in-telephone-surveys-have-resumed-their-decline/

Keusch, F. (2015). Why do people participate in Web surveys? Applying survey participation theory to Internet survey data collection. *Management Review Quarterly, 65,* 183–216.

Mavletova, D. (2015). A gamification effect in longitudinal web surveys among children and adolescents. *International Journal of Market Research., 57*(3), 413–438.

Messer, B. L., & Dillman, D. A. (2011). Surveying the general public over the internet using address-based sampling and mail contact procedures. *Public Opinion Quarterly, 75*(3), 429–457.

Millar, M. M. (2013). *Determining whether research is interdisciplinary: An analysis of new indicators* (Technical Report No. 13-049). Pullman, Washington State University, Social and Economic Sciences Research Center.

Millar, M. M., & Dillman, D. A. (2011). Improving response to web and mixed-mode surveys. *Public Opinion Quarterly, 75*(2), 249–269.

National Research Council. (2014). Measuring what we spend: Toward a new Consumer Expenditure Survey. In: D. A. Dillman, & C. C. House (Eds.), *Panel on redesigning the BLS Consumer Expenditure Surveys,* Committee on National Statistics, Division of Behavioral Social Sciences and Education. Washington, DC.

Olson, K., Lepkowski, J. M., & Garabrant, D. (2011). An experimental evaluation of the content of persuasion letters on response rates and survey estimates in a nonresponse follow-up study. *Survey Research Methods, 5*(1), 21–26. http://digitalcommons.unl.edu/sociologyfacpub/141/.

Olson, K., Smyth, J. D., & Wood, H. M. (2012). Does giving people their preferred survey mode actually increase survey participation rates? *Public Opinion Quarterly, 76*(4), 611–635.

Origgi, G. (2018). *Reputation, what it is and why it matters.* Princeton, NJ: Princeton University Press.

Puleston, J. (2012). Gamification 101—From theory to practice—Part I. Quirk's Marketing Research Review (article 20120126-1).

Schreiner, J. P. (2019, November). *Improving web-push respondent communication in the American Community Survey.* Unpublished PhD dissertation.

Scott, C. (1961). Research on mail surveys. *Journal of the Royal Statistical Society, 124,* 143–205.

Singer, E. (2011). Toward a benefit-cost theory of survey participation: Evidence, further tests, and implications. *Journal of Official Statistics, 27*(2), 379–392.

Singer, E., & Ye, C. (2013). The use and effects of incentives in surveys. *Annals of the American Academy of Political and Social Science., 645*(1), 112–141.

Smyth, J. D., Dillman, D. A., Christian, L. M., & O'Neill, A. (2010). Using the Internet to survey small towns and communities: Limitations and possibilities in the early 21st century. *American Behavioral Scientist, 53*, 1423–1448.

Williams, D., & Brick, J. M. (2018). Trends in U.S. face-to-face household survey nonresponse and level of effort. *Journal of Survey Statistics and Methodology, 6*, 186–211.

Chapter 3
Advancing Theories of Socially Desirable Responding: How Identity Processes Influence Answers to "Sensitive Questions"

Philip S. Brenner

What is a "sensitive question"? Paraphrasing Supreme Court Justice Potter Stewart, we know it when we see it.[1] We typically label questions that respondents may find objectionable in some way as "sensitive." But after a closer look at these questions, we can distinguish them into three general types. The first is a narrow subset of sensitive questions that respondents may view as intrusive and potentially threatening to their anonymity or may request that they disclose information that could be used to defraud. These types of factual questions, such as birthdate, ZIP code and other detailed location information, and personal or household income and related types of questions on personal finances, go unanswered by respondents who doubt the legitimacy of the survey, fear the consequences of their improper use, or simply do not wish to be identified. The second is another narrow subset of questions with objects to which respondents may react with repulsion or disgust may also go unanswered by respondents who find them distasteful or appalling.

The third type of questions constitute the lion's share and are labeled "sensitive" if their object is potentially threatening, controversial, or objectionable (Krumpal 2013). These sorts of questions are those that encourage socially desirable responding, the term used to describe respondents' propensity to answer in a way that aligns with social norms. For example, questions about illegal drug use are typically considered to be sensitive and believed to encourage socially desirable responding because they deal with a topic that respondents may consider threatening if their answers (reporting a non-zero or positive amount or frequency) were disclosed to outsiders.

---

[1]Jacobellis v. Ohio, 378 U.S. 184 (1964).

P. S. Brenner (✉)
Department of Sociology, Center for Survey Research, University of Massachusetts Boston, Boston, MA, USA
e-mail: philip.brenner@umb.edu

Questions about normative behaviors and attitudes are similarly labeled as "sensitive." I recently encountered resistance from an institutional review board because I wanted to include innocuous and commonly asked questions about religious behavior, such as frequency of prayer and attendance at religious services, in a survey. IRB members were uncomfortable allowing me to ask these "sensitive" questions because "religiosity (e.g., prayer frequency) may be sacred and spiritual to some individuals, and the Board is concerned that some subjects may perceive the questions as sensitive and an invasion of their privacy." While I strongly objected to this comment and defended the need to ask important questions such as these, I understand that this is a commonly voiced, although simplistic and shortsighted, sentiment from some ethics board gatekeepers and critics of survey research.

But this critique also raises an important methodological question: for whom and in which contexts are these questions sensitive? Conventional wisdom holds that this process hinges on the emotions of embarrassment, shame, or guilt felt during the survey interview. Respondents feel shame admitting to an interviewer that they did something that they feel they should not have done, or guilt for admitting that they failed to do something that they feel they should have done. For example, respondents may fail to report a counternormative behavior, such as drug use, to an interviewer to avoid the feeling of shame or embarrassment or the threat of admitting to an illicit or illegal activity (Tourangeau and Yan 2007). But respondents who haven't used drugs during the reference period would be highly unlikely to consider these questions sensitive. "No" and "never" are easy answers to recall and report when the question is about a counternormative behavior (Fowler 1995). Moreover, respondents who used drugs many years before the reference period would also be unlikely to consider the question sensitive given the relative comfort of their "no" answer.

The only respondents who may *potentially* find the question sensitive are those respondents who used drugs during the reference period but that they will find the question to be sensitive is not guaranteed. Some number of respondents may have used drugs very early in the reference period and may see themselves as being very different people since that time. Or they may see drug use as an acceptable and harmless personal choice and not be ashamed to admit it. Or they may see their drug use as justifiable behavior against unreasonable social norms. Whatever the reason, not all respondents for whom the answer is "yes" will feel threatened by this question. Thus, for a sizable majority of the population, a question about drug use is not sensitive. Similar arguments could be readily drawn against other question objects commonly thought to be sensitive, such as sexual behavior, abortion, and illegal or illicit activity. Arguably, few respondents will feel threatened by these questions. So why paint with such a broad brush by calling them all "sensitive questions"?

This chapter reviews the theory behind sensitive questions and related concepts, social desirability and impression management, in survey data collection. The limitations of conventional understandings are outlined and a novel theoretical approach is introduced based in the self-views of the respondent. I argue that the time has come to retire the terminology of "sensitive questions" as too nebulous and encompassing to be of social scientific use. At the same time, I will argue that conventional understandings of sensitive questions that rely on subjective external assessments of threat, controversiality, or objectionability and respondents' concern over the interviewer's impression (and related personality constructs that are argued to prompt this concern) are incomplete and include residual variation that may be explained with an alternative theoretical approach. In its place, I argue for an understanding based in how respondents see themselves vis-à-vis their identities. This identity-based approach affords a more complete and effective understanding of socially desirable responding than conventional explanations.

Theories of Socially Desirable Responding

The classical psychological approach to understanding sensitive questions links the perceived sensitivity of the question and the potential for response bias (e.g., false negative reports of drug use or false positive reports of voting) to the personality of the respondent (Crowne and Marlowe 1960; DeMaio 1984). This perspective, called "impression management," originated in the work of Erving Goffman (1959) and was adopted by psychological social psychology (Leary and Kowalski 1990) and included in social desirability theory (Crowne and Marlowe 1960; Marlow and Crowne 1961), self-presentation theory (Leary 1996), self-monitoring theory (Snyder 1974), among other related psychological theories. Each of these theories posits that impression management is the manifestation of an inherent personality construct that leads some people to be more attentive to the expectations of social norms and the opinions of others.

The psychological interpretation and development of impression management has dominated survey methodologists' views on socially desirable responding. Survey respondents who score highly on the social desirability personality construct enter the survey interview as they would other social interactions, with a deep underlying concern for the impression the interviewer has of them. They feel a strong need to be seen as a good person, one who meets social norms and does not violate them. Thus, when questions are asked about normative behaviors, respondents are likely to report having performed them even if they have not, or report performing them at a socially acceptable frequency if their actual level of behavior is somewhat less than that. Similarly, their reported rates of counternormative behavior will be lower than their actual frequencies. These "defensive practices" as Goffman described them, allow respondents to save face (1959).

As a form of impression management, saving face is argued to occur late in the four-stage question answering process. Respondents must first correctly comprehend the question, interpreting it in a way that matches its intended meaning (see Fig. 3.1). Next, respondents must recall the appropriate information needed to formulate an answer. They must then process this information in order to enumerate or estimate a response (Tourangeau et al. 2000). The respondent with an exaggerated socially desirable personality construct may proceed through the first two steps without error

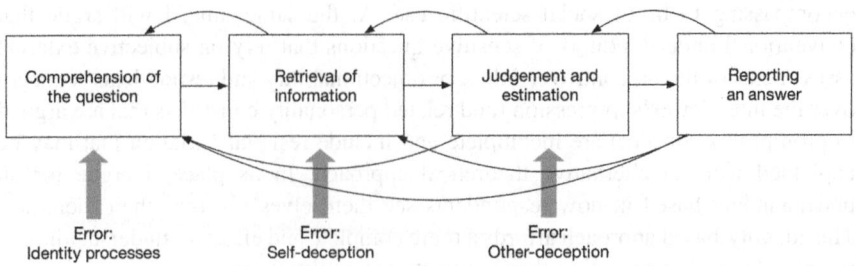

Fig. 3.1 Question answering process and sources of response error

but then introduce error to their response by intentionally adjusting their answer after reflecting on social norms (Holtgraves 2004).

Two important inferences follow these premises. First, because socially desirable responding is generated by impression management and hinges on interaction with the interviewer, we should not see errors like these on self-administered questionnaires, such as web surveys, mail surveys, and interactive voice response (IVR) interviews, in which interviewers are not present. Much of the survey methodological literature assumes this to be the case. Although some studies suggest that respondents report lower rates of normative behavior (Holbrook and Krosnick 2010; Stocké 2007a), higher rates of counternormative behavior (Aquilino 1994; Aquilino and LoSciuto 1990), and express less normative and more counternormative attitudes (Krysan 1998) on self-administered surveys, the evidence on the whole is somewhat mixed. For example, evidence suggests that respondents may exaggerate their normative activity even on self-administered surveys (Brenner 2019; Brenner and DeLamater 2014, 2016a, b; Kreuter et al. 2008). Moreover, even where self-administered surveys relieve socially desirable responding, they may only partially do so. Thus, self-administration may not correct reported normative behaviors to their true values; rather, a substantial portion of bias remains in estimates.

The relative scarcity of primary research specifically designed to address survey methodological problems contributes to the uncertainty in this line of inquiry. Much of the survey methodological literature investigating survey artifacts such as social desirability effects, analyzes data from production surveys originally designed for other purposes (Groves et al. 2009). Thus, these studies are typically limited by designs that are not true experiments. For example, one such study compared rates of religious behavior between two surveys—a web panel and a phone survey—and attributed a small effect to mode (specifically, comparing interviewer-administered and self-administered modes) without controlling for differing nonresponse and coverage error profiles or other factors of the survey designs that could cause observed differences (Cox et al. 2014). In addition, publication bias and the "file drawer problem" (Franco et al. 2014) may further muddy our perspective on this problem as null findings (e.g., no differences between interviewer- and self-administered modes) may go unpublished.

Second, respondents who score high on the social desirability personality construct should have a strong tendency to exaggerate all their reports on objects linked to social norms. They should tend to overreport all behavior and attitudes considered normative in their society or community and underreport all behavior that is considered counternormative. The corollary to this argument is that those who score low on the social desirability personality construct should tend to not exaggerate any of their reports linked to social norms. They should report all behavior and attitudes honestly in line with their true values on these topics. This explanation, focused only on a single personality construct in ignorance of the content of the survey question, is arguably naïve. Why would any respondent report so consistently with or without error regardless of the content of the question? Social norms are not uniform across time and space and are not evenly adhered to across individuals. Moreover, even individual respondents may report inconsistently, in a socially desirable direction on some questions and not on others. Undoubtedly, survey respondents care about some norms, attitudes, opinions, and behaviors a great deal, others less, and still others not at all and the variation in their feelings across these topics should influence their responses. Thus, the subject of the survey questions should weigh into respondents' answers and be reflected in their idiosyncratic errors.

Self-Deception

An extension to the personality-based explanation of socially desirable responding further distinguishes two factors in the phenomenon (Paulhus 1984). Where impression management, as has been discussed, has been referred to as "other-deception" given its focus on the interviewer as the object for or recipient of the deception (Sackeim and Gur 1978), "self-deception" refocuses the motivation for error back to the respondents themselves. Rather than editing a response for the benefit of the interviewer's impression, respondents edit their report for their own benefit; that is, for their own view of themselves.

Thus, this process is argued to occur earlier in the question answering response process (see Fig. 3.1). Rather than editing information recalled potentially without error (the process involved in other-deception), self-deception assumes that the information respondents recall includes systematic error which in turn biases survey estimates (Holtgraves 2004). The respondent arguably semantically interprets the question in a way that matches the researcher's intent but then engages in a biased recall process that generates information skewed toward and motivated by their own pre-existing self-views. Thus, self-deception is arguably an unconscious phenomenon in contrast with other-deception which is deliberate and intentional, although research has not supported this assumption.

If we accept that respondents recall information selectively in a way that supports their self-views, then the importance of the self-views should certainly matter. Therefore any tendency toward socially desirable responding must acknowledge the specific concepts or topics being measured beyond some generic notion of their sensitivity. Such an approach would correctly assume variation in respondents' attention to "sensitive questions" and social norms. Indeed, evidence suggests that social desirability fails to influence reporting on all questions for all respondents equally. When and where it occurs, its influence is uneven (Stocké 2007b; Stocké and Hunkler 2007). The literature has repeatedly demonstrated that people of different demographic groups and subpopulations, as well as those of different countries and cultures, approach and respond to questions about socially desirable topics differently (Lalwani et al. 2006; Ross and Mirowsky 1984; Steenkamp et al. 2010). Similarly we should expect that people in other groups, such as those with different political orientations (i.e., liberals/progressives v. conservatives), will see different objects as socially desirable. For example, a respondent who is disinterested in politics (perhaps holding "they're all alike" or "voting only encourages them" views on politicians across the political spectrum), would be unlikely to find questions about voting sensitive. This respondent would simply not care enough to bother overreporting voting. Similarly, a respondent who sees recycling and other "green" behaviors as a waste of time would be unlikely to find questions about green behaviors sensitive and would be unlikely to say that she recycles when she does not.

Similarly, attitudes may hold varying levels of sensitivity. Some attitudes may be socially desirable for some, but not necessarily all, people in particular communities, subgroups, or even within families. The current political environment, saturated with the openly racist, sexist, xenophobic, and anti-immigrant rhetoric of a polarizing American president, evinces a weakening of the social norms that made expressing these types of attitudes undesirable (Pettigrew 2017). If this shift in social norms is reflected in responses to questions in survey interviews and on self-administered survey questionnaires it may reduce the occurrence of socially desirable responding as some respondents feel emboldened to report honestly given the precedent set by this ugly political rhetoric (Valentino et al. 2018). For example, a survey respondent who holds anti-immigrant views may be less likely to report in a socially desirable direction, counter to their "true value," given the example repeatedly set by the extremely harsh anti-immigrant rhetoric of Fox News commentators, conservative talk radio hosts, and the White House.

Survey methodology already has a literature on the contexts in which respondents feel comfortable expressing counternormative attitudes. Research on interviewer effects gives equal weight to the content of the question and the context in which questions are asked; here, the observable characteristics of the respondent and interviewer. In an interviewer-administered survey, the respondent may be especially attentive to the potentially observable characteristics of the interviewer, such as their race (Finkel et al. 1991) and ethnicity (Reese et al. 1986), sex or gender (Kane and Macaulay 1993), sexuality (Kemph and Kasser 1996), age (Ehrlich and Riesman 1961), and religion or religiosity (Benstead 2014). Respondents may adapt their answers to meet the social norms expected from the interviewer based on these characteristics. While well established in the literature, this phenomenon is relatively circumscribed, linked only to questions related to the salient characteristic that is shared or discrepant between the respondent and interviewer (Groves et al. 2009; Schaeffer 1980). For example, a white respondent who does not support affirmative action may report supporting it to an African American interviewer but not to a white interviewer (An and Winship 2017). Similarly, a male respondent who adheres to traditionalist gender norms may report more gender egalitarian viewpoints to a female interviewer but report more honestly to a male interviewer (Huddy et al. 1997).

Unfortunately, this type of interactional and contextual approach has not been widely adapted to other problems and topics in survey methodology. Where the interviewer effects literature wisely focuses on the relationship between the topic of the question and the physical characteristics of the interviewer and respondent, research into other types of "sensitive questions" focuses on an external subjective evaluation of question sensitivity and the respondents' personality trait that motivates a predilection for socially desirable responding. Arguably, any understanding of social desirability error and the measurement of sensitive topics is incomplete without acknowledging that both the topic of the question and the respondent's contextual interpretation of it are important.

In summary, conventional understandings of socially desirable responding are incomplete. The problem is not that some questions are inherently "sensitive," leading all respondents to feel threatened by them. Nor is the sensitivity of the question the fault of a personality construct that leads some respondents tend to lie to all such questions in a consistent fashion. Nor is it the fault of respondents and their desire to be seen as good people by interviewers. Each of these is only a partial explanation at best. Clearly, there is some residual variation within conventional understandings of socially desirable responding that suggests additional explanation, or a better theory, is needed. I argue for a more complete and robust explanation founded in identity. This approach, rooted in social interaction, allows us to understand why some respondents respond in socially desirable ways on some questions but not others and in both interviewer-administered and self-administered modes of data collection.

Symbolic Interactionism and Identity Theory

Impression management was originally conceptualized and coined by Erving Goffman (1959), a sociologist and symbolic interactionist. Symbolic interactionism is a sociological perspective and one of the three faces of social psychology, along with psychological social psychology and the sociological perspective called social structure and personality (House 1977). Symbolic interactionism understands society as rooted in human interaction and human interaction as a product of society. In brief, it posits that meanings are created and shared in interaction, which is the basis for the existence and persistence of society (Cooley 1902; James 1890; Mead 1934). Meanings are created within and inform social interaction in our daily lives: garnered from and applied to the roles we play, to our physical and verbal characteristics, to the tangible and intangible objects we encounter, and so on. For example, individuals in one such role, those employed as physicians, achieve a sense of meaning by performing their duties, such as caring for the sick and helping well patients to maintain their health, and by using and displaying the objects of their profession, such as wearing a white lab coat and a stethoscope. In interaction with other individuals who are themselves taking on the roles of patients, the physician creates and enjoys the meanings attributed to practicing medicine.

This approach to symbolic interactionism has been critiqued for giving individuals nearly limitless agency to generate meaning that creates, maintains, alters, and can even completely overturn, society within interaction (Blumer 1969; Stryker 1980). However, the agency of the individual is not unlimited but rather is constrained by the social structure in which interaction occurs. Structural symbolic interactionism critiques and amends the tenets of symbolic interactionism by acknowledging that social structure determines interactional opportunities and that interaction occurs within the confines of a social structure that informs and constrains individuals' behavior (Stryker 1980). Thus, interactions don't occur in isolation; interactional partners don't enter each interaction *tabula rasa*. Rather, every interaction takes place in a world in which other interactions have occurred and are occurring. The influence of previous interactions extends beyond their immediate situations and into other interactional situations. Individuals and their interactional partners bring with them the summary of their prior interactions into subsequent ones. Moreover, interactional partners enter interactions with unequal power to guide the interaction and determine its outcome (Berger et al. 1972). For example, being a physician carries with it meanings—such as being a knowledgable, wise, and high status member of the community—that extend beyond examination rooms and hospital corridors into other interactional situations unrelated to their profession (Abbott 1981).[2]

Ensuring that others see us in the ways we see ourselves provides us a motivation for interaction. Individuals enter social interactions with the goal of ensuring that their interactional partner's view matches their own view of themselves. Verification of one's own view of oneself—or one's self-appraisal—by others generates positive emotions while a discrepancy between other and self appraisals yield negative emotions (Burke 1991; Burke and Stets 1999; Goffman 1959). This process spans interactions of all types, from informal interactions within our homes with our own family members, those with our close friends and acquaintances, to interactions as a professional or with other professionals, such as an interaction as a teacher with a student or an interaction as a patient with a physician.

The survey interview itself is a novel type of interaction [and a notably unusual and potentially awkward one (Schaeffer 1991)] in which this process is played out. In the survey interview, the respondent wants to ensure that the interviewer sees her in the same way that she sees herself, as a concerned and engaged (rather than disinterested) citizen, an attentive and caring (rather than negligent) mother, a respected and effective physician (rather than a quack), and so on. Note that, thus

---

[2]Note that these meanings are durable but not unchanging. For example, physicians were not always held in such esteem. The professionalization of medicine altered it and the way in which its practitioners were seen by the public (Waddington 1990).

far, this understanding shares much in common with more conventional understandings based on impression management. A primary difference, however, is that this process does not rely on a personality characteristic or construct.

Of course, we cannot read the minds of others and know with certainty what impression of us they hold. We rely instead on our own perceptions of their impressions, called reflected appraisals (Cooley 1902). Reflected appraisals are formed from our interpretation of the direct (e.g., verbal or written) and indirect feedback (e.g., nonverbal or gestural), as well as hearsay or gossip (second-hand information from other interactional partners) and information from other sources. For example, the student's reflected appraisal from their teacher might come from multiple sources: test scores and letter grades, as well as verbal comments (e.g., "good job!"), gestures (e.g., a wide, approving smile and affirming head nod), and actions (e.g., asking the student to assist or tutor their peers) of the teacher and comments from other students. If the student views herself as a good student, these pieces of feedback may contribute to a positive reflected appraisal that verifies of the student's positive self-appraisal. Note that not all reflected appraisals are based on such clear feedback, such as test scores and letter grades. Rather, reflected appraisals may, by necessity, be founded in less clear or even ambiguous evidence.

In a similar way, the survey respondent gleans a reflected appraisal from interaction with the interviewer. For example, if the respondent sees herself as a concerned and conscientious citizen, her affirmative answer to a question about voting in the last election may lead to a positive reflected appraisal that matches her own self-view. Granted, interviewers trained in standardized interviewing techniques only respond non-directively, using neutral utterances that avoid expressing any judgment, positive or negative, of the response (Fowler and Mangione 1990). Even though well-trained interviewers avoid either providing a positive and affirming response or openly challenging the respondent's answer, the unconditional acceptance of the respondent's answer (as long as it fits into close-ended response categories offered to the respondent) may still yield a positive reflected appraisal as, from the respondents' viewpoint, a self-view has been expressed and accepted.

Conversely, a reflected appraisal may fail to match the individual's self-appraisal. A student with bad marks and failing letter grades encountering a teacher's shaking head and heavy sighs may result in a negative reflected appraisal that is discrepant from the student's "good student" self-view.[3] Similarly, survey respondents may encounter discrepant reflected appraisals if their answers to survey questions are discrepant from their self-views. For example, if respondents see themselves as

---

[3]Note that individuals holding negative self-views (that is, those others may view as undesirable) would want them verified just the same. A student with a self-view as a poor student (e.g., the stereotypical "rebel" or class clown from *The Breakfast Club* or other John Hughes movies) would, however, see this reflected appraisal as verification of their self-view. Poor grades, critical comments, and even punishment for misbehavior (e.g., detention or visits to the principal's office) would be seen as positive reflected appraisals thereby verifying the self-view. Thus the evaluation of the reflected appraisal as positive or negative depends on its relationship to the self-view rather than our subjective assessment of it.

concerned and conscientious citizens but failed to vote in the last election, their answers to a question about voting would lead to a discrepancy between their reflected appraisals of the interviewer's view and their own self-views.

In the face of a discrepant reflected appraisal, the individual has a number of options. First, the individual might take action to correct the discrepancy and bring the other's and one's own views into agreement. In more typical types of everyday interactions, the individual can change their behavior, improve their skills, argue their case with their interactional partner, or take any other number of tacks to ensure that the reflected and self appraisals agree. For example, in a conversation with a friend or colleague, the physician from a previous example who failed to vote may attempt to use these types of "defensive or protective practices" to save face (Goffman 1959: 14) and ensure a positive evaluation (Holtgraves 2004) by telling her friend that she "usually votes" but failed to do so this election for some important reason, such as being out-of-town for an emergency or the like. But unfortunately for respondents, the standardized survey interview doesn't leave much, if any, room for these sorts of justifications.[4] The respondent may try to hedge or amend her answer, but survey interviewers are trained to clarify and probe answers until they receive one that fits the response set (Fowler and Mangione 1990).

Second, the individual might dismiss the reflected appraisal as incorrect or unimportant. This approach may be successful if the interactional partner is unimportant to the individual or whose opinion can be readily dismissed or if the reflected appraisal is reflecting something unimportant to the respondent. For example, a student whose reflected appraisal from their teacher is negative might discount that information as partial and unfair (e.g., "she just doesn't like me" or "he has it out for me") in order to maintain their self-view as a good student.

While disregarding a reflected appraisal by discounting the interviewer and their opinion is certainly an option for the respondent in the survey interview, the respondent has another option that is perhaps more easily taken. The problem of a discrepant reflected appraisal may be avoided completely by a respondent who reports honestly about her self-view as a good citizen by reporting voting in the election. When the question is asked, the respondent may interpret the question to a pragmatic meaning ("Are you the kind of person who votes?") (Belli et al. 2001) rather than its semantic meaning ("Did you vote in the last election?"), placing the source of this error in the first stage of the question answering process (see Fig. 3.1). This interpretation allows the respondent to report on her self-view as a good citizen and regular voter rather than reporting that she did not (for good reasons) vote. Research on error in reports of religious behavior suggest that explanation may better illustrate the response process. Using a series of cognitive interviews, Brenner (2017a) found that respondents apply pragmatic interpretations to report on self-views as religious people rather than actual behavior which may fail to live up to those self-views.

---

[4]Many self-administered surveys leave even less room for these justifications, other than writing in the margins of a mail survey.

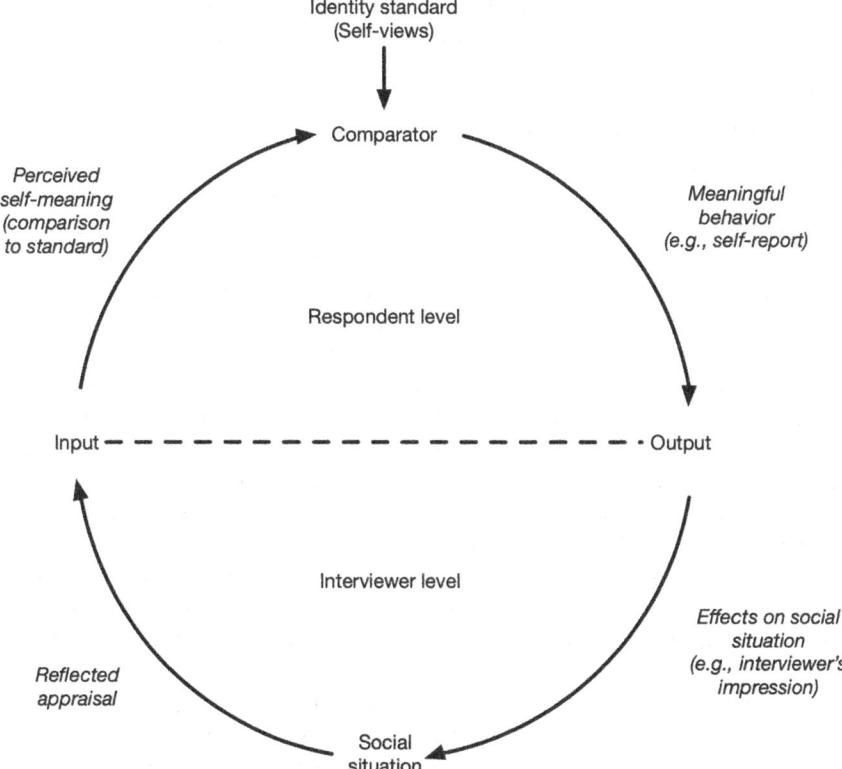

Fig. 3.2 Cybernetic identity model for survey response

This process by which one compares reflected appraisals to a self-view is represented in identity theory as a cybernetic model (see Fig. 3.2). Individuals enter social interactions with the goal of ensuring that the interactional partner's view of the individual matches that held by the individual. Individuals compare the reflected appraisals of others to a standard, one's self-view. If the comparison yields a positive match between the self-view and the reflected appraisal, called identity verification, positive emotions are the result (Burke 1991; Burke and Stets 1999; Goffman 1959). If the comparison yields a mismatch (one's self-appraisal is not verified) between the self-view and the reflected appraisal, called identity discrepancy, negative emotions are the result.

The outcome of this process is deeply important as it involves key components of how individuals see themselves: of who we are at our cores. We define ourselves by the roles we fill, such as physician, parent, or professor; the groups to which we belong, such as being Jewish or Catholic or being Democrat or Republican; and the other personal characteristics we hold, such as being artistic or devout. But each of us plays multiple roles, holds multiple group memberships, and characterizes ourselves in multiple ways; not all of which are equally important or valuable in how we define ourselves. As an application of structural symbolic interactionism, identity theory helps us to understand how we view and manage each of these parts of the self.

According to identity theory, "identities are 'parts' of the self, internalized positional designations (that) exist insofar as the person is a participant in structured role relationships" (Stryker 1980: 60). Each of us is an amalgamation of identities, the exact mixture of which is a function of the roles we fill in social interaction (James 1890). We may have as many identities as we have roles that are performed with others who are themselves performing counter-roles (e.g., parent-child, employer-employee, teacher-student). In conjunction with our social identities (i.e., group memberships) and personal identities (i.e., personal characteristics), each of these identities contributes to, and altogether comprise, the self.

Identity theory's focus is on understanding behavior and why individuals call forward and perform the identities that they do in interactional situations. Three concepts from the theory that detail the relationship between the identity and behavior related to it are also helpful for understanding how behavior is measured on surveys. The first of these concepts, identity commitments, was introduced in the previous paragraph. Commitments are the quantity and quality of connections the individual has to the identity through relationships with others. These two forms of commitments, called extensivity and intensivity, are one way to describe the identity. Commitments to an identity may be few in number (low extensivity) but very affectively strong (high intensivity), such as the connections to one's children through one's parent identity. Commitments may also be of relatively lower affective strength (low intensivity) but greater in number (high extensivity), such as for a priest with his parishioners and other clergy. The higher the number or intensity of the connections to the identity, the higher one's commitment to it. Commitments inform the other two key constructs of identity theory: identity prominence and identity salience.

The second construct, identity prominence, is the individual's affective connection to an identity, reflecting the value the individual places on the identity (Ervin and Stryker 2001; McCall and Simmons 1978). Prominence is typically equated with two complimentary or even synonymous concepts, identity importance (Ervin and Stryker 2001) and psychological centrality (Rosenberg 1979). What these concepts share is their focus on the affective; the value the individual places on the identity and its relative ranking among other identities in the self-concept. Thus, identities are hierarchically ordered based on their subjective value to the individual with highly ranked identities reflecting the individual's ideal self; the person one wants to be (Brenner et al. 2014; McCall and Simmons 1978). Individuals may have many identities for which they care very little but are obliged to maintain, such as an identity as a student if their approach to their own education is one of perfunctory obligation, or as an employee if they work begrudgingly for a paycheck at a job they dislike. Such identities would fall low on the prominence hierarchy. Conversely, other identities may be highly valued, such a professional identity as a professor or physician, or as a spouse or parent. Accordingly, these highly valued identities would place high in the individual's prominence hierarchy.

The third concept, identity salience, is the probability of an identity being enacted or the propensity to define a situation as relevant for identity enactment (Stryker 1980). Like the prominence hierarchy, identities are similarly arranged into a salience hierarchy. Highly salient identities are those that the individual is very likely to enact or to interpret a situation as relevant for their enactment. These identities are nearly certain to be called up and enacted in situations that are relevant to the identity (e.g., a person employed as a professor enacting their "professor identity" in the classroom, during a faculty meeting, or at an academic conference). Moreover, they may also be called up and enacted in situations that are not necessarily relevant (e.g., the professor discussing their research at a cocktail party, with a fellow passenger on an airplane, or with their hairdresser). Such an identity may be so highly salient that it subsumes the self and is nearly universally and continuously enacted, even in situations in which it is inappropriate (Turner 1978). For example, a former co-worker at a utility company for which I worked during the summer while an undergraduate had such a highly salient religious identity that it overrode and endangered his employee identity. On multiple occasions, he used his job as a service representative to proselytize customers who called to inquire about billing matters or changes to their service. Even after multiple warnings from supervisors, he continued this behavior in accordance with his highly salient religious identity, to the preclusion of his employee identity, and was eventually dismissed.

Unlike prominence, which is by definition at the level of the individual's awareness, the individual may not necessarily know the salience of an identity (Brenner et al. 2014; Serpe 1987; Stryker and Serpe 1994). Consequently, identity theory posits and research confirms that the prominence of the identity informs its likelihood of being enacted (Brenner et al. 2014; Nuttbrock and Freudinger 1991; Stryker and Serpe 1994). The higher the value placed on the identity, the more likely the individual will see a situation as relevant to the identity and thus call it forward and enact it. In this way, a highly prominent identity may be ubiquitously enacted across situations, whether it is appropriate or inappropriate, similar to the highly religious co-worker from the previous example.

Applying Identity Theory in Survey Methodology

Understanding the relationship between identity prominence and identity salience may be immensely beneficial for survey methodologists grappling with measurement error, socially desirable responding, and "sensitive questions." Although prominence and salience are typically concordant, they need not be. An identity may be of little or no value to an individual but may be enacted frequently and regularly given social obligations. An obligatory but disvalued identity, such as an identity as a prisoner or an employee at disliked job, may be oft-enacted but of low value to the individual. Conversely, an identity may be strongly valued but unlikely or rarely enacted given the constraints of daily life. Individuals may see themselves as athletes or physically active or fit and may strongly value this identity but have little time to enact it given their work schedules, demands of children and family, and the other rigmarole of daily life (Brenner 2016, 2017b).

Yet, even in this latter situation, survey measures based on self-reports may indicate high consistency between the prominence and salience of this sort of identity. However, this consistency may be an artifact of measurement (Stryker and Serpe 1994). High identity prominence may motivate bias in measures of behavior related to identities with discrepancy between (high) importance and (relatively lower) salience (Brenner 2011, 2012a, 2014). For example, the respondent who values religiosity and sees himself or herself as the "kind of person" who attends religious services regularly, may not enact the focal identity at a rate consistent with the identity given the costs of its enactment. These costs may include getting up early on a Sunday morning, spending hours at services instead of doing obligatory (e.g., running errands and doing housework) and leisure (e.g., getting brunch, going to the beach) activities missed during the busy work week (Brenner 2016). But in such a situation in which (high) prominence and (low) salience are discrepant, a survey question may be seen by the respondent as a low-cost opportunity to enact the identity. Asking a survey question about religious service attendance lacks the "normal situational constraints" that characterize the everyday situations in which identity performance does (or does not) occur (Burke 1980: 28). Respondents' answers to a survey question may reflect on their ideal selves linked to their religious identities rather than on their actual behavior as constrained by the lack of time, money, and other resources (Brenner 2016, 2017b). Thus, conventional survey measures of behavior that ask the respondent to report on typical or current behavior, or behavior over a long reference period, may encounter substantial measurement bias, especially if the identity and its consequential behavior are normative (Brenner 2011, 2012a, 2014).

Religious behavior is not solely affected by this source of bias. Indeed, other types of normative behaviors are also affected by survey respondents' identities. Survey respondents overreport voting by reporting that they voted when they did not or by saying that they vote more regularly than they do. Respondents' identities as good citizens (Brenner 2012b; Silver et al. 1986; Tourangeau et al. 2010) increase the social pressure to vote (Bernstein et al. 2001; Presser and Traugott 1992) and to answer the question about voting in line with this identity regardless of actual behavior (Belli et al. 2001; Brenner 2012b; Green and Shachar 2000; Silver et al. 1986).

Survey respondents similarly overreport their pro-environmental "green" behaviors such as recycling given their environmentalist or "green" identity. A number of studies examining the overreporting of recycling have compared survey self-reports of typical behavior with observation data, like the appearance of recycle bins on the curbside and the volume or weight of recycled material (Corral-Verdugo 1997; Gamba and Oskamp 1994; Vining and Ebreo 1992). Other articles compared self-reports to proxy reports to estimate and explain overreporting (Chao and Lam 2011; Lam and Cheng 2002). However, relatively few studies have compared an observed, discrete behavior to self-reported behavior to estimate overreporting (Barker et al.

1994; Corral-Verdugo 1997), but all suggest the contribution of a green identity to systematic error in survey reports (Terry et al. 1999).

Survey respondents may also overreport their physical activity (Durante and Ainsworth 1996; Sallis and Saelens 2000; Shephard 2003) for a similar reason. Reports of exercising and playing sports are strongly linked to respondents' identities as physically active people, as demonstrated by time diaries (Brenner 2017b), reverse record checks (Chase and Godbey 1983; Chase and Harada 1984), and experimental designs that manipulate the priming effect of the framing of the study (Brenner and DeLamater 2014, 2016a). These studies demonstrate that respondents' identities as physically active individuals motivate them to report a rate of activity that better reflects their identity as an active person in contrast to their actual behavior. Indeed, those with very prominent identities are very likely to also have high salience and a high likelihood to perform their identities. Work that manipulated the directiveness of the measurement process found that respondents with moderately prominent athlete identities were the most likely to overreport their physical activity. Conversely, respondents with low athlete identity prominence were less likely to overreport, presumably because they do not care enough about sports and exercise to do so. Moreover, respondents with very or extremely prominent athlete identities did not need to overreport as their actual behavior matched their reported salience (Brenner and DeLamater 2016a).

In each of these examples, respondents answer the "sensitive" question about normative behavior with error given reflection on their relevant (religious, civic, ecological, athlete) identity. All of these questions ask about normative behavior as, to my knowledge, no research has directly investigated the role of identity in the underreporting of counternormative behavior. It is likely that respondents may underreport some types of counternormative behavior for a similar reason. They do not see themselves as "kind of person" who engages in one of many counternormative behaviors, even if it is something that they had done in the more distant past. An identity-based approach may be fruitful for improving our understanding of how respondents report past abortion experiences, drug, alcohol, and tobacco use, criminal arrests, and the like. Moreover, this approach may help researchers to better understand stability and instability in self-reports of these behaviors over time (Shillington et al. 2011a, b, 2012). As time passes and one moves away (temporally, spatially, emotionally, etc.) from past behavior, the shame and embarrassment fades as we become different person. As a result, one's reporting on these behaviors change as one's view of the behavior, and the person they were when they behaved in that fashion, evolves.

Conclusion

Conventional wisdom labels questions that are intrusive or threatening, or whose object is controversial or objectionable, as "sensitive." These questions are seen as difficult to ask and even more difficult to answer as their answers may be embarrassing or make the respondent feel guilty or shameful. As a result, they have an increased likelihood of being answered in a socially desirable way, either falsely negative (claiming to have not done something one actually did, typically because it is frowned upon) or falsely positive (claiming to have done something that one did not, typically because it is obligatory or seen as beneficial).

This terminology, "sensitive questions," makes sense from the conventional perspective which focuses on subjective and external assessments of questions. The question itself, or more specifically its object, is seen as threatening, controversial, intrusive, or objectionable. These objects include behaviors, attitudes, and opinions that society or the respondent's community or family views as (or that not having or doing them is) undesirable, sinful, or wrong. They are met with disapproval, denunciation, or disgust by society which engenders in the transgressor feelings of embarrassment, shame, or guilt. Moreover, some respondents are more attuned to and desirous of the approval of others, and more cautious and avoidant of their disapproval. These respondents are argued to be more likely to mislead interviewers when asked questions about these types of topics.

Conventional explanations taking this perspective focus on the latter stages of the question answering process—flawed recall or estimation—as they view the phenomenon as a intention to deceive the interviewer or one's own self. These understandings assume that respondents correctly comprehend the intended semantic meaning of the question but recall information selectively or compile the recalled intimation in a way that shines the best possible light on their behavior, attitude, and so on. As a result, conventional best practices suggest relieving the potential for embarrassment, shame, or guilt by substituting all or part of a survey interview with a self-administered survey, such as a paper-and-pencil questionnaire.

However, this conventional approach, focused on personality constructs and subjective assessments of question sensitivity, is arguably incomplete. An identity-based approach, as was presented in this chapter, offers survey methodologists a deeper and more complete understanding of respondents' motivations for misreporting. An explanation based in identity shifts the focus earlier, to the question comprehension stage and does not assume a deception, either other-deception or self-deception, motivation. Rather, respondents reflect on their self-views and pragmatically interpret questions in ways that allow them to honestly report on these self-views.

This application of identity theory offers practical advice for the use of these self-reported survey data and insight on how the influence of identity may be avoided to improve measurement in the future. If these measures are being used to reflect the self-view of the individual, they may do so well. For example, a self-reported religious behavior measure, such frequency of church attendance, may be effectively used as an independent variable to control for religiosity in general, or self-reported physical activity may be used as an indicator of an athlete identity. However, the identity approach suggests that these measures may not reflect well the true value of their objects for which we need a measure with criterion validity. Achieving this requires some additional work. Research has demonstrated that some measurement procedures better reflect the true value of their objects. Using non-direct (and nondirective) measurement does not flag the attention of the respondent to the topic under study thereby avoiding the potentially biasing influence of the identity process. For example, chronological measurement, such as time diaries and extensions of the experience sampling method (ESM) can provide unbiased measurement of some objective objects, such as behaviors (Brenner and DeLamater 2014, 2016a, b; Hadaway et al. 1993, 1998; Presser and Stinson 1998) by obscuring the object under study from the respondent. Some of these procedures were originally developed to measure contextual and subjective states, such as mood, and may be effectively and fruitfully extended to the measurement of attitudes.

However, these specialized procedures may not work well in conventional production surveys given their typical limitations (i.e., restrictions on respondent time, attention, and cognitive complexity). Thus, the holy grail of questionnaire design is a technique that uses conventional, direct survey questions but does not prompt respondent self-reflection or one that provides an excuse that permits the respondent to disclose truthfully. Unfortunately, findings in this line of research have been, at best, mixed (DeBell and Figueroa 2011; Holtgraves et al. 1997; Näher and Krumpal 2012; Presser 1990). It remains unclear whether it is possible to write conventional, direct survey questions on topics such as these that avoid prompting the respondent to consider prominent identities thus becoming directive and encouraging measurement biases. But if we set aside the focus on question sensitivity and focus instead on the role of identity in the phenomenon of socially desirable responding, we may be able to progress in our understanding of the social sources of this form of measurement error.

References

Abbott, A. (1981). Status and status strain in the professions. *American Journal of Sociology, 86*(4), 819–835.
An, W., & Winship, C. (2017). Causal inference in panel data with application to estimating race-of-interviewer effects in the general social survey. *Sociological Methods and Research, 46*(1), 68–102.
Aquilino, W. S. (1994). Interview mode effects in survey of drug and alcohol use: A field experiment. *Public Opinion Quarterly, 58*, 210–240.
Aquilino, W. S., & LoSciuto, L. (1990). Effects of interview mode on self-reported drug use. *Public Opinion Quarterly, 54*, 362–395.
Barker, K., Fong, L., Grossman, S., Quin, C., & Reid, R. (1994). Comparison of self-reported recycling attitudes and behaviors with actual behavior. *Psychological Reports, 75*, 571–577.
Belli, R. F., Traugott, M. W., & Beckmann, M. N. (2001). What leads to voting overreports? Contrasts of overreporters to validated voters and admitted nonvoters in the American National Election Studies. *Journal of Official Statistics, 17*, 479–498.
Benstead, L. J. (2014). Does interviewer religious dress affect survey responses? Evidence from morocco. *Politics and Religion, 7*, 734–760.
Berger, J., Cohen, B. P., & Zelditch, M., Jr. (1972). Status characteristics and social interaction. *American Sociological Review, 37*(3), 241–255.
Bernstein, R., Chadha, A., & Montjoy, R. (2001). Overreporting voting: Why it happens and why it matters. *Public Opinion Quarterly, 65*, 22–44.

Blumer, H. (1969). *Symbolic interactionism: Perspective and method.* Berkeley, CA: University of California Press.

Brenner, P. S. (2011). Identity importance and the overreporting of religious service attendance: Multiple imputation of religious attendance using American Time Use Study and the General Social Survey. *Journal for the Scientific Study of Religion, 50*(1), 103–115.

Brenner, P. S. (2012a). Identity as a determinant of the overreporting of church attendance in Canada. *Journal for the Scientific Study of Religion, 51*(2), 377–385.

Brenner, P. S. (2012b). Overreporting of voting participation as a function of identity salience. *Social Science Journal, 49,* 421–429.

Brenner, P. S. (2014). Testing the veracity of self-reported religious behavior in the Muslim world. *Social Forces, 92*(3), 1009–1037.

Brenner, P. S. (2016). Time as a situational constraint on role-identity performance. In J. E. Stets & R. T. Serpe (Eds.), *New directions in identity theory and research* (pp. 279–307). New York: Oxford University Press.

Brenner, P. S. (2017a). Narratives of error from cognitive interviews of survey questions about normative behavior. *Sociological Methods & Research, 46*(3), 540–564.

Brenner, P. S. (2017b). Differential effects of time constraints on athletic behavior and survey reports of athletic behavior. *Sociological Spectrum, 37,* 97–110.

Brenner, P. S. (2019). On the rolls and at the polls: Survey estimates of voting in a total survey error framework. In *74th meeting of the American Association for Public Opinion Research.* Toronto: ON (May).

Brenner, P. S., & DeLamater, J. (2014). Social desirability bias in self-reports of physical activity: Is an exercise identity the culprit? *Social Indicators Research, 117*(2), 489–504.

Brenner, P. S., & DeLamater, J. (2016a). Lies, damned lies, and survey self-reports? Identity as a cause of measurement bias. *Social Psychology Quarterly, 79*(4), 333–354.

Brenner, P. S., & DeLamater, J. (2016b). Measurement directiveness as a cause of response bias: Evidence from two survey experiments. *Sociological Methods and Research, 45*(2), 348–371.

Brenner, P. S., Serpe, R. T., & Stryker, S. (2014). The causal ordering of prominence and salience in identity theory: An empirical examination. *Social Psychology Quarterly, 77*(3), 231–252.

Burke, P. J. (1980). The self: Measurement implications from a symbolic interactionist perspective. *Social Psychology Quarterly, 43,* 18–29.

Burke, P. J. (1991). Identity processes and social stress. *American Sociological Review, 56,* 836–849.

Burke, P. J., & Stets, J. E. (1999). Trust and commitment through self-verification. *Social Psychology Quarterly, 62*(4), 347–366.

Chao, Y. L., & Lam, S. P. (2011). Measuring responsible environmental behavior: Self-reported and other-reported measures and their differences in testing a behavioral mode. *Environment and Behavior, 43,* 53–71.

Chase, D. R., & Godbey, G. C. (1983). The accuracy of self-reported participation rates. *Leisure Studies, 2,* 231–235.

Chase, D. R., & Harada, M. (1984). Response error in self-reported recreation participation. *Journal of Leisure Research, 16,* 322–329.

Cooley, C. H. (1902). *Human nature and the social order.* New York: Charles Scribner.

Corral-Verdugo, V. (1997). Dual realities of conservation behavior: Self-reports vs observations of re-use and recycling behavior. *Journal of Environmental Behavior, 17,* 135–145.

Cox, D., Jones, R. P., & Navarro-Rivera, J. (2014). I know what you did last Sunday: Measuring social desirability bias in self-reported religious behavior, belief, and identity. In *Paper presented at the 69th annual meeting of the American Association for Public Opinion Research.* CA: Anaheim.

Crowne, D. P., & Marlowe, D. (1960). A new scale of social desirability independent of psychopathology. *Journal of Consulting Psychology, 24,* 349–354.

DeBell, M. & Figueroa, L. (2011). Results of a survey experiment on frequency reporting: Religious service attendance from the 2010 ANES panel recontact survey. Paper presented at the *66th annual conference of the American Association for Public Opinion Research*, Phoenix, AZ

DeMaio, T. J. (1984). Social desirability and survey measurement: A review. In C. F. Turner & E. Martin (Eds.), *Surveying subjective phenomena* (pp. 257–282). New York: Russell Sage.

Durante, R., & Ainsworth, B. E. (1996). The recall of physical activity: Using a cognitive model of the question-answering process. *Medicine and Science in Sports and Exercise, 28*(10), 1282–1291.

Ehrlich, J., & Riesman, D. (1961). Age and authority in the interview. *Public Opinion Quarterly, 25*, 39–56.

Ervin, L. H., & Stryker, S. (2001). Theorizing the relationship between self-esteem and identity. In T. J. Owens, S. Stryker, & N. Goodman (Eds.), *Extending self-esteem theory and research: Sociological and psychological currents* (pp. 29–55). New York: Cambridge University Press.

Finkel, S. E., Gutterbock, T. M., & Borg, M. J. (1991). Race-of-interviewer effects in a Preelection Poll: Virginia 1989. *Public Opinion Quarterly, 55*, 313–330.

Fowler, F. J., Jr. (1995). *Improving survey questions: Design and evaluation*. Thousand Oaks, CA: Sage.

Fowler, F. J., Jr., & Mangione, T. W. (1990). *Standardized survey interviewing: Minimizing interviewer-related error*. Thousand Oaks, CA: Sage.

Franco, A., Malhotra, N., & Simonvits, G. (2014). Publication bias in the social sciences: Unlocking the file drawer. *Science, 345*(6203), 1502–1505.

Gamba, R. J., & Oskamp, S. (1994). Factors influencing community residents' participation in commingled curbside recycling programs. *Environment and Behavior, 26*, 587–612.

Goffman, E. (1959). *The presentation of self in everyday life*. New York: Anchor.

Green, D. P., & Shachar, R. (2000). Habit formation and political behavior: Evidence of consuetude in voter turnout. *British Journal of Political Science, 30*, 561–573.

Groves, R. M., Fowler, F. J., Jr., Couper, M. P., Lepkowski, J. M., Singer, E., & Tourangeau, R. (2009). *Survey methodology* (2nd ed.). New York: Wiley.

Hadaway, C. K., Marler, P. L., & Chaves, M. (1993). What the polls don't show: A closer look as US church attendance. *American Sociological Review, 58*, 741–752.

Hadaway, C. K., Marler, P. L., & Chaves, M. (1998). Overreporting church attendance in America: Evidence that demands the same verdict. *American Sociological Review, 63*, 122–130.

Holbrook, A. L., & Krosnick, J. A. (2010). Social desirability bias in voter turnout reports: Tests using the item count technique. *Public Opinion Quarterly, 74*, 37–67.

Holtgraves, T. (2004). Social desirability and self-reports: Testing models of socially desirable responding. *Personality and Social Psychology Bulletin, 30*(2), 161–172.

Holtgraves, T., Eck, J., & Lasky, B. (1997). Face management, question wording and social desirability. *Journal of Applied Social Psychology, 27*, 1650–1671.

House, J. S. (1977). The three faces of social psychology. *Sociometry, 40*, 161–177.

Huddy, L., Billig, J., Bracciodieta, J., Hoeffler, L., Moynihan, P. J., & Pugliani, P. (1997). The effect of interviewer gender on the survey response. *Political Behavior, 19*(3), 197–220.

James, W. (1890/1950). *Principles of psychology*. New York: Dover.

Kane, E. W., & Macaulay, L. J. (1993). interviewer gender and gender attitudes. *Public Opinion Quarterly, 57*(1), 1–28.

Kemph, B. T., & Kasser, T. (1996). Effects of sexual orientation of interviewer on expressed attitudes toward male homosexuality. *Journal of Social Psychology, 136*(3), 401–403.

Kreuter, F., Presser, S., & Tourangeau, R. (2008). Social desirability bias in CATI, IVR, and web surveys: The effects of mode and question sensitivity. *Public Opinion Quarterly, 72*, 847–865.

Krumpal, I. (2013). Determinants of social desirability bias in sensitive surveys: A literature review. *Quality and Quantity, 47*(4), 2025–2047.

Krysan, M. (1998). Privacy and the expression of white racial attitudes: A comparison across three contexts. *Public Opinion Quarterly, 62*(4), 506–544.

Lalwani, A. L., Shavitt, S., & Johnson, T. (2006). What is the relation between cultural orientation and socially desirable responding? *Journal of Personality and Social Psychology, 90*(1), 165–178.

Lam, S. P., & Cheng, S. I. (2002). Cross-informant agreement in reports of environmental behavior and the effect of cross-questioning on report accuracy. *Environment and Behavior, 34*, 508–520.

Leary, M. R. (1996). *Self-presentation: impression management and interpersonal behavior*. Boulder, CO: Westview.

Leary, M. R., & Kowalski, R. M. (1990). Impression management: A literature review and two-component model. *Psychological Bulletin, 107*(1), 34–47.

Marlow, D., & Crowne, D. P. (1961). Social desirability and response to perceived situational demands. *Journal of Consulting Psychology, 25*(2), 109–115.

McCall, G. J., & Simmons, J. L. (1978). *Identities and interactions: An examination of human associations in everyday life*. New York: Free Press.

Mead, G. H. (1934). *Mind, Self, and Society*. Chicago: University of Chicago Press.

Näher, A. F., & Krumpal, I. (2012). Asking sensitive questions: The impact of forgiving wording and question context on social desirability bias. *Quality and Quantity, 46*, 1601–1616.

Nuttbrock, L., & Freudinger, P. (1991). Identity Salience and mothering: A test of Stryker's theory. *Social Psychology Quarterly, 54*, 146–157.

Paulhus, D. L. (1984). Two-component models of socially desirable responding. *Journal of Personality and Social Psychology, 46*(3), 598–609.

Pettigrew, T. F. (2017). Social psychological perspectives on Trump supporters. *Journal of Social and Political Psychology, 5*(1), 107–116.

Presser, S. (1990). Can changes in context reduce vote overreporting in surveys? *Public Opinion Quarterly, 54*(4), 586–593.

Presser, S., & Stinson, L. (1998). Data collection mode and social desirability bias in self-reported religious attendance. *American Sociological Review, 63*, 137–145.

Presser, S., & Traugott, M. (1992). Little White Lies and social science models: Correlated response errors in a panel study of voting. *Public Opinion Quarterly, 56*, 77–86.

Reese, S. D., Danielson, W. A., Shoemaker, P. J., Chang, T. K., & Hsu, H. L. (1986). Ethnicity-of-interviewer effects among Mexican-Americans and Anglos. *Public Opinion Quarterly, 50*, 563–572.

Rosenberg, M. (1979). *Conceiving the self*. New York: Basic Books.

Ross, C. E., & Mirowsky, J. (1984). Socially-desirable response and acquiescence in a cross-cultural survey of mental health. *Journal of Health and Social Behavior, 25*(2), 189–197.

Sackeim, H. A., & Gur, R. C. (1978). Self-deception, self-confrontation, and consciousness. In G. E. Schwartz & D. Shapiro (Eds.), *Consciousness and self-regulation* (pp. 139–197). Boston, MA: Plenum.

Sallis, J. F., & Saelens, B. E. (2000). Assessment of physical activity by self-reports: Status, limitations, and future directions. *Research Quarterly for Exercise and Sport, 71*, 1–14.

Schaeffer, N. C. (1980). Evaluating race-of-interviewer effects in a national survey. *Sociological Methods and Research, 8*(4), 400–419.

Schaeffer, N. C. (1991). Conversation with a purpose-or conversation? Interaction in the standardized interview. In P. P. Biemer, R. M. Groves, L. E. Lyberg, N. A. Mathiowetz, & S. Sudman (Eds.), *Survey measurement and process quality* (pp. 365–391). New York: Wiley.

Serpe, R. T. (1987). Stability and change in self: A structural symbolic interactionism explanation. *Social Psychology Quarterly, 50*(1), 44–55.

Shephard, R. J. (2003). Limits to the measurement of habitual physical activity by questionnaires. *British Journal of Sports Medicine, 37*, 197–206.

Shillington, A. M., Reed, M. B., Clapp, J. D., & Woodruff, S. I. (2011a). Testing the length of time theory of recall decay: Examining substance use report stability with 10 years of national longitudinal survey of youth data. *Substance Use and Misuse, 46*(9), 1105–1112.

Shillington, A. M., Reed, M. B., Clapp, J. D., & Woodruff, S. I. (2011b). Adolescent alcohol use self-report stability: A decade of panel study data. *Journal of Child and Adolescent Substance Abuse, 20*(1), 63–81.

Shillington, A. M., Woodruff, S. I., Clapp, J. D., Reed, M. B., & Lemus, H. (2012). Self-reported age of onset and telescoping for cigarettes, alcohol, and marijuana: Across eight years of the national longitudinal survey of youth. *Journal of Child and Adolescent Substance Abuse, 21*(4), 333–348.

Silver, B. D., Anderson, B. A., & Abramson, P. R. (1986). Who overreports voting? *American Political Science Review, 80*, 613–634.

Snyder, M. (1974). Self-monitoring of expressive behavior. *Journal of Personality and Social Psychology, 30*, 526–537.

Steenkamp, J. B. E. M., de Jong, M. G., & Baumgartner, H. (2010). Socially desirable response tendencies in survey research. *Journal of Marketing Research, 47*(2), 199–214.

Stocké, V. (2007a). Response privacy and elapsed time since election day as determinants for vote overreporting. *International Journal of Public Opinion Research, 19*(2), 237–246.

Stocké, V. (2007b). Determinants and consequences of survey respondents' social desirability beliefs about racial attitudes. *Methodology, 3*, 125–138.

Stocké, V., & Hunkler, C. (2007). Measures of desirability beliefs and their validity as indicators for socially desirable responding. *Field Methods, 19*(3), 313–336.

Stryker, S. (1980/2003). *Symbolic interactionism: A social structural version.* Caldwell, NJ: Blackburn.

Stryker, S., & Serpe, R. T. (1994). Identity salience and psychological centrality: Equivalent, overlapping, or complimentary concepts? *Social Psychology Quarterly, 57*(1), 16–35.

Terry, D. J., Hogg, M. A., & White, K. M. (1999). The theory of planned behaviour: Self-identity, social identity, and group norms. *British Journal of Social Psychology, 38*, 225–244.

Tourangeau, R., & Yan, T. (2007). Sensitive questions in surveys. *Psychological Bulletin, 133*, 859–883.

Tourangeau, R., Rips, L. J., & Rasinski, K. (2000). *The psychology of survey response.* New York: Cambridge University Press.

Tourangeau, R., Groves, R. M., & Redline, C. D. (2010). Sensitive topics and reluctant respondents. *Public Opinion Quarterly, 74*(3), 413–432.

Turner, R. H. (1978). The role and the person. *American Journal of Sociology, 84*(1), 1–23.

Valentino, N. A., Neuner, F. G., & Vandenbroek, L. M. (2018). The changing norms of racial political rhetoric and the end of racial priming. *Journal of Politics, 80*(3), 757–771.

Vining, J., & Ebreo, A. (1992). Predicting recycling behavior from global and specific environmental attitudes and changes in recycling opportunities. *Journal of Applied Social Psychology, 22*(20), 1580–1607.

Waddington, I. (1990). The movement towards the professionalization of medicine. *BMJ: British Medical Journal, 301*(6754), 688.

Chapter 4
Culture and Response Behavior: An Overview of Cultural Mechanisms Explaining Survey Error

Henning Silber and Timothy P. Johnson

Introduction

Over the course of several centuries, culture has been conceived in many different ways with literally hundreds of definitions debated (Borofsky et al. 2001; Kroeber and Kluckhohm 1966). In contrast, awareness that culture may influence survey behavior is a comparatively recent phenomenon. Early recognition that social surveys may be influenced by cultural processes dates back to the immediate post-World War II years, when cross-national survey research studies first began to be fielded (Duijker and Rokkan 1954; Ervin and Bower 1952–1953; Lowenthal 1952–1953; Stern 1948–1949; Wallace and Woodward 1948–1949). At about the same time, there was similar recognition that respondent culture, typically operationalized via proxy indicators of race and/or ethnicity, may be associated with variations in the quality of self-reported survey data (Collins 1946). During the ensuing decades, the rapid growth and development of social survey methodologies, coupled with increased opportunities for cross-national and multi-ethnic investigations, led to growing awareness that often poorly-understood cultural processes may intervene to influence the survey-related behaviors of respondents (and researchers) at multiple points during the data collection process (Harkness et al. 2003; Smith 2010).

In this chapter, we provide a brief overview of some of the more well-known theoretical frameworks for conceptualizing cultural values and orientations. We then present the available evidence that links these various cultural processes with selected survey response and nonresponse behaviors within the total survey error

---

H. Silber (✉)
Department of Survey Design and Methodology, GESIS – Leibniz Institute for the Social Sciences, Mannheim, Germany
e-mail: Henning.Silber@gesis.org

T. P. Johnson
Department of Public Administration, University of Illinois at Chicago, Chicago, IL, USA

framework (Biemer 2010; Groves and Lyberg 2010), the most common framework that is used to differentiate between various sources of errors in surveys.

Dimensions of Culture

Triandis (2007: 63–64) has observed that virtually all conceptualizations of culture have in common the belief that culture is a product of "adaptive interactions between humans and environments," that it consists of shared elements, such as language, norms, values beliefs, expectations and life experiences, that these elements are passed down from generation-to-generation. These conceptualizations ironically stand in contrast to the approach commonly used to operationalize culture in empirical research, one that emphasizes objective biological traits (e.g., race or ethnicity) or residential status (e.g., nation or region), rather than subjective social norms. Considerable progress has been in recent decades towards "unpackaging" these rather crude measures of culture by identifying various values and behaviors that may prove useful for interpreting similarities and differences in beliefs, values and behaviors across broad social groups. We selected three of the more prominent cultural frameworks that have been outlined by Hofstede (1980, 2001), Schwartz (1994), and Inglehart (1997) to explain them in more detail (see summary overview provided in Table 4.1). Other important cultural dimensions and frameworks proposed by Minkov (2011), Nisbett and Cohen (1996), Steenkamp (2001), Triandis (1996) and Trompenaars and Hampden-Turner (1998) are not addressed in this chapter.

Table 4.1 Three selected cultural frameworks and their dimensions

Cultural framework	Dimension
Cultural orientations (Hofstede 2001; Hofstede et al. 2010)	Individualism vs. collectivism
	Power distance
	Uncertainty avoidance
	Masculinity vs. femininity
	Long-term vs. short-term orientation
	Indulgence vs. restraint
Universal Values (Schwartz 1994)	Embeddedness vs. autonomy
	Mastery vs. harmony
	Hierarchy vs. egalitarianism
National Values (Inglehart 1997; Inglehart and Baker 2000)	Tradition vs. secular-rational
	Survival vs. self-expression

Hofstede's Cultural Orientations

Perhaps the most widely recognized of these cultural frameworks was first proposed by Hofstede (1980), who initially identified four dimensions that were believed to vary systematically across national cultures. These dimensions were labeled individualism-collectivism, power distance, uncertainty avoidance and masculine vs. feminine cultures. When outlining this framework, Hofstede (2001) refers to "mental programs" as culture-specific social norms that are shared by large social groups. Those social norms are most relevant for actions of an individual within a society and cultural values are at the heart of the social norm spectrum.

Briefly, *individualism* was posited to represent a self-enhancement orientation, whereas *collectivism* represented a group-enhancement perspective. According to Triandis (1995), persons from individualist cultures most commonly behave as independent actors who emphasize their personal interests. Persons within collectivist cultures, in contrast, have more interdependent social relationships, and emphasize membership and duties within well-defined social groups to a much greater degree than do those within individualist cultures. Within collectivist societies, much sharper distinctions are also made between members of one's own in-group vs. members of out-groups and these distinctions are believed to influence behavior to a much greater degree than within individualist societies (Gudykunst 1997). This dimension of culture has probably received the most attention by scholars over the past several decades (c.f., Oyserman et al. 2002; Schimmack et al. 2005; Triandis 1995).

Hofstede's dimension of *power distance* addresses the degree to which the unequal distribution of power within a society is accepted and considered legitimate by that society's less powerful members (Hofstede and Bond 1984). This dimension is largely concerned with the nature of relationships between persons of different social status. High power distance cultures are believed to be more authoritarian and to emphasize conformity. In contrast, low power distance cultures are viewed as less authoritarian and as emphasizing independence. There are also more opportunities for social mobility available within low power distance cultures.

Uncertainty avoidance is concerned with the degree to which uncertainty and ambiguity can be tolerated within a society. Consensus is highly valued within cultures high in uncertainty avoidance. These societies also generally have more formal rules, laws and regulations, and there is less tolerance of deviance (Gudykunst and Kim 1997).

Masculine vs. feminine orientations identify the degree of nurturance within a society. Assertiveness, competition and material success are encouraged and highly valued within masculine societies. In contrast, a much greater emphasis is placed on cooperation and quality of life considerations, and competition and personal success are less important, in feminine societies (Hofstede 1998). Sharp occupational stratification by gender is also commonly found in masculine cultures, whereas there is less differentiation of occupational opportunities within feminine cultures.

In the second edition of *Culture's Consequences*, Hofstede (2001) added another cultural value to his framework, which he labeled *long vs. short-term orientation*. Long-term orientations, common in China and other Eastern countries, value thrift, persistence and pragmatism, and demonstrate a willingness to adapt traditions to changing conditions when necessary (Chinese Culture Connection 1987). Short-term orientations, in contrast, do not focus as strongly on these values, emphasizing instead respect for traditions. Consequently, they are less able to change and adapt quickly.

More recently, a sixth dimension of the Hofstede model—*indulgence vs. restraint*—has also been conceptualized (Hofstede et al. 2010). Indulgent cultures are those in which there is an emphasis on life satisfaction and fulfilment of personal needs. More restrained cultures, in contrast, demonstrate less concern for personal satisfaction and are more likely to have social norms that restrict personal gratification.

Schwartz's Universal Values

Drawing from social psychological theory, Schwartz (1992) has proposed a theory of human values as well as an extension regarding cultural differences in values (for the theoretical background see: Schwartz and Bilsky 1987, 1990). The value theory proposes a psychological universe that includes a set of ten universal and motivationally distinguishable value dimensions which have been postulated and validated across a broad variety of nations (Steenkamp 2001). The ten individual level values include the values of *power* (emphasizing social status and prestige), *achievement* (emphasizing personal success), *hedonism* (pleasure and gratification), *stimulation* (excitement and novelty), *self-direction* (autonomy, independent thoughts and actions), *universalism* (appreciation and tolerance for the welfare of nature and all people), *benevolence* (concern for the welfare of persons in contact with), *tradition* (respect and commitment for traditional culture or religion), *conformity* (unwillingness to violate social norms), and *security* (concern for the stability of society, self, and relationships). These ten values underlie four higher order values that represent two orthogonal dimensions: *self-enhancement* vs. *self-transcendence* and *openness-to-change* vs. *conservatism*.

In addition, Schwartz (1994, 2006) has proposed a cross-national universe of values that describe basic problems with which all societies are challenged. These include *embeddedness* (emphasizing the status-quo and group unity), *hierarchy* (emphasizing unequal distribution of societal roles), *mastery* (emphasizing the achievement of goals), *affective and intellectual autonomy* (emphasizing own feelings, ideas, and preferences), *egalitarianism* (emphasizing moral equality), and *harmony* (emphasizing understanding and appreciation of the world). These dimensions can be combined into three bipolar value dimensions: *autonomy* vs. *embeddedness*, *egalitarianism* vs. *hierarchy*, and *harmony* vs. *mastery*.

Both the individual and the societal level concepts have been linked in practice to study response behavior in surveys. Since the concept on the societal level was explicitly proposed to study cross-national differences, we have decided to include this concept in Table 4.1.

Inglehart's National Values

Work on the delineation of national values has also been reported by Inglehart (1990, 1997), who has proposed a cultural framework grounded in theories from sociology and political science. His work follows a modernization paradigm that builds upon two main hypotheses: the scarcity and the socialization thesis. The scarcity thesis, based on Maslow's theory of needs (1970), proposes that humans prioritize their basic physiological and safety needs such as the needs for air, water, food, shelter, sleep, clothing, security, and safety and only when those basic needs are fulfilled do they aspire to needs that are higher in the hierarchy. These higher needs relate to psychological and self-fulfillment needs such as morality, creativity, and quality of relationships with others. Additionally, Inglehart's socialization thesis proposes that everyone's value orientations are predominantly acquired during childhood and early adulthood and are relatively stable throughout adulthood.

Based on the scarcity and the socialization hypotheses, Inglehart (1990, 1997) proposed to order the value orientations of nations along the *Postmaterialism Index*, which helps to identify countries with a materialist/economic vs. a post-materialist/ non-economic orientation (see also Inglehart and Baker 2000). Later this concept has been expanded by including the dimensions *tradition* vs. *secular-rational* and *survival* vs. *self-expression* to be able to illustrate a greater verity of change in values over time (Inglehart and Oyserman 2004).

The *traditional vs. secular-rational* dimension is primarily concerned with acceptance of different values related to authorities such as family, gender roles, and religion as fundamental principles. And the *survival vs. self-expression* dimension is primarily concerned with societal emphasis on values related to physical and economic safety as well as consideration regarding the quality of someone's life.

Overlap of the Selected Cultural Frameworks

There is considerable similarity and overlap between the three selected cultural frameworks (see for example: Hsu et al. 2013). The authors identified four main dimensions—'authority,' 'self and group,' 'social/natural environment,' and 'uncertainty'—that capture each dimension of the three selected cultural frameworks concerned with cultural orientations (Hofstede 2001), universal values (Schwartz 1994), and national values (Inglehart 1997). First, with respect to the authority dimension, there is overlap regarding power distance within Hofstede's framework, egalitarianism vs. hierarchy within Schwartz's framework, and traditional vs. secular-rational within Inglehart's framework. Second, with respect to the self and group dimension, overlap exists with regard to individualism vs. collectivism as well as indulgence vs. restraint within Hofstede's framework, autonomy vs. embeddedness within Schwartz's framework, and survival vs. self-expression within Inglehart's framework. Third, regarding the social/natural environment dimension, we see overlap among the masculinity vs. femininity dimension within Hofstede's framework and mastery vs. harmony within Schwartz's framework. Finally, the uncertainty dimension seems to relate solely to uncertainty avoidance within Hofstede's framework. Also, other researchers have done considerable work on comparing and synthesizing the three cultural frameworks (for example recently Beugelsdijk and Welzel 2018).

Total Survey Error Framework

The cultural frameworks outlined above provide measures of cultural dimensions, which can be used as predictors in explanatory concepts to understand cultural differences in survey response behavior. As acknowledged earlier, a well-established theoretical framework to understand response behavior in surveys is the total survey error framework (Biemer 2010; Groves et al. 2011; Groves and Lyberg 2010), which distinguishes between survey related errors due to measurement and due to representation in the sample. Relevant error sources for this contribution include measurement error within the measurement category and nonresponse error within the representation category. A cultural adaption of Groves et al.'s (2011) framework has been proposed by Smith (2018), who described comparability issues in the multicultural context by using a slightly different terminology. He divided survey error into error due to sampling and nonsampling. Again, relevant error sources are cognitive and presentational error with respect to the respondent and nonresponse error within the nonsampling error category.

Building on both contributions regarding the total survey error framework, we propose that measurement error with respect to culture-specific response behavior is very much related to response effects, which are defined as instances when the respondent's answer differs from the true answer due to some factor (Sudman and Bradburn 1974). In a cross-cultural context those factors can be expected to include variability in cultural environments, in addition to traditional error sources. More formally, if respondents in Country A and Country B respond to survey questions in a way that does not relate to the content of the question but rather is due to cultural differences, we consider that as a culture-specific response effect and measurement error. This error is especially problematic for cross-cultural analyses where data from respondents with different cultures are combined and/or compared because different respondents from Country A may answer in a different culture-specific way to a question than respondents from Country B. Similarly, for nonresponse error, respondents from Country A may introduce a different culture-specific representation error than respondents from Country B and this error may be especially problematic for making cross-group comparisons.

Often the term "culture-specific response styles" has been used to describe some culture-specific response behaviors (see Johnson et al. 2010b; Yang et al. 2010). Even though we see value in using a more neutral term such as response style, we have decided to make use of the more global total survey error framework instead. This is because we believe that culture-specific response behavior introduces measurement and nonresponse error into survey estimates. Thus, relating culture-specific response behavior directly to survey error allows a more consistent classification of the relationship between culture and response behavior.

Culture and Survey Error

In this chapter, we explore how these various cultural values and dimensions may be relevant for understanding several survey-related behaviors, primarily measurement error (i.e., extreme responding, acquiescence, socially desirable responding, and item nonresponse),[1] and nonresponse error (referring to unit nonresponse). A summary of studies that have linked culture to survey error is provided in Table 4.2.

Measurement Error

A growing body of empirical literature is now available that suggests a range of processes by which culture might influence survey response, including extreme responding (e.g., Greenleaf 1992), acquiescence (e.g., Schuman and Presser 1981), item nonresponse (e.g., Shoemaker et al. 2002), and socially desirable responding (e.g., Lensvelt-Mulders 2008). Investigating cultural influences on these processes is critical, as cultural group variability in response style behaviors may be misinterpreted as differences in substantive variables if the nature of these relationships is not understood.

---

[1]There are many other response effects that influence measurement error due to culture that could be included such as disacquiescence, middling response style, mild response style, non-contingent response style, net acquiescence response style, response range, and straightlining (see Roberts 2016; van Vaerenbergh and Thomas 2013; Yang et al. 2010, for overviews). We decided to limit our description to the three most prominent response effects: extreme responding, acquiescence, and socially desirable responding.

Table 4.2 Literature overview: number of studies using culture to explain survey error

Survey error		Cultural framework		
		Cultural orientations (Hofstede 2001)	Universal values (Schwartz 2004)	National values (Inglehart 1997)
Measurement error	Extreme responding	17	None	None
	Acquiescence	17	2	None
	Socially desirable responding	10	1	None
	Item nonresponse	2	None	None
Nonresponse error	Unit nonresponse	4	None	None
Measurement and nonresponse error	Total	45	3	None

Note. The literature review was done in a non-systematic way by authors. Thus, we cannot be sure that we have missed studies nor did we approach the literature search in a documented way

Extreme Responding

Extreme responding refers to respondents who systematically choose endpoints of response scales regardless of the substantive content of the question (Yang et al. 2010). Extreme responding refers to both the negative as well as the positive end point of any given rating scale.

Positive associations between extreme responding and individualism, measured at both the respondent level (Chen et al. 1995; Gibbons et al. 1997; Marshall and Lee 1998; van Herk et al. 2004) and at the national level (DeJong et al. 2008; Lamm and Keller 2007; Smith and Fisher 2008), have been reported. Extreme responding has also been found to be associated (in a positive direction) with national-level indicators of power distance (Johnson et al. 2005), uncertainty avoidance (DeJong et al. 2008; Harzing 2006; van de Vijver et al. 2004), and masculinity (DeJong et al. 2008; Johnson et al. 2005). Overall, this research is consistent with the interpretation that respondents most likely to exhibit extreme response style behavior are those embedded within cultures that have low tolerance for ambiguity and which emphasize distinct, independent, competitive, assertive, decisive and sincere behavior (Hamilton 1968; Johnson et al. 2010b; Liu 2015; Marín et al. 1992; Soueif 1958; van Herk et al. 2004). Conversely, extreme responding is found to be less common within cultures where modesty, moderation, interpersonal harmony and being nonjudgmental are more valued (Chia et al. 1997; Kitayama et al. 1997; Riordan and Vandenberg 1994).

Acquiescence

Acquiescence refers to a respondent's tendency toward an affirmative answer to a survey question that offers agree/disagree, yes/no, or true/false response categories. Possible causes of acquiescence are general norms of conduct regarding being polite and agreeable, the status differential that defers to the higher social status of the researcher, and satisficing that suggests that a respondent chooses the easiest response option in order to minimize cognitive effort (see Krosnick 1991).

Evidence suggests that acquiescence is associated with various aspects of collectivism (Harzing 2006; Hofstede 2001; Hoffmann et al. 2013; Johnson et al. 2005; Smith 2004; Smith and Fisher 2008; van de Vijver et al. 2004; Van Dijk et al. 2009; van Herk et al. 2004). It is possible that acquiescence is more typical in collectivist environments because such cultures are more likely to emphasize deference, agreeableness, politeness, and hospitality (Javeline 1999; Wong et al. 2003). Collectivist cultures also tend to employ holistic and dialectical thought processes, which are believed to better tolerate contradictory ideas (Peng and Nisbett 1999; Wong et al. 2003).

Evidence also comes from research employing Schwartz value measures. Specifically, Lechner et al. (2019) investigated acquiescence among respondents to the World Values Survey from 60 nations and reported that acquiescent responding was more common in those nations exhibiting greater social deference norms, as assessed by the Schwartz dimensions of tradition and conformity. In addition, Rammstedt et al. (2017) reported increased individual acquiescence to be associated with individual level conservatism, which integrates the Schwartz values of tradition, conformity and security, as well as national level collectivism, assessed using Hofstede values, across 22 nations participating in the 2002 round of the European Social Survey (ESS).

Johnson et al. (2005) have also documented a negative association between acquiescence and the masculine cultural orientation, a finding that may be interpreted as conforming with masculine emphasis on decisive behavior. Interestingly, when examining interviewer effects, Liu and Wang (2016) report that across multiple Asian nations, male interviewers elicit greater levels of acquiescence from both genders in patterns consistent with cultural emphases on Masculinity in some nations and Confucian emphasis on the privileged social status of males in others.

Associations between acquiescence and other cultural orientations have also been identified, although these findings are not consistent across all studies. Several investigators have found positive relationships between acquiescence and indicators of power distance (Harzing 2006; Hoffmann et al. 2013; Krautz and Hoffmann 2018; van de Vijver et al. 2004), consistent with the expectation of greater deference among high power distance respondents. Contrary to expectations, however, Johnson et al. (2005) reported an inverse association between these constructs.

Several studies have also linked acquiescence with uncertainly avoidance. Smith (2004), Harzing (2006), and van de Vijver et al. (2004) have each presented evidence suggesting that acquiescence is more common in high uncertainty avoidant cultural settings. In contrast, research by Johnson et al. (2005) found individual-level acquiescence to be greater within cultures low in uncertainty avoidance, a finding suggesting that acquiescence may be less common in cultural settings where uncertainty and ambiguity are not tolerated. Additional research will be necessary to resolve these differential patterns of findings.

Additional work by He et al. (2014), He and van de Vijver (2016) has identified a generalized response style factor that incorporates acquiescent, extreme and middling response styles into a single unified dimension. Analyzing multi-level and multi-year data from the European Values Survey, the International Social Survey Program, and the World Values Survey, He et al. (2014) reported findings consistent with most findings reported earlier, and added additional insights regarding cultural dimensions that can be linked to these response behaviors. Specifically, they found two clusters of variables associated with generalized response styles. One was labeled "fitting in," that includes indicators of collectivism, embeddedness, traditionalism, agreeableness and social desirability. A second cluster is labeled "avoiding ambiguity," which seems similar to Hofstede's dimension of Uncertainty Avoidance.

Other work by Grau et al. (2019) has examined a concept we view as similar to acquiescence labeled "careless responding," which is defined as a content-free response set involving a lack of motivation to read and answer survey questions accurately. At the national level, this construct was found to be negatively associated with a composite measure of three of the original Hofstede items, including individualism, gender inequality, and power distance, along with the human development index.

Socially Desirable Responding

Socially desirable responding refers to a respondent's answer that confirms with or endorses social norms or socially preferred behaviors (see Tourangeau et al. 2000; Lensvelt-Mulders 2008). This process of social editing of a respondent's true answer can be deliberate or undeliberate (see Lalwani et al. 2006). Although most often assumed to be an intentional attempt at impression management, socially desirable responding can also be an unconscious form of self-deception (Paulhus 1984).

The effects of socially desirable responding on the quality of self-reports has been a concern for many years (DeMaio 1984; Nederhof 1985). Answering survey questions in a socially desirable manner is uniquely relevant to culture, as knowledge of cultural values and norms is a prerequisite for responding in a manner consistent with them (Malham and Saucier 2016). Indeed, one of the earliest conceptualizations of social desirability specifically emphasized the importance of conformity with culturally sanctioned behavior (Crowne and Marlowe 1964). Differences in perceptions of social desirability across cultures are also now acknowledged as an important area warranting additional investigation (Johnson and van de Vijver 2003). This issue has taken on some urgency given findings from numerous validation studies that have documented race and ethnic differences in the accuracy of self-reports of sensitive topics such as drug and alcohol use in the United States, a problem that may also lead to erroneous conclusions regarding substantive differences across cultural groups (Johnson and Bowman 2003).

There is some evidence that responding in a socially desirable manner tends to be greater in collectivist cultural settings, which are known to place greater emphasis on conformity (Bond and Smith 1996), harmonious social interactions (Church 1987; Triandis et al. 1984), and willingness to present oneself in normatively appropriate ways (Lalwani et al. 2006). Relatedly, in their discussion of cognitive interviewing protocols, Park and Goerman (2019) observed that respondents with collectivist cultural backgrounds seem less willing to provide interviewers with candid answers and more likely to provide evasive answers during cognitive interviews. Persons embedded within individualist cultures, in contrast, may feel less pressure to conform and provide socially desirable information. Evidence consistent with this interpretation comes from studies reported by van Hemert et al. (2002), who found an inverse association between a nation's individualism score and mean scores on the Lie scale of the Eysenck Personality Inventory (Eysenck and Eysenck 1964) across 23 nations, Bernardi (2006), who also found social desirability scores to decrease with national individualism scores, and Schwartz et al. (1997), who found positive associations between the Marlowe-Crowne social desirability measure and the Schwartz values of conformity and tradition.

An important aspect of individualism that may also be relevant to social desirability concerns is the greater value placed on personal privacy. In contrast, persons in collectivistic cultures have fewer expectations regarding privacy and are more accustomed to social monitoring. Using data from the World Mental Health Initiative, Mneimneh et al. (2018) have reported direct and indirect effects of country-level individualism and wealth on rates of interview privacy across 14 nations. As they observe, the likelihood that others would be in attendance during a survey interview is lower in those societies that place a greater emphasis on individual privacy rights.

Lalwani et al. (2006) have demonstrated that both individualism and collectivism predict desirable responding, but in distinct ways. Using the two-dimensional Balanced Inventory of Desirable Responding (BIDR, Paulhus 1991), collectivism was associated with impression management (i.e., the tendency to misrepresent one's actions to conform more closely with perceived social norms) in a manner consistent with the studies described above. Individualism, however, was additionally found to be associated with self-deceptive enhancement (i.e., the tendency to hold and express inflated views of one's skills and abilities), suggesting that culture influences multiple dimensions of socially desirable behavior.

Although little direct evidence is currently available, it has been hypothesized that persons within high power distance cultures may feel more pressure to respond in a socially desirable manner, compared to those embedded in low power distance cultures (Bernardi 2006; Middleton and Jones 2000). Middleton and Jones (2000) have also suggested that persons in high uncertainty avoidance environments may feel greater pressure to conform by providing socially desirable responses when faced with ambiguous survey situations. Bernardi (2006) presents evidence consistent with this idea. Respondents within cultures with long-term time orientations may also feel greater pressure to provide socially desirable answers in order to maintain important social relationships.

Interestingly, alternative hypotheses regarding the potential association between feminine cultural orientation and social desirability have been posited. Middleton and Jones (2000) suggest that those in feminine cultures may be more likely to respond in a socially desirable manner in order to also maintain positive and harmonious social relationships. Bernardi (2006), in contrast, anticipated more socially desirable responding within more competitive masculine cultures, although no association between these variables was found in his study. Clearly, research into the potential effects of cultural orientations on socially desirable response behavior is only beginning.

Item Nonresponse

Item nonresponse error refers to questions left unanswered by a respondent (Shoemaker et al. 2002). Depending on the survey mode, the processes leading to item nonresponse differ slightly. In an interviewer administered survey such as telephone and face-to-face surveys, a respondent has to let the interviewer know that he or she refuses to answer a specific question, whereas in a self-administered survey a respondent can simply refuse to answer a question by skipping this particular question.

There is only now some emerging evidence regarding how culture might influence survey item nonresponse. Using survey data from multiple international sources, a recent paper by Lee et al. (2017) demonstrated cultural differences in Hofstede's time orientation dimension to be associated with item nonresponse for subjective probability questions. Meitinger and Johnson (see Chap. 8) also examined cultural variability in item nonresponse across 32 nations participating in the 2016 International Social Survey Programme (ISSP). They reported item nonresponse to be greater in those nations with less of an emphasis on uncertainty avoidance. Such nations, they reason, would have a greater tolerance for ambiguity. Although measures of collectivism and power distance were associated with item nonresponse in the hypothesized direction, neither was significant in the multi-level models examined.

Nonresponse Error

Nonresponse error refers to sampled individuals not participating in a survey due either to intentional refusal or failure to contact, which can lead to bias when this nonparticipation is associated with the survey's variables of interest (see Groves et al. 2011). In addition, sometimes respondents who only partially complete a survey interview are considered nonrespondents when their percentage of completed questions with respect to the full questionnaire is below a specific threshold such as 30%.

Unit Nonresponse

Although Johnson et al. (2002) have previously speculated as to potential associations between cultural orientations and survey participation, only in recent years has empirical evidence become available regarding this topic. In a mail survey conducted in 22 nations, Harzing (2000) found that a country's level of power distance was negatively associated with that country's survey response rate (no other cultural dimensions were examined). In the U.S., Johnson et al. (2010a) investigated associations between county-level indices of three of Hofstede's dimensions and county mail-back response rates of 2000 Census questionnaires. Although power distance and femininity were not significantly associated with response rates, collectivism was found to have a negative association with rates of survey response. Jans et al. (2019), using data from the California Health Interview Survey, also investigated associations between several of Hofstede's measures and community level screener and interview response rates. Consistent with Johnson et al. (2010a, b), they found community collectivism scores to be negatively correlated with response rates for both the survey screener and interview. They also observed power distance to be negatively associated with screener response rates, consistent with Harzing (2000), but negatively associated with interview response. Jans et al. (2019) also reported community femininity scores to be negatively associated with screener, but not interview, response rates. In contrast, a 20-nation survey in Europe of business managers, Lyness and Kropf (2007) reported that a national level gender equality index, composed of indicators of education, life expectancy, and standard of living, which can be interpreted as a proxy measure of Hofstede's femininity dimension, was predictive of higher survey response rates. Although not entirely consistent, these findings offer evidence suggestive of a model in which unit survey response can be expected to be greater within geographic areas where the population is less likely to differentiate in-groups from out-groups and to treat representatives from each differently.

Discussion

In conducting this overview, we note that there are many criticisms of Hofstede's and the other cultural frameworks discussed. Among McSweeney's (2002) critiques of the Hofstede model, for example, is the concern that his work over-generalizes cultural dimensions at the national level and ignores what in many cases is likely to be considerable heterogeneity at the subnational level. Another concern is that the dimensions he identifies are based on a very small set of survey items that could not be expected to adequately sample the diverse components of the values he claims they represent. It is also notable that the data set employed by Hofstede to develop his framework was limited to employees working for the IBM Corporation almost 50 years ago and that the degree to which these employees are equally representative of their various cultures can be easily questioned. Given the alternative frameworks now available (noted earlier in this chapter), it is important to recognize that there is no consensus on the most appropriate strategy for conceptualizing and assessing cultural values and orientations. That being said, it should also be acknowledged that Hofstede's framework is robust and appears to have remained relatively intact despite decades of empirical scrutiny, has been applied productively to a wide variety of practical research problems across multiple fields of study, and has had a "profound influence on the development of cross-cultural studies ... in the social sciences..." (Smith 2002: 119). While critical assessment will always be appropriate, and alternative cultural frameworks certainly warrant careful consideration, Hofstede's dimensions have provided valuable insights into variability in several survey-related sources of error and deserve further attention. We also note that critiques of the frameworks developed by Schwartz and by Inglehart similarly exist (e.g., Beugelsdijk and Welzel 2018; Lakatos 2015).

There are several sources of survey error beyond those considered here that may also be moderated by cultural processes. Schwarz and colleagues, for example, have demonstrated mechanisms by which culture may influence memory retrieval processes (Haberstroh et al. 2002; Ji et al. 2000). Other areas, however, remain largely unexplored. One might expect, for example, that the greater social monitoring known to take place within collectivist cultures (Oyserman et al. 2002) might produce more accurate proxy reporting, compared to what might be obtained within individualist cultures where there is less emphasis on observation of the actions of other persons. Similarly, the effects that interviewers may have on socially desirable responding might be expected to be moderated by a cultural group's level of collectivism, given that persons within collectivist cultures tend to draw sharper distinctions between members of in-groups vs. out-groups. As was noted in Table 4.1, there are only a modest number of existing studies now available that examine relationships between theoretically derived indicators of culture and one or more sources of total survey error, and most of these employ only one of the available cultural frameworks (Hofstede 2001).

Looking to the future, although there are multiple excellent synthesis and review articles on response styles (e.g., Podsakoff et al. 2012; Roberts 2016; van Vaerenbergh and Thomas 2013) and nonresponse (e.g., Couper and De Leeuw 2003; Wagner and Stoop 2018) as sources of survey error, there have been relatively few efforts to provide a comprehensive review on how to integrate culture into the survey error framework in order to account for the needs of cross-national and cross-cultural survey research (e.g., van Vaerenbergh and Thomas 2013; Yang et al. 2010). Since our world becomes increasingly connected in an area of globalization and internationalization, also surveys on all topics (must) aim at providing a global understanding of our society. Recent work on the sociology of culture, for example, suggests important linkages between the diffusion of social behaviors associated with adoption of Christianity and the subsequent development of individualistic cultural values and social practices (Schulz et al. 2019). In this context, we urgently need to integrate theoretical concepts of culture into the detection, measurement, and explanation of survey error to ensure the reliable measurement of our concepts of interest. Even though awareness of the relationship between culture and response behavior is not new, there is much empirical and theoretical work that remains to be done.

References

Bernardi, R. A. (2006). Associations between Hofstede's cultural constructs and social desirability response bias. *Journal of Business Ethics, 65*, 43–53.

Beugelsdijk, S., & Welzel, C. (2018). Dimensions and dynamics of national culture: Synthesizing Hofstede with Inglehart. *Journal of Cross-Cultural Psychology, 49*(10), 1469–1505.

Biemer, P. P. (2010). Total survey error: Design, implementation, and evaluation. *Public Opinion Quarterly, 74*(5), 817–884.

Bond, R., & Smith, P. B. (1996). Culture and conformity: A meta-analysis of studies using Asch's (1952b, 1956) line judgment task. *Psychological Bulletin, 119*(1), 111–137.

Borofsky, R., Barth, F., Shweder, R., Rodseth, F., & Stolzenberg, N. M. (2001). When: A conversation about culture. *American Anthropologist, 103*, 432–446.

Chen, C., Lee, S.-Y., & Stevenson, H. W. (1995). Response style and cross-cultural comparisons of rating scales among East Asian and North American students. *Psychological Science, 6*(3), 170–175.

Chia, R. C., Allred, L. J., & Jerzak, P. A. (1997). Attitudes toward women in Taiwan and China. *Psychology of Women Quarterly, 21*, 137–150.

Chinese Culture Connection. (1987). Chinese values and the search for culture-free dimensions of culture. *Journal of Cross-Cultural Psychology, 18*, 143–164.

Church, A. T. (1987). Personality research in a non-Western culture: The Philippines. *Psychological Bulletin, 102*, 272–292.

Collins, S. D. (1946). The incidence of poliomyelitis and its crippling effects, as recorded in family surveys. *Public Health Reports, 61*(10), 327–355.

Couper, M. P., & De Leeuw, E. D. (2003). Nonresponse in cross-cultural and cross-national surveys. In J. A. Harkness, F. J. R. Van de Vijver, & P. P. Mohler (Eds.), *Cross-cultural survey methods* (pp. 157–177). Hoboken, NJ: Wiley.

Crowne, D. P., & Marlowe, D. (1964). *The approval motive: Studies in evaluative dependence.* New York: Wiley.

DeJong, M. G., Steenkamp, J.-B. E. M., Fox, J. P., & Baumgartner, H. (2008). Using item response theory to measure extreme response style in marketing research: A global investigation. *Journal of Marketing Research, 45*, 104–115.

DeMaio, T. J. (1984). Social desirability and survey measurement: A review. In C. F. Turner & E. Martin (Eds.), *Surveying subjective phenomena* (pp. 257–282). New York: Russell Sage Foundation.

Duijker, H. C. J., & Rokkan, S. (1954). Organizational aspects of cross-national social research. *Journal of Social Issues, 10*, 8–24.

Ervin, S., & Bower, R. T. (1952–1953) Translation problems in international surveys. *Public Opinion Quarterly, 16*, 595–604.

Eysenck, H. J., & Eysenck, S. B. G. (1964). *The manual of the eysenck personality inventory.* London: University of London Press.

Gibbons, J. L., Hamby, B. A., & Dennis, W. D. (1997). Researching gender-role ideologies internationally and cross-culturally. *Psychology of Women Quarterly, 21*, 151–170.

Grau, I., Ebbeler, C., & Banse, R. (2019). Cultural differences in careless responding. *Journal of Cross-Cultural Psychology, 50*(3), 336–357.

Greenleaf, E. A. (1992). Measuring extreme response style. *Public Opinion Quarterly, 56*, 328–351.

Groves, R. M., & Lyberg, L. (2010). Total survey error: Past, present, and future. *Public Opinion Quarterly, 74*(5), 849–879.

Groves, R. M., Fowler, F. J., Jr., Couper, M. P., Lepkowski, J. M., Singer, E., & Tourangeau, R. (2011). *Survey methodology* (Vol. 561). New Jersey: Wiley.

Gudykunst, W. B. (1997). Cultural variability in communication: An introduction. *Communications Research, 24*, 327–348.

Gudykunst, W. B., & Kim, Y. Y. (1997). *Communicating with strangers* (3rd ed.). Boston: McGraw-Hill.

Haberstroh, S., Oyserman, D., Schwarz, N., Kühnen, U., & Ji, L. (2002). Is the interdependent self more sensitive to question context than the independent self? Self-construal and the observation of conversational norms. *Journal of Experimental Social Psychology, 38*, 323–329.

Hamilton, D. L. (1968). Personality attributes associated with extreme response style. *Psychological Bulletin, 69*(3), 192–203.

Harkness, J. A., van de Vijver, F. J. R., & Mohler, P. P. (2003). *Cross-cultural survey methods.* New York: Wiley.

Harzing, A. W. (2000). Cross-national industrial mail surveys: Why do response rates differ between countries? *Industrial Marketing Management, 29*, 243–254.

Harzing, A. W. (2006). Response styles in cross-national survey research: A 26-country study. *International Journal of Cross-Cultural Management, 6*(2), 243–266.

He, J., & van de Vijver, F. J. R. (2016). Response styles in factual items: Personal, contextual and cultural correlates. *International Journal of Psychology, 51*(6), 445–452.

He, J., Van de Vijver, F. J. R., Dominguez Espinosa, A., & Mui, P. H. C. (2014). Toward a unification of acquiescent, extreme, and midpoint response styles: A multilevel study. *International Journal of Cross Cultural Management, 14*, 306–322.

Hoffmann, S., Mai, R., & Cristescu, A. (2013). Do culture-dependent response styles distort substantial relationships? *International Business Review, 22*, 814–827.

Hofstede, G. (1980). *Culture's consequences.* Beverly Hills, CA: Sage.

Hofstede, G. (1998). *Masculinity and femininity: The Taboo dimension of national cultures.* Thousand Oaks, CA: Sage.

Hofstede, G. (2001). *Culture's consequences* (2nd ed.). Thousand Oaks, CA: Sage.

Hofstede, G., & Bond, M. (1984). Hofstede's culture dimensions. *Journal of Cross-Cultural Psychology, 15*, 417–433.

Hofstede, G., Hofstede, G. J., & Minkov, M. (2010). *Cultures and organizations: Software of the mind* (3rd ed.). New York: McGraw-Hill.

Hsu, S. Y., Woodside, A. G., & Marshall, R. (2013). Critical tests of multiple theories of cultures' consequences: Comparing the usefulness of models by Hofstede, Inglehart and Baker, Schwartz, Steenkamp, as well as GDP and distance for explaining overseas tourism behavior. *Journal of Travel Research, 52*(6), 679–704.

Inglehart, R. (1990). Values, ideology, and cognitive mobilization in new social movements. In R. J. Dalton & M. Kuechler (Eds.), *Challenging the political order* (pp. 43–66). New York: Oxford University Press.

Inglehart, R. (1997). *Modernization and postmodernization: Cultural, economic, and political change in 43 societies.* Princeton, NJ: Princeton University Press.

Inglehart, R., & Baker, W. E. (2000). Modernization, cultural change, and the persistence of traditional values. *American Sociological Review, 65*(1), 19–51.

Inglehart, R., & Oyserman, D. (2004). Individualism, autonomy and self-expression: The human development syndrome. In H. Vinken, J. Soeters, & P. Ester (Eds.), *Comparing cultures: Dimensions of culture in a comparative perspective* (pp. 74–96). Leiden: Brill.

Jans, M., McLaughlin, K., Viana, J., Grant, D., Park, R., & Ponce, N. A. (2019). Geographic correlates of nonresponse in California: A cultural ecosystems perspective. In T. P. Johnson, B.-E. Pennell, I. A. L. Stoop, & B. Dorer (Eds.), *Advances in comparative survey methods: Multinational, multiregional, and multicultural contexts (3MC)* (pp. 835–858). Hoboken, NJ: Wiley.

Javeline, D. (1999). Response effects in polite cultures. *Public Opinion Quarterly, 63*, 1–28.

Ji, L.-J., Schwarz, N., & Nisbett, R. E. (2000). Culture, autobiographical memory, and behavioral frequency reports: Measurement issues in cross-cultural studies. *Personality and Social Psychology, 26*, 585–593.

Johnson, T. P., & Bowman, P. J. (2003). Cross-cultural sources of measurement error in substance use surveys. *Substance Use and Misuse, 38*, 1447–1490.

Johnson, T. P., & van de Vijver, F. J. R. (2003). Social desirability in cross-cultural research. In J. A. Harkness, F. J. R. van de Vijver, & P. P. Mohler (Eds.), *Cross-cultural survey methods* (pp. 195–204). New York: Wiley.

Johnson, T. P., O'Rourke, D., Burris, J., & Owens, L. (2002). Culture and survey nonresponse. In R. M. Groves, D. A. Dillman, J. L. Eltinge, & R. J. A. Little (Eds.), *Survey nonresponse* (pp. 55–69). New York: Wiley.

Johnson, T. P., Kulesa, P., Cho, Y. I., & Shavitt, S. (2005). The relation between culture and response styles: Evidence from 19 countries. *Journal of Cross-Cultural Psychology, 36*, 264–277.

Johnson, T. P., Cho, Y. I., & Lee, G. (2010a). Examining the association between cultural environments and survey nonresponse. *Survey Practice, 3*, 3. https://www.surveypractice.org/article/3006.

Johnson, T. P., Shavitt, S., & Holbrook, A. L. (2010b). Culture and response styles in survey research. In D. Matsumoto & F. J. R. van de Vijver (Eds.), *Cross-cultural research methods in psychology* (pp. 130–178). Oxford: Oxford University Press.

Kitayama, S., Markus, H. R., Matsumoto, H., & Norasakkunkit, V. (1997). Individual and collective processes in the construction of the self: Self-enhancement in the United States and self-criticism in Japan. *Journal of Personality and Social Psychology, 72*, 1245–1267.

Krautz, G., & Hoffmann, S. (2018). Cross-cultural application of a practice-oriented acquiescence measure. *International Marketing Review, 36*(3), 391–415. https://doi.org/10.1108/IMR-03-2018-0091.

Kroeber, A. L., & Kluckhohm, C. (1966). *Culture: A critical review of concepts and definitions.* New York: Vintage.

Krosnick, J. A. (1991). Response strategies for coping with the cognitive demands of attitude measures in surveys. *Applied Cognitive Psychology, 5*(3), 213–236.

Lakatos, Z. (2015). Traditional values and the Inglehart constructs. *Public Opinion Quarterly, 79* (S1), 291–324.

Lalwani, A. K., Shavitt, S., & Johnson, T. (2006). What is the relation between cultural orientation and socially desirable responding? *Journal of Personality and Social Psychology, 90*, 165–178.

Lamm, B., & Keller, H. (2007). Understanding cultural models of parenting: The role of intracultural variation and response style. *Journal of Cross-Cultural Psychology, 38*, 50–57.

Lechner, C. M., Partsch, M. V., Danner, D., & Rammstedt, B. (2019). Individual, situational, and cultural correlates of acquiescent responding: Towards a unified conceptual framework. *British Journal of Mathematical and Statistical Psychology, 72*(3), 426–446. https://doi.org/10.1111/bmsp.12164.

Lee, S., Liu, M., & Hu, M. (2017). Relationship between future time orientation and item nonresponse on subjective probability questions: A cross-cultural analysis. *Journal of Cross-Cultural Psychology, 48*(5), 698–717.

Lensvelt-Mulders, G. J. L. M. (2008). Surveying sensitive topics. In E. D. De Leeuw, J. J. Hox, & D. A. Dillman (Eds.), *The international handbook of survey methodology*. Erlbaum/Taylor & Francis: New York/London.
Liu, M. (2015). *Response style and rating scales: The effects of data collection mode, scale format, and acculturation*. Ph.D. Dissertation. University of Michigan.
Liu, M., & Wang, Y. (2016). Interviewer gender effect on acquiescent response style in 11 Asian countries and societies. *Field Methods, 28*(4), 327–344.
Lowenthal, L. (1952–1953). Introduction, special issue on international communications research. *Public Opinion Quarterly, 16*: v–x.
Lyness, K. S., & Kropf, M. B. (2007). Cultural values and potential nonresponse bias: A multilevel examination of cross-national differences in mail survey response rates. *Organizational Research Methods, 10*(2), 210–224.
Malham, P. B., & Saucier, G. (2016). The conceptual link between social desirability and cultural normativity. *International Journal of Psychology, 51*(6), 474–480.
Marín, G., Gamba, R. J., & Marín, B. V. (1992). Extreme response style and acquiescence among Hispanics: The role of acculturation and education. *Journal of Cross-Cultural Psychology, 23* (4), 498–509.
Marshall, R., & Lee, C. (1998). A cross-cultural, between-gender study of extreme response style. *European Advances in Consumer Research, 3*, 90–95.
Maslow, A. H. (1970). *Motivation and personality*. New York: Harper & Row.
McSweeney, B. (2002). Hofstede's model of national cultural differences and their consequences: A triumph of faith – a failure of analysis. *Human Relations, 55*, 89–118.
Middleton, K. L., & Jones, J. L. (2000). Socially desirable response sets: The impact of country culture. *Psychology and Marketing, 17*(2), 149–163.
Minkov, M. (2011). *Cultural differences in a globalizing world*. Bradford: Emerald.
Mneimneh, Z. M., Elliott, M. R., Tourangeau, R., & Heeringa, S. G. (2018). Culture and interviewer effects on interview privacy: Individualism and national wealth. *Cross-Cultural Research, 52*(5), 496–523.
Nederhof, A. J. (1985). Methods of coping with social desirability bias: A review. *European Journal of Social Psychiatry, 15*, 263–280.
Nisbett, R. E., & Cohen, D. (1996). *Culture of honor: The psychology of violence in the South*. Boulder, CO: Westview Press.
Oyserman, D., Coon, H. M., & Kemmelmeier, M. (2002). Rethinking individualism and collectivism: Evaluation of theoretical assumptions and meta-analyses. *Psychological Bulletin, 128*, 3–72.
Park, H., & Goerman, P. L. (2019). Setting up the cognitive interview task for non-English-speaking participants in the United States. In T. P. Johnson, B.-E. Pennell, I. A. L. Stoop, & B. Dorer (Eds.), *Advances in comparative survey methods: Multinational, multiregional, and multicultural contexts (3MC)* (pp. 227–250). Hoboken, NJ: Wiley.
Paulhus, D. L. (1984). Two-component models of socially desirable responding. *Journal of Personality and Social Psychology, 46*, 598–609.
Paulhus, D. L. (1991). Measurement and control of response bias. In J. P. Robinson, P. R. Shaver, & L. S. Wrightsman (Eds.), *Measures of personality and social psychology attitudes* (pp. 17–59). New York: Academic Press.
Peng, K., & Nisbett, R. E. (1999). Culture, dialectics, and reasoning about contradiction. *American Psychologist, 54*, 741–754.
Podsakoff, P. M., MacKenzie, S. B., & Podsakoff, N. P. (2012). Sources of method bias in social science research and recommendations on how to control it. *Annual Review of Psychology, 63*, 539–569.
Rammstedt, B., Danner, D., & Bosnjak, M. (2017). Acquiescent response styles: A multilevel model explaining individual-level and country-level differences. *Personality and Individual Differences, 107*, 190–114.

Riordan, C., & Vandenberg, R. (1994). A central question in cross-cultural research: Do employees of different cultures interpret work-related measures in an equivalent manner? *Journal of Management, 20*, 643–671.

Roberts, C. (2016). Response styles in surveys: understanding their causes and mitigating their impact on data quality. In C. Wolf, D. Joye, T. W. Smith, & Y.-C. Fu (Eds.), *The Sage handbook of survey methodology*. Thousand Oaks, CA: Sage.

Schimmack, U., Oishi, S., & Diener, E. (2005). Individualism: A valid and important dimension of cultural differences between nations. *Personality and Social Psychology Review, 9*, 17–31.

Schulz, J. F., Bahrami-Rad, D., Beauchamp, J. P., & Henrich, J. (2019). The Church, intensive kinship, and global psychological variation. *Science, 366*, eaau5141.

Schuman, H., & Presser, S. (1981). *Questions and answers in attitude surveys: Experiments in question form, wording, and context*. New York: Academic Press.

Schwartz, S. H. (1992). Universals in the content and structure of values: Theoretical advances and empirical tests in 20 countries. In *Advances in experimental social psychology* (Vol. 25, pp. 1–65). New York: Academic Press.

Schwartz, S. H. (1994). Beyond individualism/collectivism: New cultural dimensions of values. In U. Kim, H. C. Triandis, Ç. Kâğitçibaşi, S.-C. Choi, & G. Yoon (Eds.), *Cross-cultural research and methodology series, Vol. 18. Individualism and collectivism: Theory, method, and applications* (pp. 85–119). Thousand Oaks, CA: Sage.

Schwartz, S. H. (2004). Mapping and interpreting cultural differences around the world. In H. Vinken, J. Soeters, & P. Ester (Eds.), *Comparing cultures: Dimensions of culture in a comparative perspective* (pp. 43–73). Leiden: Brill.

Schwartz, S. (2006). A theory of cultural value orientations: Explication and applications. *Comparative Sociology, 5*(2–3), 137–182.

Schwartz, S. H., & Bilsky, W. (1987). Toward a universal psychological structure of human values. *Journal of Personality and Social Psychology, 53*(3), 550.

Schwartz, S. H., & Bilsky, W. (1990). Toward a theory of the universal content and structure of values: Extensions and cross-cultural replications. *Journal of Personality and Social Psychology, 58*(5), 878.

Schwartz, S. H., Verkasalo, M., Antonovsky, A., & Sagiv, L. (1997). Value priorities and social desirability: Much substance, some style. *British Journal of Social Psychology, 36*, 3–18.

Shoemaker, P. J., Eichholz, M., & Skewes, E. A. (2002). Item nonresponse: Distinguishing between don't know and refuse. *International Journal of Public Opinion Research, 14*(2), 193–201.

Smith, P. B. (2002). Culture's consequences: Something old and something new. *Human Relations, 55*, 119–135.

Smith, P. B. (2004). Acquiescent response bias as an aspect of cultural communication style. *Journal of Cross-Cultural Psychology, 35*, 50–61.

Smith, T. W. (2010). The globalization of survey research. In J. A. Harkness, M. Braun, B. Edwards, T. P. Johnson, L. E. Lyberg, P. P. Mohler, B.-E. Pennell, & T. W. Smith (Eds.), *Multinational, multicultural, and multiregional survey methods* (pp. 477–484). New York: Wiley.

Smith, T. W. (2018). Improving multinational, multiregional, and multicultural (3MC) comparability using the total survey error (TSE) paradigm. In T. P. Johnson, B.-E. Pennell, I. A. L. Stoop, & B. Dorer (Eds.), *Advances in comparative survey methods: multinational, multiregional, and multicultural contexts (3MC)* (pp. 13–43). Hoboken, NJ: Wiley.

Smith, P. B., & Fisher, R. (2008). Acquiescence, extreme response bias and culture: A multilevel analysis. In F. J. van de Vijver, D. A. van Hemert, & Y. H. Poortinga (Eds.), *Multilevel analysis of individuals and cultures* (pp. 285–314). New York: Lawrence Erlbaum Associates.

Soueif, M. I. (1958). Extreme response sets as a measure of intolerance of ambiguity. *British Journal of Psychology, 49*, 329–333.

Steenkamp, J. B. E. M. (2001). The role of national culture in international mar-keting research. *International Marketing Review, 18*, 30–44.

Stern, E. (1948–1949). The universe, translation, and timing. *Public Opinion Quarterly, 12*, 711–715.

Sudman, S., & Bradburn, N. M. (1974). *Response effects in surveys: A review and synthesis* (No. 16). Chicago: Aldine.

Tourangeau, R., Rips, L. J., & Rasinski, K. (2000). *The psychology of survey response*. Cambridge: Cambridge University Press.

Triandis, H. C. (1995). *Individualism-collectivism*. Boulder, CO: Westview Press.

Triandis, H. C. (1996). The psychological measurement of cultural syndromes. *American Psychologist, 51*, 407–415.

Triandis, H. C. (2007). Culture and psychology: A history of the study of their relationship. In S. Kitayama & D. Cohen (Eds.), *Handbook of cultural psychology* (pp. 59–76). New York: Guilford Press.

Triandis, H. C., Marín, G., Lisansky, J., & Betancourt, H. (1984). Simpatía as a cultural script of Hispanics. *Journal of Personality and Social Psychology, 47*(6), 1363–1375.

Trompenaars, F., & Hampden-Turner, C. (1998). *Riding the waves of culture: Understanding diversity in global business* (2nd ed.). New York: McGraw-Hill.

van de Vijver, F. J. R., Ploubidis, G., & van Hemert, D. A. (2004). Toward an understanding of cross-cultural differences in acquiescence and extremity scoring. Paper presented at the *Sheth/Sudman Symposium on Cross-Cultural Survey Research Methodology*, Urbana, IL.

Van Dijk, T. K., Datema, F., Welten, S., & Van de Vijver, F. J. (2009). Acquiescence and extremity in cross-national surveys: domain dependence and country-level correlates. In A. Gari & K. Mylonas (Eds.), *Quod erat Demonstran dum: From Herodotus' ethnographic journeys to cross-cultural research* (pp. 137–147). Athens: Pedio Books.

van Hemert, D. A., van de Vijver, F. J., Poortinga, Y. H., & Georgas, J. (2002). Structural and functional equivalence of the Eysenck Personality Questionnaire within and between countries. *Personality and Individual Differences, 33*, 1229–1249.

van Herk, H., Portinga, Y. H., & Verhallen, T. M. M. (2004). Response styles in rating scales: Evidence of method bias in data from six EU countries. *Journal of Cross-Cultural Psychology, 35*(3), 346–360.

van Vaerenbergh, Y., & Thomas, T. (2013). Response styles in survey research: A literature review of antecedents, consequences and remedies. *International Journal of Public Opinion Research, 25*(3), 195–217.

Wagner, J., & Stoop, I. A. (2018). Comparing nonresponse and nonresponse biases in multinational, multiregional, and multicultural contexts. In T. P. Johnson, B.-E. Pennell, I. A. L. Stoop, & B. Dorer (Eds.), *Advances in comparative survey methods: Multinational, multiregional, and multicultural contexts (3MC)* (pp. 807–833). Hoboken, NJ: Wiley.

Wallace, D., Woodward, J. L. (1948–1949) Experience in the time international survey: A symposium. *Public Opinion Quarterly, 12*, 709–711

Wong, N., Rindfleisch, A., & Burroughs, J. E. (2003). Do reverse-worded items confound measures in cross-cultural consumer research? The case of the Material Values Scale. *Journal of Consumer Research, 30*(1), 72–91.

Yang, Y., Harkness, J. A., Chin, T.-C., & Villar, A. (2010). Response styles and culture. In J. A. Harkness, M. Braun, B. Edwards, T. P. Johnson, L. E. Lyberg, P. P. Mohler, B.-E. Pennell, & T. W. Smith (Eds.), *Multinational, multicultural, and multiregional survey methods* (pp. 203–223). New York: Wiley.

Chapter 5
Translating Lessons from Status Characteristics and Expectation States Theory to Survey Methods

Bianca Manago

Status characteristics and expectation states theory (SC-EST) is a theoretical program that predicts individuals' behaviors in dyads and groups. Specifically, SC-EST research can predict who, in a group of individuals with mixed statuses (e.g., those who differ on race, gender, age, etc.), will be listened to, agreed with, and whose ideas will be solicited. It does so by examining the characteristics of the individuals in these groups relative to others, and the general expectations associated with these characteristics. Because SC-EST research is most often conducted in an experimental setting, it is probably unfamiliar to most survey methodologists. This lack of integration is unfortunate because SC-EST can both inform and be informed by survey research.

SC-EST can inform survey research both theoretically and methodologically. Theoretically, SC-EST is driven by empirical research questions and relies heavily on the power of formalization. By formalization, I am referring to "a restricted set of explicit propositions that yield deductive implications that can be empirically confirmed or refuted" (Lee Freese 1981, p. 346). This reliance on formalization allows for the development of a vast body of literature for which the findings not only accumulate, but also advance the broader theory. An examination of the way that SC-EST has developed as a theoretical research program, and in particular its reliance on initial and scope conditions, provides guidance for survey methodologists who seek to develop and test theory. Methodologically, SC-EST can provide concrete guidance to survey methodologists whose survey methodology has some sort of human interaction, e.g., in-person surveys, phone surveys, focus groups, etc. Specifically, because SC-EST can predict how humans will interact in group settings, it can foresee some of the dynamics that could take place. Furthermore,

B. Manago (✉)
Department of Sociology, Vanderbilt University, Nashville, TN, USA
e-mail: bianca.manago@vanderbilt.edu

SC-EST research provides insights as to how researchers can avoid interactions that may negatively affect data quality.

Finally, survey methods research can help to inform SC-EST research. First, the strengths of surveys make them ideal for providing SC-EST researchers with a broad understanding of the general public's perceptions about certain status characteristics. Second, as a methodological discipline that is concerned with the details of the way questions are asked and answered, survey methodologists can help SC-EST researchers (who often conduct laboratory-based experiments) with questionnaires that are administered before, during, and/or after the study. In summary, survey methodology is well positioned to examine the initial and scope conditions of SC-EST research.

In what follows, I first summarize status characteristics and expectation states (SC-EST) theory. Second, I outline how SC-EST, as an example of an advanced theoretical paradigm, can broadly inform survey methodology, paying particular attention to initial and scope conditions. Third, I discuss the methodological implications of SC-EST for survey methodologists. Finally, I suggest some ways that survey methodologists can contribute to SC-EST.

Status Characteristics and Expectation States Theory

I will first provide a broad introduction to status characteristics and expectation states (SC-EST) theory, followed by specific and thorough explanations of the theory. Of importance, SC-EST is a theoretical paradigm with several very precise definitions. I will define all of these concepts throughout the chapter, providing examples along the way. In addition, I have also created a table that readers can refer to which has these concepts and their definitions (see Table 5.1).

SC-EST explains the process by which certain status characteristics (e.g., race and gender differences) affect social interactions (Berger and Zelditch Jr 1985; Berger and Fişek 1974, 2006; Berger et al. 1977, 1980). *Status characteristics* may vary throughout time and can encompass a wide range of social distinctions. To meet the definition of a "status characteristic," a social distinction must: (1) have at least two states [e.g., gender (man, woman, non-binary) or race/ethnicity (Asian, black, white, Latinx/e], and (2) these states must be associated with different assumptions about individuals' competence. Even though these assumptions are generally not based in fact and many individuals may not believe them, these assumptions, which are called *performance expectations,* will still organize group interactions. This is because individuals are aware that others hold these ideas, and thus, behave according to them. By "organize group interactions", I am referring to the way that groups of individuals function when working on a task. SC-EST theorizes that individuals with the high state of the characteristic will be listened to, agreed with, and have their ideas solicited more than the person with the low state

Table 5.1 Terms and definitions for expectation states theory

Term	Definition[a]
Status characteristic	Individual attributes that are socially significant
Diffuse (DSC)	Carry general cultural expectations for overall competence on a number of tasks
Specific (SSC)	Carry cultural expectations for performance on a limited number/array of tasks.
Performance expectations	Implicit, often unconscious, anticipations of the relative quality of individual members' future performance
Status generalization process	The process of attributing abilities to individuals based on the status characteristics they posses
Burden of proof	Suggests status hierarchies and processes will occur unless something else intervenes.
Observable power and prestige order (OPPO)	Inequalities in social interactions that are based on status characteristics, and take the form of deference, agreement, disagreement, etc.

[a]Definitions from Correll and Ridgeway (2003)

of the characteristic. This process is known as the *status generalization process* and results in high status individuals having more influence in groups than their lower status counterparts. In summary, the status generalization process occurs when: (1) socially evaluated characteristics, known as *status characteristics*, differ among individuals; (2) these differences lead to expectations about the performance of group members (known as *performance expectations*); and these (3) performance expectations affect group interactions such that high-status individuals have more influence in group interactions than low-status individuals.

Status characteristics and expectation states theory (SC-EST) research is typically conducted in a laboratory experimental setting in which at least two, but often more, participants work on a group task. Researchers sometimes assign individuals to different statuses; for example, having participants fill out a questionnaire and then telling participants that one individual performed better than the other (when in fact there was no difference). Other times, researchers will bring individuals to the laboratory who already have status differences; for example, bringing in people of color and white individuals to work on a task. Then, researchers have these participants work on a task together, examining either the group social dynamics—known as observable power and prestige— (e.g., who speaks most, who agrees with whom, etc.) or *deference* (i.e., the amount that participants change their answers to match other participants). Although surveys are rarely used to examine SC-EST, there is the potential for survey methodology to contribute to SC-EST and for some of the principals and findings of SC-EST to contribute to survey methodology.

Status Characteristics and Performance Expectations

Status characteristics are social distinctions, such as race, gender, or age, that are associated with differing levels of expected competence. There are at least two levels of a status characteristic: *high or low*. The high state of a status characteristic is associated with competence whereas the low state of a status characteristic is associated with incompetence.[1] These associations with competence set expectations for performance, i.e., individuals who are perceived as competent are expected to perform well at most tasks.

There are two kinds of status characteristics, diffuse and specific. Specific status characteristics are often reflected in the single dimension of a specific ability that people possess. A specific status characteristic is most salient, and most powerful, when it is directly related to the task at hand. For example, an individual who has a reputation for being an extraordinary athlete may be considered competent when participating on a task that is associated with athletics. If the task is related to mathematics, however, the athlete may not be perceived as similarly competent.

Diffuse status characteristics, on the other hand, hold performance expectations of both limited and unlimited scope. These types of status characteristics are considered *diffuse* because they are not particular to just one task, but set general expectations of performance on a variety of tasks. In past research, diffuse status characteristics have included characteristics such as race (Brezina and Winder 2003; Cohen and Roper 1972; Goar et al. 2013; Goar and Sell 2005; Manago et al. 2019; Thye and Harrell 2017; Webster and Driskell 1978), gender[2] (Correll and Benard 2006; Gerber 1996; Lockheed and Hall 1976; Cecilia L Ridgeway and Diekema 1992; Wagner et al. 1986), age (Freese and Cohen 1973), physical attractiveness (Webster and Driskell 1983), and education (Moore 1968; Zelditch et al. 1980).

In summary, a diffuse status characteristic is one that has both specific and general expectations for performance. In and of itself, that broad description could fit thousands of characteristics. While this most certainly *describes* a status characteristic—it does not *define* a status characteristic. More specifically, a characteristic is a diffuse status characteristic if it has three properties (Berger et al. 1972):

1. Individuals must believe "that it is better to possess one state of the characteristic than another; that is, the states of the characteristic are differentially valued" (Berger et al. 1972: p. 244). Although many characteristics carry hierarchical connotations, others do not. For example, at this time in society, there is little

---

[1] Importantly, there are some situations in which there are more than two states, such as race, where there are many different racial and ethnic identities. Some research suggests that in these cases, there is a hegemonic state which is differentiated from all other states (Mize and Manago 2018a, b). More research is needed in this area.

[2] To date, research on gender as a status characteristic has focused cisgender men and women. Another example could be cis vs. transgender individuals. At this time in the United States, cisgender individuals would be considered the high state and transgender individuals the low state of the status characteristic: gender.

differentiation in the evaluation of dog vs. cat owners. In contrast, there are many characteristics that are generally valued, such as race, gender, beauty, etc. For these status characteristics, individuals recognize there is a high and low state of the characteristic. As an example, in today's society, being a man is generally more highly evaluated than being a woman (Ridgeway 1991; Ridgeway and Correll 2004; Ridgeway and Diekema 1992). This is not to say that there is anything inherently about men and women that mark them as high or low status group members, respectively. At another time, or in another society, these categorizations may be reversed; however, at this time and in this society, men are generally viewed as better than women.

2. Individuals must associate one or more specific expectations for behavior with the states of the characteristic; and the "states of the expectation, like the states of the characteristic, are valued, either positively or negatively" (Berger et al. 1972: p. 244). For example, there are no perceptions of specific differentially evaluated behaviors associated with being a dog owner. In contrast, there are perceptions of differentially evaluated behaviors associated with being a man or woman (Biernat and Kobrynowicz 1997; Ridgeway and Diekema 1992). For example, men are perceived to be better at math than women (Gonzales et al. 2002; Steele 1997).

3. Individuals must associate "with each state of the characteristic a general expectation state; for example, that people who possess the high state of the characteristic are smart, or moral" (Berger et al. 1972: p. 244). Neither dog nor cat owners are thought to be broadly better than the other in any way. In contrast, however, men are generally thought to be smarter, or more competent, than women (Berger et al. 1980; Biernat and Kobrynowicz 1997; Fiske et al. 2002; Mize and Manago 2018b).

In summary, a characteristic is a diffuse status characteristic if it possesses these three components: (1) differentially evaluated states, (2) specific expectations for behavior, and (3) general expectations for ability. As an example, race is considered to be a diffuse status characteristic (Brezina and Winder 2003; Goar and Sell 2005; Manago et al. 2019; Thye and Harrell 2017; Webster and Driskell 1978). For race, there are at least two differentially evaluated states (as an example): white and black. At this time in the United States, there are more negative stereotypes of Black individuals than of White individuals (Allport 1954; Brezina and Winder 2003; Fiske et al. 2002; Goar and Sell 2005; Thye and Harrell 2017). As such, Black is the low state of the status characteristic, race, and White is the high state of the status characteristic, race. In addition to there being differentially evaluated states of the characteristic, there are different specific stereotypes related to being Black and White. For example, White individuals are thought to be better at abstract thinking than Black individuals (Plous and Williams 1995). This results in general beliefs about competence, with individuals perceiving White individuals to be broadly more competent than Black individuals (Fiske et al. 1999, 2002).

Importantly, these differentially evaluated states and expectations for behavior are based on broadly shared stereotypes rather than individual beliefs. Said otherwise, status beliefs are grounded in culturally salient stereotypes (Ridgeway 2008;

Ridgeway and Diekema 1992). Because these stereotypes are culturally salient, even if individuals do not endorse these stereotypes merely being aware of them can affect expectations for performance and behavior in group interactions (Correll 2004; Ridgeway and Correll 2004).

Observable Power and Prestige

Expectations for performance are revealed to the extent that individuals' status characteristics shape social interactions. For example, if two individuals of differential levels of status are working together on a task and they disagree on an answer, SC-EST predicts that the lower status group member will defer to the opinion of the higher status group member more often than not. In addition, higher status individuals will be agreed with to a higher extent, have their ideas solicited more often, and speak more than lower status individuals. In contrast, lower status individuals will be disagreed with to a greater extent than their higher status counterparts. These social dynamics organize behavior despite the quality of individuals' ideas.

The distribution of speaking opportunities, disagreements, and deference in group interactions is known as the observable power and prestige order (OPPO). The observable power and prestige order (OPPO) is the behavioral measurement framework associated with the status characteristic and expectation states theory framework. The OPPO offers objective and precise measurement of the information exchange process and allows researchers to measure team structure by quantifying behaviors that define group hierarchy. SC-EST defines four conceptual categories of the OPPO: performance outputs (task contributions), action opportunities (invitations to make task contributions), influence (given a disagreement, whose contribution is accepted) and compliance (voluntary agreement). The quantity of performance outputs, action opportunities, influence, and compliance, which are measured by counting specific statement types for each group member determine the power and prestige order, the rank-order of members based on their status characteristics, and a team member's relative influence on the team.

In general, SC-EST predicts that lower status group members will have fewer performance outputs and action opportunities than higher status group members. Similarly, SC-EST predicts that lower status group members will have less influence and receive less compliance than higher status group members. This will occur because low status individuals will defer to high status individuals at higher rates than high status individuals defer to low status individuals. In addition, SC-EST predicts that low status individuals will defer less to other low status individuals than they will to high status individuals. Similarly, high status individuals will defer more to high status individuals than low status individuals. This is known as the *burden-of-proof* process; that is, all of these processes will occur, with high status individuals having more deference than low status individuals, unless something else intervenes.

As an illustration, consider gender as a diffuse status characteristic. In terms of SC-EST, the status characteristic "gender" has two[3] levels: high, which is occupied by men, and low, which is occupied by women (Ridgeway 1991, 2008; Ridgeway and Diekema 1992). Status characteristics and expectation states theory would hypothesize that, all else being equal, when men and women are working together in groups: women would defer to men more often than to other women, and men would also defer to other men more often than to women. That is to say, men will have more observable power and prestige in small group interactions than women.

In summary, status characteristics and expectation states theory predicts individuals' influence in group interactions. These group interactions are based on the status of individuals relative to other in the group. Status differences affect whose ideas are heard, agreed with, and solicited. That is, those who are evaluated as having more ability will also have more influence in the group interactions. This operates in the opposite direction as well, with those who are perceived to have less ability having less influence (Berger et al. 1977; Webster and Foschi 1988).

Theoretical Implications of Status Characteristics and Expectation States Theory for Survey Methodologists

The theoretical implications of status characteristics and expectation states theory (SC-EST) for survey methodologists stems from its series of *initial* and *scope conditions*. These conditions state when the theory will apply, and when it will not. When conditions are implied rather than explicitly stated, researchers are unable to either detail the conditions under which a certain theory will apply, or explain discrepancies that may occur between things that are expected and what is observed (Cohen 1980). In this section of the chapter, I will describe the initial and scope conditions for SC-EST and explain how these concepts may be helpful for survey methodologists.

Initial Conditions

Initial conditions define particular circumstances, such as the time and place, under which a theory will be relevant (Cohen 1980, 1989; Sell and Martin 1983a; Walker and Cohen 1985). For instance, when I used gender as an example of a diffuse status characteristic, I stated: "At this time in the United States, the status characteristic "gender" has two levels: high, which is occupied by men and low, which is occupied by women." I went on to emphasize that just because men are the high-status members of the diffuse status characteristic, 'gender', this does not mean that men

---

[3]For cisgender individuals.

are inherently superior–it is simply that at this time in history in the United States, men are treated with higher regard than women. Specifically, I said "At another time, or in another society, these levels may be reversed; however, at this time and in this society, we expect men to be given more deference than women." This caveat is an example of an *initial condition*.

Scope Conditions

Scope conditions are the abstractly defined conditions under which a theory is expected to be true (Cohen 1980, 1989; Foschi 1997; Freese 1980; Lucas 2003; Sell and Martin 1983b; Walker and Cohen 1985; Webster and Kervin 1971). Said otherwise, scope conditions "indicate what constitutes an appropriate test and an appropriate application of a proposition or theory" (Sell and Martin 1983b) (p. 347). Scope conditions are like initial conditions, but more abstract in nature.

As an example,[4] status characteristics and expectation states theory generally has four scope conditions: (1) groups have no prior history of interaction; (2) individuals are group-oriented and task-oriented; (3) there exists one (and generally only one) status difference among group members and group members are aware of it; and (4) *ceteris paribus* (i.e., all else being equal) (Foschi 1997). These are the conditions under which a status characteristic would be expected to operate as theorized. That is, under these conditions, researchers would expect that higher status individuals would be deferred to more often than lower status individuals. Below, I list these scope conditions, explain their relevance for SC-EST, and finally their potential relevance for survey methodologists.

Scope Condition 1: No Prior History of Interaction

The first scope condition of SC-EST is that groups must have no prior history of interaction. This is theoretically relevant for SC-EST because if individuals have extensive information about the other group members, the diffuse status characteristic may carry less influence. That is, if I am examining the effect of gender, but research participants have more information about a fellow group member than "woman" or "man" and they know something like "astrophysicist" or "statistician" it may affect their evaluations of the group member and the ability for gender to organize social interaction.

Although survey participants will not likely have had interaction with other participants or the interviewer, this scope condition could be relevant in a number of ways. First, in terms of personal interaction, it may be important that the

---

[4]Expectation states theory is not the only sociological theory to take advantage of scope conditions. It is but one theory that is used to examine scope conditions fruitfully.

interviewer is both: (1) a stranger to the interviewee and (2) a person with whom the interviewee will be unlikely to have future interactions. This is important to reduce social desirability bias in which respondents give answers for which they think other will judge them positively. For example, if a parent is interviewing a child about drug and alcohol habits, the child may be unlikely to report their actual habits to the parent. This example is not a common survey method, but remains a clear illustration of the general principle.

Another way in which a prior history of interaction may be relevant for survey methodologists is regarding respondents' previous interaction with the survey instrument. For example, a large body of research has examined the effects of asking a question in an earlier survey on future responses to this same question in later years (such as in panel studies) (Halpern-Manners et al. 2014, 2017; Halpern-Manners and Warren 2012; Lazarsfeld 1940; Struminskaya 2016) and on future behavior (Levav and Fitzsimons 2006; Struminskaya 2016). Although this process happens to varying degrees for different kinds of questions (Axinn et al. 2015), researchers should consider the relevance of this phenomenon for their particular research question. As noted by Struminskaya (2016), at times, this conditioning may be advantageous, increasing data quality based on respondents understanding the survey instrument or procedure. In others, it could be disadvantageous, with respondents answering questions in ways that avoid follow-up questions. For both, it is important that researchers explicitly state if the effect of past responses on future responses is relevant for their research question as a scope condition.

Scope Condition 2: Attentiveness and Task-Orientation

The second scope condition, task-orientation, states that individuals must care about the outcome of the task for status characteristics to affect group interactions. Specifically, if participants do not care about the task, then they will not worry about getting the best possible score. If participants do not care about getting the best score, the expectations for their group members' performance will not affect the extent to which they defer (or listen) to them. Thus, the predictions of SC-EST may not come to pass.

The scope condition of task-orientation is also relevant for survey methodologists because responding to surveys requires considerable cognitive effort (Krosnick 1991; Krosnick et al. 1996). The problem of inattentive responses, also referred to as insufficient effort or careless responding, has received considerable attention from survey methodologists (Berry et al. 1992; Curran 2016; Hauser and Schwarz 2016; Huang et al. 2012; Meade and Craig 2012; Oppenheimer et al. 2009). Generally, this research is concerned with data quality and has noted that inattentive respondents increase statistical noise, such as standard error.

Less research has considered the theoretical implications of inattentive responses. The little research that has examined this question, however, has found interesting trends. For example, across multiple studies, research has found that women, individuals with more education, and white respondents, were more likely to pass attention checks (i.e., Screeners) than men, individuals with a high school degree or less, and respondents of color (Berinsky et al. 2014). These differences may be important, especially for researchers who are interested in issues that may be affected by these demographic differences.

Of additional theoretical relevance is the effect of attention check measures on respondents' future responses. Some research finds that Instructional Manipulation Checks (one of the most common forms of an attention check) affect future responses (Hauser and Schwarz 2015). For example, some IMCs may promote more systematic reasoning on future tasks, which, could reduce effects that may come from intuitive thinking (Hauser and Schwarz 2015). If intuitive vs. systematic reasoning is important for a specific research question, then this should definitely be considered as part of the scope conditions. Researchers could state the scope condition as "Participants are not prompted into thinking systematically."

Scope Condition 3: If There Is a Manipulation, Participants Notice It

In SC-EST theory, there must be variation on a status characteristic for it to function as such. For example, if there are only women in a room, we would not see gender function as a status characteristic. There would be no higher (or lower) status group to elicit status processes. Importantly, however, these differences must not only exist, but participants must notice them.[5] If I am studying race and the participants in my study do not accurately identify the race of their group members, then my study will not function as intended (Manago et al. 2019). Thus, closely related to checks for attentiveness are checks for acknowledging the manipulation. For survey experiments and other kinds of studies in which participants are subject to a manipulation, researchers should ensure that respondents noticed the manipulation (Oppenheimer et al. 2009). The reason for failed manipulation/attention checks should also be considered.

In some circumstances, a failed manipulation check may relate to the carelessness of respondents; however, in other circumstances, the inability for participants to accurately remember a manipulation is a result of the survey design. If a large portion of respondents are not able to recall the manipulation, it may be the case that the manipulation is too subtle for participants to perceive. Regardless, researchers should measure if respondents did, or did not, remember the manipulation.

Alternatively, other research in which the researcher is measuring things like discrimination may be affected by manipulation checks. If the researcher asks respondents to recall the race or gender of a vignette character prior to asking

---

[5]This point has also been made regarding the race of the interviewer relative to that of the respondent. Researchers are most likely to find effects when these characteristics obviously differ, however, also see the section entitled "Methodological Implications of Status Characteristics and Expectation States Theory for Survey Methodologists."

important questions to measure discrimination—these manipulation checks may reveal what the researchers are really interested in. This may, in turn, result in biased responses because the respondents may be more likely to edit their initial responses to address the researchers' intention.

For these reasons, it may be wise for researchers to include checks of manipulation at the end of a survey instrument. Of importance, placing the IMC at the end of the survey may also have drawbacks. For example, towards the end of a long survey, participants may be fatigued, more likely to satisfice, and thus, more likely to fail such checks (Hauser and Schwarz 2015; Krosnick et al. 1996; Oppenheimer et al. 2009). Thus, researchers must consider the length of the survey when including manipulations to ensure any failure is not simply attributable to response fatigue.

Scope Condition 4: Ceteris Paribus

The fourth scope condition, *ceteris paribus*, applies to all theories and encompasses conditions that are not explicitly stated but are undeniably important for being held constant. Although researchers may try, we cannot think of every possible thing that could go wrong in a study—and this is especially true for things that are otherwise unrelated to the study's design. For example, *ceteris paribus* would cover such unpredictable occurrences such as the respondent's cat walking across the keyboard and answering questions randomly without the respondent noticing prior to submission. Ceteris paribus would also cover instances in which the color of the survey or the size of the dots unexpectedly affects research findings.

A more likely use for ceteris paribus (than ornery cats) is to capitalize on the work that cognitive aspects of survey methodology (CASM) researchers are doing (Schwarz 2007). For example, theory itself may not suggest that a certain question wording or ordering would affect research findings. Ceteris paribus would cover this. For this reason, CASM research is extremely important. The most important survey methods research, however, is the research that is grounded in theory. Thus, studying all of the ways a question may be interpreted is less helpful than understanding how this interpretation would affect a specific theory.

General Scope Conditions for Survey Methodologists

There are some scope conditions that likely apply to all survey methodology. While this list may not be exhaustive, I suggest it gives the bare minimum for all survey methodology. Specifically, these conditions are inspired by Dillman et al. (2014):

> Asking questions of a sample of individuals and deriving estimates from them sounds simple in theory. However, in reality, to generate a good estimate, we have to write a question that every potential respondent will be willing to answer, will be able to respond to accurately, and will interpret in the way the surveyor intends (p. 94).

Said otherwise, if a survey is going to be able to answer the questions it proposes, it must meet the following broad scope conditions: (1) that respondents are willing to answer these questions honestly, (2) have the capacity to accurately answer questions, and (3) that respondents interpret the question in the way the surveyor intends. Below, I describe each broad scope condition and provide some additional nuance.

Willingness to Honestly Answer Questions and Social Desirability

Social desirability is the extent to which individuals are likely to provide responses that they think present them in a positive light (Ballard 1992; Crowne and Marlowe 1960; Fischer and Fick 1993; Kassarjian 1974; Loo and Loewen 2004; Strahan and Gerbasi 1972). In social science research, social desirability often results in respondents being unwilling to either report holding negative views of various groups (Fiske et al. 2002; Kassarjian 1974) or unflattering things about themselves (Brenner 2011; Brenner and Delamater 2014). This unwillingness to answer honestly often results in biased estimates.

Ability to Answer Questions Honestly

To address the issue of social desirability researchers have adopted a number of strategies. For example, one advantage of the increasing number of surveys being self-administered online is that compared to surveys administered over the phone or in-person, social desirability bias is reduced, presumably due to additional perceived anonymity (Tourangeau 2014). Researchers have also used different kinds of question forms to reduce social desirability bias. These include: asking individuals what they think most people believe (Most People Projective Questioning -MPPQ) (Fiske et al. 2002; Ostapczuk and Musch 2011), using vignettes to provide reasonable doubt as to what the study is asking about (Pescosolido et al. 2008), item count or list response (Coffman et al. 2016), using tests designed to measure implicit bias (e.g., Melamed et al. 2019), and nondirective measurement (Brenner and DeLamater 2016). Researchers have also included measures, such as the Marlowe-Crowne scale, that is designed to measure the extent to which respondents provide socially desirable responses to questions (Ballard 1992; Crowne and Marlowe 1960; Fischer and Fick 1993; Loo and Loewen 2004; Strahan and Gerbasi 1972). Finally, researchers often include statements within a survey instrument to remind respondents that their responses are anonymous and examined in the aggregate.

Some research suggests that most people projective questioning (MPPQ), or the method by which researchers ask respondents to answer as they believe "most people" would answer, overestimates individual-level discrimination and negative sentiments (Ostapczuk and Musch 2011). If researchers are interested in an estimate for what respondents believe about societal norms (or what is termed in the theory of planned behavior as 'subjective norms') MPPQ methods may be appropriate. If, however, researchers are interested in participants' views, they may seek to avoid

MPPQ methods. In summary, when choosing the method for which to circumvent social desirability, researchers should carefully attend to their own research questions.

Capacity to Answer Questions

To have the capacity to answer questions, respondents must be self-aware and able to recall relevant information (Glasman and Albarracín 2006; Nisbett and Wilson 1977). Without these two conditions, respondents' answers to survey questions cannot be considered accurate.

One point that most researchers agree on is that since survey methodology typically relies on verbal reports, researchers who employ survey methods should limit their inquiries to processes about which people have some awareness (Nisbett and Wilson 1977). For example, it would be unlikely that a survey would ask individuals about the chemical processes occurring in their brains. This chemical process is not something that individuals could possibly be aware of; and therefore, individuals would not be able to report it on a survey. In summary, this scope condition that must be met by survey methodologists is: *Any question that is being asked of respondents must be about a topic about which they can have a degree of awareness or ability to recall.*

While it is obvious that we cannot ask individuals about biological processes of which they could have no knowledge, there are other examples that are less clear-cut. At times, researchers may expect that respondents are aware of opinions towards things that they had not previously considered. Similarly, individuals may form opinions in the moment about things that they have not previously seriously considered. If this is the case, it is unlikely that the respondents' reported opinions are particularly strong or consistent, but instead, their response may be developed in the moment and as a result, likely to change. This would negatively affect the reliability of the measure.

In addition to self-awareness, when considering if individuals have the capacity to accurately answer research questions, researchers must consider respondents' ability to recall relevant information (Dykema and Schaeffer 2000; Glasman and Albarracín 2006; Menon 1994; Schaeffer 1994). Recall refers to an individual's ability to remember the information we are asking of them. If we say: "In the last week, how many times did you check your email?" do we expect individuals to accurately be able to account for this information? Yes, individuals may estimate this answer by estimating how many times they check their email and multiply that by seven, but this is unlikely to be an accurate answer. Perhaps there is a difference on the weekend compared to weekdays. All of these factors must be considered in research and fit under this general scope condition.

Of course, researchers have sought best practices for eliciting correct information from survey respondents. Indeed, considerable research has examined how accuracy of responses is affected by things such as the complexity of the question (Dykema and Schaeffer 2000; Menon 1994) and the affect towards the behavior in question

(Brenner and DeLamater 2016; Dykema and Schaeffer 2000; Thompson et al. 1996). Depending on the kinds of questions that are being asked of respondents, these factors should be considered, and best practices incorporated. Rather than examine specific behaviors, future research in this area should try to consider broad classes of behavior. For example, "what kinds of questions increase affect?"; and "how do we define affect?" (as an example, see Brenner and DeLamater 2016).

Interpretation of Survey Instrument and Research Questions

Finally, researchers must ensure that respondents are interpreting questions as they are intended. Prior to developing the research question, it is important for researchers to determine what it is they are—*and what they are not*—interested in knowing. By knowing exactly what is of importance, the researcher can be careful to obviate any ambiguity in the wording of questions. This scope condition could be stated as:

respondents interpret the question as researcher intended.

One example of this work is research on how individuals perceive the sexual behavior of men and women (Mize and Manago 2018a, b). Researchers asked respondents to read a vignette and report their perceptions of the vignette characters. The vignettes described an individual with a dating history of different gender partners, who "hooked-up" with a same-gender person for the first time. The issue with this vignette is that "hook-up" may be understood differently based on: the ages of the respondents (for example, older respondents may consider a "hook-up" to mean meeting for a date; while younger respondents may consider a "hook-up" to mean having sex) or the gender of the vignette characters (e.g., do respondents think of different sexual acts occurring between two women compared to two men?). For these reasons, the authors went on to specifically describe two different sexual encounters, either "kissing passionately" or "oral sex." By doing so, the researchers were able to control for respondents' interpretation of the sexual behavior (Mize and Manago 2018a, b). Note, this kind of question requires considerable pre-testing to identify that both scope and initial conditions are met.

Overview

In summary, initial and scope conditions may be of great importance to survey methodologists and even though research on SC-EST is often conducted in a laboratory, many of SC-EST's scope conditions may apply to survey methodology. Of importance, these conditions will not apply equally for all survey methodologists. Instead, each of these scope conditions should be considered and adopted while devising the research questions or hypotheses of interest. That is because the importance of any one scope condition is dependent on the question that is being asked. Additionally, if researchers conduct a study and do not find support for their hypotheses and believe that one of the conditions below is the reason, they may conduct another study to test that condition—but should do so in the context of their specific research question. This follow-up study (and post hoc theorizing) needs to be conducted within the original theoretical framework. Rather than getting findings that say: "this factor might have affected research findings"; researchers should aim for findings that say "given the context of this theory, we might expect this factor to affect findings and, indeed, it does (or does not)." Even more ideally, however, researchers would consider these factors before fielding the survey. They would conduct survey methods-based research that would be relevant for other theorists of the same tradition and surveys would be designed with these factors in mind.

Methodological Implications of Status Characteristics and Expectation States Theory for Survey Methodologists

Now that status characteristics and expectation states theory (SC-EST) and its scope conditions are clear, I will discuss its methodological implications for survey methodologists, mostly in terms of research artifacts. *Research artifacts* are uncontrolled, systematic biases that threaten the validity of research findings. Although there are many kinds of research artifacts, SC-EST is best poised to speak to biases that are a result of the interaction between the demographic characteristics of respondents and researchers that may affect data quality.

Researchers have long detailed the effects of experimenter characteristics on research participants' responses and behavior. Much of this research has examined how the gender and race of the respondent interacts with the gender and race of the interviewer to affect data. The effect on data is especially apparent when the questions are directly related to obvious interviewer characteristics (Groves et al. 2009) and has been found to have a relatively limited scope. For example, as would be expected, respondents' reports of attitudes about gender are affected by the gender of the interviewer (Kane and Macaulay 1993). Similarly, respondents' reports of attitudes about race are often affected by the race of the interviewer (Campbell 1981; Cotter et al. 1982; Robinson and Rohde 1946; Schaeffer 1980; Schuman and Converse 1971; Schuman and Johnson 1976).

While these findings may seem unsurprising, research affects can also appear when the question is subtly related to interviewer or respondent characteristics. For example, some research has found that when interviewed or observed by women, men reported more sexual partners than when asked the same question by men (Fisher 2007). Other research has found that men tend to work harder and report less physical distress during cardiovascular workouts when being observed by women interviewers (compared to interviewers who are men) (Siegwarth et al. 2012). Although less obviously related to gender than respondents' reported gender attitudes (such as in Kane and Macaulay 1993), these questions/behaviors are still relevant for gender. Specifically, in these studies, both the gender of the interviewer and that of the participant may affect data because the dependent variable of interest—here, sexuality or athletic ability—are often gendered constructs.[6]

There are also race-based interviewer effects for questions that may not appear to be directly relevant to race. For example, the race of the interviewer relative to the race of the participant has been found to affect responses about likelihood to vote (Anderson et al. 1988) and disclosure of suicidality (Samples et al. 2014) or risky health behaviors (Davis et al. 2010). Again, while these topics may not seem directly related to race, there may be racial overtones. For example, with regard to likelihood to vote, black respondents reported a higher intention to vote to black interviewers than to white respondents. Because of the Fifteenth Amendment, the history of Jim Crow laws, mass incarceration of black men (Alexander 2010), and other factors, black individuals may feel a higher civic burden to vote when asked by a black interviewer who shares this same history of black voter suppression in the United States. Similarly, in a society that blames black and brown individuals for their own disenfranchisement, black individuals may hesitate to report risky health behaviors to a white interviewer. Thus, while not explicitly about race, many kinds of questions have racial overtones that may be just below the surface and important for researchers to consider.

Status characteristics and expectation states theory may have some insights into these processes and suggestions for ways to intervene. In instances in which the status characteristics of respondents (relative to those of interviewers) may affect responses, SC-EST might recommend matching respondents with interviewers that share relevant status characteristics. This is because unless the status characteristic is made not salient (by removing differences between respondent and interviewer), SC-EST would predict that these characteristics will organize behavior. Specifically, even if the diffuse status characteristic is not directly related to the questions at hand, SC-EST would predict that there might be some data quality artifacts. If there are no differences on the basis of diffuse status characteristics, then the status characteristic is not salient and therefore will not affect the interaction. Thus, one way to avoid such data biases is to match on diffuse status characteristics.

Matching on the basis of status characteristics is not the only solution, however. To review, SC-EST states that the statuses of individuals may structure interactions when individuals are interacting with those whose status characteristics differ from their own. These phenomena have been found for differences in race (Brezina and Winder 2003; Cohen and Roper 1972; Goar et al. 2013; Goar and Sell 2005; Manago et al. 2019; Thye and Harrell 2017; Webster and Driskell 1978), gender (Correll and Benard 2006; Gerber 1996; Lockheed and Hall 1976; Ridgeway and Diekema 1992; Wagner et al. 1986), age (Freese and Cohen 1973), physical attractiveness (Webster and Driskell 1983), and education (Moore 1968; Zelditch et al. 1980). Specifically, status differences affect perceptions of competence and in turn, the observable power and prestige order; i.e., the extent to which individuals are listened to, agreed with,

---

[6]I encourage future researchers interested in these kinds of questions to examine how the sexual orientation, gender identity, and other features of the participants affect these kinds of findings.

and have their ideas solicited. The power and prestige order is not only affected by diffuse status characteristics, but also specific status characteristics.

For example, consider a situation in which the interviewer is a woman (the presumed low state of the DSC) and the participant is a man (the presumed high state of the DSC). In this situation, there is no additional information, so the general expectation state is determined by the diffuse status characteristic on which the participant and interviewer differ (i.e., gender). This expectation will affect interactions by making it so the woman researcher has lower observable power and prestige than the participant who is a man. For example, the man participant may not defer as often or listen as closely to the woman interviewer as he might to a man interviewer. Thus, principal investigators (PIs) might find lower quality data from the women interviewer's participants (if they are primarily men) than her counterparts who are men. Upon finding this data quality issue, the PIs may attribute the low-quality data to the interviewer herself, when in fact, it is an artifact of the participants' reactions to the interviewer.

To circumvent this kind of issue, many researchers have considered methods to dismantle interactional hierarchy. The majority of this research focuses on adding information about other status characteristics possessed by group members. So, for example, some studies have examined how evidence of superior performance (a specific status characteristic) might decrease the negative effects of the low state of the diffuse status characteristic (Cohen and Roper 1972; Freese and Cohen 1973; Markovsky et al. 1984; Pugh and Wahrman 1983; Wagner et al. 1986; Webster and Driskell 1978). By introducing information about task ability, the researchers are able to reduce the bias that may result from diffuse status characteristic differences.

This general principal can apply to survey research methods. For example, if interviewer and participant are both told that the interviewer is an expert in survey administration, the participant might defer to the interviewer more than he would if he only knew the interviewer was a woman.[7] This knowledge about the *specific status* characteristic would modify the expectations of the researcher and participant. Once the expectations change, then their behavior would change and the interaction between participant and interviewer would be more equal than if they knew *only* each other's diffuse status characteristics. Thus, the participant may defer more often and listen more closely to the interviewer than he otherwise would. Due to this change in the power and prestige order that results from additional information, differences in data quality between interviewers with high and low states of diffuse status characteristics may become less relevant.

Alternatively, PIs may find that interviewers do not listen as carefully to participants who have lower status characteristics than them. For example, white

---

[7]Importantly, research on legitimacy would suggest that the research assistant him or herself should not share this information with the participant (Johansson and Sell 2004; Johnson et al. 2006; Ridgeway et al. 1994; Walker and Zelditch 1993; Younts 2008). Instead, a third party with high external status should provide this information about the research assistant. For example, information about the interviewer's educational status may be introduced in the invitation letter, which is ostensibly sent by the PI.

interviewers may listen less carefully to participants of color than to white participants; or, interviewers who are middle-aged may not listen carefully to participants who are young.

To prevent this kind of error, it may be important to introduce a specific status characteristic about the participant. PIs should reiterate that the participant is the expert of their own thoughts and experiences—increasing the respondent's specific status of task expertise—improving the participant's relative status in the task of completing the survey.

In summary, the demographic characteristics of research assistants, relative to participants, may affect interactions. These interactions may primarily be determined by the diffuse status characteristics of the research assistant and participant if they differ and both the interviewer and participant are aware of these differences. This could negatively affect data quality, especially if the interviewer is of lower status than the participant. The effect on data quality is not inevitable. Considerable SC-EST research has found ways to intervene in these status processes. One such way might be to make participants (and interviewers) aware of interviewers' expertise (i.e., a relevant specific status characteristic). In doing so, researchers may be able to reduce research artifacts. Of course, status dynamics are not the only things researchers must contend with when interviewers and participants have different statuses. Status dynamics, and the ways they are addressed, must be considered in the context of a number of different factors.

Survey Methodology's Implications for Status Characteristics and Expectation States Researchers

Although the bulk of this chapter has been spent introducing survey methodologists to SC-EST and explaining how SC-EST can contribute both theoretically and methodologically to survey research, there are many ways in which expectation states theory could greatly benefit from survey methodology. Specifically, surveys are well-poised to examine both initial conditions and scope conditions on which SC-EST depends. Below, I detail some of these areas for future research—encouraging survey methodologists to seriously engage with expectation states research.

Examination of Status Beliefs and Initial Conditions

Although most SC-EST research is conducted in labs, the status beliefs on which this research relies, exist on a societal level. Specifically, status beliefs are based in *third order inferences*, which are what individuals think "most people" believe (Correll et al. 2017; Ridgeway and Correll 2006). Research finds that third order inferences organize behavior in small group interactions, even if individuals do not actually believe them (Correll et al. 2017; Ridgeway and Correll 2006). So, for example, a Black person may not think that Black people are actually less competent than white people, but may know that many people in their society (i.e., primarily white individuals) tend to believe that. Because third order inferences are so important for predicting status processes, it is important that researchers have a clear idea of third order inferences.

Surveys are ideal for examining third order inferences, because they allow researchers to 'get the pulse' of a specific, intended population. Moreover, with their ability to examine phenomena across cultures and periods of time, surveys are the best poised of all social science research methods to examine and test initial conditions. A test of initial condition would answer questions such as: "Is gender (still) a status characteristic?" or "Is gender a status characteristic in countries with a history of women as heads of state?" To get third order inferences and establish initial conditions, researchers would ask individuals what they think "most people" think about certain groups of people relative to others.

Scope Conditions, Manipulation, and Attention Checks

Although SC-EST research is often conducted in laboratories, during these studies researchers will often collect some information using survey instruments. Survey instruments are used in SC-EST experiments to: (1) establish scope conditions are met; (2) determine if participants noticed experimental manipulations; and (3) in some cases, make sure respondents are paying attention or are group/task oriented. Survey methodologists, with their careful attention to question wording, ordering, and answer choices, likely have the expertise to develop ways for researchers to measure these questions.

First, surveys are used to measure scope conditions. For example, using a survey, SC-EST researchers will ask participants to answer questions about their group members, ensuring that they accurately assessed individuals' status characteristics. For example, SC-EST research that studies race in a laboratory setting must ensure that group members accurately assessed each other's race. If, for example, the white participants did not accurately identify their white group members as white or their Mexican American group members as Mexican American, then the theory would not apply. As a result, these groups would not meet the scope conditions of SC-EST theory and would not be analyzed with the rest of the data (Manago et al. 2019). For a number of reasons, it may be difficult for researchers to assess participants' observations/understandings of other group members' race.

Second, surveys are used to determine if participants noticed experimental manipulations. In the same study described above, the researchers were not only interested if race/ethnicity organized group processes, but also, if there was a way to intervene in these processes (Manago et al. 2019). Specifically, the researchers randomly assigned groups of three participants to one of two conditions: a control condition and an "inconsistent complexity" condition. In the control condition, participants were told that some people do better on these tasks than other people. In the inconsistent complexity condition, participants were told that the task on which groups would be working required a variety of skills and abilities and that it would be impossible for any one person to possess all of these skills. An important scope condition for the study's hypotheses was that participants listened to and absorbed this information about the task. The researchers gave the participants a survey that asked them to respond with true/false answers to questions about the manipulation including: (1) some people just seem to do better, overall, than others at the task, and (2) there are many different abilities and skills important for the task. While these questions allowed Manago et al. (2019) to determine if groups absorbed the manipulation (which they did)—survey methodologists may have additional insights about the way these questions can be asked and what kinds of questions are the best measures of manipulation checks.

Finally, many researchers, including those who use SC-EST, are increasingly venturing into online experiments (Kalkhoff and Thye 2006). In this work, researchers will need to be sure that participants are group and task oriented (scope conditions)—among other things (e.g., other scope conditions, manipulation checks, and attitudinal or behavioral measures). As SC-EST researchers conduct research not only in laboratories, but also online, the expertise of survey methodologists will be paramount. In summary, survey methodology cannot only benefit from—but also contribute to—SC-EST research in myriad ways that are only preliminarily outlined here.

Discussion and Conclusion

In conclusion, status characteristics and expectations states theory (SC-EST) is a formal theoretical paradigm that is used to predict individuals' behavior in groups. SC-EST has both theoretical and methodological implications for survey methodologists. Theoretically, SC-EST research is deductive, precise, formalized, and cumulative—features that enhance the research findings. Although survey methodology is not, in and of itself a theoretical paradigm, the formal aspects of SC-EST, such as scope conditions and initial conditions apply to and should be employed by survey methodologists. In doing so, survey methodologists have another way to ensure that their data is both precise and accurate—goals that are paramount in cognitive aspects of survey methodology (CASM) research. Methodologically, SC-EST details the ways in which status characteristics such as race, gender, age, and attractiveness affect group interactions. The insights from SC-EST research have concrete recommendations for survey methodologists with regards to the race, gender, and other status characteristics of research assistants relative to/in combination with participants. Finally, SC-EST can benefit from the expertise of survey methodologists to establish third order inferences/status beliefs, confirm experimental manipulations are noticed, and ensure scope conditions are met. This is especially true as SC-EST research is conducted in online experiments. Over time, the symbiosis between survey methodologists and SC-EST can and should advance. This chapter suggests a few ways for this relationship to progress.

Acknowledgement I would like to thank Jane Sell, Anne Groggel, Erin Macke, Trenton Mize, and Long Doan for their feedback with various parts of this manuscript. The best projects are a collaboration of multiple people and I feel fortunate to have some of the most disciplined minds and considerate individuals who are willing to give me both support and feedback on my work. I would also like to thank Hannah Regan for excellent editorial assistance.

References

Alexander, M. (2010). *The new Jim Crow: Mass incarceration in the age of color blindness*. The New Press.
Allport, G. W. (1954). *The nature of prejudice*. Perseus Books Publishing.
Anderson, B. A., Silver, B. D., & Abramson, P. R. (1988). The effects of race of the interviewer on measures of electoral participation by Blacks in SRC National Election Studies. *Public Opinion Quarterly, 52*(1), 53. https://doi.org/10.1086/269082.
Axinn, W. G., Jennings, E. A., & Couper, M. P. (2015). Response of sensitive behaviors to frequent measurement. *Social Science Research, 49*, 1–15. https://doi.org/10.1016/j.ssresearch.2014.07.002.
Ballard, R. (1992). Short forms of the Marlowe-Crowne social desirability scale. *Psychological Reports, 71*(3), 1155–1160.
Berger, J., & Fişek, M. H. (1974). A model for the evolution of status structures in task-oriented discussion groups. In J. Berger, T. Conner, & M. Fisek (Eds.), *Expectation states theory: A theoretical research program* (pp. 53–84). Winthrop Publishers.
Berger, J., & Fişek, M. H. (2006). Diffuse status characteristics and the spread of status value: A formal theory. *American Journal of Sociology, 111*(4), 1038–1079. https://doi.org/10.1086/498633.
Berger, J., & Zelditch, M., Jr. (Eds.). (1985). *Status, rewards, and influence: How expectations organize behavior*. San Francisco: Jossey-Bass.
Berger, J., Cohen, B. P., & Zelditch, M., Jr. (1972). Status characteristics and social interaction. *American Sociological Review, 37*(3), 241–255.
Berger, J., Fişek, M. H., Norman, R. Z., & Zelditch, M. (1977). *Status characteristics and social interaction: An expectation-states approach*. Elsevier Scientific Publishing Company.
Berger, J., Rosenholtz, S. J., & Zelditch, M., Jr. (1980). Status organizing processes. *Annual Review of Sociology, 6*(1980), 479–508.
Berinsky, A. J., Margolis, M. F., & Sances, M. W. (2014). Separating the shirkers from the workers? Making sure respondents pay attention on self-administered surveys. *American Journal of Political Science, 58*(3), 739–753. https://doi.org/10.1111/ajps.12081.
Berry, D. T. R., Wetter, M. W., Baer, R. A., Larsen, L., Clark, C., & Monroe, K. (1992). MMPI-2 random responding indices: Validation using a self-report methodology. *Psychological Assessment, 4*(3), 340–345. https://doi.org/10.1037/1040-3590.4.3.340.
Biernat, M., & Kobrynowicz, D. (1997). Gender- and race-based standards of competence: Lower minimum standards but higher ability standards for devalued groups. *Journal of Personality and Social Psychology, 72*(3), 544–557. https://doi.org/10.1037/0022-3514.72.3.544.
Brenner, P. S. (2011). Identity importance and the overreporting of religious service attendance: Multiple imputation of religious attendance using the American time use study and the general social survey. *Journal for the Scientific Study of Religion, 50*(1), 103–115. https://doi.org/10.1111/j.1468-5906.2010.01554.x.

Brenner, P. S., & Delamater, J. (2014). Social desirability bias in self-reports of physical activity: Is exercise identity the culprit. *Social Indicators Research, 117*(2), 489–504.

Brenner, P. S., & DeLamater, J. (2016). Lies, damned lies, and survey self-reports? identity as a cause of measurement bias. *Social Psychology Quarterly, 79*(4), 333–354. https://doi.org/10.1177/0190272516628298.

Brezina, T., & Winder, K. (2003). Economic disadvantage, status generalization, and negative racial stereotyping by White Americans. *Social Psychology Quarterly, 66*(4), 402–418.

Campbell, B. A. (1981). Race-of-interviewer effects among southern adolescents. *Public Opinion Quarterly, 45*(2), 231. https://doi.org/10.1086/268654.

Coffman, K. B., Coffman, L. C., & Ericson, K. M. M. (2016). The size of the LGBT population and the magnitude of antigay sentiment are substantially underestimated. *Management Science, 63* (10), 3168–3186. https://doi.org/10.1287/mnsc.2016.2503.

Cohen, B. P. (1980). The conditional nature of scientific knowledge. In L. Freese (Ed.), *Theoretical methods in sociology: seven essays*. University of Pittsburgh Press.

Cohen, B. P. (1989). *Developing sociological knowledge: Theory and method* (2nd ed.). Chicago: Nelson-Hall.

Cohen, E. G., & Roper, S. S. (1972). Modification of interracial interaction disability: An application of status characteristic theory. *American Sociological Review, 37*(6), 643–657.

Correll, S. J. (2004). Constraints into preferences: Gender, status, and emerging career aspirations. *American Sociological Review, 69*, 93–113. https://doi.org/10.1177/000312240406900106.

Correll, S. J., & Benard, S. (2006). Biased estimators? Comparing status and statistical theories of gender discrimination. *Advances in Group Processes, 23*, 89–116.

Correll, S. J., & Ridgeway, C. L. (2003). Expectation states theory. In J. Delamater (Ed.), *Handbook of social psychology* (pp. 29–51). New York: Kluwer Academic/Plenum Publishers.

Correll, S. J., Ridgeway, C. L., Zuckerman, E. W., Jank, S., Jordan-Bloch, S., & Nakagawa, S. (2017). It's the conventional thought that counts: How third-order inference produces status advantage. *American Sociological Review, 82*(2), 297–327. https://doi.org/10.1177/0003122417691503.

Cotter, P. R., Cohen, J., & Coulter, P. B. (1982). Race-of-interviewer effects in telephone interviews. *Public Opinion Quarterly, 46*(2), 278. https://doi.org/10.1086/268719.

Crowne, D. P., & Marlowe, D. (1960). A new scale of social desirability independent of psychopathology. *Journal of Consulting Psychology, 24*(4), 349–354.

Curran, P. G. (2016). Methods for the detection of carelessly invalid responses in survey data. *Journal of Experimental Social Psychology, 66*, 4–19. https://doi.org/10.1016/j.jesp.2015.07.006.

Davis, R. E., Couper, M. P., Janz, N. K., Caldwell, C. H., & Resnicow, K. (2010). Interviewer effects in public health surveys. *Health Education Research, 25*(1), 14–26. https://doi.org/10.1093/her/cyp046.

Dillman, D. A., Smyth, J. D., & Christian, L. M. (2014). *Internet, phone, mail, and mixed-mode surveys: The tailored design method*. Hoboken, NJ: John Wiley & Sons.

Dykema, J., & Schaeffer, N. C. (2000). Events, instruments, and reporting errors. *American Sociological Review, 65*(4), 619–629. https://doi.org/10.2307/2657386.

Fischer, D. G., & Fick, C. (1993). Measuring social desirability: short forms of the Marlowe-Crowne social desirability scale. *Educational and Psychological Measurement, 53*, 417–424. https://doi.org/0803973233.

Fisher, T. D. (2007). Sex of experimenter and social norm effects on reports of sexual behavior in young men and women. *Archives of Sexual Behavior, 36*(1), 89–100. https://doi.org/10.1007/s10508-006-9094-7.

Fiske, S. T., Xu, J., Cuddy, A. C., & Glick, P. (1999). (Dis)respecting versus (Dis)liking: Status and interdependence predict ambivalent stereotypes of competence and warmth. *Journal of Social Issues, 55*(3), 473–489. https://doi.org/10.1111/0022-4537.00128.

Fiske, S. T., Cuddy, A. J. C. C., Glick, P., & Xu, J. (2002). A model of (often mixed) stereotype content: Competence and warmth respectively follow from perceived status and competition.

Journal of Personality and Social Psychology, 82(6), 878–902. https://doi.org/10.1037/0022-3514.82.6.878.

Foschi, M. (1997). On scope conditions. *Small Group Research, 28*(4), 535–555. https://doi.org/10.1177/1046496497284004.

Freese, L. (1980). The problem of cumulative knowledge. In L. Freese (Ed.), *Theoretical methods in sociology: Seven essays* (pp. 13–69). Pittsburgh, PA: University of Pittsburgh Press.

Freese, L. (1981). The formalization of theory and method. *American Behavioral Scientist, 24*(3), 345–363. https://doi.org/10.1177/000276428102400303.

Freese, L., & Cohen, B. P. (1973). Eliminating status generalization. *Sociometry, 36*(2), 177–193. https://doi.org/10.2307/2786565.

Gerber, G. L. (1996). Status in same-gender and mixed-gender police dyads: Effects on personality attributions. *Social Psychology Quarterly, 59*(4), 350. https://doi.org/10.2307/2787076.

Glasman, L. R., & Albarracín, D. (2006). Forming attitudes that predict future behavior: A meta-analysis of the attitude-behavior relation. *Psychological Bulletin, 132*(5), 778–822. https://doi.org/10.1037/0033-2909.132.5.778.Forming.

Goar, C., & Sell, J. (2005). Using task definition to modify racial inequality within task groups. *The Sociological Quarterly, 46*(815), 525–543.

Goar, C., Sell, J., Manago, B., Melero, C., & Reidinger, B. (2013). Race and ethnic composition of groups: Experimental investigations. In S. R. Thye & E. J. Lawler (Eds.) *Advances in group processes* (Vol. 30). Bingley: Emerald Group Publishing. https://doi.org/10.1108/S0882-6145(2013)0000030006.

Gonzales, P. M., Blanton, H., & Williams, K. J. (2002). The effects of stereotype threat and double-minority status on the test performance of Latino women. *Personality and Social Psychology Bulletin, 28*(5), 659–670. https://doi.org/10.1177/0146167202288010.

Groves, R. M., Fowler, F. J., Couper, M. P., Lepkowski, J. M., Singer, E., & Tourangeau, R. (2009). *Survey methodology* (2nd ed.). New York: Wiley.

Halpern-Manners, A., & Warren, J. R. (2012). Panel conditioning in longitudinal studies: evidence from labor force items in the current population survey. *Demography, 49*(4), 1499–1519. https://doi.org/10.1007/s13524-012-0124-x.

Halpern-Manners, A., Warren, J. R., & Torche, F. (2014). Panel conditioning in a longitudinal study of illicit behaviors. *Public Opinion Quarterly, 78*(3), 565–590. https://doi.org/10.1093/poq/nfu029.

Halpern-Manners, A., Warren, J. R., & Torche, F. (2017). Panel conditioning in the general social survey. *Sociological Methods and Research, 46*(1), 103–124. https://doi.org/10.1177/0049124114532445.

Hauser, D. J., & Schwarz, N. (2015). It's a trap! Instructional manipulation checks prompt systematic thinking on "tricky" tasks. *SAGE Open, 5*(2), 215824401558461. https://doi.org/10.1177/2158244015584617.

Hauser, D. J., & Schwarz, N. (2016). Attentive Turkers: MTurk participants perform better on online attention checks than do subject pool participants. *Behavior Research Methods, 48*(1), 400–407. https://doi.org/10.3758/s13428-015-0578-z.

Huang, J. L., Curran, P. G., Keeney, J., Poposki, E. M., & DeShon, R. P. (2012). Detecting and deterring insufficient effort responding to surveys. *Journal of Business and Psychology, 27*(1), 99–114. https://doi.org/10.1007/s10869-011-9231-8.

Johansson, A. C., & Sell, J. (2004). Sources of legitimation and their effects of group routines: A theoretical analysis. In C. Johnson (Ed.), *Legitimacy processes in organizations: Research in the sociology of organizations* (Vol. 22, pp. 89–116). Bingley: Emerald Group Publishing Limited. https://doi.org/10.1016/S0733-558X(04)22003-1.

Johnson, C., Dowd, T. J., & Ridgeway, C. L. (2006). Legitimacy as a social process. *Annual Review of Sociology, 32*(1), 53–78. https://doi.org/10.1146/annurev.soc.32.061604.123101.

Kalkhoff, W., & Thye, S. R. (2006). Expectation states theory and research. *Sociological Methods and Research, 35*(2), 219–249. https://doi.org/10.1177/0049124106290311.

Kane, E. W., & Macaulay, L. J. (1993). Interviewer gender and gender attitudes. *Public Opinion Quarterly, 57*(1), 1. https://doi.org/10.1086/269352.

Kassarjian, H. H. (1974). Projective methods. In R. Ferber (Ed.), *Handbook of marketing research* (pp. 85–100). New York, NY: McGraw-Hill Book Company.

Krosnick, J. A. (1991). Response strategies for coping with the cognitive demands of attitude measures in surveys. *Applied Cognitive Psychology, 5*(3), 213–236. https://doi.org/10.1002/acp.2350050305.

Krosnick, J. A., Narayan, S., & Smith, W. R. (1996). Satisficing in surveys: Initial evidence. *New Directions for Evaluation, 1996*(70), 29–44. https://doi.org/10.1002/ev.1033.

Lazarsfeld, P. (1940). "Panel" studies. *Public Opinion Quarterly, 4*(1), 122–128.

Levav, J., & Fitzsimons, G. J. (2006). When questions change behavior: The role of ease of representation. *Psychological Science, 17*(3), 207–213. https://doi.org/10.1111/j.1467-9280.2006.01687.x.

Lockheed, M. E., & Hall, K. P. (1976). Conceptualizing sex as a status characteristic: Applications to leadership training strategies. *Journal of Social Issues, 32*(3), 111–124. https://doi.org/10.1111/j.1540-4560.1976.tb02600.x.

Loo, R., & Loewen, P. (2004). Confirmatory factor analyses of scores from full and short versions of the Marlowe-Crowne social desirability scale. *Journal of Applied Social Psychology, 34* (Oct), 2343–2352. https://doi.org/10.1080/00224540009600503.

Lucas, J. W. (2003). Theory-testing, generalization, and the problem of external validity. *Sociological Theory, 21*(3), 236–253. https://doi.org/10.1111/1467-9558.00187.

Manago, B., Sell, J., & Goar, C. (2019). Groups, inequality, and synergy. *Social Forces, 97*(3), 1365–1388.

Markovsky, B., Smith, L. R. F., & Berger, J. (1984). Do status interventions persist? *American Sociological Review, 49*(3), 373–382.

Meade, A. W., & Craig, S. B. (2012). Identifying careless responses in survey data. *Psychological Methods, 17*(3), 437–455. https://doi.org/10.1037/a0028085.

Melamed, D., Munn, C. W., Barry, L., Montgomery, B., & Okuwobi, O. F. (2019). Status characteristics, implicit bias, and the production of racial inequality. *American Sociological Review, 84*(6), 1013–1036. https://doi.org/10.1177/0003122419879101.

Menon, G. (1994). Judgements of behavioral frequencies: Memory search and retrieval. In N. Schwarz & S. Sudman (Eds.), *Autobiographical memory and the validity of retrospective reports* (pp. 161–172). New York: Springer.

Mize, T. D., & Manago, B. (2018a). Precarious sexuality: How men and women are differentially categorized for similar sexual behavior. *American Sociological Review, 83*(2), 305–330. https://doi.org/10.1177/0003122418759544.

Mize, Trenton D, & Manago, B. (2018b). The stereotype content of sexual orientation. *Social Currents, 5*(5), 458–478. https://doi.org/10.1177/2329496518761999

Moore, J. C. (1968). Status and influence in small group interactions. *Sociometry, 31*(1), 47–63.

Nisbett, R. E., & Wilson, T. D. (1977). Telling more than we can know: Verbal reports on mental processes. *Psychological Review, 84*(3), 231–259. https://doi.org/10.1037/0033-295X.84.3.231.

Oppenheimer, D. M., Meyvis, T., & Davidenko, N. (2009). Instructional manipulation checks: Detecting satisficing to increase statistical power. *Journal of Experimental Social Psychology, 45*(4), 867–872. https://doi.org/10.1016/j.jesp.2009.03.009.

Ostapczuk, M., & Musch, J. (2011). Estimating the prevalence of negative attitudes towards people with disability: A comparison of direct questioning, projective questioning and randomised response. *Disability and Rehabilitation, 33*(5), 399–411. https://doi.org/10.3109/09638288.2010.492067.

Pescosolido, B. A., Jensen, P. S., Martin, J. K., Perry, B. L., Olafsdottir, S., & Fettes, D. (2008). Public knowledge and assessment of child mental health problems: Findings from the National Stigma Study-Children. *Journal of the American Academy of Child and Adolescent Psychiatry, 47*(3), 339–349. https://doi.org/10.1097/CHI.0b013e318160e3a0.

Plous, S., & Williams, T. (1995). Racial stereotypes from the days of American slavery: A continuing legacy1. *Journal of Applied Social Psychology, 25*(9), 795–817. https://doi.org/10.1111/j.1559-1816.1995.tb01776.x.

Pugh, M. D., & Wahrman, R. (1983). Neutralizing sexism in mixed-sex groups: Do women have to be better than men? *American Journal of Sociology, 88*(4), 746. https://doi.org/10.1086/227731.

Ridgeway, C. L. (1991). The social construction of status value: Gender and other nominal characteristics. *Social Forces, 70*(2), 367–386. https://doi.org/10.1093/sf/70.2.367.

Ridgeway, C. L. (2008). Framed before we know it: How gender shapes social relations. *Gender and Society, 23*(2), 145–160. https://doi.org/10.1177/0891243208330313.

Ridgeway, C. L., & Correll, S. J. (2004). Unpacking the gender system: A theoretical perspective on gender beliefs and social relations. *Gender & Society, 18*(4), 510–530. https://doi.org/10.1177/0891243204265269.

Ridgeway, C., & Correll, S. J. (2006). Consensus and the creation of status beliefs. *Social Forces, 85*, 431–454.

Ridgeway, C. L., & Diekema, D. (1992). Are gender differences status differences? In C. Ridgeway (Ed.), *Gender, interaction, and inequality* (pp. 157–180). New York: Springer.

Ridgeway, C. L., Johnson, C., & Diekema, D. (1994). External status, legitimacy, and compliance in male and female groups. *Social Forces, 72*(4), 1051–1077. https://doi.org/10.2307/2580292.

Robinson, D., & Rohde, S. (1946). Two experiments with an anti-Semitism poll. *The Journal of Abnormal and Social Psychology, 41*(2), 136–144. https://doi.org/10.1037/h0053559.

Samples, T. C., Woods, A., Davis, T. A., Rhodes, M., Shahane, A., & Kaslow, N. J. (2014). Race of interviewer effect on disclosures of suicidal low-income African American women. *Journal of Black Psychology, 40*(1), 27–46. https://doi.org/10.1177/0095798412469228.

Schaeffer, N. C. (1980). Evaluating race-of-interviewer effects in a national survey. *Sociological Methods and Research, 8*(4), 400–419. https://doi.org/10.1177/004912418000800403.

Schaeffer, N. C. (1994). Errors of experience: response errors in reports about child support and their implications for questionnaire design. In N. Schwarz & S. Sudman (Eds.), *Autobiographical memory and the validity of retrospective reports* (pp. 141–160). Berlin: Springer.

Schuman, H., & Converse, J. (1971). The effects of black and white interviewers on black responses in 1968. *Public Opinion Quarterly, 35*(1), 44–68.

Schuman, H., & Johnson, M. P. (1976). Attitudes and behavior.

Schwarz, N. (2007). Cognitive aspects of survey methodology. *Applied Cognitive Psychology, 21*, 277–287. https://doi.org/10.1002/acp.1340.

Sell, J., & Martin, M. W. (1983a). The effects of group benefits and type of distribution rule on noncompliance to legitimate authority. *Social Forces, 61*(4), 1168–1185.

Sell, J., & Martin, M. W. (1983b). An acultural perspective on experimental social psychology. *Personality and Social Psychology Bulletin, 9*(3), 345–350. https://doi.org/10.1177/0146167283093003.

Siegwarth, N., Larkin, K. T., & Kemmner, C. (2012). Experimenter effects on cardiovascular reactivity and task performance during mental stress testing. *The Psychological Record, 62*(1), 69–82. https://doi.org/10.1007/BF03395787.

Steele, C. M. (1997). A threat in the air: How stereotypes shape intellectual identity and performance. *American Psychologist, 52*(6), 613–629. https://doi.org/10.1037/0003-066X.52.6.613.

Strahan, R., & Gerbasi, K. C. (1972). Short, homogeneous versions of the Marlow-Crowne social desirability scale. *Journal of Clinical Psychology, 28*(2), 191–193.

Struminskaya, B. (2016). Respondent conditioning in online panel surveys: results of two field experiments. *Social Science Computer Review, 34*(1), 95–115. https://doi.org/10.1177/0894439315574022.

Thompson, C. P., Skowronski, J. J., Larsen, S. F., & Betz, A. L. (1996). *Autobiographical memory: remembering what and remembering when*. Mahwah, NJ: Lawrence Erlbaum.

Thye, S. R., & Harrell, A. (2017). The status value theory of power and mechanisms of micro stratification: Theory and new experimental evidence. *Social Science Research, 63*, 54–66. https://doi.org/10.1016/j.ssresearch.2016.09.008.

Tourangeau, R. (2014). Measurement properties of web surveys. In: *Proceedings of statistics Canada symposium*.

Wagner, D. G., Ford, R. S., & Ford, T. W. (1986). Can gender inequalities be reduced? *American Sociological Review, 51*(1), 47. https://doi.org/10.2307/2095477.

Walker, H. A., & Cohen, B. P. (1985). Scope statements: Imperatives for evaluating theory. *American Sociological Review, 50*(3), 288. https://doi.org/10.2307/2095540.

Walker, H. A., & Zelditch, M., Jr. (1993). Power, legitimacy, and the stability of authority: A theoretical research program. In J. Berger & M. Zelditch Jr. (Eds.), *Theoretical research programs: Studies in the growth of theory* (pp. 364–381). Stanford, CA: Stanford University Press.

Webster, M., & Driskell, J. E. (1978). Status generalization: A review and some new data. *American Sociological Review, 43*, 220–336.

Webster, M., & Driskell, J. E. (1983). Beauty as status. *American Journal of Sociology, 89*(1), 140–165.

Webster, M., & Foschi, M. (1988). *Status generalization: New theory and research*. Stanford, CA: Stanford University Press.

Webster, M., & Kervin, J. B. (1971). Artificiality in experimental sociology. *Canadian Review of Sociology and Anthropology, 8*, 263–273.

Younts, C. W. (2008). Status, endorsement, and the legitimacy of deviance. *Social Forces, 87*(1), 561–590. https://doi.org/10.1353/sof.0.0088.

Zelditch, M., Lauderdale, P., & Stublarec, S. (1980). How are inconsistencies between status and ability resolved? *Social Forces, 58*(4), 1025–1043. https://doi.org/10.1093/sf/58.4.1025.

Part II
Applications

Chapter 6
Stigma and the Meaning of Social Desirability: Concealed Islamophobia in the Netherlands

Mathew J. Creighton

The selective presentation of self can entail a significant difference between what is expressed openly (i.e., front-stage) and what emerges under conditions of absolute anonymity (i.e., back-stage). Theoretically, this chapter links notions of *stigma*, rooted in the symbolic interactionist tradition in sociology, and the concept of *social desirability bias*, which emerged from the literature on survey methodology. The result is a coherent framework by which social pressure to offer a desirable response is developed as an object of study in of itself rather than simply a form of bias. Empirically, this work employs a population-level survey experiment in the Netherlands to see how predictions framed by stigma theory result in distinct interpretations of a seemingly well-understood correlate with tolerance—education. If more educated respondents anticipate the *stigma* of Islamophobia, greater masking will positively correlate with higher levels of attained education as the more educated as more susceptible to social desirability pressure—a pattern of educated liars. However, if more education, via conditioning or selection, shapes a more accepting outlook toward others, the differences between education levels in support for Muslim immigrants should remain although the absolute levels of support could vary by how stigmatised intolerance is in the Dutch context. Results reveal two patterns. Intolerance is clearly stigmatized and when conditions mitigate the risk of exposure, more intolerant sentiment is expressed—regardless of education. In other words, all levels of schooling are subject to the normative pressure of stigma and, evidence suggests, elect to differentiate their front-stage and back-stage response patterns.

Why do we selectively present our opinions to others? A standard response from the literature in survey methods is social desirability, which is a phenomenon whereby responses conform to social norms. The idea is based on an absolute notion

M. J. Creighton (✉)
University College Dublin, UCD Geary Institute for Public Policy, Dublin, Ireland
e-mail: mathew.creighton@ucd.ie

of truth in that response patterns are *biased* by social desirability pressure and efforts to improve the veracity of the response is improved if social desirability pressure is alleviated. Akin to notions underpinning True Score Theory (Shultz and Whitney 2005), the supposition is that a single objective truthful measure exists and efforts to ascertain it should focus on mitigating measurement error. Building upon scepticism of the existence of an underlying, stable reality (Wikman 2006),[1] this chapter argues that another, more situational, interpretation is equally legitimate. Theoretically rooted in the symbolic interactionist tradition, this perspective sees social stigma as the mechanism by which distinct versions of oneself are presented. Rather than seeing one's presentation of self as more or less true, the interest is in understanding how the anticipation of stigma shapes what is expressed (or left unexpressed) in a given interaction. This theoretical framework is not typically applied to the type of interaction a survey entails, but its application underlines the tension between a sociological understanding of situational truth, rooted in the expression/maintenance of identity (Brenner 2017), and the subtext of absolute truth and notions of measurement error inherent in survey methodology.

Empirically, this work operationalizes stigma-oriented theoretical frames in the following ways. *The first* considers the overt[2] expression of support for Muslim immigrants. *The second* assesses opposition that is only covertly[3] expressed under conditions of absolute anonymity. This work considers how education, a consistent factor in shaping anti-immigrant sentiment, can also play a role in the extent to which this sentiment is concealed. In other words, we test the extent to which opposition is hidden by levels of schooling, reflecting a layered model of anti-immigrant sentiment.

There are theoretical and empirical reasons to think the gap between overt and covert attitudes toward Muslim immigrants varies significantly by level of education. This has real implications for our understanding of the importance of education as a proximate determinant hostility/moderation toward immigrants—Muslim or otherwise. Based largely on the analysis of overtly expressed opposition, there is a widely observed pattern of tolerance among the better educated (Manevska and Achterberg 2013; Hainmueller and Hiscox 2007). However, there might also be stronger normative pressure among those with more education to perform tolerance (Kuppens and Spears 2014) while covertly holding more restrictionist perspectives. The logic here is that the process of being educated—either via the greater labour-market mobility it affords and/or a process of selection—reflects a normatively more

---

[1] Wikman (2006) sucintly summarizes the concern by pointing out that "...a stable and comprehensible reality is often only a theoretical construction."

[2] *Overt* expression of attitudes refers to opinions articulated in an interaction where anonymity is not permanently guaranteed. This includes responses to opinion polls and/or interviews where anonymity might be offered, but still requires individual-level preferences to be expressed in some form.

[3] *Covert* expression of attitudes refers to opinions articulated in an interaction where absolute and permanent anonymity is guaranteed. This requires that individual-level opinions be concealed even from the individual collecting the information.

outward and accepting mindset. The question becomes, are the more educated relatively more tolerant or simply more reluctant to express intolerance?

Two insights result from this work. *The first* is that support for Muslim immigration is overstated. Even when considering conservative measures of overt support, public opinion in the Netherlands deviates significantly and substantively from that which is expressed under conditions of absolute and permanent anonymity. *The second* insight is that an education gradient persists even when covert sentiment is being considered. This is an interesting finding as there is no evidence that the more educated are more likely to mask their opinions nor are the less/least educated more forthright. Instead, the more educated are indeed more supportive of Muslim immigration and, at the same time, are no more likely to mask their opinions. Succinctly put, the less/least educated are shaped by the same normative pressure as those further up the education ladder.

Social Desirability Bias: Norms, Stigma and the Selective Expression of Educated Preferences

Succinctly put, the relevant norms for a specific context or society are internalized via a life course process of socialization (Mazar et al. 2008; Henrich et al. 2001; Campbell 1964). Variation in what a context accepts/expects results determines the extent to which certain behaviours or held beliefs are expressed (Major and O'Brian 2005). As Goffman's points out in his work on self (1959) and stigma (1963), the strategic presentation of information is an effort to conform or circumvent to contextual norms[4] (for a recent review of the literature on stigma see Pescosolido and Martin 2015). A parallel literature on social desirability bias resides at the intersection of sociology and survey methodology. The implications of social desirability bias influenced and continue to influence an expansive literature focused on measurement (for a recent summary see Krumpal 2013). Aside from general assessments of reporting bias (Phillips and Clancy 1972; Presser and Stinson 1998; Arnold and Feldman 1981; Kuklinski et al. 1997c; Davis and Silver 2003; Kuran and McCaffery 2008; Heerwegh 2009; Brenner and DeLamater 2014), research specifically focused on immigration finds that social desirability bias biases estimates of support for a closed border (Janus 2010; Creighton et al. 2015), immigration policy preferences (Knoll 2013b), nativism (Knoll 2013a) and racism (Kuklinski et al. 1997a, b) and anti-immigrant sentiment (Janus 2010; Creighton et al. 2015; Creighton and Jamal 2015) in the US.

Overall, the literature suggests that for intolerance to shape behaviour, two theoretical mechanisms need be at play: (1) The stigmatization of a given

---

[4]"[W]hen the individual presents himself before others, his performance will tend to incorporate and exemplify the officially accredited values of the society, more so, in fact, than does his behavior as a whole (Goffman 1959: 35)."

sentiment—Islamophobia in this case—must be able to be anticipated and (2) this potentially stigmatizing sentiment need be concealable.[5] Moreover, this notion of stigma allows the mitigation of stigma to be separated from efforts at measurement correction. In other words, changing the situational dynamics under which interpretably Islamophobic sentiment is expressed does leads to distinct interpretations of patterns (e.g., education gradients), but is not a truth serum.

Context: Muslim Immigration and Opposition to Immigration in The Netherlands

Three overlapping phases define Muslim immigration to the Netherlands. The first, which started in the 1950s, consists of colonial (e.g., Suriname until 1975) and post-colonial migration—both independent and via family re-unification (FORUM 2010). The second, which began in earnest in the early 1970s, includes participants in guest worker programmes, which draw largely from Morocco and Turkey and constitutes the majority of Muslims in the Netherlands today (Forum 2010; Eurostat 2015). The third, gaining momentum in the 1980s, consists of refugees and asylum seekers from the Middle East and parts of East Africa (FORUM 2010; Eurostat 2015). With some variation depending on the data source and definition, estimates of the Muslims constitute about 6% of the total population (FORUM 2010) and half of the total foreign-born population, which is estimated at about 12% in 2015 (Eurostat 2015).

This backdrop underline two dynamic that make the Netherlands ideal for understanding the role/meaning of overt and covert expression of attitudes toward Muslim immigrants. First, Muslim immigration is not new and consists of a mix of colonial/post-colonial, labour and refugee migrants. This is distinct from contexts like the US, where Muslim immigration is relatively recent and concentrated in specific geographies (Jamal and Naber 2008). Second, it is a non-trivial proportion of overall migration, constituting a large (if not the largest) immigrant group in the Netherlands. In other words, the Muslim population is relevant and of a duration of residence sufficient that individuals are plausibly socialized into the norms governing the overt expression of positive and negative attitudes.

In fact, social and political currents in the Netherlands suggest that a gap between the expressed opposition to immigration and anonymously expressed sentiment is wide and, potentially, widening. Outwardly, over two thirds (65%) of residents in the Netherlands consider immigration to contribute to tolerance. Only 35% of the Netherlands maintain a negative view of Muslims, which is less than Hungary (72%), Poland (69%), Italy (66%) and Greece (65%) (Wike et al. 2016). There is a clear education gradient with nearly twice as many Dutch having favourable

---

[5]Goffman (1963) uses the term "discreditable" to refer to potentially stigmatizing characteristics that, at least in some situations, can be selectively revealed and/or concealed.

opinions of diversity among those with more relative to less than a secondary-school education (43% vs. 22%) (Wike et al. 2016).

However, some suggest that high-profile events such as the 2004 murder of Theo van Gogh potentially shifted public opinion (Savelkoul et al. 2011). Sniderman and Hagendoorn (2007) point to a similar contradictory expression of attitudes toward immigrants and immigration, specifically on the issue of Islam. Covert (i.e., anonymous) expression of attitudes toward immigrants, namely voting, suggests a hardening of sentiment, with the Party for Freedom/Partij voor de Vrijheid (PVV), an overtly anti-Muslim party headed by Geert Wilders, rising in influence and representation somewhat steadily from 2008 forward. Geert Wilders' recent conviction for hate speech underlines the disconnection between the rise of the PVV and contextual norms, embedded in the legal code, about acceptable expression of intolerance toward immigrants, immigration and religion in the Netherlands. What is clear is that the Netherlands offers a context in which the stigmatization of Islamophobia can be anticipated, reflected in legal and social normative pressure.

The Anti-Immigrant Sentiment and the Role of Education

What follows is a brief overview of an extensive literature—both quantitative and qualitative—on attitudes toward immigrants (for a recent, systematic review see Hainmueller and Hopkins 2014). Typically, economic determinants of opposition, framed as labour-market competition, are distinguished from sociocultural[6] determinants, which are rooted in values and beliefs (Ceobanu and Escandell 2010; Schneider et al. 2008; Hainmueller and Hiscox 2007). The role of education is prominent in both perspectives with the difference being more about the interpretation of what education means rather than whether education matters.

From the perspective of labour-market competition, education is a marker of human capital with greater attained education being analogous to greater skills (Borjas 1999). Highly cited works by Scheve and Slaughter (2001) and Mayda (2006) clearly articulate this human-capital perspective, which adheres closely to a structural functionalist[7] understanding of schooling. For instance, work that privileges a skills-based interpretation of education by Scheve and Slaughter (2001), Mayda (2006), Hanson et al. (2007) and McLaren and Johnson (2007) consistently find a negative correlation between anti-immigrant/immigration sentiment and years/level of schooling.

---

[6]In some work, sociocultural determinants are referred to as sociotropic (Hainmueller and Hopkins 2014). In this work, sociocultural will be used throughout and can be considered synonymous.

[7]See Collins (1971) for concise summery of the implications of a functionalist perspective on educational attainment.

Comparative work in Europe by Rustenbach (2010) points out the interpretation of education is ambiguous, supporting both a skills-based and status-based reading.[8] Some find that once cultural values and beliefs are considered, overt expression of opposition to immigration is no longer significantly associated with education in a number of European contexts (Hainmueller and Hiscox 2007), reinforced in work that suggests education is best understood as a marker of cultural capital rather than skills (Manevska and Achterberg 2013). Others, also comparing multiple European contexts, find that education remains significantly and negatively associated with the perception of threat after the risk of job loss and income are taken into account (McLaren 2003).

The primacy of sociocultural determinants is echoed by two studies in the Netherlands by Sniderman et al. (2004) and Sniderman and Hagendoorn (2007) that find cultural markers (e.g., language) to be relatively more salient than economic markers in determining attitudes toward immigration. This emphasis on cultural attributes of the immigrant—religion in general and Islam in particular—underlies comparative work in Europe that finds prejudice toward Muslims, independent of immigrant status, is more prevalent than prejudice toward immigrants in general (Strabac and Listhaug 2007).

Evidence linking education and perception of immigration in Europe, from the sociocultural perspective, is somewhat more consistent (Manevska and Achterberg 2013; Hainmueller and Hiscox 2007). In the case of the Netherlands, Savelkoul et al. (2011) find that the interpretation of Islam as a threat significantly predicts anti-Muslim sentiment and is inversely related to the educational attainment of the respondent. The religiosity (i.e., frequency of practice) of the non-immigrant population, which is negatively correlated with education, is emphasized by some with traditional and culturally conservative non-Muslim faiths in Europe being significantly more likely to express negative attitudes (Davidov et al. 2008; Sides and Citrin 2007). Helbling (2014) concludes that the religiosity of non-immigrants is of particular salience, but only associated with general opposition to Muslim immigrants and not phenotypical symbols such as a headscarf.[9] Of note, accounting for social desirability bias results in similar and, in some cases, stronger evidence that education is associated with a more tolerant attitude (Heerwig and McCabe 2009; Ostapczuk et al. 2009; Wagner and Zick 1995). That said, others conclude that higher levels of education are associated with a greater reluctance to *express* racist sentiment in the US, but do not find a strong case that the more educated are in fact more tolerant (Kuppens and Spears 2014).[10]

---

[8]Of note, this work refers to education as "Human Capital", but makes explicit that cosmopolitanism, described as when "...higher levels of education are related to higher tolerance toward different races and cultures and a more international outlook," is an alternative interpretation (Rustenbach 2010: 57).

[9]In Switzerland, Helbling (2010) goes further and concludes that Islamophobia (i.e., the targeted opposition to Muslims) is of limited definitional value above the broader frame of xenophobia.

[10]Kuppens and Spears (2014) use an implicit association test (IAT) and find that the more educated are not necessarily more racially tolerant but aversive in their expression of racial intolerance.

In sum, education, rather than a straightforward accumulation of human capital, entails the socialization into a constellation of norms, accumulation of social and cultural capital. When considering the expression of intolerance, different educational trajectories shape distinct subsequent perceptions of social expectations. Two perspectives emerge, which parallel closely the dramaturgical vocabulary systematized by Goffman (1959). To the extent to which education is a marker of a more cosmopolitan orientation, the difference between levels of schooling in expressed intolerance is essentially a "back-stage" phenomenon. However, to the extent that an education gradient determines an increasing sensitivity to the stigmatisation of intolerance, the resulting masking of intolerance is best understood as a performance (i.e., "front-stage") better acted by the better educated.

Hypotheses

Given that public opinion in the Netherlands is notably moderate in standard polls, but support for an overtly anti-immigrant political platform (i.e., the PVV vote share) is steady, there is a reasonable expectation that social desirability pressure results in non-trivial over-statement of support for Muslim immigration. Therefore, the following hypothesis is expected to hold: (H1) *Overt support for Muslim Immigration is significantly higher than covert support.*

The general expectation defined by H1 overlays a more nuanced prediction of significant variation in overt/covert support for Muslim immigration by levels of education. Specifically, either for reasons of reduced perception of economic competition or a generally more open, accepting outlook, the following hypothesis is expected to hold: (H2) *More educated respondents are more overtly AND covertly tolerant of Muslim immigration.*

That said, this work considers opposition/support for Muslim immigration on two levels with different expectations for overtly and covertly expressed sentiment. Are the better educated more tolerant, overtly and covertly, as H2 suggests or are the better educated simple more averse to expressing intolerance? If yes, under conditions of absolute anonymity, the observed education gradient should be reduced and/or eliminated, resulting in the following hypothesis: (H3) *More educated respondents are more tolerant of Muslim immigrants only when asked directly. When anonymity is protected, no gradient in tolerance by level of education remains.*

Formally, as presented, the second and third hypotheses are mutually exclusive. If the education gradient disappears under the list condition, H3 would be fully supported. If the gradient remains unchanged, H2 would be preferred. However, it is possible that the more educated can be more tolerant overall AND subject to the same normative pressure to present themselves as tolerant, resulting in an interpretation whereby there is significant masking AND the gradient remains. This would be interpretable as a case of "tolerant liars" in that it would couple greater relative tolerance with significant masking.

Method: An Intuitive Introduction to the List Experiment

Concern about the veracity of responses to surveys that target controversial topics has been pointed out for more than four decades (Phillips and Clancy 1972; Krumpal 2013). In fact, the research design pursued in this work, termed the *list experiment*, reflects only one of a number of available options. Other approaches focus on the mode of interaction (e.g., phone vs. online vs. in-person) or sub-conscious/unconscious mechanisms (e.g., implicit association test). However, the list experiment offers a reasonable method for concerns about anti-immigrant sentiment as it (1) guarantees absolute anonymity, (2) is easily implemented with a representative sample and (3) is directly comparable with measures used in standard survey data, which offers a clear measure of the extent to which support for Muslim immigration is over-stated in direct measurement.

To offer the intuition, the list experiment works by only asking respondents to offer the number of items in a provided list with which they agree. A control sample is given a list of three items, covering topics like assistance to the poor, taxation and environmental regulation A treatment group is presented this same list, but with the addition of a *focal* item that asks about support for the controversial topic of interest—Muslim immigration in this case. Because, both samples are presented the same control list items, any difference between the average response to the control and treatment is due to the additional item. At the group-level, simply subtracting the average response to the control from the average response to the treatment offers an covert way to ascertain support for the focal item (i.e., support for Muslim immigration).

The key to the success of the survey experiment is that respondents are never asked to articulate support for any specific item in the list, which guarantees permanent anonymity at the individual level. An additional step, which is taken in this work, is to ask a subset of respondents to directly express their support for Muslim immigration via the presentation of a standard survey question, which measures *overt* support as it is measured at the individual-level in the absence of absolute, permanent anonymity. The difference between *covert* support and *overt* support is interpretable as a measure of the extent to which support for Muslim immigration is over-stated. In addition, variation in the extent to which masking of intolerance occurs can be observed by subgroups (e.g., levels of education).

Method: A Formal Introduction to the List Experiment

Building from intuition, the list experiment is designed specifically to manipulate the amount of anonymity guaranteed respondents. As with any experiment, the basic design involves independent samples designated as treatment(s) and control (see Fig. 6.1). The control sample is presented with the following list question A, translated from Dutch (original placed in the associated footnote):

Fig. 6.1 Design of experiment. Source: Author's own elaboration

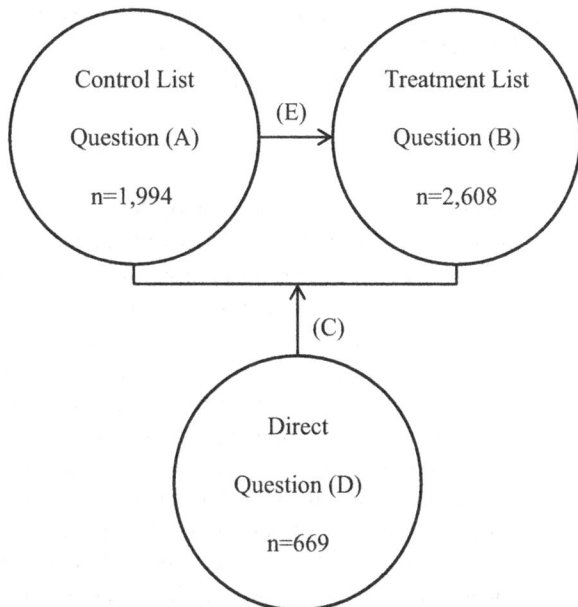

A. Of the following three statements, HOW MANY of them do you AGREE with? We don't want to know which statements, just HOW MANY?

- The Netherlands should increase assistance to the poor
- The Netherlands should decrease the tax on petrol and diesel
- The Netherlands should allow large corporations to pollute the environment

Responses range from zero and three. These items establish a baseline distribution, from which a mean response and standard deviation can be calculated. An independent treatment group is presented a similar list question B, but with the following additional focal item included:

B. Of the following four statements, HOW MANY of them do you AGREE with? We don't want to know which statements, just HOW MANY?

- The Netherlands should increase assistance to the poor
- The Netherlands should decrease the tax on petrol and diesel
- The Netherlands should allow large corporations to pollute the environment
- The Netherlands should allow Muslim people to come and live here[11]

Responses to the treatment list range from zero to four.[12] As with the control list question A, group-level measures of central tendency (e.g., mean and

---

[11]The statement in Dutch is worded as follows: "Nederland zou moslims moeten toelaten om hier te komen wonen en leven"

[12]Selecting all or none of the items in a list question is called ceiling or floor effects, respectively. In either case a respondent reveals her/his preferences, which limits the utility of a list experiment. A

standard deviation) can be calculated for the treatment list question B. The difference between these two means gives the proportion that select the focal item and is formalized with (Eq. 6.1)

$$E = \overline{Y}_B - \overline{Y}_A \qquad (6.1)$$

where E represents the proportion of the sample that select the focal item in the treatment, which is derived from the difference between the mean response to the treatment list ($\overline{Y}_B$) and the mean response to the control list ($\overline{Y}_A$). A two-sample, one-sided[13] t-test is sufficient to test whether the proportion selecting the focal item in the treatment is significantly greater than zero. Although the difference between the two list questions provides a measure of covert support for the focal item (i.e., tolerance of Muslim immigration), the extent to which attitudes are hidden requires comparing the estimate of E to a direct question (C) about perception of Muslim immigrants to the Netherlands:

Of note, the direct question C offers four response options. This is in-line with other effort to assess attitudes toward immigrants,[14] but is rarely deployed in a list experiment as (Eq. 6.1) can only derive a proportion, which must be compared to a binary response. In an effort to retain the range of options typically offered in a standard survey question, two coding schemes to generate a binary are pursued.

D. To what extent do you think the Netherlands should allow Muslim people to come and live here?[15]

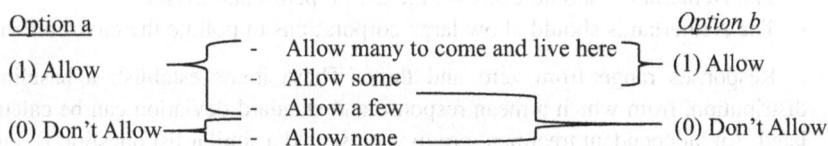

Option a
(1) Allow
(0) Don't Allow

- Allow many to come and live here
- Allow some
- Allow a few
- Allow none

Option b
(1) Allow
(0) Don't Allow

The first, designated *option a*, considers respondents that select the allowance of many, some and few Muslim immigrants to be comparable to those who select the focal item (i.e., agree that the Netherlands should allow Muslim people to come and live). This option considers any respondent that does not select complete opposition

---

discussion of the potential biases these two options could entail is included in the concluding section on limitations.

[13] A one-sided test is used as the mean response to question B should always be equal to or greater than the mean response to question A.

[14] For example, see question B30a in European Social Survey Wave 7 (2014).

[15] The question in Dutch is worded as follows: "In welke mate vindt u dat Nederland moslims zou moeten toelaten om hier te komen wonen en leven?".

(i.e., allow none) to be tolerant of Muslim immigration at least in some amount. *Option b* is a more conservative approach, which considers only those who support many or some Muslim immigrants to be comparable in perspective to those who select the focal item in the list experiment. Although there is value in presenting both options, *option a* is the most analogous to the binary response required of the list experiment as all levels of support (i.e., few, some, many) are considered distinct from a clear negative response (i.e., none). It is worth noting that this issue is present in any list experiment, but it is typically hidden via the presentation of a simple binary direct question. This experiment offers a more transparent approach, but at the cost of complexity in the interpretation. Regardless of the how the binary measure (both are presented throughout) is determined, the resulting measure can be subtracted from the proportion derived from the list experiment to assess the extent to which intolerance is concealed when giving a direct response, which is formalized by (Eq. 6.2):

$$C = E - \overline{Y}_D \qquad (6.2)$$

where C measures the difference between the proportion expressing tolerance toward Muslim immigrants when asked directly (i.e., $\overline{Y}_D$, where the subscript D refers to the binary derivation of question C), and the proportion who express tolerance when assessed via the list experiment (i.e., E, which is calculated using Eq. 6.1). When converted to a percentage scale, C is interpretable as the percentage-point difference between overtly expressed tolerance and that which is expressed when permanent anonymity is offered.

In sum, (Eqs. 6.1 and 6.2) provide three key measures: (1) tolerance expressed when asked directly, (2) tolerance when offered absolute anonymity and (3) the difference between the two, which measures the extent to which intolerance is concealed. These components can be estimated for the entire sample or by levels of education. The list experiment is not without limitations and two are of particular concern (Blair and Imai 2012). First, if all (*ceiling effect*) or none (*floor effect*) of the items in the list question are selected, anonymity is no longer plausible. Second, if the response pattern to the control list items changes due to the addition of the additional, focal item in the treatment (*design effect*), interpretation of E (Eq. 6.1) is problematic. These concerns are addressed in detail in Appendix 2.

Data

Representative of the adult population of the Netherlands in 2014, the survey experiment was a component of the Longitudinal Internet Studies for the Social Sciences (LISS) panel, initiated in 2007 as part of the Measurement and Experimentation in the Social Sciences (MESS) project. The full LISS panel, drawn from the population register held by Statistics Netherlands,[16] is a true probability sample and includes approximately 8000 individuals residing in 5000 households. All participants are non-immigrant residents of the Netherlands this analysis as the focus is on the autochthonous population's perception of immigrants. That said, LISS maintains a separate panel that provides an oversample the immigrant population, which was not included in this experiment. Respondents participated via a web survey and, aside from initial contact, did not interact directly with survey takers. The LISS panel is available to outside researchers, conditional on approval of a submitted research proposal, and all collected data, including the experiment used in this work, is publicly available to registered users via the LISS Data Archive (Scherpenzeel and Das 2011).[17] Complete technical details of the sample design and maintenance across waves can be found in Scherpenzeel (2011).

The experiment that informs this work entered (and exited) the field in September of 2014 as part of a larger data collection comprised of eight distinct experimental groups. The total number of usable cases for the entire data collection, of which only a subset are used in this analysis, was 5615. This total sample reflects the number of non-missing cases out of a total of 6558 selected individuals from the full LISS panel with non-response of 14.3% and 3 incompletes. The control group (n = 1994) received a list question with three items. The treatment group (n = 2608) was presented with an identical list with an additional focal item. The final group (n = 669) received a direct question, which is needed for direct comparison to the focal item in the list question. This results in a total, across all independent samples, of 5271 respondents. The variables used in the main analysis and the supplementary multivariate models (Appendix 1) are reported for each treatment and control sample in Table 6.1.[18]

Direct and List Responses

When considering overt expression, few support the arrival of many Muslim immigrants to the Netherlands (8%; Table 6.1). About a third of respondents consider "some" (36%) or "few" (34%) Muslim immigrants to be preferable and over a fifth of respondents (22%) in the direct group oppose the arrival and residency of any Muslim immigrant (Table 6.1). Clearly, the selection of *option a* (i.e., many + some + few) or *option b* (i.e., many + some) for the conversion of question C to a binary

---

[16]Link to technical details of the Population Register of the Netherlands: https://www.cbs.nl/nl-nl/achtergrond/2016/01/population-register-data-basis-for-the-netherlands-population-statistics.

[17]Link to LISS Data Archive: http://www.lissdata.nl/dataarchive.

[18]A test of proportions was conducted for each comparable value in Table 6.1 (e.g., unemployed in treatment vs. control) to assess differences in the groups for included observed characteristics. Although the percentage male in the control (44%) and the direct (49%) and the percentage with no income in the treatment (11%) and the direct (7%) are notable, the differences did not approach significance at the 0.10 level.

Table 6.1 Descriptive statistics

	Treatment		Control		Direct
	Mean (standard error) or percentage				
List (question A and B)	1.70	(0.01)	1.44	(0.01)	
Direct (question C)					
Allow [insert] Muslim immigrants to come and live in the Netherlands					
[Many]					7.92
[Some]					36.32
[Few]					33.93
[No]					21.82
Education (highest attained)					
Primary	7.02		6.72		7.47
Lower secondary	23.54		23.47		23.47
Upper secondary	12.23		9.93		11.06
Junior college	23.96		24.92		24.81
College/University	33.24		34.95		33.18
Occupation (primary)					
Wage labour	43.67		44.43		44.69
Independent employment	14.11		14.34		12.71
Unemployed	2.68		3.46		2.54
State supported	26.34		26.13		29.60
Other/Enrolled	13.19		11.63		10.46
Monthly income (euros)					
None	11.23		9.83		7.03
1–1000	23.43		23.02		23.32
1001–1500	19.25		21.46		19.43
1501–2000	21.17		20.86		24.66
2001+	24.92		24.82		25.56
Sex					
Male	46.40		43.88		49.18
Female	53.60		56.12		50.82
n	2608		1994		669

Source: LISS 2015

makes a substantive difference. It is worth noting that this implications of offering respondents only a binary response, which is more easily compared directly to the covert estimate derived from the list experiment, would obfuscated the differences shown by *option a* and *b* above.

Education

The Netherlands has experienced a large and sustained expansion of higher education since the 1960s, covering the education period most relevant for the sampled population. A two-tiered system was introduced in the early 1980s, consisting of academic and vocational institutions of higher learning, which was paralleled by an expansion of financial support for enrolled students (for a comprehensive discussion see Rijken et al. 2010). As seen in Table 6.1, a majority complete some form of tertiary degree (i.e., junior college, college or university) affirming the substantively expanded education landscape. That said, nearly a quarter of respondents have a lower-secondary education and over 5% report only a primary education, indicating substantial variation across the education spectrum.

Results

For purposes of illustration, the interpretation will focus on the predicted tolerance of Muslim immigrants depicted in Fig. 6.2 and associated evidence of social desirability bias presented in Fig. 6.3. Of note, multivariate models that control for socio-economic and demographic characteristics constant are presented in Figs. 6.4 and

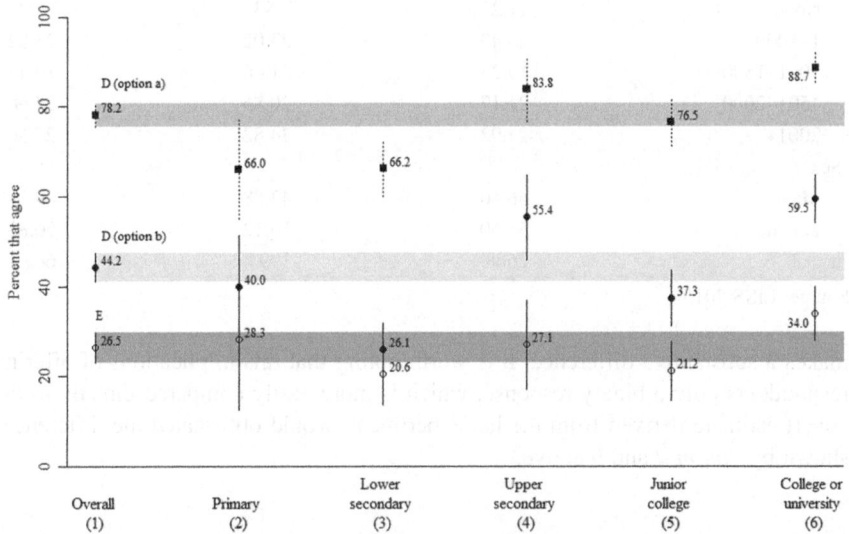

Fig. 6.2 Direct and list experiment estimates of the proportion who agree that Muslim immigrants should be allowed to come and live in the Netherlands—predicted percentage in agreement and related 90 per cent confidence interval. Source: LISS 2015; author's own elaboration. Note: Column 1 is for a model with no controls and is estimated using (Eq. 6.1). Columns 2–6 are derived from models that control only for education, estimated by (Eq. 6.3)

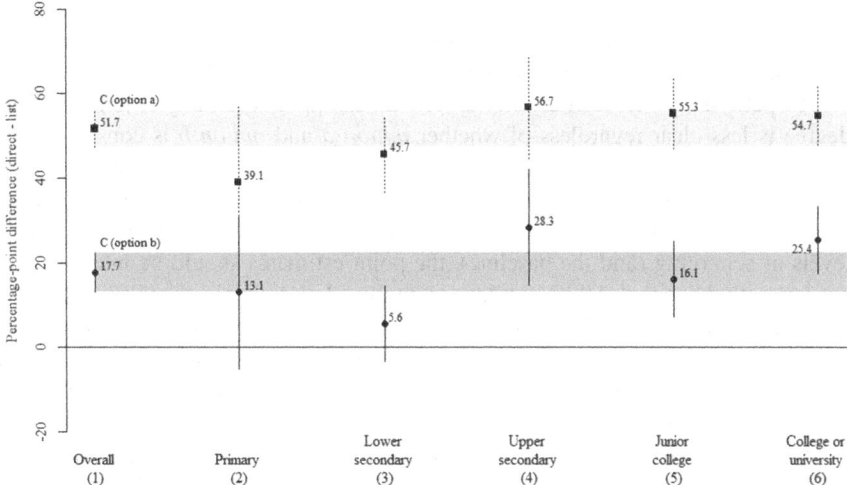

Fig. 6.3 The extent to which opposition to Muslim immigration is hidden in the Netherlands—predicted percentage-point difference and related 90 per cent confidence interval. Source: LISS 2015; author's own elaboration. Note: As with Fig. 6.2, column 1 is for a model with no controls and is estimated using (Eq. 6.1). Columns 2–6 are derived from models that control for education, estimated by (Eq. 6.3)

6.5 of Appendix 1 along with an interpretation of the observed pattern overall and by levels of education. As the results in the models with controls are notably consistent with Fig. 6.2 and the multivariate approach requires a number of additional assumptions to calculate predicted values, the pattern by level of education without controls is preferable.

Overt and Covert Intolerance

The first column in Fig. 6.2 shows the predicted value and 90% confidence interval for overt opposition to Muslim immigrants (D) and covert opposition (E), which is calculated using (Eq. 6.1). The remaining columns in Fig. 6.2 show the same two estimates by level of education. The upward education gradient in both overt (D) and covert (E) acceptance of Muslim immigrants to the Netherlands is evident. When considering *option a*, the percentage that overtly support Muslim immigrants increases along with attained education. Greatest overt tolerance is found among the college educated respondents with about 88.7% in agreement that Muslim immigrants should be allowed to reside in the Netherlands, which is significantly higher than the least educated and the baseline percentage (78.2%). Specifically, primary educated respondents (66%) are similar in their reported tolerance to those with a lower secondary education (66.2%). The pattern is similar for *option b* of overt support (D). Relative to the 59.5% who support Muslim immigration among the college educated, the less educated are significantly less supportive at 40% and 30% for the primary and lower-secondary educated, respectively. The college/ university educated differ significantly from the baseline (44.2%) as well.

The pattern of overt tolerance for those with an upper-secondary or junior college degree is less clear regardless of whether *option a* and *option b* is considered. At 83.8% (*option a*) and 55.4% (*option b*), the point estimates of those with an upper-secondary education appear to be more tolerant relative to those with completed junior college who report 76.5% (*option a*) and 37.3% (*option b*) respectively. For all levels of schooling (and the baseline), the point estimates should be interpreted in concert with the reported 90% confidence interval. For example, the 90% confidence internals of upper-secondary educated respondents and the most educated overlap (column 4 vs. column 6). That said, for all overt estimates, the 90% confidence intervals do not overall when the highest and lowest levels of schooling are compared (column 6 vs. column 2).

When considering covert support (E), derived from the list experiment, the gradient in the point estimates is notably less pronounced and significance and no significant difference is observed. It is notable that the point estimate for college/ university educated respondents is notably higher relative to other levels, which range between 28.3% (primary) and 24.2% (lower secondary), but the 90% confidence intervals clearly overlap. Simply put, highly educated respondents are more covertly tolerant, but the gradient is less evident and the significant difference is observed only when compared to the baseline. In other words, these results offer some evidence that that the positive gradient in tolerance is explained, at least in part, by a greater tendency among the most educated to over-report support for Muslim immigration. Appendix 1 reports supplementary analysis that considers the educational gradient derived from models that include controls for income, occupational status and a number of core sociodemographic characteristics. As the multivariate results are notably consistent but require that predicted values be derived using assumed values for controls, the results reported in Fig. 6.2 are preferable.

Masking and Social Desirability Bias

Figure 6.3 depicts the extent to which intolerance is concealed by level of education. The baseline estimate (column 1) is derived from the bivariate model described by (Eq. 6.1). Identical to Fig. 6.1, estimates by level of education (column 2–6). With the possible exception of participants with an upper-secondary education, social desirability pressure is noticeably similar across levels of education. Overall (column 1), a 17.7 percentage-point difference (*option b*) and a 51.7 percentage-point difference (*option a*) underline that fact that significantly and substantively fewer respondents report tolerance when offered permanent and absolute anonymity. That said, in general, rather than explaining the gradient, the stigma attached to expressing intolerance is somewhat uniformly observed. One comparison deviates slightly from the general interpretation—the percentage over-stating their tolerance for contrast of the covert estimates with *option b* of the overt estimates does seem to differ significantly from the percentage observed for those with a lower-secondary education.

The extent to which support for Muslim immigration is overstated, comparable to what is shown in Fig. 6.3, is reported for models that control for socioeconomic and sociodemographic attributes of respondents in Fig. 6.5 of Appendix 1. The results are notably consistent, deviating only slightly in terms of point estimates, but not in terms of relative magnitude nor overall pattern. As a result, the estimates reported in Fig. 6.3 are preferred.

Conclusion

As part of a broader effort to underline the theoretical importance of stigma for the interpretation of survey responses, this work tests three hypotheses about the education gradients and perception of Muslim immigrants. The first (H1), which predicts the Netherlands to be a context in which tolerance toward Muslim immigrants is significantly higher when expressed in situations where stigma is anticipated. Regardless of the way in which overt support for Muslim immigration was measured, it deviated significantly and substantively from that measured under conditions of permanent and absolute anonymity. The implications are clear in that the expression of tolerance is shaped by situational norms. This is different than interpreting covert expression if Islamophobic sentiment as closer to the truth. Instead, the greater prevalence of anonymously expressed anti-Muslim attitudes is better understood as an alternative context of reception that operates under distinct situational conditions—akin to rhetoric on anonymous online forum rather than a measure of an underlying absolute truth.

The second hypothesis (H2) is premised on the theoretical argument that education reflects an open and accepting outlook toward Muslim immigrants, regardless of whether support is overtly or covertly expressed. This is partially supported by the evidence. The most educated in the Netherlands are, in some cases, more open to Muslim immigration, but the manipulation of the anonymity afforded participants results in significant and substantive differences in the extent to which opposition to Muslim immigrants is expressed. Covert sentiment, rather than reflecting a clear gradient, is notably flatter with little substantive difference by levels of schooling. Here, the theoretical importance of the selective presentation some into sharper relief. Clearly, the interpretation of the role of education demands greater scrutiny if the role of stigma is meaningfully considered, which brings us to the next conclusion.

The third hypothesis (H3) assesses whether some levels of schooling are more likely to mask their intolerance relative to others. Rather than finding that the most educated are the only group to reluctantly express less support for Muslim immigration, evidence suggests that all levels of schooling significantly mask their opposition. The implication is that contextually determined stigma does not vary too much by level of education. Again, the moderating *effect* of more school cannot be extrapolated from the observed education gradient. Instead, overt and covert estimates suggest that those who receive more education are the same people who, in the end, maintain a more tolerant stance toward Muslim immigration. This fits the expectation that the more educated are more open-minded in their outlook regardless of whether education conditions those who participate, or educational mobility is disproportionately selected by the more tolerant. The less and least educated feel similar pressure to that of the more and most educated and this pressure is reflected in the near uniform underestimation of intolerance when explicit measures are used.

Discussion

In addition to unique empirical insight into the case of selective revelation of Islamophobic sentiment in the Netherlands, this work underlies the pitfalls, rooted in the systematic masking of discreditable attributes, of taking overt responses to surveys measuring attitudes toward immigrants at face value. The more educated are not disproportionately hiding their intolerance and the college educated, at least overtly, do reflect a relatively more accepting attitude toward Muslim immigrants, even when labour-market position (i.e., income and occupation) are taken into account (see Appendix 1). That said, the relevance of these findings extends beyond measurement, offering a theoretical framework that avoids the need to consider the elimination/reduction of stigma to reflect a truer version of reality.

What does this mean for our understanding of social desirability bias? First, this work moves beyond a perspective that looks at social desirability as a form of measurement error. Anonymity is a powerful tool for reducing the anticipation of scrutiny (and associated stigmatization) of a response to a controversial question, but responses that are performed overtly need not be dismissed as biased in the strict sense of the word. Instead, they are selective presentations of self and, in some cases, are more indicative of the prevalence of a given response pattern than their covertly measured equivalents.

Fundamentally, this work evidences a pattern by which education shapes the extent to which social desirability leads to a gap between overt and covert antipathy towards Muslim newcomers. This is distinct from a perspective that see social desirability as a fixed attribute of the individual. Instead, social desirability is better understood as a contextually defined response to a specific interaction. Future work would do well to consider that being strategic in the presentation of some attitudes might not determine a general reluctance to mitigate social desirability pressure in all cases. The hope is that, as sociologists, the meaning of being adverse to the overt expression of certain sentiment and the way that this hesitancy is structured by other attributes of an individual, remain a subject of study and inquiry rather than being overlooked as a component of measurement error. In the literature on social stigma, we do find the tools to understand the theoretical motivations and distinct situational logics that offer a more robust and complete picture of the origin and performance of socially desirable response patterns to surveys.

Acknowledgments I would like to thank the team of the Longitudinal Internet Studies for the Social Sciences (LISS) panel who accepted this proposal and offered guidance before, during and after its time in the field. Also, this experiment is a small part of a larger project that reflects the fruitful and ongoing collaboration with Philip Brenner, Diana Zavala-Rojas and Peter Schmidt.

Appendix 1: Multivariate Analysis

Interpretations of education are not limited to cosmopolitanism nor status (Rustenbach 2010) and, instead, can encompass differences in acquired skills directly translatable into labour-market outcomes (e.g., occupation, salary). To better distinguish labour-market position from the status component of education, occupation, monthly income and sex were asked of all sampled respondents. This allows an interpretation of education, albeit imperfect, independent of the labour-market position of respondents. If the gradient in education remains, the implication would be that education is a marker of a tolerant and openminded outlook. To be clear, a causal interpretation of differences between levels of education, net of other socio-economic characteristics or not, does not offer a causal interpretation. The exercise is helpful as large deviations between the pattern show by levels of schooling (i.e., Fig. 6.2) and those observed when additional controls are added would indicate that education is unlikely to have a plausibly independent role. To these ends, recent work to extend the basic list experiment, defined by (Eqs. 6.1 and 6.2), to a multivariate framework allows the inclusion of controls (Imai 2011), described by (Eq. 6.3):

$$Y = X\beta_A + TX\beta_B + \epsilon \qquad (6.3)$$

where the outcome of interest, Y, is the response to the list question determined by a vector of covariates, X. The indicator T can take a value of 0 or 1 depending on whether the treatment (T = 1) or control (T = 0) group is considered. The parameters β_A and β_B, which are assumed to have a linear[19] relationship with Y, are estimated from the model. One way to understand this estimation strategy is in two steps. The first uses the observed response to the three-question list given to the control group

---

[19]This approach has also been extended to include nonlinear and maximum likelihood estimation strategies (Imai 2011). In some cases (e.g., non-linear outcomes), the nonlinear, two-step model is advantageous. The maximum-likelihood approach allows for the modelling of the joint distribution of the covariates, but is computationally intensive and, for these models, does not offer a clear advantage. As a result, the linear model was selected for its parsimony, intuitiveness and direct link to the simple difference in means (Eq. 6.16.1). As Imai (2011) acknowledges, when the parameters β_A and β_B are the same, the equation reduces to the difference in means formalized in (Eq. 6.1).

(T = 0) to estimate $\widehat{\beta}_A$ for covariates X. The expected value of Y (i.e., $\widehat{Y}$) in this first step, averaged across all respondents in the control sample, is comparable to $\overline{Y}_A$ in (Eq. 6.1). In the second step, because X and the individual response to the four-question treatment list question are observed in the treatment group (T = 1), an estimate of $\widehat{\beta}_B$ can be independently obtained by setting β_A from the first step equal to $\widehat{\beta}_A$.[20] Similar to the first step, $\widehat{Y}$, derived from the parameters $\widehat{\beta}_B$, averaged across all individuals in the treatment group, is comparable to $\overline{Y}_B$ in (Eq. 6.1). For all estimates, $E(\epsilon | X, T) = 0$.

For multivariate estimates of direct tolerance (i.e., question C), a binomial logit model with covariates X identical to those included in (Eq. 6.3) is sufficient. Given the ubiquity of this approach in the literature, a formal presentation of the model is forgone, but Pampel (2000) offers a thorough introduction to the logic and interpretation of logistic regression. Equations (6.1–6.3) are estimated using the package -list-[21] and the binomial logit model is estimated using the package -glm—in R version 3.3.2.

Control Variables: Income, Occupation and Sex

To take into account observed differences in labour-market position, income and primary occupation are measured at the time of the experiment. Occupation defines the labour-market status of the participant in terms of work, which is the self-reported primary employment at the time of the interview. Two types of active employment are identified—wage labour and independent employment. Three additional categories account for those inactive, recipients of state transfers and other/enrolled in school. Being employed for a wage (44%) is the largest category among those active in the labour market and overall. Income is measured as bracketed monthly earnings in Euros ranging across five brackets from 0 to 2001+ Euros per month. Among those with some income, the distribution is notably even with between 20% and 25% of respondents in each of the four non-zero wage brackets. A narrow measure of the sex of the respondent, limited to a binary, is also included.

To estimate a predicted probability, values must be assumed for each covariate, allowing only education to vary. The specific coefficients for each covariate are reported in Table 6.2a and b. To offer an intuitive interpretation and plausible predicted values, the most frequent response for each independent variable held constant. As a result the predicted value is interpretable as women, engaged in wage labour who earn between €1501 and €2000, inclusive, per month.

---

[20] As Imai (2011) points out, the two-step approach can also be articulated as an interaction between the indicator for the treatment (T_i) and all covariates (X) that are present in both the treatment and the control groups.

[21] Link to technical details and download of the -list- package: https://cran.r-project.org/web/packages/list/index.html.

6 Stigma and the Meaning of Social Desirability: Concealed Islamophobia in the...

Table 6.2 Logistic regression models of agreement that Muslim immigrants should be allowed to come and live in the Netherlands

	Direct/Overt (option a)				Direct/Overt (option b)			
	Model 1		Model 2		Model 3		Model 4	
	Coefficient (standard error)							
Intercept	1.28 ***	(0.09)	1.14 **	(0.41)	−0.23 **	(0.08)	−0.59 +	(0.34)
Education (ref. = upper secondary)								
Primary			−0.61	(0.37)			0.14	(0.35)
Lower secondary			−0.50 +	(0.26)			−0.46 +	(0.25)
Junior college			0.40	(0.38)			0.76 *	(0.30)
College/University			0.97 ***	(0.29)			1.01 ***	(0.23)
Occupation (ref. = wage labour)								
Ind. Employment			−0.06	(0.33)			−0.13	(0.28)
Unemployed			0.04	(0.69)			−0.25	(0.54)
State supported			−0.18	(0.24)			−0.38 +	(0.21)
Other/enrolled			0.33	(0.44)			−0.01	(0.34)
Monthly income (euros; ref. = 1501–2000)								
None			0.20	(0.52)			0.11	(0.41)
1–1000			−0.17	(0.31)			−0.25	(0.27)
1001–1500			0.04	(0.31)			−0.02	(0.26)
2001+			−0.33	(0.29)			−0.40 +	(0.24)
Sex (ref. = female)								
Male			0.11	(0.23)			0.20	(0.19)
n	669		669		669		669	
AIC	704.00		689.35		920.55		884.34	

+p < 0.10, * p < 0.05, ** p < 0.01, *** p < 0.001
Source: LISS 2015

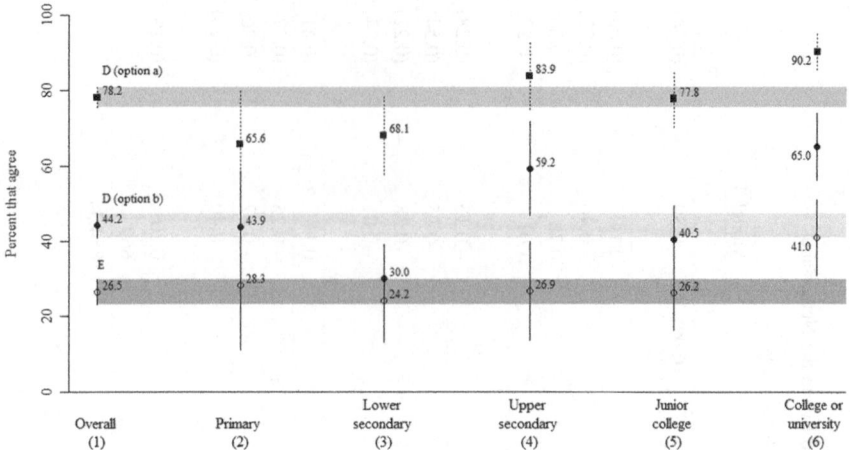

Fig. 6.4 Direct and list experiment estimates of the proportion who agree that Muslim immigrants should be allowed to come and live in the Netherlands—predicted percentage in agreement and related 90 per cent confidence interval. Source: LISS 2015; author's own elaboration. Note: Column 1 is for a model with no controls and is estimated using (Eq. 6.1). Columns 2–6 are derived from models that control for occupation, income and sex, estimated by (Eq. 6.3). For estimates with controls, the reported predicted values are for women, engaged in wage labour who earn between €1501 and €2000, inclusive, per month

Figure 6.4 reports the estimated overt (option a and b) and covert support for Muslim immigration with no controls and for each level of schooling. The results are notably consistent with those presented without controls (Table 6.2). There is no evidence that the pattern observed in which the more educated report greater overt AND covert support relative to the less educated is explained by variation across education levels in occupational status or income. As the multivariate models require a number of assumptions both in the estimation and in the derivation of predicted values, the straightforward depiction of the results from the list experiment, presented in Table 6.2, is preferred.

Figure 6.5 requires little elaboration as it does not deviate substantively from the estimates of social desirability bias ascertained without controls and reported in Table 6.3. The pattern appears consistent in that all levels of schooling significantly overstate their support for Muslim immigration.

Table 6.3 List models of agreement that Muslim immigrants should be allowed to come and live in the Netherlands

	List/Covert					
	Model 5			Model 6		
	Coefficient (standard error)					
Intercept	1.44	***	(0.01)	1.33	***	(0.06)
Education (ref. = upper secondary)						
Primary				0.08		(0.07)
Lower secondary				0.08	*	(0.04)
Junior college				−0.03		(0.05)
College/University				−0.14	***	(0.04)
Occupation (ref. = wage labour)						
Ind. Employment				0.07	+	(0.05)
Unemployed				0.03		(0.08)
State supported				0.06	*	(0.04)
Other/enrolled				−0.04		(0.06)
Monthly income (euros; ref. = 1501–2000)						
None				−0.11	*	(0.06)
1–1000				0.00		(0.05)
1001–1500				0.04		(0.04)
2001+				0.01		(0.04)
Sex (ref. = female)						
Male				0.07	*	(0.03)
n (total)	4602			4602		
n (treatment)	2608			2608		
n (control)	1994			1994		
Residual standard error	0.71			0.70		

+$p < 0.10$, *$p < 0.05$, **$p < 0.01$, ***$p < 0.001$
Source: LISS 2015

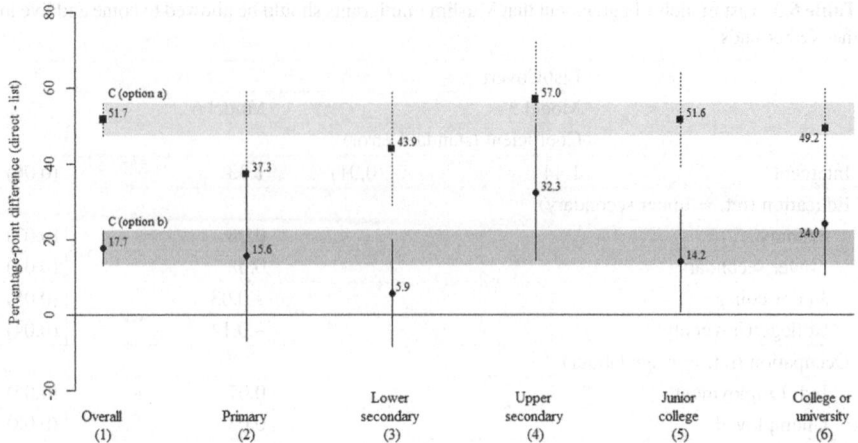

Fig. 6.5 The extent to which opposition to Muslim immigration is hidden in the Netherlands—predicted percentage-point difference and related 90 per cent confidence interval. Source: LISS 2015; author's own elaboration. Note: As with Fig. 6.2, column 1 is for a model with no controls and is estimated using (Eq. 6.1). Columns 2–6 are derived from models that control for occupation, income and sex, estimated by (Eq. 6.3). For estimates with controls, the reported predicted values are for women, engaged in wage labour who earn between €1501 and €2000, inclusive, per month

Appendix 2: Limitations of the List Experiment

This work offers a way forward in our efforts to reveal the determinants of intolerance, but not without some caveats. A primary concern of any list experiment is if the response is zero (i.e., floor effect) or equal to the total number of list items (i.e., ceiling effect) the preferences for any given item, including the focal item in the treatment group, are revealed (Imai 2011; de Jonge and Nickerson 2014). One assessment for the presence of floor or ceiling effects is to consider the observed proportion of the sample that selects zero/three in the control or zero/four in the treatment. This does not account for respondents who changed their response when confronted with the option of agreeing with all or none of the list items, but it can give an indication of a tendency as some would not alter their response even if anonymity cannot be guaranteed. As seen in Table 6.4, the proportion selecting all items in the treatment or control list is rather low, never constituting more than 2% of the sample in either. However, the risk of a floor effect is somewhat more evident with 5 and 6% selecting no items in the control and treatment respectively.

Blair and Imai (2012) offer a test for the potential bias due to floor effects, but its application requires one to assume a participant's answer to the focal list item is independent of a response to the other items in the list. This assumption should hold when there is little thematic overlap between the list items, which is a plausible in

Table 6.4 Ceiling and floor effect estimates

	Control list Question (A)		Treatment list Question (B)	
	n	(%)	n	(%)
# of list items				
0	111	(6)	126	(5)
1	944	(47)	864	(33)
2	896	(45)	1297	(50)
3	43	(2)	303	(12)
4	–	–	18	(1)
Total	1994	(100)	2608	(100)

Maximum-likelihood estimate of floor liars = 0.20%
Quasi-Bayesian approximation of floor liars = 0.23%
Source: LISS 2015

this case as the reference to religion is limited to the focal item. Below Table 6.4 the estimated percentage "floor liars" is reported, which, at between 0.20 and 0.23%,[22] suggests that floor effects are unlikely to significantly nor substantively bias the estimates.

A second consideration is the interpretation of causality. An experiment, which by definition involves some form of manipulation, offers a straightforward causal interpretation. In this case, the causal interpretation is limited to the difference between the treatment and control list question, which is the comparison used to estimate the overt measure of tolerance (i.e., E in Eq. 6.1). This difference is caused by the manipulation and, assuming an interpretation of social desirability pressure, when compared to the direct measure, a causal interpretation holds. That said, comparison of attributes that are not manipulated (e.g., less educated vs. more educated) does not offer a causal interpretation. Therefore, the role of education as a conditioning process (i.e., more education results in a more tolerant outlook) relative to a pathway selected by the most tolerant cannot be assessed in this research design.

References

Arnold, H. J., & Feldman, D. C. (1981). Social desirability response bias in self-report choice situations. *The Academy of Management Journal, 24*, 377–385.
Blair, G., & Imai, K. (2012). Statistical analysis of list experiments. *Political Analysis, 20*, 47–77.
Borjas, G. J. (1999). The economic analysis of immigration. In D. Card & O. Ashenfelter (Eds.), *Handbook of labour economics*. Amsterdam: Elsevier Science B.V..
Brenner, P. S. (2017). Toward a social psychology of survey methodology: An application of the approach and directions for the future. *Sociological Compass, 11*(17), 1–13.

---

[22]The range of values reflects two estimation options, which are outlined in greater detail in Blaire and Imai (2011). The first uses a maximum-likelihood estimator. The second is a quasi-Bayesian approach, which results in a slightly higher estimate. Still, neither approach nor exceed 1%.

Brenner, P. S., & DeLamater, J. D. (2014). Social desirability Bias in self-reports of physical activity: Is an exercise identity the culprit? *Social Indicators Research, 117*, 489–504.

Campbell, E. Q. (1964). The internalization of moral norms. *Sociometry, 27*(4), 391–412.

Ceobanu, A. M., & Escandell, X. (2010). Comparative analyses of public attitudes toward immigrants and immigration using multinational survey data: a review of theories and research. *Annual Review of Sociology, 36*, 309–328.

Collins, R. (1971). Functional and conflict theories of educational stratification. *American Sociological Review, 36*, 1002–1019.

Creighton, M. J., & Jamal, A. (2015). Does Islam play a role in anti-immigrant sentiment? An experimental approach. *Social Science Research, 53*, 89–103.

Creighton, M. J., Jamal, A., & Malancu, N. C. (2015). Has opposition to immigration increased in the United States after the economic crisis? An experimental approach. *International Migration Review, 49*, 727–756.

Davidov, E., Meuleman, B., Billiet, J., & Schmidt, P. (2008). Values and support for immigration: A cross-country comparison. *European Sociological Review, 24*, 583–599.

Davis, D. W., & Silver, B. D. (2003). Stereotype threat and race of interviewer effects in a survey on political knowledge. *American Journal of Political Science, 47*, 33–45.

de Jonge, C. P. K., & Nickerson, D. W. (2014). Artificial inflation or deflation? Assessing the item count technique in comparative surveys. *Political Behavior, 36*, 659–682.

Eurostat. (2015). *Migration and migrant population statistics*. Accessed March 14, 2018, from http://ec.europa.eu/eurostat/statistics-explained/index.php/Migration_and_migrant_population_statistics.

FORUM – Institute for Multicultural Affairs. (2010). *The position of Muslims in the Netherlands: Facts and figures – fact book 2010*. Accessed March 14, 2018, from http://www.eukn.eu/fileadmin/Lib/files/EUKN/2010/0_linkclick.pdf.

Goffman, E. (1959). *The presentation of self in everyday life*. New York: Random House.

Goffman, E. (1963). *Stigma: Notes on the management of spoiled identity*. New York: Simon and Schuster.

Hainmueller, J., & Hiscox, M. J. (2007). Educated preferences: Explaining attitudes toward immigration in Europe. *International Organization, 61*, 399–442.

Hainmueller, J., & Hopkins, D. J. (2014). Public attitudes toward immigration. *Annual Review of Political Science, 17*, 225–249.

Hanson, G. H., Scheve, K. F., & Slaughter, M. J. (2007). Public finance and individual preferences over globalization strategies. *Economics and Politics, 19*, 1–33.

Heerwegh, D. (2009). Mode differences between face-to-face and web surveys: An experimental investigation of data quality and social desirability effects. *International Journal of Public Opinion Research, 21*, 111–121.

Heerwig, J. A., & McCabe, B. J. (2009). Education and social desirability bias: The case of a black presidential candidate. *Social Science Quarterly, 90*, 674–686.

Helbling, M. (2010). Islamophobia in Switzerland: A new phenomenon or a new name for xenophobia. In S. Hug & K. H. Lanham (Eds.), *Value change in Switzerland*. Lanham, MD: Lexington Press.

Helbling, M. (2014). Opposing Muslims and the Muslim headscarf in Western Europe. *European Sociological Review, 30*, 242–257.

Henrich, J., Boyd, R., Bowles, S., Camerer, C., Fehr, E., Gintis, H., & McElreath, R. (2001). In search of Homo Economicus: Behavioral experiments in 15 small-scale societies. *American Economic Review, 91*(2), 73–78.

Imai, K. (2011). Multivariate regression analysis for the item count technique. *Journal of the American Statistical Association, 106*, 407–416.

Jamal, A., & Naber, N. (2008). *Race and Arab Americans before and after 9/11 Syracuse*. New York: Syracuse University Press.

Janus, A. L. (2010). The influence of social desirability pressures on expressed immigration attitudes. *Social Science Quarterly, 91*, 928–946.

Knoll, B. R. (2013a). Implicit nativist attitudes, social desirability, and immigration policy preferences. *International Migration Review, 47*, 1–34.
Knoll, B. R. (2013b). Assessing the effect of social desirability on nativism attitude responses. *Social Science Research, 42*, 1587–1598.
Krumpal, I. (2013). Determinants of social desirability bias in sensitive surveys: A literature review. *Quality and Quantity, 47*, 2025–2047.
Kuklinski, J. H., Cobb, M. D., & Gilens, M. (1997a). Racial attitudes and the 'new south'. *The Journal of Politics, 59*, 323–349.
Kuklinski, J. H., Sniderman, P. M., Knight, K., Piazza, T., Tetlock, P. E., Lawrence, G. R., & Mellers, B. (1997b). Racial prejudice and attitudes toward affirmative action. *Political Science, 41*, 402–419.
Kuklinski, J. H., Sniderman, P. M., Knight, K., Piazza, T., Tetlock, P. E., Lawrence, G. R., & Mellers, B. (1997c). Racial prejudice and attitudes toward affirmative action. *American Journal of Political Science, 41*, 402–419.
Kuppens, T., & Spears, R. (2014). You don't have to be well-educated to be an aversive racist, but it helps. *Social Science Research, 45*, 211–223.
Kuran, T., & McCaffery, E. J. (2008). Sex differences in the acceptability of discrimination. *Political Research Quarterly, 61*, 228–238.
Major, B., & O'Brian, L. T. (2005). The social psychology of stigma. *Annual Review of Psychology, 56*, 393–421.
Manevska, K., & Achterberg, P. (2013). Immigration and perceived ethnic threat: Cultural capital and economic explanations. *European Sociological Review, 29*, 437–449.
Mayda, A. M. (2006). Who is against immigration? A cross-country investigation of individual attitudes towards immigrants. *Review of Economic and Statistics, 88*, 510–530.
Mazar, N., Amir, O., & Ariely, D. (2008). The dishonesty of honest people: A theory of self-concept maintenance. *Journal of Marketing Research, 45*, 633–644.
McLaren, L. M. (2003). Anti-immigrant prejudice in Europe: Contact, threat perception, and preferences for the exclusion of migrants. *Social Forces, 81*, 909–936.
McLaren, L. M., & Johnson, M. (2007). Resources, group conflict and symbols: Explaining anti-immigration hostility in Britain. *Political Studies, 55*, 709–732.
Ostapczuk, M., Musch, J., & Moshagen, M. (2009). A randomized-response investigation of the education effect of in attitudes toward foreigners. *European Journal of Social Psychology, 39*, 920–931.
Pampel, F. C. (2000). Logistic regression: A primer. In *Sage university series on quantitative applications in social sciences* (pp. 7–132). Thousand Oaks, CA: Sage.
Pescosolido, B. A., & Martin, J. K. (2015). The stigma complex. *Annual Review of Sociology, 41*, 87–116.
Phillips, D. L., & Clancy, K. J. (1972). Some effects of 'social desirability' in survey studies. *American Journal of Sociology, 77*, 921–940.
Presser, S., & Stinson, L. (1998). Data collection mode and social desirability bias in self-reported religious attendance. *American Sociological Review, 63*, 137–145.
Rijken, S., Maas, I., & Ganzeboom, H. B. G. (2010). The Netherlands: Access to higher education, institutional arrangements and inequality of opportunity. In Y. Shavit, R. Arum, & A. Gamoran (Eds.), *Stratification in higher education: A comparative study*. Stanford University Press: Stanford CA.
Rustenbach, E. (2010). Sources of negative attitudes toward immigrants in Europe: A multi-level analysis. *International Migration Review, 44*, 53–77.
Savelkoul, M., Scheepers, P., Tolsma, J., & Hagendoorn, L. (2011). Anti-Muslim attitudes in the Netherlands: Tests of contradictory hypotheses derived from ethnic competition theory and intergroup contact theory. *European Sociological Review, 27*, 741–758.
Scherpenzeel, A. C. (2011). Data collection in a probability-based internet panel: How the LISS panel was built and how it can be used. *Bulletin de Méthodologie Sociologique, 109*, 56–61.

Scherpenzeel, A. C., & Das, M. (2011). True longitudinal and probability-based internet panels: Evidence from the Netherlands. In M. Das, P. Ester, & L. Kaczmirek (Eds.), *Social and behavioral research and the internet: Advances in applied methods and research strategies*. New York: Routledge.

Scheve, K., & Slaughter, M. (2001). Labor market competition and individual preferences over immigration policy. *Review of Economics and Statistics, 83*, 133–145.

Schneider, P. M., Hagendooorn, L., & Prior, M. (2008). Anti-immigrant attitudes in Europe: Outgroup size and perceived ethnic threat. *European Sociological Review, 24*, 53–67.

Shultz, K. S. And Whitney, D. J. (2005). Classical true score theory and reliability, in *Measurement theory in action: Case studies and exercises* edited by Shultz, K. S. and Whitney, D. J. Sage, Thousand Oaks, CA

Sides, J., & Citrin, J. C. (2007). European opinion about immigration: The role of identities, interests and information. *British Journal of Political Science, 37*, 477–504.

Sniderman, P. M., & Hagendoorn, L. (2007). *When ways of life collide: Multiculturalism and its discontents in the Netherlands*. Princeton, NJ: Princeton University Press.

Sniderman, P. M., Hagendoorn, L., & Prior, M. (2004). Predispositional factors and situational triggers: Exclusionary reactions to immigrant minorities. *American Political Science Review, 98*, 35–50.

Strabac, Z., & Listhaug, O. (2007). Anti-Muslim prejudice in Europe: A multilevel analysis of survey data from 30 countries. *Social Science Research, 37*, 268–286.

Wagner, U., & Zick, A. (1995). The relation of formal education to ethnic prejudice: Its reliability, validity and explanation. *European Journal of Social Psychology, 25*, 41–56.

Wike, R., Stokes, B., & Simmons, K. (2016). Europeans fear wave of refugees will mean more terrorism, fewer jobs. *Pew research center: Numbers, facts and trends shaping the world* (Release July 11, 2016).

Wikman, A. (2006). Reliability, validity and true values in surveys. *Social Indicators Research, 78*, 85–110.

Chapter 7
Is Not Knowing the Same as Being Incorrect? An Examination of 'Don't Know' Responses to Questions about Immigrant Population Size

Daniel Herda

Introduction

A nearly ubiquitous problem for survey researchers is that of item nonresponse. When subjects refuse to answer a question or respond with a "don't know," it is often treated as a frustrating nuisance. These empty cells do not fit easily into our statistical techniques. Listwise deletion—or simply dropping affected cases—is common but sacrifices statistical power and risks introducing bias. More complex solutions, like multiple imputation, estimate likely responses for individuals by fitting a particular profile of non-missing variables. However, such solutions are not a panacea as they are found to underestimate standard errors, and thus overestimate the significance of test statistics (Allison 2002). The current study takes a step back and considers an example where "don't know" responses may actually be substantively meaningful and perhaps should be treated as a valid observation rather than a technical nuisance. In particular, there are many instances where social scientists ask respondents about their factual knowledge regarding various social and political realities (Nadeau and Niemi 1995; de Vreese and Boomgaarden 2006; Henriks Vettehen et al. 2004; Johann 2012; Fraile 2013; Kunovich and Kunovich 2016; Simon 2017; Goetzmann 2017; Ipsos 2015). When being correct becomes a characteristic of interest, "don't know" becomes relevant. It represents ignorance alongside being incorrect, but is it a distinct and meaningful form of ignorance?

Over the last two decades there has been a growing interest in respondents' misperceptions of demographic realities and the consequences of viewing the world inaccurately. Since 2000 there have been dozens of published papers on the topics of overestimating racial and ethnic minority populations (Alba et al. 2005; Sigelman and Niemi 2001; Wong 2007; Schlueter and Scheepers 2010; Hooghe and

D. Herda (✉)
Merrimack College, North Andover, MA, USA
e-mail: herdad@merrimack.edu

de Vroome 2013; Kunovich 2017; Herda 2013a; Lameris et al. 2018a; Lameris et al. 2018b; Chiricos et al. 2001; Gallagher 2003), immigrant populations (Hjerm 2007; Semyonov et al. 2004; Citrin and Sides 2008; Sides and Citrin 2007; Semyonov et al. 2008; Strabac 2011; Herda 2010, 2013b, 2015, 2018), as well as other groups (Herda 2017; Martinez et al. 2008). There are also now several national and international surveys that include questions eliciting population size estimates from the European Social Survey (ESS), Ipsos MORI, the Center for American Progress, the Transatlantic Trends Studies (TATS), the General Social Survey (GSS), as well as many smaller national election studies.

Most survey respondents display ignorance, typically by overestimating minority populations and underestimating the majority (Ipsos 2015). Further, many researchers demonstrate connections between this factual ignorance and more hostile policy preferences regarding the group being estimated (Sides and Citrin 2007; Semyonov et al. 2004; Nadeau et al. 1993; Sigelman and Niemi 2001; Kunovich 2017; Wong 2007; Alba et al. 2005). The demographically innumerate arguably use incorrect information to inform and justify their policy positions in opposition to the group in question. A large imagined immigrant population may seem more frightening or threatening, regardless of the actual size (Pottie-Sherman and Wilkes 2018).

While the overestimators, and to a lesser extent the underestimators, have received a great deal of attention, there exists another, largely overlooked form of ignorance: those who do not provide an estimate. Substantively such individuals are interesting because they, like over- and underestimators, lack factual knowledge on the question of interest. Yet, this form of ignorance is distinct, since its magnitude and direction (larger or smaller than the correct answer) cannot be known due to a lack of information. Nevertheless, when ignorance is the variable of focus, "don't know" responses represent a potentially meaningful category that should not be neglected, despite the difficulties including it in statistical models.

The current study sets out to understand those who choose "don't know" when prompted to estimate the immigrant population size (henceforth DK respondents). The analysis develops in four parts. First, it considers the question: What is the extent of DK responses across countries? Through combining data from four international surveys, the current study displays "don't know" patterns across Europe and North America. Second, what factors characterize DK respondents? Several independent variables, gathered from the 2014 ESS are hypothesized to influence the likelihood of DK responses and are used to predict its variation. The goal is to generate a basic profile of those who answer "don't know." Third, do DK responses have any consequences for anti-immigrant policy positions? Respondent type ("don't know," overestimator, and correct/underestimator) will serve as the primary independent variable in a model predicting in an index of restrictionist immigration policy preferences. Finally, what is the best strategy for dealing with DK responses in population innumeracy research? This final analysis re-estimates the models from question 3, addressing "don't knows" with both listwise deletion and multiple imputation to determine how different the findings would look with these commonly used strategies.

Part I: The Extent and Variability of DK Responses

It is first necessary to establish how often respondents neglect to provide an answer to immigrant population size questions. Among the published innumeracy studies cited above, many do not specify anything about missing cases. Among those that do, there is wide variation in the number responding with "don't know." On the high end, 41% of Spanish respondents did not provide an immigrant population size estimate in the 2002 ESS, as reported by Citrin and Sides (2008). By contrast, in this same multi-nation study that used similar interviewing protocols, only 6% of Swiss respondents did not estimate. Other European examples include about 28% missing cases in the 1996 German Allbus survey (Semyonov et al. 2004) and only 4.1% in the 2011 Finnish National Election Survey (Herda 2015).

Immigrant population innumeracy is studied less frequently in the US, so there exists little published information about the specific DK responses examined here. More often research with American samples examines racial population size perceptions. In Lameris et al. (2018a) analysis of the 2013 American Social Fabric Study, about 6% of respondents failed to estimate the white population size. Similarly, Wong (2007) identifies a maximum of 5% missing cases among all of the questions regarding various racial groups in the GSS. Finally, in a study considering the perceived size of the LGBQ population, nearly 18% did not provide an answer (Martinez et al. 2008).

Clearly DK responses occur with innumeracy questions and sometimes reach levels that raise concerns about measurement validity. However, since the aforementioned estimates come from a patchwork of studies with different approaches, it would be useful to examine the extent of DK responses in a standardized way. Since researchers have been gathering relevant data across Europe and North America for over a decade, we can now thoroughly document these patterns for a large portion of Western countries.

The current study combines results from similar interviewer-administered immigrant population size questions across four multi-nation surveys: the 2002 and 2014 ESS (Jowell 2003; European 2014), as well as the 2009 and 2013 TATS (Kennedy et al. 2009; Stelzenmueller et al. 2013). The two former ask: "Out of every 100 people living in [country] how many were born outside [country]." The TATS question wording differs: "In your opinion, what percentage of the total [country] population are immigrants?" ESS and TATS respondents were prompted to write in an estimate from 0 to 100. This approach permits the documentation of DK response patterns across 28 countries. Most are in Europe, but estimates are also included for the US, Canada, Turkey, and Israel. Several countries were included more than once across the four surveys. In such cases, the bar chart in Fig. 7.1 presents the mean level of DK responses across surveys.

In the full sample 17.0% of subjects responded with "don't know." The standard deviation of 11.5 percentage points, suggests substantial variation that is apparent in Fig. 7.1. Within country item DK response percentages range from only 4.5% in Norway to a maximum of 50.5% in Romania.

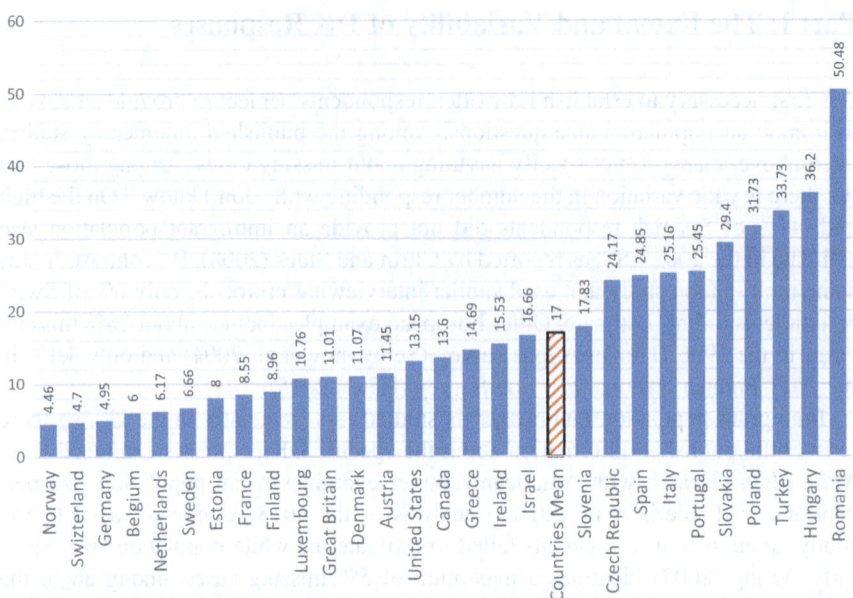

Fig. 7.1 Bar chart of immigrant population DK response rates across countries (Sources: ESS 2002, ESS 2014, TATS 2009; TATS 2013)

There is clear regional difference with those in Northern and Central Europe being the most likely to provide an estimate. The German, Norwegian, and Swiss percentages are all under 5%. Belgium, the Netherlands, and Sweden follow close behind with rates below 7%. Eastern and Southern European subjects are the most likely to provide no estimate. In Italy, Spain and Portugal, DK response rates hover around 25%. In the Eastern nations of Slovakia, Poland, Hungary, Romania, and Turkey, 29% or more failed to provide a size estimate. Outside of continental Europe, the US and Canada exhibit DK response rates above 13%, which places them below the average for the sample.

Overall, the regional patterns could indicate cultural, historical, or demographic reasons for greater or lesser DK response rates. One classic explanation comes from Sicinski (1970) who argued that cultures differ in their willingness to admit a lack of knowledge about a subject, and thus the willingness to say "don't know" on a survey, notably finding Norwegians least likely to select "don't know." Thus, the propensity to provide a size estimate is arguably not a random process. Rather, "don't know" seems to vary in patterned ways. The following section considers this possibility in detail with several independent variables hypothesized to influence the likelihood of not responding.

Part II: Characterizing DK Respondents

Missing data is not necessarily a problem. If the mechanism causing it is unrelated to any of the variables in the data, DK responses would be missing completely at random (MCAR). One could simply drop the cases and the sample will remain representative, albeit with weakened statistical power due to a smaller number of observations. However, survey researchers have known for decades that, when it comes to questions of factual knowledge, the selection of "don't know" is not random, but systematically related to respondent characteristics (Ferber 1966; Krosnick et al. 2002). For example, in their analysis of three US presidential election surveys from the 1960s, Francis and Busch (1975) found that female, lower income, less educated, and politically uninvolved respondents were all significantly more likely to respond with "don't know."

Extant research suggests that DK response patterns for population size questions are similarly non-random. Herda (2013b) included a "don't know" category in a multinomial logistic regression model focused on overestimation in his analysis of 2002 ESS data. Likewise, Nadeau and Niemi (1995) considered DK respondents in their analysis of the Francophone population in Canada and the Hispanic population in the US using surveys from the early 1990s. Both found several independent variables that predicted DK responses, indicating non-random variation. The current study considers several independent variables hypothesized to predict "don't knows."

Each measure described below comes from the 2014/2015 iteration of the ESS. These data were gathered through face-to-face interviews selected via probability sampling in each of the included countries. The current study focuses on the 14 countries[1] that participated in the relevant survey modules and had missing data[2] on the population innumeracy question. The wording is the same as described earlier. Variable distributions for the full sample and across countries are presented in Table 7.1. The vast majority, 92.4%, provided an estimate, leaving only 7.6% as DK respondents. Among estimators, the mean perceived immigrant population size is 19.8%. Across countries, DK response rates range from 1.0% in Ireland to 31.2% in Poland. The following paragraphs outline several theories used to hypothesize links between DK responses and various independent variables.

---

[1]The countries included in this and all subsequent portions of the analysis are Austria, Switzerland, the Czech Republic, Germany, Denmark, Estonia, Finland, France, Ireland, the Netherlands, Norway, Poland, Sweden, and Slovenia. Belgium was excluded because there were no missing observations on the innumeracy variable.

[2]In the ESS data innumeracy question, missing observations are classified as either "don't know" (n = 2047), "refusal" (n = 12), or "no answer" (n = 15). The current analysis includes only the "don't know" respondents and drops the rest. The other categories cannot be categorized as ignorance as these individuals could have responded correctly if they provided an answer. Models that include the refusals and no answer (not shown) are nearly identical to those presented.

Table 7.1 Proportions of DK Respondents and Estimators (Over- and Correct/Underestimators) in the 2014 ESS Sample

	DK respondents	Estimators		
	Don't know	Under/Correct estimation	Over-estimation	N
Full sample	7.6%	51.1%	41.3%	26,425
Countries				
Austria	8.9%	44.1%	46.9%	1795
Switzerland	4.5%	59.9%	35.6%	1532
Czech Republic	14.8%	53.3%	31.9%	2148
Germany	3.4%	39.9%	56.7%	3041
Denmark	3.9%	69.8%	26.2%	1498
Estonia	8.0%	41.9%	50.1%	2051
Finland	7.3%	72.2%	20.5%	2086
France	6.6%	34.2%	59.2%	1912
Ireland	1.0%	63.8%	35.2%	2390
Netherlands	3.4%	38.9%	57.7%	1918
Norway	2.3%	62.6%	35.2%	1435
Poland	31.2%	41.5%	27.3%	1608
Sweden	3.2%	61.3%	35.5%	1791
Slovenia	13.9%	36.0%	50.1%	1220

Variables

Cognitive Availability When confronted with questions of fact, people often look to examples in their memory to use as evidence in formulating a quick answer. This strategy, known as the cognitive availability heuristic, is a mental shortcut that allows one to come to an answer through minimal effort (Tversky and Kahneman 1973, 1974; Nadeau and Niemi 1995). Respondents answering questions about immigrant population size may employ this strategy, with their cognitive availability being populated by the number of immigrants that they observe and remember as they navigate their social world. Contact with immigrants on the street, in social networks, at work, or perhaps in the media are all relevant bits of evidence that one can use to generate an estimate. The more examples one has in their memory, the larger their estimate will likely be. Using data from the 2002 ESS, Herda (2010) finds that contact with neighbors (but not with friends) was significantly associated with larger population size estimates. Further, greater exposure to the visual medium of television, particularly news broadcasts, also increased size estimates. It is likely that these individuals view more representations of immigrants and use these as evidence in a manner similar to interpersonal contact.

The underlying assumption is that those with more exposure to immigrants will have more examples in their memory, leading to larger estimates. Logically then, fewer contacts will produce lower estimates. However, it is also possible that if fewer contacts result in weaker cognitive availability, they will make respondents less confident in formulating an estimate (they have less evidence from which to draw),

Table 7.2 Sample means (with standard deviations) and percentages

	Mean/Percentage	Std. Deviation
Cognitive availability		
Immigrant	10.8%	
Immigrant parents	0.3	0.7
Intergroup contact	4.6	2.2
Neighborhood diversity	1.9	0.7
Friendship diversity	1.6	0.8
Television hours	4.0	2.2
Negative affect		
Perceived threat	6.4	1.7
Social distance	2.7	2.9
Bio Racism (Intelligence)	15.7%	
Bio Racism (Work ethic)	39.3%	
Survey satisficing		
Missing total	2.7	6.3
Interview length	58.8	21.8
Demographics		
Age	47.9	19.5
Female	52.1%	
Education	13.1	3.8
Suburban	13.2%	
Small city	31.3%	
Village	28.7%	
Rural	8.6%	
Conservatism	5.1	2.4
Income	5.4	3.7
Unemployment	5.8%	
Voted	68.8%	
Political interest	2.5	1.0
Religiosity	4.3	3.2
Life satisfaction	7.3	2.2

producing a DK response. Herda's (2013b) analysis found that measures of interpersonal contact (friends, neighbors, and co-workers) more effectively differentiate overestimators from "don't knows" than they do overestimators from underestimators. Thus, the current study expects to find higher DK response rates among those with the lowest levels of cognitive availability—measured through intergroup contact and media exposure.

This analysis considers five intergroup contact measures (Table 7.2 displays the means, proportions, and standard deviations for these and all other independent variables). The first captures general contact with individuals of a different ethnic or racial background than the respondent when they are "out and about." The variable ranges from 1, indicating "never," to 7, indicating "every day." The next two measures both consist of three categories capturing one's level of exposure to racial or ethnic others inside their neighborhood and among friends. The variables are coded such that 0 indicates "none" and 2 indicates "many." Next, the analysis uses parents' birthplace as a proxy for familial contact. It is assumed that having foreigners in one's family will be associated with greater contacts overall with foreigners. The variable is measured on a 3-point scale ranging from 0, indicating no foreign-born parents, to 2 indicating that both parents are foreign born. Finally, if the respondent is him or herself an immigrant, it is assumed that he or she will have more contact with other immigrants, making them more likely to provide a response. The variable is dichotomous with immigrants coded as 1, and 0 otherwise.

In the absence of interpersonal contact, respondents may also draw heuristically from what they observe in the mass media. Images of immigrants on television or in film may provide evidence to formulate a population size estimate. In previous research, television exposure predicts larger immigrant population size estimates (Herda 2010), and significantly differentiates overestimators and DK respondents (Herda 2013b). The current study considers this association with a variable measuring television viewing time. Categories range from 0, indicating no time, and 7, indicating more than 3 h/day.

Affect Heuristics A relatively consistent correlate of immigrant population overestimates is negative affect toward the group in question (Hjerm 2007; Sides and Citrin 2007; Semyonov et al. 2008; Herda 2010). Those who find immigrants more threatening or have a greater dislike of foreigners, tend to think that there are more of them. Herda (2013b) argues that this association is explained by another heuristic device: the affect heuristic (Finucane et al. 2000). According to Zajonc (1980, 1984), individuals experience an emotional response to various representations (immigrants in this case) before answering any questions of fact. Thus, respondents with particularly negative attitudes toward foreigners will react emotionally to a question about their population size. This logic, combined with theories about motivated reasoning (Kunda 1990; Hart and Nisbet 2011) predict that xenophobic and threatened individuals will provide larger estimates because a reality with an overly large immigrant population confirms and justifies their threatened views.

It is possible that the same emotional response thought to prompt inflated estimates could also motivate individuals to avoid the question completely, by responding with "don't know." Evidencing this possibility, Herda (2013b) found that these two groups displayed equal levels of threat. But, both expressed threat levels that were significantly lower than underestimators.

The current study considers four affect heuristic variables. The first, perceptions of threat felt from immigrants, combines responses from four questions measuring immigrants' impact on various aspects of society—(1) job creation, (2) taxes and services, (3) crime, and (4) religious beliefs and practices. Items range from 0 to 10 with higher scores representing more threatened feelings. The scale has a Cronbach's alpha value of 0.7 and is combined into a mean index of threat. The second variable focuses on xenophobia by combining two questions measuring comfort if an immigrant: (1) became your boss; or (2) married a close family member. Both items are scaled from 0 to 10 with high values indicating greater discomfort. The items have a Cronbach's alpha of 0.8 and are combined into a mean index of xenophobia. The final two variables address biologically racist views, but since their alpha value was relatively low (0.5), they are included separately in the analysis. The first measures agreement with the statement "some race or ethnic groups are born less intelligent." The second measures agreement with the statement: "some race or ethnic groups are born harder working." Both have dichotomous response options with a score of 1 indicating agreement and 0 otherwise.

Survey Satisficing The survey satisficing theory holds that providing accurate survey responses requires cognitive effort, which many subjects are not willing to expend (Krosnick 1991; Krosnick et al. 2002). Offering a "don't know" response option provides a quick and easy answer for those who lack the ability or motivation to exert the mental effort necessary to express an opinion. Estimating the immigrant population size requires that respondents tap into their memory (cognitive availability heuristics) or emotions (affect heuristics). These cognitively taxing tasks encourage respondents to simply select "don't know" so they can move on with the survey, while still appearing that they are responding appropriately to the questionnaire. These satisficing tendencies may be revealed in a subject's overall pattern of nonresponse throughout the survey or the speed with which they complete the survey. More omitted questions and slower completion time (suggesting greater cognitive effort expended) indicate a greater propensity to satisfice and would suggest that DK respondents' ignorance is independent of attitudes toward immigrants or immigration.

These satisficing measures are operationalized through two variables. This first is the total time in minutes needed for the respondent to complete the survey. Values on this variable range from 4 to 696 min.[3] The second variable is a count of survey questions refused or answered "don't know" by the subject. Only questions asked of every research subject were included in the count. Follow-up questions within skip patterns are not included. This variable ranges from 0 to 118 questions.

Demographics The analysis includes several demographic controls found to increase the likelihood of DK responses in the literature, but some may be particularly relevant for predicting population innumeracy. Logically, education level should be associated with greater knowledge, which will likely lead one to have more confidence in providing an estimate. This association has been known in the item nonresponse literature for decades. For example, Francis and Busch (1975) found a consistent, negative association between education and the likelihood of nonresponse. In the current study, education is measured in years.

A similar logic can be applied to political knowledge and participation (Nadeau and Niemi 1995). Respondents who are more interested in politics or who have voted in the past election are assumed to feel more confident in providing a size

---

[3]This wide range with a mean of 58.8 suggests potential outliers. However, models that remove the extremely long interview lengths (100 min or more) yield coefficients that are similar to those presented suggesting that the outlying cases do not overly influence the results. The same is true for models that omit outlying cases on the total number of missing survey questions variable (50 missed questions or more).

estimate and, thus, will be more likely to do so. Those less involved and interested may be more reticent to specify a number, opting for "don't know." Political interest is operationalized with a single item measuring the respondent's interest in politics. Scores range from 1, indicating "not interested at all" to 4, indicating "very interested." Political involvement is measured with a question asking if the respondent voted in the previous national election. Responses of "yes" are coded as 1, and 0 otherwise.

Additional demographic factors include age, which is measured in years. Gender is coded such that female is equal to 1 and male equal to zero. Unemployment is dichotomous with those without work and not actively seeking work coded as 1. Residence type is measured with five categories with the first acting as the reference: (1) big city; (2) suburbs; (3) small city; (4) village; and (5) rural. Finally, all analyses include measures of political conservatism, religiosity, and life satisfaction. All three range from 0 to 10 with higher values indicating higher levels of the respective variable.

In order to understand DK respondents, this analysis considers two approaches. The first uses logistic regression to distinguish estimators from DK respondents. Second, the analysis considers the nuances between DK respondents and two categories of estimators—correct/underestimation and overestimation—using multinomial logistic regression. Table 7.4 presents the results for each of these models. All coefficients are estimated using sample weights to ensure representativeness both within and across countries. In addition, missing values for all variables, save for the population innumeracy categories, are replaced via multiple imputation.

Results: Characterizing DK Respondents Relative to Estimators

For the logistic regression models, a positive coefficient indicates greater predicted log odds of being an DK respondent versus an estimator. Several significant regression effects emerge. Those who do not guess the immigrant population size are more likely to be female. Specifically, women are 30.5% ($e^{.266}$) more likely to respond with "don't know" than men, net of controls. Likewise, DK respondents tend to be older, displaying an 8.3% greater odds of "don't know" for each 10 year increase in age. They also tend to be less educated and less interested in politics on average. Each additional year of education decreases the odds of DK response by 6% and each unit increase in political interest decreases the odds by 24%. Both these associations suggest that DK respondents are less knowledgeable than estimators, which could explain their reticence to offer an estimate. Further, DK respondents tend to earn less income, indicate greater levels of religiosity, and are less likely to reside in suburbs or rural areas, relative to cities, but more likely to reside in villages. Overall, these significant patterns suggest that DK responses on the population size question are not simply a random phenomenon but vary in patterned ways.

All of these significant effects exist net of the distinct survey satisficing patterns displayed by DK respondents. Following the predictions of satisficing theory, those who fail to estimate the immigrant population size, also fail to answer more survey questions overall. For each additional omitted question, respondents' likelihood of not answering the immigrant population size question increases by 9.3%. This finding ostensibly supports the argument that DK responses on this question reflect an overall propensity for item nonresponse. DK respondents take longer to complete the survey on average, which could reflect greater cognitive effort on their part, which ultimately fails to produce an estimate. For each additional 10 min spent competing the survey, respondents become 4% more likely to skip the immigrant population size question.

DK respondents also have fewer diverse contacts than those who provide an estimate. Greater reported frequencies of overall intergroup contact and neighborhood diversity both make one less likely to be a DK respondent. Each unit increase in these variables increases the odds of offering an estimate by 18.2 and 14.7% respectively. The relative lack of intergroup exposure suggests that they have less cognitively available evidence about immigrants from which they can draw when formulating an answer. This could explain their reticence to estimate.

DK respondents exhibit equivalent levels of perceived threat and xenophobia relative to estimators. The only significant association that emerges is for the biological racism measure regarding work ethic. Those who endorse this idea are 12.7% less likely to answer "don't know" relative to those who disagree with the statement.

Analysis: Characterizing DK Respondents Relative to Over- and Underestimators

The right side of Table 7.3 contains an additional multinomial logistic regression model that distinguishes DK respondents from correct/underestimators and overestimators. This single model yields two sets of coefficients, one for each comparison with DK respondents. A correct/underestimator is defined as someone who estimates either correctly or perceives the immigrant population to be smaller than the reality.[4] For the purposes of this analysis, this category includes all underestimates, exactly correct responses, and estimates up to 5 percentage points larger than the correct answer. Therefore, overestimators are those whose estimates are more than 5 percentage points larger than the correct answer. Table 7.1 indicates that among the estimators, a slight majority (51.1%) are correct/underestimators. In

---

[4]For simplicity, the current author decided to combine underestimators and correct estimators into a single category. Doing so focuses the analysis on the most important theoretical distinction: those with inflated size perceptions versus those without. An alternative strategy would be to include correct- and underestimators separately. However, the ±5% zone of correctness (see Herda 2013b) makes underestimation impossible in the Czech Republic, Finland, and Poland where the actual immigrant population is 5% or less. Nevertheless, models that include separate correct and underestimation categories (not shown) are largely similar to those presented.

Table 7.3 Logistic regression model predicting DK responses and multinomial logistic regression model distinguishing DK response from over- and correct/underestimators (n = 26,425)

	Logistic regression model		Multinomial logistic regression model			
			Overestimators v. DK respondents		Correct/ Underestimators v. DK respondents	
	B	SE	B	SE	B	SE
Cognitive availability factors						
Immigrant	−0.281*	0.144	0.210	0.148	0.358*	0.149
Immigrant parents	0.056	0.064	0.097	0.066	−0.237***	0.067
Intergroup contact	−0.167***	0.016	0.173***	0.017	0.161***	0.016
Neighborhood diversity	−0.137**	0.047	0.239***	0.048	0.030	0.048
Friendship diversity	−0.063	0.050	0.127*	0.052	−0.001	0.052
Television time	0.014	0.014	0.011	0.015	−0.037*	0.015
Survey satisficing						
Missing total	0.089***	0.004	−0.093***	0.004	−0.086***	0.004
Interview length	0.004**	0.001	−0.002	0.001	−0.005***	0.001
Negative affect						
Perceived threat	0.005	0.020	0.035	0.021	−0.043*	0.020
Social distance	0.003	0.011	0.011	0.011	−0.016	0.011
Bio. Racism (Intelligence)	−0.128	0.084	0.150	0.086	0.103	0.087
Bio. Racism (Work Ethic)	−0.120*	0.061	0.134*	0.063	0.112	0.062
Demographics						
Age	0.008***	0.002	−0.011***	0.002	−0.005**	0.002
Female	0.266***	0.056	0.017	0.058	−0.507***	0.057
Years of education	−0.057***	0.009	0.035***	0.009	0.076***	0.009
Conservatism	0.012	0.015	−0.017	0.015	−0.007	0.015
Suburb	−0.374***	0.114	0.341**	0.117	0.411***	116
Small city	0.093	0.081	−0.143	0.084	−0.041	0.084
Village	0.174*	0.084	−0.167	0.086	−0.171*	0.086
Rural	−0.462***	0.125	0.232	0.130	0.624***	0.127
Income	−0.040**	0.014	0.030*	0.014	0.048***	0.014
Unemployment	0.044	0.115	−0.021	0.118	−0.076	0.120
Religiosity	0.041***	0.009	−0.031**	0.010	−0.052***	0.010
Life satisfaction	−0.009	0.013	−0.011	0.014	0.030*	0.014
Voted	−0.107	0.065	0.062	0.068	0.154*	0.068
Political interest	−0.215***	0.035	0.186***	0.036	0.240***	0.036
Constant	−1.417***	0.294	0.350	0.305	1.053***	0.303
Fit statistics						
Pseudo R-squared	0.174		0.089			
AIC	12094.310		43761.367			
BIC	11873.003		44203.253			

Note: *p < 0.05, **p < 0.01, ***p < 0.001

the multinomial models a positive coefficient indicates a greater likelihood of falling into the comparison category (over- or correct/underestimators) versus DK respondents. Conversely a negative coefficient indicates a greater likelihood of "don't know."

Many of the associations from the previous model are consistent across comparisons. For instance, DK respondents differ similarly and significantly from both over- and correct/underestimators in age, education, political interest, and in the overall number of missed survey questions. However, several coefficients distinguish the "don't knows" from the other categories. For example, women are more likely to be DK respondents compared to correct/underestimators, but there is no gender association distinguishing overestimators and DK respondents.

DK respondents express significantly greater perceived threat than correct/underestimators. Specifically, for each unit increase in threat, the odds of answering "don't know" increases by 4.4. Conversely, perceived threat fails to distinguish DK respondents and overestimators. In addition, DK respondents are less likely to endorse biological racism arguments compared to both over- and correct/underestimators.

While the difference in frequency of contact is consistent, nonrespondents tend to have less diverse neighborhood contact compared to overestimators only. They also are less likely to be immigrants and spend more time watching television, compared to correct/underestimators only. However, DK respondents are more likely to have immigrant parents compared to correct/underestimators.

Overall, these analyses indicate that DK respondents can be differentiated from estimators on several characteristics. The "don't know" patterns are not random, or attributable simply to survey completion tendencies (i.e., survey satisficing). Rather, DK respondents appear to be a distinct category of ignorance displayed by those with low levels of education, political interest, and intergroup contact. But, are there any consequences associated with this ignorance? The following section considers whether DK responses predict support for an index of hypothetical immigration policy positions.

Part III: Consequences for DK Responses?

The general fear about overestimation among researchers is that such warped perceptions of reality will inform policy positions. Researchers often find this to be the case. An analysis of data from the 2000 GSS found that overestimation of African American and Latino population sizes in the US was associated with greater opposition to affirmative action and greater support for immigration restrictions respectively (Alba et al. 2005). Across Europe, exaggerated perceptions of immigrant population size are similarly linked to support for immigration restrictions and the curtailment of immigrants' rights (Semyonov et al. 2004; Sides and Citrin 2007). While this has been the case with ignorance in the form of overestimation, what about ignorance in the form of "don't know"? The following analysis tests whether DK responses are also associated with more restrictionist attitudes toward immigrants relative to over- and correct/underestimation. It will also examine whether the correlates of nonresponse from Table 7.3 can explain any significant differences between these three categories of interest.

The link between overestimation and anti-immigrant policy preferences is often explained as a function of affect heuristics, particularly threat perceptions. Threat typically explains much, if not all of the difference between over- and correct/ underestimators' support of anti-immigrant policy (Semyonov et al. 2004; Blumer 1958; Bobo 1983). However, since overestimators and DK respondents are similarly threatened by immigration, it may not explain any differences between the categories.

Alternatively, the comparatively low levels of cognitive availability among DK respondents relative to over- and correct/underestimators may distinguish between these groups. Intergroup contact is related to the likelihood of estimating as well as and sympathy for and understanding of out-groups. The intergroup contact theory holds that direct interpersonal exposure to individuals from different backgrounds can be effective for reducing intergroup prejudice (Allport 1954; Pettigrew 1998; Pettigrew and Tropp 2006); the same types of prejudice that predict support for anti-immigrant policies. Thus, differences between DK respondents and the other categories may be mediated by a lack of prejudice-reducing contact among those reporting "don't know."

DK respondents are more likely to satisfice with the "don't know" option compared to estimators. Thus, any differences between these categories may simply result from the way DK respondents' approach the survey. The following analysis will test this possibility. The primary goal is to determine whether the independent variables from Part II can mediate the relationship between the innumeracy categories and an index of restrictionist immigration policy preferences.

Outcome Variable: Restrictionist Immigration Policy Preferences

Three ESS questions measure the respondents' willingness to allow immigrants into their country if they are: (1) of the same race or ethnicity as the majority; (2) of a different race or ethnicity; or (3) Muslims. All three items have 4-point scales ranging from "allow many to come and live" to "allow none." The three variables are highly correlated and load onto a single principal components factor with an eigenvalue above 1. The variables are combined into a mean index with a Cronbach's alpha value of 0.9, indicating high internal consistency.

The final variable ranges from 1 to 4 with the higher values meaning a greater desire to restrict immigration. The sample mean is equal to 2.3 with a standard deviation of 0.8. Within country means vary between 1.7 in Sweden where restrictionist leanings are least common and 3.0 in the Czech Republic where they are most common.

The index of restrictionist immigration attitudes is used as an outcome in the regression analyses below. These least squares models, presented in Table 7.4, develop in 5 steps. The first distinguishes between overestimators, correct/underestimators, and DK respondents, net of demographic factors, with overestimators acting as the reference category. The subsequent models add groups of independent variables separately and then together in the final model. The goal is to examine and explain the effect of DK responses with the independent variables described earlier.

Results: Examining the Consequences of DK Response

The first model of Table 7.4 demonstrates that restrictionism differs significantly between the estimators and DK respondents. Correct/underestimators display significantly lower restrictionist attitudes, roughly 0.03 points lower compared to overestimators (the reference category), net of demographic controls. The effect for DK respondents, however, is in the opposite direction and is statistically significant, suggesting that those not providing an estimate actually exhibit more restrictionist attitudes that those overestimating. Specifically, DK respondents display restrictionist attitudes scores that are 0.13 points higher on average relative to overestimators, net of demographic factors.

The second model attempts to explain the significant innumeracy category effects with the cognitive availability controls. Several of these have significant associations with the outcome. As would be expected in the intergroup contact theory, increased exposure to immigrants and ethnic diversity (immigrant parents, overall intergroup contact, and diverse friendships) reduces support for restrictionism. Conversely, more time spent watching television increases restrictionist attitudes. Including cognitive factors reduces the difference between the DK respondents and overestimators by 53.8%. However, the DK respondent association remains significant. The same cognitive factors do not explain any of the difference between over- and correct/underestimators.

Model 3 introduces the survey satisficing measures. Only the total number of omitted survey questions is associated with the outcome, with more predicting increased support for restrictionist immigration policy. The satisficing variables explain some of the DK response association with the outcome, reducing the effect

Table 7.4 Regression model predicting immigrant restrictionist attitudes (n = 26,425)

	Model 1		Model 2		Model 3		Model 4		Model 5	
	B	SE	B	SE	B	SE	B	SE	B	SE
Innumeracy category (v. over)										
Correct/Underestimators	−0.030**	0.010	−0.045***	0.009	−0.032***	0.010	0.015	0.008	0.006	0.008
DK respondents	0.130***	0.019	0.060***	0.019	0.071***	0.020	0.122***	0.016	0.053***	0.016
Cognitive availability factors										
Immigrant			−0.045*	0.022					0.025	0.019
Immigrant parents			−0.009	0.010					0.009	0.009
Intergroup contact			−0.049***	0.003					−0.031***	0.002
Neighborhood diversity			0.015*	0.008					−0.005	0.006
Friendship diversity			−0.160***	0.007					−0.059***	0.006
Television time			0.036***	0.002					0.019***	0.002
Survey satisficing										
Missing total					0.010***	0.001			0.006***	0.001
Interview length					−0.000	0.000			−0.001	0.000
Negative affect										
Perceived threat							−0.101***	0.005	0.164***	0.003
Social distance							0.169***	0.003	0.070***	0.002
Biological racism (Intelligence)							0.077***	0.002	0.156***	0.012
Biological racism (Work ethic)							0.170***	0.012	0.074***	0.009
Demographics										
Age	0.006***	0.000	0.002***	0.000	0.006***	0.000	0.003***	0.000	0.001***	0.000
Female	−0.045***	0.009	−0.052***	0.009	−0.043***	0.009	−0.010	0.008	−0.014	0.008
Years of education	−0.028***	0.001	−0.021***	0.001	−0.027***	0.001	−0.013***	0.001	−0.010***	0.001
Suburb	−0.074***	0.016	−0.062***	0.016	−0.069***	0.016	−0.062***	0.013	−0.053***	0.013
Small City	0.009	0.013	−0.030*	0.013	0.011	0.013	−0.022*	0.011	−0.037***	0.011
Village	0.023	0.014	−0.037**	0.014	0.024	0.014	−0.025*	0.011	−0.053***	0.012

Rural	0.058**	0.019	−0.005	0.019	0.063***	0.019	0.021	0.016	−0.011	0.016
Conservatism	0.066***	0.002	0.058***	0.002	0.066***	0.002	0.034***	0.002	0.032***	0.002
Income	−0.020***	0.002	−0.016***	0.002	−0.020***	0.002	−0.013***	0.002	−0.010***	0.002
Unemployment	−0.039	0.021	−0.051*	0.020	−0.036	0.021	−0.028	0.017	−0.038*	0.017
Religiosity	−0.011***	0.002	−0.007***	0.002	−0.011***	0.002	−0.001	0.001	−0.001	0.001
Life satisfaction	−0.051***	0.003	−0.043***	0.002	−0.050***	0.002	−0.019***	0.002	−0.016***	0.002
Voted	−0.025*	0.011	−0.054***	0.011	−0.016	0.011	−0.018	0.009	−0.010	0.010
Political interest	−0.188***	0.006	−0.155***	0.006	−0.178***	0.006	0.003***	0.000	−0.084***	0.005
Constant	3.113***	0.034	3.453	0.040	3.063***	0.036	1.341***	0.035	1.595***	0.042
R-Squared	0.193		0.251		0.197		0.446		0.461	

*p < .05; **p < .01; ***p < .001

by 45.4%. However, the association remains significant and these factors do not explain as much as the cognitive availability controls from the previous model. Also like the previous model, these satisficing measures explain none of the difference between over- and correct/underestimators.

The fourth model adds the affect heuristic factors, which yield significant and positive associations. Notably, the affective factors reduce the difference between over- and correct/underestimators to statistical insignificance. Conversely, the difference in restrictionism between overestimators and DK respondents remains stable net of negative affect. The coefficient for "don't know" is reduced by only 6.2%, which is the smallest amount relative to the previous models.

The final model combines all of the explanatory variables included in the study. The difference in restrictionist views between over- and correct/underestimators remains nonsignificant, mostly due to the mediating effect of negative affect. Conversely, the coefficient for DK response, although greatly reduced from the initial model (59.2% decrease), remains statistically significant. Even net of all the controls considered, those who respond with "don't know" expressed significantly greater restrictionism compared to those who overestimated. This finding highlights the importance of treating "don't know" as a substantive response category in innumeracy studies.

Part IV: What Happens When Researchers Delete or Replace DK Respondents?

DK responses on the immigrant population size question clearly arise from a non-random and consequential process. Net of controls, those answering "don't know" express the highest levels of immigrant restrictionism. This finding suggests that much of the existing research, which focuses on a continuous measure of population innumeracy (computed as the difference between the respondent's estimate of immigrant population size and its actual size) without a focus on DK respondents, has not told the entire story. Thus, this final section will reexamine the current data using the most common strategies in the innumeracy literature. The goal is to see whether treating DK responses as a nuisance produces different results and conclusions.

Among 23 existing studies that analyze innumeracy measures, about one-third address DK responses through listwise deletion. This strategy simply drops observations with any missing data from the analysis. This common and simple approach requires the strong assumption that DK respondents are missing completely at random (MCAR) (Allison 2002). The current study demonstrates that this assumption does not hold and may also fail in other existing innumeracy studies.

About one-fifth of existing innumeracy research multiply impute missing values for "don't know" responses. This approach involves the substitution of the missing observations based on patterns of values for the non-missing variables. This

Table 7.5 Continuous population innumeracy slopes from regression models predicting restrictionist attitudes using multiple imputation and listwise deletion

	Full imputed sample (n = 26,425)		Listwise deletion (n = 24,378)		Imputed DK respondents (n = 2047)	
Innumeracy	−0.0006*	0.0003	−0.0005*	0.0003	−0.0006	0.001
Constant	1.613***	0.041	1.585***	0.043	1.890***	0.159

*p < .05; ***p < .001

technique is conducted through an iterative process, creating several new datasets with complete data, which differ by design based on the inclusion of a random component.[5] The approach does not require the MCAR assumption, but rather only that the missingness not depend on the variable with missing cases itself (i.e. missingness on innumeracy does not depend on the magnitude of one's estimate), but it can be related to other independent variables. This assumption is known as missing at random (MAR) (Allison 2002).

Table 7.5 examines how the current results would look if these more conventional approaches were applied. The first model replaces the "don't knows" using multiple imputation via Stata's ice command. All of the independent variables listed above were included in the imputation equation. The analyses combine the results from 35 imputed datasets to generate slope coefficients and standard errors in models predicting restrictionist policy leanings. Also included in Table 7.5 are estimates from a listwise deletion model. The final column includes only the imputed DK respondents for comparison. All models in Table 7.5 control for full list of independent variables from Table 7.4, but they are omitted from presentation.

After constructing the imputed sample, the mean levels of innumeracy for all respondents combined is 19.9. For just the estimators the mean perceptions is 19.8 and for the replaced DK responders it is 21.0. These two means are statistically equivalent. However, there exists more than 1.7 times more variation around the respective means for the imputed estimates of DK respondents (sd = 30.0) compared to the actual estimates of the estimators (sd = 17.2). This reflects the stochastic component built into the multiple imputation procedure.

The point estimates are nearly identical in the imputed and listwise deletion models. The coefficient from the replaced DK respondent model, while not statistically significant, is also nearly the same as the other two comparisons. Notably though, all the effect sizes are quite small, amounting to 8 tenths of 1% of a standard deviation on the restrictionism scale for a 10-percentage point increase. Also interesting is that these associations are negative in direction, suggesting that the larger an individual's immigrant population size estimate, the lower their restrictionist attitude. This finding is counter to much of the existing literature, but must be interpreted cautiously given its small magnitude combined with the large sample

---

[5] It should be noted that some innumeracy studies find no substantial differences between models using listwise deletion and multiple imputation (see Sides and Citrin 2007; Citrin and Sides 2008).

sizes in the first two models. The negative association is actually the result of a suppression effect involving education. When years of education is removed from the model, the population innumeracy slopes are no longer significant, which mirrors the result from Table 7.4 suggesting that there is no difference in restrictionist attitudes between over- and correct/underestimators, net of affect controls. Regardless, the replacing or dropping item DK respondents obscures the unique consequences of answering "don't know" demonstrated in Table 7.4.

Discussion and Conclusion

At some point, every survey researcher will face the problem of missing observations. Failing to address it can have consequences for the accuracy of estimates and standard errors. However, sometimes these missing observations may be substantively meaningful. The current study set out to understand one such case when subjects are prompted to estimate the size of immigrant populations. With the existing research's nearly exclusive focus on overestimation, DK responses are usually ignored or treated as a nuisance. However, "don't know" appears to be consequential for actions and policy positions. When considering research questions about factual knowledge, whether about immigrant populations or other demographic facts, political realities, or historical events, DK responses should be treated as substantive and included in analyses. Failing to do so can produce biases in results and errors in inferences. The main findings of the current analysis are as follows.

Varying DK Response Levels

DK response on the immigrant population size question is high enough to be concerning, particularly in Eastern and Southern Europe, where well over one-quarter of respondents do not provide an answer. However, in other places, particularly Northern Europe, rates are typically less than 5%. Regardless, wherever researchers are considering respondents' factual knowledge, it is essential to also understand and report the level of missingness and consider whether not estimating represents a meaningful or consequential category.

Profile of the DK Respondent

What is clear from the current analysis is that the DK response patterns are not a random process. Rather, we can predict the likelihood of selecting "don't know" using several independent variables. The current study considered many, allowing for the development of a basic profile of DK respondents that can be used to differentiate them from over- and underestimators.

DK respondents are less educated and less interested in politics relative to both over- and correct/underestimators. This could correspond to lower knowledge levels and lower confidence in their ability to estimate the immigrant population size. DK respondents are older on average and more likely to be female. They also tend to identify themselves as more religious than both over- and underestimators.

DK respondents have particularly low levels of inter-group contact. They have fewer out-group neighbors and are less likely to encounter racial and ethnic others as they navigate their social worlds. These provide a much weaker cognitive availability compared to estimators. They are more likely to populate their cognitive availability with images from the television, as they watch significantly more than correct/underestimators.

While overestimation is often thought to associate with greater out-group prejudice and perceptions of threat from the group being estimated, DK respondents actually express similar levels of negative affect. Both groups were equivalent on measures of threat and xenophobia. But, DK respondents are more threatened by immigrants on average than correct/underestimators.

DK respondents also show evidence of satisficing as they complete the survey. They omit many more questions than their over- and correct/underestimating counterparts. They also take more time to complete the survey, which may reflect greater cognitive difficulties as they advance through the questions.

If one considers all of these characteristics simultaneously, it suggests that "don't know" is a substantive response that identifies an important group. Like over- and underestimators, they do not know the correct answer, but their ignorance is more difficult to classify as they provide no information. These patterns will hopefully further convince future researchers to pay attention to DK respondents. The next logical question though is whether or not this ignorance is consequential.

DK Respondents Express the Most Restrictionist Attitudes

The current study considered support for an index of hypothetical restrictionist policy positions as a potential consequence for ignorance in the form of "don't know." While much of the focus in the existing literature has been on the connection between overestimation and a desire to block immigrants or take away their rights, the current analysis revealed the DK respondents actually exhibit the most restrictionist leanings. When controlling for all of the independent variables in the model, over- and correct/underestimators exhibit statistically equivalent levels of restrictionist support, yet DK respondents are still significantly more likely to want to block various immigrants from entering their country.

This pattern is interesting, particularly given the tendency in the research to drop these cases or assign them an estimate through a multiple imputation process. The effect suggests that those most willing to exclude immigrants are those who know so little about them that they are not confident enough to provide an estimate. This assertion is supported by DK respondents relatively low levels of inter-group contact. According to the intergroup contact theory, exposure to out-groups are important for generating knowledge and understanding, a lack of which can produce support for anti-immigrant policy. The largest portion of the DK respondent association was mediated by the cognitive availability factors (i.e.: intergroup contact measures).

Overall, these patterns provide further evidence that future immigrant population size innumeracy studies should not neglect item DK respondents. Not only are "don't know" patterns predictable with various independent variables, but the category is the most strongly linked to policy preference consequences. Any efforts to reduce innumeracy to improve intergroup relations must pay special attention to DK respondents. Some researchers have specifically advocated the dissemination of correct demographic information to better inform the public and improve intergroup relations (Alba et al. 2005; Nadeau et al. 1993; Sides and Citrin 2007; Sigelman and Niemi 2001). However, such a strategy is unlikely to produce the same effects as inter-group contact, which is a major source of DK respondents' ignorance.

Common Missing Value Fixes Ignore the Important Category of DK Respondents

As a final exploration, the current study considered how the results would look after applying the usual approaches in population innumeracy analyses: a continuous immigrant population size variable in which the DK respondents are either dropped or imputed. Such approaches were effective in producing results that were consistent across strategies. However, they completely miss the distinct patterns exhibited by DK respondents. In fact, they produce a different set of conclusions in which larger estimates are actually associated with more welcoming attitudes toward immigrants (net of education).

While in the current data listwise deletion replicated the multiple imputation results well, it cannot be recommended as a technique for handling the DK respondents. The current study clearly demonstrates that the innumeracy variable is not MCAR, which listwise deletion assumes. Therefore, simply dropping "don't knows" presents a risk of introducing sample bias, even if it did not come to fruition here or in other research. Those doing so will be dropping respondents with the lowest levels of intergroup contact, education, and political interest.

The same assumptions are not necessary for multiple imputation approaches, which make them more appropriate for innumeracy analyses. However, the technique artificially turns DK respondents into estimators, which is problematic given that the current study found them to be a distinct category of ignorance. Future studies of immigrant population size innumeracy and respondent knowledge in general should include parallel or supplementary analyses that explore patterns among those who do not provide an estimate. Dismissing them off hand cannot be recommended.

Conclusion

Item nonresponse is all but guaranteed for most survey instruments. If questions pertain to factual knowledge, where it is expected that one will not know the correct answer, it may be even more likely that subject will respond with "don't know." The current study has found that this category is more than just a statistical nuisance. It should be considered as substantively meaningful and interesting. Future research should continue to explore such DK responses as a category worthy of understanding, rather than simply dropping or assigning them artificial estimates. Neglecting them will only hinder our ability to create a more knowledgeable and tolerant public.

References

Alba, R., Rumbaut, R. G., & Marotz, K. (2005). A distorted nation: Perceptions of racial/ethnic group sizes and attitudes toward immigrants and other minorities. *Social Forces, 84*(2), 901–919.

Allison, P. D. (2002). *Missing data: Quantitative applications in the social sciences*. Thousand Oaks, CA: Sage.

Allport, G. W. (1954 [1979]). The nature of prejudice. New York: Basic Books.

Blumer, H. (1958). Race prejudice as a sense of group position. *Pacific Sociological Review, 1*(1), 3–7.

Bobo, L. (1983). Whites' opposition to busing: Symbolic racism or realistic group conflict? *Journal of Personality and Social Psychology, 45*(6), 1196–1210.

Chiricos, T., McEntire, R., & Gertz, M. (2001). Perceived racial and ethnic composition of neighborhood and perceived risk of crime. *Social Problems, 48*(3), 322–340.

Citrin, J., & Sides, J. (2008). Immigration and the imagined community in Europe and the United States. *Political Studies, 56*(1), 33–56. http://onlinelibrary.wiley.com/doi/10.1111/j.1467-9248.2007.00716.x/abstract.

De Vreese, C. H., & Boomgaarden, H. (2006). News, political knowledge and participation: The differential effects of news media exposure on political knowledge and participation. *Acta Politica, 41*(4), 317–341.

European Social Survey Round 7 Data. (2014). *Data file edition 2.1. NSD – Norwegian center for research data, Norway – Data archive and distributor of ESS data for ESS ERIC*.

Ferber, R. (1966). Item nonresponse in a consumer survey. *Public Opinion Quarterly, 30*(3), 399–415.

Finucane, M. L., Alhakami, A., Slovic, P., & Johnson, S. M. (2000). The affect heuristic in judgments of risks and benefits. *Journal of Behavioral Decision Making, 13*(1), 1–17.

Fraile, M. (2013). do information-rich contexts reduce knowledge inequalities? The contextual determinants of political knowledge in Europe. *Acta Politica, 48*(2), 119–143.

Francis, J. D., & Busch, L. (1975). What we know about 'i don't knows'. *Public Opinion Quarterly, 39*(2), 207–218.

Gallagher, C. A. (2003). Miscounting race: Exploring whites' misperceptions of racial group size. *Sociological Perspectives, 46*(3), 381–396.

Goetzmann, A. (2017). elementary school children's political knowledge. *The American Behavioral Scientist, 61*(2), 238–253.

Hart, P. S., Nisbet, E. C. (2011) Boomerang Effects in Science Communication. *Communication Research 39*(6), 701–723

Henriks Vettehen, P. G. J., Hagemann, C. P. M., & van Snippenburg, L. B. (2004). Political knowledge and media use in the Netherlands. *European Sociological Review, 20*(5), 415–424.

Herda, D. (2010). 'How many immigrants?' Foreign born population innumeracy in Europe. *Public Opinion Quarterly, 74*, 674–695.

Herda, D. (2013a). Innocuous Ignorance?: Perceptions of the American Jewish Population Size. *Contemporary Jewry, 33*, 241–245.

Herda, D. (2013b). Too many immigrants? Examining alternative forms of immigrant population innumeracy. *Sociological Perspectives, 56*, 213–240.

Herda, D. (2015). Beyond innumeracy: Heuristic decision-making and qualitative misperceptions about immigrants in Finland. *Ethnic and Racial Studies, 38*(9), 1627–1645.

Herda, D. (2017). Correcting misperceptions: An in-class exercise for reducing population innumeracy using student response systems and a test of its effectiveness. *Teaching Sociology, 45*(2), 150–162.

Herda, D. (2018). Comparing ignorance: Misperceptions about immigrants in the United States and Western Europe. *Societies Without Borders: Human Rights and the Social Sciences, 12*(1).

Hjerm, M. (2007). Do numbers really count? Group threat theory revisited. *Journal of Ethnic and Migration Studies, 33*(8), 1253–1275. https://www.tandfonline.com/doi/abs/10.1080/13691830701614056.

Hooghe, M., & de Vroome, T. (2013). The perception of ethnic diversity and anti-immigrant sentiments: A multilevel analysis of local communities in Belgium. *Ethnic and Racial Studies, 38*(1), 38–56.

Ipsos MORI. (2015). Perceptions are not reality: What the world gets wrong. *Perils of perception.* Retrieved January 5, 2016, from https://www.ipsos.com/ipsos-mori/en-uk/perils-perception-2015.

Johann, D. (2012). Specific political knowledge and Citizens' participation: Evidence from Germany. *Acta Politica, 47*(1), 42–66.

Jowell, R., & The Central Co-ordinating Team. (2003). *European social survey 2002/2003: Technical report*. London: Centre for Comparative Social Surveys, City University.

Kennedy, C., Nyiri, Z., La Balme, N., Isernia, P., Everts, P., & Eichenberg, R. (2009). *Transatlantic trends survey*. Ann Arbor, MI: Inter-university Consortium for Political and Social Research. [distributor], 2011-07-01. https://doi.org/10.3886/ICPSR28462.v1.

Krosnick, J. A. (1991). Response strategies for coping with the cognitive demands of attitude measures in surveys. *Applied Cognitive Psychology, 5*, 213–236.

Krosnick, J. A., Hollbrook, A. L., Brent, M. K., Carson, R. T., Hanemann, W. M., Kopp, R. J., Mitchell, R. C., Presser, S., Rudd, P. A., Smith, V. K., Moody, W. R., Green, M. C., & Conaway, M. (2002). The impact of 'no opinion' response options on data quality: Non-attitude reduction or an invitation to satisfice? *Public Opinion Quarterly, 66*, 371–403.

Kunda, Z. (1990). The case for motivated reasoning. *Psychological Bulletin, 108*, 480–498.

Kunovich, R. M. (2017). Perceptions of racial group size in a minority-majority area. *Sociological Perspectives, 60*(3), 479–496. http://journals.sagepub.com/doi/abs/10.1177/0731121416675869.

Kunovich, R. M., & Kunovich, S. (2016). The gender gap in political knowledge in Poland. *Polish Sociological Review, 193*, 33–49.

Lameris, J., Hipp, J. R., & Tolsma, J. (2018a). Perceptions as the crucial link? The mediating role of neighborhood perceptions in the relationship between the neighborhood context and neighborhood cohesion. *Social Science Research, 72*, 53–68.

Lameris, J., Kraaykamp, G., Ruiter, S., & Tolsma, J. (2018b). Size is in the eye of the beholder: How differences between neighborhoods and individuals explain variation in estimations of the ethnic out-group size in the neighborhood. *International Journal of Intercultural Relations, 63*, 80–94.

Martinez, M.D., Wald, K.D., & Craig, S.C. (2008). Homophobic innumeracy? Estimating the size of the gay and lesbian population. *Public Opinion Quarterly, 72*(4), 753–767. https://doi.org/10.1093/poq/nfn049

Nadeau, R., & Niemi, R. (1995). Educated guesses: The process of answering factual knowledge questions in surveys. *Public Opinion Quarterly, 59*(3), 323–346.

Nadeau, R., Niemi, R. G., & Levine, J. (1993). Innumeracy about minority populations. *The Public Opinion Quarterly, 57*(3), 332–347. https://academic.oup.com/poq/article/57/3/332/1888468.

Pettigrew, T. F. (1998). Intergroup contact theory. *Annual Review of Psychology, 49*, 65–85. https://doi.org/10.1146/annurev.psych.49.1.65.

Pettigrew, T. F., & Tropp, L. R. (2006). A meta-analytic test of intergroup contact theory. *Journal of Personality and Social Psychology, 90*(5), 751–783. https://doi.org/10.1037/0022-3514.90.5.751.

Pottie-Sherman, Y., & Wilkes, R. (2018). Does size really matter? On the relationship between immigrant group size and anti-immigrant prejudice. *International Migration Review, 51*(1), 218–250.

Schlueter, E., & Scheepers, P. (2010). The relationship between outgroup size and anti-outgroup attitudes: A theoretical synthesis and empirical test of group threat and intergroup contact theory. *Social Science Research, 39*(2), 285–295.

Semyonov, M., Raijman, R., Tov, A. Y., & Schmidt, P. (2004). Population size, perceived threat and exclusion: A multiple-indicators analysis of attitudes toward foreigners in Germany. *Social Science Research, 33*(4), 681–701. https://www.sciencedirect.com/science/article/pii/S0049089X03000875.

Semyonov, M., Raijman, R., & Gorodzeisky, A. (2008). Foreigners' impact on European societies: Public views and perceptions in a cross-national comparative perspective. *International Journal of Comparative Sociology, 49*(3), 5–29. http://journals.sagepub.com/doi/abs/10.1177/0020715207088585?journalCode=cosa.

Sicinski, A. (1970). 'Don't know' answers in cross-national surveys. *Public Opinion Quarterly, 34*(1), 126–129. https://www.jstor.org/stable/pdf/2747891.pdf.

Sides, J., & Citrin, J. (2007). European opinion about immigration: The role of identities, interests and information. *British Journal of Political Science, 37*(3), 477–504. https://www.cambridge.org/core/journals/british-journal-of-political-science/article/european-opinion-about-immigration-the-role-of-identities-interests-and-information/C1BF2F7978F9FEA75A5BCD3CED0CF90F.

Sigelman, L., & Niemi, R. G. (2001). Innumeracy about minority populations: African Americans and whites compared. *The Public Opinion Quarterly, 65*(1), 86–94. https://academic.oup.com/poq/article-abstract/65/1/86/1888954?redirectedFrom=PDF.

Simon, A. (2017). How can we explain the gender gap in children's political knowledge? *The American Behavioral Scientist, 61*(2), 222–237.

Stelzenmueller, C., Eichenberg, R., Kennedy, C., & Isernia, P. (2013). *Transatlantic trends survey.* Ann Arbor, MI: Inter-university Consortium for Political and Social Research. [distributor], 2014-04-02. https://doi.org/10.3886/ICPSR34973.v1.

Strabac, Z. (2011). It is the eyes and not the size that matter. *European Societies, 13*(4), 559–582.

Tversky, A., & Kahneman, D. (1973). Availability: A heuristic for judging frequency and probability. *Cognitive Psychology, 5*, 207–232.

Tversky, A., & Kahneman, D. (1974). Judgment under uncertainty: Heuristics and biases. *Science, 185*, 1124–1131.

Wong, C. J. (2007). 'Little' and 'Big' pictures in our heads: Race, local context, and innumeracy about racial groups in the United States. *Public Opinion Quarterly, 71*(3), 392–412. https://www.jstor.org/stable/4500384?seq=1#page_scan_tab_contents.

Zajonc, R. B. (1980). Feelings and Thinking: Preferences Need No Inferences. *American Psychologist, 35*, 151–175.

Zajonc, R. B. (1984). On the Primacy of Affect. *American Psychologist, 39*, 117–123.

Chapter 8
Power, Culture and Item Nonresponse in Social Surveys

Katharina M. Meitinger and Timothy P. Johnson

Introduction

It is somewhat ironic that attention to survey unit nonresponse (UNR)—defined as "the failure to obtain any survey measurements on a sample unit" (Dillman et al. 2002: 6)—is pervasive in the survey methodology literature, whereas item nonresponse (INR)—defined as "the failure to obtain substantive answers to individual survey questions when a unit response is obtained" (Dillman et al. 2002: 12)—is much less frequently considered. It is equally ironic that considerable sociologic theory is available to account for patterns of survey UNR (e.g., Goyder et al. 2006; Groves and Couper 1998), while underlying theoretical explanations for INR are less developed.

In this chapter, we address this imbalance by examining INR within cross-national social surveys and considering its relationship to several sociological constructs which may advance our understanding of the INR process. These include social status, power, diversity and culture. We focus on these aspects because they enable us to take into account the social contexts within which individuals make decisions as to whether or not they will participate in survey interviews or complete self-administered questionnaires. In doing so, we employ a rich source of international social data that affords us the opportunity to integrate the existing evidence concerned with INR—much of which is limited to a single national setting—and

---

The original version of this chapter was revised. A correction to this chapter can be found at https://doi.org/10.1007/978-3-030-47256-6_15

K. M. Meitinger
University of Utrecht, JE, Utrecht, Netherlands
e-mail: k.m.meitinger@uu.nl

T. P. Johnson (✉)
University of Illinois at Chicago, Chicago, IL, USA
e-mail: timj@uic.edu

examine its generalizability across a more diverse set of social contexts. It also enables us to investigate new hypotheses concerned with the potential effects of culture that can only be examined using multi-national data sets. We begin with an overview of existing research regarding INR.

Item Nonresponse in Social Surveys

While the increased attention afforded to UNR is perhaps excusable given the dramatic declines in survey response rates witnessed in recent decades (Stoop 2016), INR nonetheless remains an important potential source of nonresponse error as well. Most importantly, item-level missing data can result in biased survey estimates or incorrect conclusions when mistakenly treated as being missing completely at random (MCAR) (Little and Rubin 2014; Schafer and Graham 2002). INR also reduces the effective sample size available for analyses, resulting in reductions in statistical power (Callens and Loosveldt 2018; McKnight et al. 2007). As virtually all social surveys experience some degree of INR and are thus vulnerable to these threats, we believe it is essential that greater effort be invested in understanding the sociological processes associated with it.

Available research highlights the relevance of INR for data quality, demonstrating it to be associated with variables at multiple levels of analysis. At the item level, evidence suggests that use of branching questions increases INR (Messmer and Seymour 1982; Turner et al. 1992). Question sensitivity can also increase INR, particularly during interviewer-assisted surveys (Rässler and Riphahn 2006; Tourangeau et al. 2000). In contrast, topic salience or relevance can decrease INR (Adua and Sharp 2010). Mode differences in INR are also well-known. In general, INR is more common in self-administered surveys (Heerwegh and Loosveldt 2008; Tourangeau et al. 2000), where it has been associated with poor visual design and questionnaire layout (Jenkins and Dillman 1997) and where interviewers who can encourage respondents to answer every question are absent (Dillman et al. 2002).

Rates of INR have also been shown to vary systematically across interviewers (Callens and Loosveldt 2018; Pickery and Loosveldt 1998). The speed at which interviewers read survey questions has been found to influence INR, with faster speeds leading to higher rates of 'don't know' responses (Vandenplas et al. 2018). Interviewer job experience, though, has not been shown to be consistently associated with INR (Tu and Liao 2007; Vandenplas et al. 2018). Some research suggests higher levels of INR obtained from female interviewers (Riphahn and Serfling 2005). Other findings indicate that social distance between interviewers and respondents may be reduced when interviewer-respondent dyads are matched on demographic characteristics, potentially decreasing INR. Indeed, some evidence finds reduced social distance in terms of variables such as gender, age, ethnicity and education to be associated with INR (Tu and Liao 2007; Vercruyssen et al. 2017). Other investigators, in contrast, have concluded there are few if any effects on INR of interviewer-respondent matching (Lipps 2007; Rässler and Riphahn 2006; Riphahn and Serfling 2005).

Item Nonresponse and Marginalized Populations

Several respondent characteristics have in addition been found to be associated with increased rates of INR. Females, older persons, those with lower levels of education, the unemployed, and those who are otherwise socially disadvantaged all demonstrate greater INR (Adua and Sharp 2010; Callens and Loosveldt 2018; Candido et al. 2011; Colsher and Wallace 1989; Elliott et al. 2005; Frick and Grabka 2007; Klein et al. 2011; Koch and Blohm 2009; Kupek 1998; Messer et al. 2012; Pickery and Loosveldt 1998; Riphahn and Serfling 2005; Struminskaya et al. 2015; Vercruyssen et al. 2017; Yan et al. 2010). In the U.S., numerous studies have also documented race and ethnic differences in patterns of INR. Specifically, in the U.S., African American, Asian, Hispanic, and Native American respondents have each demonstrated higher levels of INR, compared to non-Hispanic whites, in social surveys (Elliott et al. 2005; Klein et al. 2011; Lee et al. 2017; Owens et al. 2001; Yan et al. 2010). Similar differences in INR between German vs. other ethnic groups in Germany have also been reported (Struminskaya et al. 2015). Alexander (2018) interprets these findings from a marginalized group perspective, attributing the INR differences to group variations in abilities and access to the information resources needed, in some cases, to answer survey questions. These social group differences in INR rates are also consistent with Berinsky's (2002) discussion of "exclusion bias," which suggests that INR differentials reflect broader patterns of social inequality. It is notable that most of this existing INR research has been conducted within single countries. Here, we propose several new hypotheses that seek to expand the group marginalization explanation by suggesting it can be generalized across countries:

H1: Across countries, women provide more INR than men.
H2: Across countries, older respondents provide more INR than younger respondents.
H3: Across countries, lower educated respondents provide more INR than higher educated respondents.

Group marginalization also leads to social inequalities, and we expect levels of social inequalities within countries to be associated with INR across countries:

H4: Across countries, INR will be higher in those with greater levels of inequality.

Item Nonresponse and Social Power

The social inequities reviewed above all suggest power differentials. Indeed, social power, which generally refers to relationships among people and the ability of some to influence the behavior of others (Dahl 1957), is typically viewed as unbalanced, as actors are understood not to have equal levels of power over one another (Mulder 1977). At the risk of over-simplifying complex and highly variable patterns of social relationships across countries, the uneven distribution of social power within societies appears to be near-universal. The structuring of these power disparities within countries, though, is highly variable and arguably unique to each. In addition to gender, age and education, power differentials may be defined in terms of any number of other personal characteristics or social positions, including race/ethnicity, religion, migration status, language, social class, geographic residency, or some combination of them.

In general, we expect that those occupying less powerful social positions will have weaker access to the resources needed to provide adequate information during survey interviews. Many of the group differences in INR identified in the literature can be accounted for by power differentials, which are commonly attributed to majority vs. minority status. Our fifth hypothesis suggests that:

H5: Across countries, members of minority groups have higher rates of INR than do members of majority groups.

In addition to power differentials defined based on objective group membership, we also believe that subjective individual feelings of powerlessness may also be associated with INR. Hence:

H6: Across countries, individuals reporting greater feelings of powerlessness have higher rates of INR than do individuals reporting less feelings of powerlessness.

Item Nonresponse and Culture

As acknowledged earlier, most research concerned with INR has examined surveys conducted within one country, which of course limits their generalizability. This is of additional concern given that the limited cross-national research that is available suggests considerable heterogeneity in INR patterns across countries (Callens and Loosveldt 2018; Frick and Grabka 2007). There are several potential rationales to account for variations in INR across countries. Countries may train interviewers differentially regarding how to address INR when in the field. They may have differing quality control protocols and employ various modalities for data collection (Koch and Blohm 2009). Cross-national research affords the opportunity to investigate some of these potential methodological sources of variability in INR. One that has been examined within countries only is data collection mode. As discussed earlier, available evidence from single country studies suggests that INR is greater when surveys are predominantly self-administered. Our sixth hypothesis seeks to generalize these findings cross-nationally:

H7: Across countries, INR is higher in self-administered modes that do not employ interviewers.

Cross-national survey research also presents the opportunity to examine how higher-level cultural values may influence INR patterns. One of the most well-known cultural frameworks was developed by Hofstede (2001), who identified multiple cultural orientations that vary across countries. Several of these are of interest here as possible country level dimensions that may be associated with INR at the individual level. Power distance addresses the issue of unequal power distribution within countries (discussed earlier) and focuses on the degree to which this unequal distribution is accepted by those with less power. Societies high in power distance tend to be authoritarian in nature, stressing conformity. In contrast, those low in power distance more often emphasize independence and are less authoritarian in nature. As conformity seems to be of greater importance in high power distance societies, we would anticipate less INR for surveys conducted there. Thus, our eighth hypothesis is that:

H8: Across countries, INR will be higher in those with lower levels of power distance.

Another of Hofstede's cultural dimensions is individualism vs. collectivism (Triandis 1995). Briefly, individualism emphasizes self-enhancement, whereas collectivism focuses more on the well-being of the social group. Individualistic cultures view persons as individual actors who pursue their personal interests. Collectivistic cultures, in comparison, view individuals as members of social groups, and it are the interests of those social groups that are paramount. The greater personal autonomy observed in individualistic cultures suggests another hypothesis:

H9: Across countries, INR will be higher in those that are more individualistic.

Uncertainty avoidance is a third of Hofstede's dimensions that we believe is relevant for understanding INR across countries (Gudykunst and Kim 2003). This orientation focuses on the amount of uncertainty and ambiguity that is acceptable within a country or culture. In those high in uncertainty avoidance, consensus is valued, formal rules and laws are plentiful, and there is less tolerance for deviance. Countries low in uncertainty avoidance, in contrast, are less threatened by ambiguity, tend to have less interest in formal rules, and are tolerant of both deviant persons and ideas. We thus suspect that the lack of tolerance for ambiguity found in cultures with high levels of uncertainty avoidance may discourage survey respondents within those cultures from leaving survey questions unanswered. Consequently, we hypothesize that:

H10: Across countries, INR will be higher in those with lower levels of uncertainty avoidance.

Finally, we also examine the effects of cultural diversity within countries on INR. Countries that are ethnically homogeneous are typically able to lay claim to a shared historical experience and are more likely to also share language and often also religion. In contrast, ethnic diversity is found to be associated with less social cohesion, weaker national economic growth (Putnam 2007) and with greater internal conflict (Kanbur et al. 2011). The social conflict associated with cultural and ethnic diversity may also be manifest in higher rates of INR in social surveys. We thus hypothesize that:

H11: Across countries, INR will be higher in those with higher levels of ethnic diversity.

While ethnic and cultural diversity can be a source of internal conflict, we acknowledge that diversity is also an immense source of national pride and strength for many peoples in many countries.

We next turn to a description of the cross-national survey data and the methods we employ to investigate these hypotheses.

Data and Methods

In the following sections, we first introduce our survey data sets. We then describe our specific measures, followed by an overview of our multi-level analysis methods.

Data Sets

We used for our analysis de-identified data from the 2016 *International Social Survey Programme* (ISSP) Module on Role of Government IV (ISSP 2018). The target population in each country consisted of all persons aged 18 and older.[1] Overall, the data set of the 2016 ISSP module contains 48,720 respondents from 35 countries. The advantage of the ISSP data set is that it covers a large variety of countries and cultural groups. A complete list of participating countries can be found in Table 8.1.

Variables

Dependent Variable: Count of Item Nonresponse

Our dependent variable in this analysis is a count of item nonresponse in the 2016 ISSP data set. Following the approach of Callens and Loosveldt (2018), we model item nonresponse as a count variable that calculates the number of questions for which respondents provided an item nonresponse. Instead of analyzing all variables in the dataset, we selected a subset of items which exceeded the recommended threshold value of 5% INR (Little and Rubin 2002). Overall, we analyzed the count of INR for 25 variables in the 2016 ISSP data set. Therefore, the outcome variable has a value range between 0 and 25. Table 8.3 in the Online Appendix provides a list of all included variables. Although a separate analysis of "can't choose" and "refusals" would have been preferable (Shoemaker et al. 2002), this was not feasible

---

[1] Exceptions for 2016 ISSP were Finland (15–74 years), Japan (16 years and over), Latvia (18–74 years), Norway (18–79 years), Sweden (18–79 years), South Africa (16 years and over), and Suriname (21–74 years).

8 Power, Culture and Item Nonresponse in Social Surveys 175

Table 8.1 Countries of the 2016 ISSP data set and their respective minority definition

Country (N)	Majority	Minority	Minority definition
Australia (1267)	847	420	Not born in Australia or English-speaking country and parents non-Australian or born in English-speaking country
Belgium (1952)	1705	247	Both parent from non-European countries
Chile (1416)	1162	254	Self-classification in lower social classes (lowest third)
Croatia (1026)	931	95	Non-Croat
Czech Republic (1400)	1285	115	Non-Czech
Denmark (1138)	815	323	Non-Danish
Finland (1186)	1104	82	Non-Finnish
France (1501)	1241	260	Non-European
Georgia (1487)	1344	143	Non-Georgian
Germany (1689)	1569	120	Non-German
Great Britain (1563)	1460	103	Non-white
Hungary (1000)	995	5	Roma
Iceland (1322)	1126	196	Belonging to a minority
India (1508)	841	667	Non-Hindu OBC or non-Hindu other
Israel (1248)	973	275	Non-Jewish
Japan (1611)	1568	43	Non-Japanese or father or mother non-Japanese
Latvia (1002)	659	343	Non-Latvian
Lithuania (1006)	898	108	Non-Lithuanian
New Zealand (1350)	1026	324	Non-European
Norway (1260)	1116	144	Non-Norwegian
Philippines (1200)	970	230	Non-Roman Catholic
Russia (1576)	1320	256	Non-Russian
Slovakia (1150)	1027	123	Non-Slovak
Slovenia (1024)	967	57	Roma and migrants from countries from former Yugoslavia
South Africa (3063)	2207	856	Self-classification in lower social classes (lowest third)

(continued)

Table 8.1 (continued)

Country (N)	Majority	Minority	Minority definition
South Korea (1051)	913	138	Inhabitants of Gwangju Metropolitan City, South Jeolla Province, North Jeolla Province
Spain (1834)	1652	182	Both parents non-Spaniards
Suriname (1273)	1078	195	Self-classification in lower social classes (lowest third)
Sweden (1140)	996	144	Parents from non-Nordic country
Switzerland (1066)	756	310	Parents non-Swiss
Thailand (1475)	1356	119	Non-Buddhist
Taiwan (1966)	1860	106	Aborigine, Southeast Asia, other
Turkey (1535)	1291	244	Non-Turks
United States (1390)	1013	377	Non-whites (GSS race variable)
Venezuela (1045)	862	183	Self-classification in lower social classes (lowest third)
Total (48,720)	40,933	7787	

due to coding inconsistencies across countries for several variables in the ISSP data set (e.g., for the income variable).

Independent Variable

Minority Status

An important focus of our research is on the influence of minority status on INR. Which social groups are considered as minority can differ across countries and might be based on distinctions such as ethnicity, religious denomination, social class, migrant status or region. We consulted with cultural experts for advice on how to define the main cleavage in each respective country (see Acknowledgements). Table 8.1 contains a list of minority definitions by country. For our analysis, we modeled the variable minority status as a binary measure (reference category: majority group). We acknowledge that a dichotomization of this variable in one majority and one minority group might be an oversimplification in a variety of countries and does not completely adjust for the diverse realities of many societies in our analysis. Since we attempted a cross-national analysis with many countries, we had to opt for a higher level of abstraction than in a single-country study. We encourage replications of our research with a smaller subset of countries that account for the differences between minority groups within countries.

Respondent Level Characteristics

On the respondent level, we included gender (reference category: women), age (metric),[2] and education. With regard to education, we distinguish between low level, medium level, and high level of education[3] (reference category: medium level of education). We also added a variable at the individual level that addresses the respondents' feeling of powerlessness (v47; "People like me don't have any say about what the government does"; 5-point scale from "strongly agree" to "strongly disagree"; can't choose option; reverse coded). All variables are grand mean centered, see (Hox et al. 2018).

Country Level Characteristics

In addition to respondent level characteristics, we also added country level variables to our model. Since previous research revealed the influence of interviewer involvement on item nonresponse, we added a dummy variable for mode that distinguishes between countries with data collection that relies predominantly on self-completions vs. countries with data collection that features greater interviewer involvement[4] (reference category: interviewer involvement).

In addition to mode setting, we also included variables that describe the countries' particularities. The countries in our data set differ with regard to the level of inequality within each respective society. We addressed this by including the Coefficient of Human Inequality in our analysis. This indicator is collected by the United Nations Development Programme and averages inequalities in health, education, and income.[5] The coefficient ranges between 0 and 1, with lower values representing greater levels of inequality within a society. Additionally, the countries differ with regard to their gross domestic product per capita. (GDP per capita in US $). We included GDP per capita data collected by the Worldbank.[6] We adjusted the GDP to the range of the other variables in the model by dividing its value by 1000.

---

[2]Age was not collected continuously but as response categories with age ranges in Denmark. We used the middle value of these age ranges as age values for Denmark.

[3]After consultation with an expert on cross-national classifications of education, we coded the categories of the ISSP degree variables as follows: no formal education, primary school, and lower secondary as *low* educational level; upper secondary and post secondary, non-tertiary as *medium* educational level; lower level tertiary and upper level tertiary as *higher* educational level.

[4]Most of the countries have either only data collection with interviewer involvement or self-completion. Two countries, Germany and Suriname, had both types of data collection. Therefore, we assigned these countries to the mode setting that was predominant in the respective country (Germany: self-completion; Suriname: interviewer).

[5]Further documentation on the UNR inequality index can be found here: http://hdr.undp.org/en/content/what-does-coefficient-human-inequality-measure.

[6]The GDP per capita data was taken from https://data.worldbank.org/indicator/NY.GDP.PCAP.CD.

The countries also vary in their cultural orientation. We selected the Hofstede dimensions of power distance, individualism-collectivism, and uncertainty avoidance for our analysis. Country level scores for these dimensions are from Hofstede's research (2010) and appended to the data set.[7]

Finally, we believe INR might also be affected by the degree of heterogeneity of ethnic groups within a society. Therefore, we included a measure of ethnic fractionalization in our analysis. The ethnic diversity index is based on the approach of Patsiurko et al. (2012) who took data on ethnic composition from Encyclopaedia Britannica and transformed them to ethnic indices using the approach of 'one minus the Herfindahl index' (Patsiurko et al. 2012). This formula calculates the probability that two randomly selected individuals in a country belong to different ethnic groups and provides estimates ranging from 0 to 1 (Alesina et al. 2003). For example, an ethnic fractionalization score of 0.04 for a country means that the odds of two people selected randomly belonging to different ethnic groups is 4 percent. Patsiurko et al. provided values for all OECD countries. However, our data set also contains non-OECD countries. Therefore, we calculated the scores for these countries based on entries from Encyclopaedia Britannica. The data entries cover the period 2000–2007 since no newer data were available from Encyclopaedia Britannica. Although not optimal, the fractionalization indices should still provide some valuable insights since previous research indicates that these measures are highly persistent and hardly change over time (Alesina et al. 2003; Awaworyi Churchill et al. 2017).

Analysis

We estimated multilevel mixed-effects negative binomial regressions with two analytical levels (respondent and country) (Hilbe 2011) for the 2016 ISSP data set. Instead of using a simple Poisson model for count data, this model is preferable if over-dispersion is present in the data. That is, when the observed variance is much larger than expected under the Poisson model (Hox et al. 2018). We adjust for the over-dispersion in our data by adding an explicit error term α to our model which increases the variance compared to the variance implied by the Poisson model (Hox et al. 2018). We used STATA version 14 to run our model and selected the mode-curvature adaptive Gauss–Hermite quadrature[8] to calculate the log likelihood. This

---

[7] Values were retrieved from Hofstede's website: https://geerthofstede.com/research-and-vsm/dimension-data-matrix/.

[8] We opted for the mode-curvature adaptive Gauss–Hermite quadrature integration method instead of the default integration method (Gauss–Hermite quadrature integration method) because the default setting created out-of-bound values for the country variance. We cross-checked our results with the Gauss–Hermite quadrature integration method with outputs in mlwin and the gllamm command in STATA. In all outputs, we found a similar pattern of significance for the regression coefficients. Contrary to the results with the default setting, not all regression coefficients are

is an estimator with numerical integration and has the advantage of permitting likelihood-ratio tests for comparing nested models.

In an initial step, we fitted a two-level random-intercept Poisson model. The reported likelihood-ratio test indicates sufficient variability between countries to favor a mixed-effects Poisson regression over a standard Poisson regression (LR test vs. Poisson model: chi-bar-squared(01) = 9321.32; $p < 0.001$). We proceeded to fit our model with a multilevel mixed-effects negative binomial model. The Likelihood-ratio test comparing the mixed-effects negative binomial model to the mixed-effects Poisson models supports the use of the mixed-effects negative binomial model for our data (LR chi-square(1) = 30087.50; $p < 0.001$).

Results

In total, we estimate three nested models. We start with a baseline model with intercept only and then add block-wise respondent level (Model 2) and country level (Model 3) explanatory variables. We additionally report incidence rate ratios for the final model. The predictors are added block-wise at the respondent and country level to also examine the amount of INR variability explained by the added variables. The model is a purely hierarchical one, where each respondent belongs to only one country.

Null Model

We begin with a Null model with a random intercept to assess whether there is significant variation on the country level. This model does not include any explanatory variables. Results are reported in Table 8.2, model 1. The estimate of the variance component σ_u^2 is 0.22. In addition, an additional parameter α that controls the variability of the data is estimated in the negative binomial model and is reported as its log estimate (/lnalpha = -0.106; S.E. = 0.010) which equals an α of 0.90 (indication of over-dispersion). The likelihood-ratio test for this model indicates that there is enough variability in INR between countries to favor a mixed-effects negative binomial regression over a negative binomial regression without random effects (chi-bar-squared(01) = 7010.43; $p < 0.001$). Therefore, we will retain our multilevel structure in the more complex models. However, INR also might be affected by characteristics of the respondents. In particular, we are interested whether minority status has an impact on INR.

---

significant with the mode-curvature adaptive Gauss–Hermite quadrature integration method. Therefore, our results are more conservative than in the default setting.

Table 8.2 Regression results for the baseline model, the respondent-level model and the combined respondent and country-level model

	Model 1 Baseline	Model 2 + Individual	Model 3 + Country	
	Coeff. (S.E.)	Coeff. (S.E.)	Coeff. (S.E.)	IRR
FIXED PART				
Intercept	0.972 (0.079)***	0.835 (0.075)***	0.811 (0.065)***	2.251 (0.147)
Minority (reference: Majority)		0.201 (0.014)***	0.207 (0.015)***	1.230 (0.018)
Gender (reference: Women)		−0.262 (0.010)***	−0.267 (0.011)***	0.766 (0.008)
Age		0.003 (0.000)***	0.003 (0.000)***	1.003 (0.000)
Education (reference: Medium)				
Low education		0.182 (0.013)***	0.155 (0.013)***	1.168 (0.015)
High education		−0.204 (0.013)***	−0.191(0.014)***	0.826 (0.012)
Influence		0.029 (.075)***	0.029 (0.005)***	1.030 (0.005)
Mode (reference: Interviewer)			0.383 (0.190)**	1.467 (0.279)
Inequality			−0.012 (0.015)	0.988 (0.0145)
GDP per capita/1000			−0.007 (0.005)	1.000 (0.000)
Uncertainty avoidance			0.008 (0.004)**	1.001 (0.000)
Power distance			−0.003 (0.004)	0.992 (0.000)
Individualism-collectivism			0.000 (0.004)	1.002 (0.000)
Ethnic fractionalization			0.379 (0.065)	2.47 (0.076)
RANDOM PART				
Country	0.217 (0.052)	0.196 (0.047)	0.131 (0.033)	0.131 (0.033)
/lnalpha	−0.106 (0.0010)***	−0.357 (0.011)***	−0.327 (0.012)***	−0.327 (0.012)***
AIC	211342.3	189445.4	169437.8	
BIC	211368.6	189524.2	169576.2	
Log	−105668.13	−94713.701	−84702.9	
UNITS				
Respondents	48,720	46,616	42,089	42,089
Countries	35	35	32	32

Note. IRR: Incidence Rate Ratio; * $p < 0.01$, ** $p < 0.05$, *** $p < 0.001$

Respondent and Country Level Random Intercept Model

Extending the baseline model, we add minority status, gender, age, education, and the measure of the feeling of powerlessness at the respondent level (model 2). On the country level, we include the mode of data collection, the Coefficient of Human Inequality, GDP per capita, the Hofstede dimensions of uncertainty avoidance, power distance, and individualism-collectivism as well as a measure of ethnic fractionalization (model 3).

The variance between countries is reduced when demographic and attitudinal control variables on the respondent level are added to the baseline model (model 2). It substantially shrinks further when country level variables are included (model 3). The likelihood ratios tests for model comparisons are significant for the comparison between the Null model and model 2 (LR chi-square (6) = 21908.86; $p < 0.001$) and between model 2 and model 3 (LR chi-square (7) = 20021.61; $p < 0.001$). The AIC and BIC values are also decreasing for each model respectively, flagging model 3 as the 'best' model. For model 3, we also report the results as incidence-rate ratio (exponentiated coefficients). An incidence-rate ratio (IRR) of 1 suggests no difference in risk, an IRR larger than 1 suggests an increased risk and values below 1 a reduced risk. Unfortunately, no data were available for Georgia for the Hofstede values and for Taiwan and New Zealand for the inequality measure. Therefore, model 3 only includes 32 countries instead of the full sample of 35 countries.

Individual Level Variables

In model 3, all individual level variables are highly significant. Since all variables where centered on their grand mean, the reference group are women who are belonging to the majority, having mean age, a medium level education and neither agree nor disagree of what people like them have no say about what the government does. Being a member of the minority seems to increase the expected number of nonresponses by 23.0%, whereas being a male respondent reduces the expected number of nonresponses by 23.4%. A year increase in age leads to 0.3% higher expected number of nonresponses. Low education increases the expected number of nonresponses by 16.8% and high education reduces it by 17.4%. Finally, the feeling of powerlessness also increases the incidence rate ratio for nonresponse. These findings confirm H5, H3, H6, H2 and H1, respectively.

Country Level Variables

In contrast to the individual level, not many country-level predictors are significant. Respondents who answered the questionnaire in a self-completion mode have a higher risk of INR, a finding that confirms H7. In a similar vein, respondents from countries with higher values of uncertainty avoidance show higher risks of INR, a finding that is opposite of what H10 expected. Although, we could not find significant effects for individualism (H9) and power distance (H8), the directions of those effects each go in the hypothesized direction, respectively. Similarly, no significant effect was found for ethnic fractionalization (H11) and inequality (H4). Although these effects were not significant, the effect for ethnic fractionalization was also in the hypothesized direction: higher levels of ethnic diversity increases the risk of INR.

Discussion

To test our hypotheses concerned with the relationships that group marginalization, social power and culture may have with INR, we analyzed data from more than 48,000 respondents situated in 35 nations across 6 continents. Employing this diverse sample, we have uncovered support for several of our eleven hypotheses.

It has now been 40 years since Hofstede (1980) first published *Culture's Consequences*, in which he described multiple dimensions of national culture. Subsequently, these dimensions have been found to be associated with a wide variety of social phenomenon across multiple disciplines (Hofstede 2001). Yet, we are aware of only a single study that has evaluated the relationship between any of these dimensions and INR (Lee et al. 2017). In that paper, Lee and colleagues demonstrated cultural differences in Hofstede's time orientation dimension to be associated with INR for subjective probability questions. However, in the analyses reported here, we only could find a significant effect for the dimension of uncertainty avoidance, and the direction of that association was the opposite of what we had hypothesized (H10). Across the countries we examined, INR was found to be greater in those countries with less of an emphasis on uncertainty avoidance where a greater tolerance of ambiguity might be anticipated. This finding suggests that respondents embedded within uncertainty avoidant cultures might be more inclined to avoid answering, perhaps when confronted with ambiguous questions or topics. In contrast, no significant effects were found for the cultural dimensions of individualism-collectivism and power distance (H8 & H9).

However, the main focus of our study was to examine the effects of group marginalization on INR. We find evidence of a relationship using multiple indicators of marginalization. Some of these findings confirm earlier research suggesting that INR is more common among the socially disadvantaged, including females, older and less educated persons (H1-H3). Together, these findings support the marginalized group perspective (Alexander 2018) and confirm its generalizability across a broad cross-section of countries. It would appear that, in addition to the many harmful effects that social exclusion and inequality have on individual well-being, marginalization processes also appear to contribute to INR in social surveys, diminishing the representation of disadvantaged persons within this social context as well.

A marginalized status easily translates into reduced or less powerful social position. Because stratification exists within all countries (Davis and Moore 1945), we can expect to observe differences in social power as well. As discussed earlier, however, we anticipated that the stratification structures related to power would almost certainly vary in form and complexity across countries. To address this reality, we consulted with cultural "insiders" and survey experts within each country we examined to determine the most appropriate measures of social cleavage for identifying majority vs. minority populations. These were subsequently employed as country-specific measures to differentiate more- vs. less-powerful social groups. At the individual level, we observe evidence supportive of our hypothesis (H5) describing the effects of membership in groups less able to wield social power. Regardless of national variability in the definitions used, those persons belonging to nationally-defined minority groups more frequently provided non-answers to the survey questions posed to them. These findings were supported by additional analyses which demonstrated more INR among persons within each country who indicated having greater feelings of powerlessness (H6). The pervasiveness of these relationships is evident in the finding that the objective indicator of marginalized group membership *and* the subjective measure of perceived powerlessness each were independently associated with increased INR across countries.

These results indicate that the dimension of power needs to be taken seriously in survey methodological research. Respondents that take less powerful positions in the different countries show increased levels of item nonresponse. This is highly problematic because nonresponse also means that the opinions of these groups are potentially not being adequately taken into account in the substantive analysis of the data. These issues address directly aspects of an insufficient representation of less powerful members of society in general social surveys. These respondents might have diverse reasons for not providing a substantive response to a survey question, such as missing comprehension of the question, lack of knowledge or distrust of government authorities.

Questionnaire developers should consider the different motivations for item nonresponse and work to design their questionnaires to better encourage responses from members of marginalized groups. Strategies to address these issues could be, for example, cognitive interviews or focus groups with particularly marginalized groups to detect issues of missing comprehension or lack of knowledge. Other strategies might include providing questionnaires in simplified language (e.g., as adopted by the LISS panel) and developing new approaches to help increase respondents' trust of interviewers and survey programmes. An example of such a strategy is the Doorstep Training Initiative for Bilingual Interviewers at the U.S. Census Bureau that also trains interviewers to address the respondents' fear or mistrust of the U.S. Government (Goerman 2017). Of course, just as definitions and the composition of marginalized groups vary across countries, optimal strategies for addressing item nonresponse can also be expected to vary from country-to-country.

Future Research

Future research should take a more differentiated look at various forms of item nonresponse. This was unfortunately not feasible with our datasets but could perhaps be done with other data sets that provide a more detailed and consistent coding of item nonresponse. Since the goal of our analysis was to represent as much cultural variability as possible, we opted to investigate ISSP data, despite this limitation. Consequently, whether there are variations of the found effects across different types of item nonresponse is an open research question. There are also reasons to anticipate that the social and cultural processes examined here may have differential effects on the INR associated with various question topics (Alexander 2018; Kane and Macaulay 1993), and we believe this also merits further inquiry. Relatedly, the contrary findings regarding the direction of uncertainty avoidance effects requires additional investigation, as questions that are structured ambiguously or that address ambiguous topics may be more likely to produce INR within uncertainty avoidant cultures. Finally, we also acknowledge that we used a very vague distinction between minority and majority in our study. Although we built our definitions based on recommendations by culture specific experts, we are aware that a simple dichotomy is almost certainly an oversimplification of the social reality in many countries. For example, in the U.S. a more detailed analysis would most likely detect differences between races (e.g., Blacks, Hispanics, and Asians). We encourage future studies that take a more detailed look at differences between different minority groups within particular countries to better understand how positions of social marginalization, social power, and culture influence response and nonresponse patterns in social surveys.

Acknowledgements We wish to gratefully thank the many colleagues who generously provided us with advice and insights regarding social cleavages and minority populations in their respective nations. Ann Evans & Karen Kellard (Australia), Markus Hadler (Austria), Jaak Billiet, Koen Verhoest and Marleen Brans (Belgium), Lilia Dimova (Bulgaria), Ricardo González and Marta Lagos (Chile), Yanjie Bian (China), Kresimir Znidar (Croatia), Dana Hamplova (Czech Republic), Dite Shamshiri-Petersen (Denmark), Kadri Täht (Estonia), Seppo Antiainen (Finland), Frédéric Gonthier (France), Lika Tsuladze (Georgia), Evi Scholz (Germany), Miranda Phillips (Miranda Phillips), Toth Istvan Gyorgy (Hungary), Hafsteinn Birgir Einarsson (Iceland), Yashwant Deshmukh and Sowmya Anand (India), Gal Ariely (Israel), Kuniaki Shishido (Japan), Mareks Niklass (Latvia), Egle Butkevicience (Lithuania), Alejandro Moreno (Mexico), Ineke Stoop (Netherlands), Barry Milne (New Zealand), Gry Karlsen (Norway), Linda Luz Guerrero (Philippines), Marcin Zieliński (Poland), Viriato Queiroga (Portugal), Bogdan Voicu (Romania), Ekaterina Lytkina (Russian Federation), Miloslav Bahna (Slovakia), Valentina Hlebec (Slovenia), Mari Harris (South Africa), Jibum Kim (South Korea), Jose-Luis Padilla (Spain), Jonas Edlund (Sweden), Marlène Sapin (Switzerland), Stithorn Thananithichot (Thailand), Yang-chih Fu (Taiwan), Wahab Benhafaiedh (Tunisia), Bulent Kilincarslan and Melike Sarac (Turkey), and Roberto Briceno-Leon and Roberto Briceno Rosas (Venezuela). We, however, assume complete responsibility for the operational definitions employed to represent majority vs. minority group membership within each nation.

Appendix

Table 8.3 Variables included in analysis from 2016 ISSP dataset

Variable number	Question text	Response options
Q1	In general, would you say that people should obey the law without exception, or are there exceptional occasions on which people should follow their consciences even if it means breaking the law?	Obey the law without exception OR Follow conscience on occasions Can't choose
Q2a	There are many ways people or organisations can protest against a government action they strongly oppose. Please show which you think should be allowed and which should not be allowed by ticking a box on each line. Organising public meetings to protest against the government	Should it be allowed? Definitely Probably Probably not Definitely not Can't choose
Q2b	There are many ways people or organisations can protest against a government action they strongly oppose. Please show which you think should be allowed and which should not be allowed by ticking a box on each line. Organising protest marches and demonstrations	Should it be allowed? Definitely Probably Probably not Definitely not Can't choose
Q3a	There are some people whose views are considered extreme by the majority. Consider people who want to overthrow the government by revolution. Do you think such people should be allowed to ... hold public meetings to express their views?	Definitely Probably Probably not Definitely not Can't choose
Q3b	There are some people whose views are considered extreme by the majority. Consider people who want to overthrow the government by revolution. Do you think such people should be allowed to ... publish books expressing their views?	Definitely Probably Probably not Definitely not Can't choose
Q4	All systems of justice make mistakes, but which do you think is worse ...	... To convict an innocent person OR ... to let a guilty person go free? Can't choose
Q5c	Here are some things the government might do for the economy. Please show which actions you are in favour of and which you are against. Less government regulation of business	Strongly in favour of In favour of Neither in favour of nor against Against Strongly against Can't choose

(continued)

Table 8.3 (continued)

Variable number	Question text	Response options
Q5f	Here are some things the government might do for the economy. Please show which actions you are in favour of and which you are against. Reducing the working week to create more jobs	Strongly in favour of In favour of Neither in favour of nor against Against Strongly against Can't choose
Q9b	Here is a list of people and organisations that can influence government actions. Please read through the list and write in the boxes below the letters corresponding to the ones you think have the most and the second most influence on the actions of the (COUNTRY) government?	The media Trade unions Business, banks and industry Religious organisations/authorities The military/army Organised crime People who vote for the party/the parties in government Citizens in general Civic and voluntary organisations International organizations (e.g. united nations, International Monetary Fund) Can't choose
Q10	Here are two opinions about what affects policies in [COUNTRY]. Which of them comes closest to your view?	Policies in [COUNTRY] depend more on what is happening in the world economy, rather than who is in government OR Policies in [COUNTRY] depend more on who is in government, rather than what is happening in the world economy Can't choose
Q11b	Do you think that the [COUNTRY] government should or should not have the right to do the following . Monitor e-mails and any other information exchanged on the internet?	Definitely should have right Probably should have right Probably should not have right Definitely should not have right Can't choose
Q12	Here is a scale from 0 to 10 where 0 is "all government information should be publicly available, even if this meant a risk to public security" and 10 is "public security should be given priority, even if this meant limiting access to government information". Where would you place yourself on such a scale?	11 point scale ranging from 00→11. Labels of endpoints: All government information should be publicly available, even if this meant a risk to public security Public security should be given priority, even if this meant limiting access to government information Can't choose

(continued)

8 Power, Culture and Item Nonresponse in Social Surveys

Table 8.3 (continued)

Variable number	Question text	Response options
Q13b	Some people think that governments should have the right to take certain measures in the name of national security. Others disagree. Do you think that the [COUNTRY] government should or should not have the right to do the following: Collect information about anyone living in other countries without their knowledge	Definitely should have right Probably should have right Probably should not have right Definitely should not have right Can't choose
Q17a	Generally, how would you describe taxes in [country] today? ((we mean all taxes together, including [wage deductions], [income tax], [taxes on goods and services] and all the rest.)) first, for those with high incomes, are taxes	... much too high, Too high, About right, Too low, Or, are they much too low? Can't choose
Q17b	Generally, how would you describe taxes in [country] today? ((we mean all taxes together, including [wage deductions], [income tax], [taxes on goods and services] and all the rest.)) Next, for those with middle incomes, are taxes ...	... much too high, Too high, About right, Too low, Or, are they much too low? Can't choose
Q17c	Generally, how would you describe taxes in [country] today? ((we mean all taxes together, including [wage deductions], [income tax], [taxes on goods and services] and all the rest.)) Lastly, for those with low incomes, are taxes ...	... much too high, Too high, About right, Too low, Or, are they much too low? Can't choose
Q18a	In general, how often do you think that the tax authorities in [country] do the following... Make sure people pay their taxes	Almost always Often Sometimes Almost never Can't choose
Q18b	In general, how often do you think that the tax authorities in [country] do the following... ... treat everyone in accordance with the law, regardless of their contacts or position in society?	Almost always Often Sometimes Almost never Can't choose
Q19a	In general, how often do you think that major private companies in [country] do the following: a. ....Comply with laws and regulations?	Almost always Often Sometimes Almost never Can't choose

(continued)

Table 8.3 (continued)

Variable number	Question text	Response options
Q19b	In general, how often do you think that major private companies in [country] do the following: ...try to avoid paying their taxes?	Almost always Often Sometimes Almost never Can't choose
Q20	In your opinion, about how many politicians in [COUNTRY] are involved in corruption?	Almost none A few Some Quite a lot Almost all Can't choose
Q21	And in your opinion, about how many public officials in [country] are involved in corruption?	Almost none A few Some Quite a lot Almost all Can't choose
Q22	In the last five years, how often have you or a member of your immediate family come across a public official who hinted they wanted, or asked for, a bribe or favour in return for a service?	Never Seldom Occasionally Quite often Very often Can't choose
Respondent's income	Example U.S.: In which of these groups did your earnings from (OCC), from all sources for [last year] fall? That is, before taxes or other deductions. Just tell me the letter. Total income includes interest or dividends, rent, social security, other pension, alimony or child support, unemployment compensation, public aid (welfare), armed forces or veteran's allotment.	Nonresponse categories: Refused Don't know No answer Inapplicable
Household income	Example U.S.: In which of these groups did your total family income, from all sources, fall last year before taxes, that is. Just tell me the letter. Total income includes interest or dividends, rent, social security, other pensions, alimony or child support, unemployment, compensation, public aid (welfare), armed forces or veteran's allotment.	Nonresponse categories: Refused Don't know No answer Inapplicable

References

Adua, L., & Sharp, J. S. (2010). Examining survey participation and response quality: The significance of topic salience and incentives. *Survey Methodology, 26*(1), 95–109. https://www150.statcan.gc.ca/n1/en/pub/12-001-x/2010001/article/11252-eng.pdf?st=kPlsEgKD.

Alesina, A., Devleeschauwer, A., Easterly, W., Kurlat, S., & Wacziarg, R. (2003). Fractionalization. *Journal of Economic Growth, 8*(2), 155–194. https://doi.org/10.1023/A:1024471506938.

Alexander, E. C. (2018). Don't know or won't say? Exploring how colorblind norms shape item nonresponse in social surveys. *Sociology of Race and Ethnicity, 4*(3), 417–433. https://doi.org/10.1177/2332649217705145.

Awaworyi Churchill, S., Ocloo, J. E., & Siawor-Robertson, D. (2017). Ethnic diversity and health outcomes. *Social Indicators Research, 134*, 1077–1112. https://doi.org/10.1007/s11205-016-1454-7.

Berinsky, A. (2002). Silent voices: Social welfare policy opinions and political equality in America. *American Journal of Political Science, 46*(2), 276–287. https://www.jstor.org/stable/3088376.

Callens, M., & Loosveldt, G. (2018). Don't know responses to survey items on trust in police and criminal courts: A word of caution. *Survey Methods: Insights from the Field.* https://doi.org/10.13094/SMIF-2018-00002.

Candido, E., Kurdyak, P., & Alter, D. A. (2011). Item nonresponse to psychosocial questionnaires was associated with higher mortality after acute myocardial infarction. *Journal of Clinical Epidemiology, 64*(2), 213–222. https://doi.org/10.1016/j.jclinepi.2010.03.010.

Colsher, P. L., & Wallace, R. B. (1989). Data quality and age: Health and psychobehavioral correlates of item nonresponse and inconsistent responses. *Journal of Gerontology, 44*(2), 45–52. https://doi.org/10.1093/geronj/44.2.P45.

Dahl, R. A. (1957). The concept of power. *Behavioral Science, 2*, 201–215. https://doi.org/10.1002/bs.3830020303.

Davis, K., & Moore, W. E. (1945). Some principles of stratification. *American Sociological Review, 10*(2), 242–249. https://www-jstor-org.proxy.cc.uic.edu/stable/2085643.

Dillman, D. A., Eltinge, J. L., Groves, R. M., & Little, R. J. (2002). Survey nonresponse in design, data collection, and analysis. In R. M. Groves, D. A. Dillman, J. L. Eltinge, & R. J. Little (Eds.), *Survey nonresponse* (pp. 3–24). New York: Wiley. https://www.wiley.com/en-us/Survey+Nonresponse-p-9780471396277.

Elliott, M. N., Edwards, C., Angeles, J., Hambarsoomians, K., & Hays, R. D. (2005). Patterns of unit and item nonresponse in the CAHPS® hospital survey. *Health Services Research, 40*(6p2), 2096–2119. https://doi.org/10.1111/j.1475-6773.2005.00476.x.

Frick, J. R., & Grabka, M. M. (2007). *Item non-response and imputation of annual labor income in panel surveys from a cross-national perspective.* SOEPpapers on multidisciplinary panel data research, no. 49, Deutsches Institut für Wirtschaftsforschung (DIW), Berlin, Germany. https://ssrn.com/abstract=1020605.

Goerman, P. (2017). *Development of a doorstep training initiative for bilingual interviewers at the U.S. Census Bureau.* Mannheim: Presentation at the CSDI Workshop. Retrieved from https://csdiworkshop.org/wp-content/uploads/2019/01/Goerman_CSDI_2017_final_updated.pdf.

Goyder, J., Boyer, L., & Martinelli, G. (2006). Integrating exchange and heuristic theories of survey nonresponse. *Bulletin de Méthodologie Sociologique, 92*, 28–44. https://journals.openedition.org/bms/554.

Groves, R. M., & Couper, M. P. (1998). *Nonresponse in Household Interview Surveys.* New York: Wiley. https://www.wiley.com/en-us/Nonresponse+in+Household+Interview+Surveys-p-9780471182450.

Gudykunst, W. B., & Kim, Y. Y. (2003). *Communicating with strangers* (4th ed.). Boston: McGraw-Hill.

Heerwegh, D., & Loosveldt, G. (2008). Face-to-face versus web surveying in a high-internet-coverage population: Differences in response quality. *Public Opinion Quarterly, 72*(5), 836–846. https://doi.org/10.1093/poq/nfn045.

Hilbe, J. M. (2011). *Negative binomial regression* (2nd ed.). Cambridge: Cambridge University Press. https://doi.org/10.1017/CBO9780511973420.

Hofstede, G. (1980). *Culture's consequences*. Beverly Hills, CA: Sage.

Hofstede, G. (2001). *Culture's consequences* (2nd ed.). Thousand Oaks, CA: Sage. https://us.sagepub.com/en-us/nam/cultures-consequences/book9710.

Hofstede, G. (2010). Cultures and organizations: Software of the mind. *Cultures Organ, 23*, 362–365. https://doi.org/10.1057/jibs.1992.23.

Hox, J., Moerbeek, M., & van de Schoot, M. (2018). *Multilevel analysis: Techniques and applications* (2nd ed.). New York: Routledge. https://doi.org/10.4324/9780203852279.

ISSP Research Group. (2018). *International social survey programme: Role of government V – ISSP 2016*. Retrieved from https://dbk.gesis.org/dbksearch/sdesc2.asp?no=6900&db=e&doi=10.4232/1.13052.

Jenkins, C. R., & Dillman, D. A. (1997). Towards a theory of self-administered questionnaire design. In L. Lyberg, P. Biemer, M. Collings, E. de Leeuw, C. Dippo, N. Schwarz, & D. Trewin (Eds.), *Survey measurement and process quality* (pp. 165–196). New York: Wiley. https://onlinelibrary.wiley.com/doi/10.1002/9781118490013.ch7.

Kanbur, R., Rajaram, P. K., & Varshney, A. (2011). Ethnic diversity and ethnic strife. An interdisciplinary perspective. *World Development, 39*(2), 147–158. https://doi.org/10.1016/j.worlddev.2009.11.034.

Kane, E. W., & Macaulay, L. J. (1993). Interviewer gender and gender attitudes. *Public Opinion Quarterly, 57*(1), 1–28. https://doi.org/10.1086/269352.

Klein, D. J., Elliott, M. N., Haviland, A. M., Saliba, D., Burkhart, Q., Edwards, C., & Zaslavsky, A. M. (2011). Understanding nonresponse to the 2007 Medicare CAHPS survey. *The Gerontologist, 51*(6), 843–855. https://doi-org.proxy.cc.uic.edu/10.1093/geront/gnr046.

Koch, A., & Blohm, M. (2009). Item nonresponse in the European social survey. *Ask: Research & Methods, 18*(1), 45–65. http://hdl.handle.net/1811/69564.

Kupek, E. (1998). Determinants of item nonresponse in a large national sex survey. *Archives of Sexual Behavior, 27*(6), 581–594. https://doi.org/10.1023/A:1018721100903.

Lee, S., Liu, M., & Hu, M. (2017). Relationship between future time orientation and item nonresponse on subjective probability questions: A cross-cultural analysis. *Journal of Cross-Cultural Psychology, 48*(5), 698–717. https://doi.org/10.1177/0022022117698572.

Lipps, O. (2007). Interviewer and respondent survey quality effects in a CATI panel. *Bulletin de Méthologie Sociologique, 95*, 5–25. https://journals.openedition.org/bms/392.

Little, R. J. A., & Rubin, D. B. (2002). Single imputation methods. *Statistical Analysis with Missing Data*. https://doi.org/10.1002/9781119013563.ch4.

Little, R. J. A., & Rubin, D. B. (2014). *Statistical analysis with missing data* (2nd ed.). New York: Wiley. https://onlinelibrary.wiley.com/doi/book/10.1002/9781119013563.

McKnight, P. E., McKnight, K. M., SIdani, S., & Figueredo, A. J. (2007). *Missing data: A gentle introduction*. New York: Guilford Press. https://www.guilford.com/books/Missing-Data/McKnight-McKnight-Sidani-Figueredo/9781593853938.

Messer, B. L., Edwards, M. L., & Dillman, D. A. (2012). Determinants of item nonresponse to web and mail respondents in three address-based mixed-mode surveys of the general public. *Survey Practice, 5*(2). http://citeseerx.ist.psu.edu/viewdoc/download;jsessionid=A45DB36A0B8BD2FBCC02FD762FEECAC9?Doi=10.1.1.673.8650&rep=rep1&type=pdf.

Messmer, D. J., & Seymour, D. T. (1982). The effects of branching on item nonresponse. *Public Opinion Quarterly, 46*(2), 270–277. https://doi.org/10.1086/268718.

Mulder, F. (1977). *The daily power game*. Leiden: Martinus Nijhoff. https://www.springer.com/us/book/9781468469530.

Owens, L., Johnson, T. P., & O'Rourke, D. (2001). Culture and item nonresponse in health surveys. *Seventh Conference on Health Survey Research Methods*. DHHS publication no. (PHS) 01-1013. Hyattsville, MD: National Center for Health Statistics. https://www.cdc.gov/nchs/data/hsrmc/hsrmc_7th_proceedings_1999.pdf.

Patsiurko, N., Campbell, J. L., & Hall, J. A. (2012). Measuring cultural diversity: Ethnic, linguistic and religious fractionalization in the OECD. *Ethnic and Racial Studies, 35*(2), 195–217. https://doi.org/10.1080/01419870.2011.579136.

Pickery, J., & Loosveldt, G. (1998). The impact of respondent and interviewer characteristics on the number of "no opinion" answers. *Quality & Quantity, 32*(1), 31–45. https://doi.org/10.1023/A:1004268427793.

Putnam, R. D. (2007). E pluribus unum: Diversity and community in the twenty-first century the 2006 Johan Skytte prize lecture. *Scandinavian Political Studies, 30*(2), 137–174. https://doi.org/10.1111/j.1467-9477.2007.00176.x.

Rässler, S., & Riphahn, R. T. (2006). Survey item nonresponse and its treatment. *Modern Econometric Analysis: Surveys on Recent Developments.* https://doi.org/10.1007/3-540-32693-6_15.

Riphahn, R. T., & Serfling, O. (2005). Item non-response on income and wealth questions. *Empirical Economics, 30*, 521–538. https://doi.org/10.1007/s00181-005-0247-7.

Schafer, J. L., & Graham, J. W. (2002). Missing data: Our view of the state of the art. *Psychological Methods, 7*(2), 147–177. https://doi.org/10.1037/1082-989X.7.2.147.

Shoemaker, P. J., Eichholz, M., & Skewes, E. A. (2002). Item nonresponse: Distinguishing between don't know and refuse. *International Journal of Public Opinion Research, 14*(2), 193–201. https://doi.org/10.1093/ijpor/14.2.193.

Stoop, I. A. L. (2016). Unit nonresponse. In C. Wolf, D. Joye, T. W. Smith, & Y.-c. Fu (Eds.), *The SAGE handbook of survey methodology* (pp. 409–424). Los Angeles: Sage.

Struminskaya, B., Weyandt, K., & Bosnjak, M. (2015). The effects of questionnaire completion using mobile devices on data quality. Evidence from a probability-based general population panel. *Methods, Data, Analyses, 9*(2), 261–292. https://www.gesis.org/fileadmin/upload/forschung/publikationen/zeitschriften/mda/Vol.9_Heft_2/MDA_Vol9_2015-2_Struminskaya.pdf.

Tourangeau, R., Rips, L. J., & Rasinski, K. (2000). *The psychology of survey response.* Cambridge: Cambridge University Press. https://www.cambridge.org/core/books/the-psychology-of-survey-response/46DE3D6F7C1399BCDC78D9441C630372.

Triandis, H. C. (1995). *Individualism and collectivism.* Boulder, CO: Westview Press. https://www.routledge.com/Individualism-AndCollectivism/Triandis/p/book/9780813318509.

Tu, S.-H., & Liao, P.-S. (2007). Social distance, respondent cooperation and item nonresponse in sex survey. *Quality & Quantity, 41*(2), 177–199. https://doi-org.proxy.cc.uic.edu/10.1007/s11135-007-9088-0.

Turner, C. F., Lessler, J. T., George, B. J., Hubbard, M. L., & Witt, M. B. (1992). Effects of mode of administration and wording on data quality. In C. F. Turner, J. T. Lessler, & J. C. Gfroerer (Eds.), *Survey measurement of drug use: Methodological studies* (pp. 221–243). Washington, DC.: National Institute of Drug Abuse, U.S. Department of Health and Human Services. http://qcpages.qc.cuny.edu/~cturner/TechPDFs/NIDA_BOOK.pdf.

Vandenplas, C., Loosveldt, G., Beullens, K., & Denies, K. (2018). Are interviewer effects on interview speed related to interviewer effects on straight-lining tendency in the European social survey? An interviewer-related analysis. *Journal of Survey Statistics and Methodology, 6*(4), 516–538. https://doi.org/10.1093/jssam/smx034.

Vercruyssen, A., Wuyts, C., & Loosveldt, G. (2017). The effect of sociodemographic (mis)match between interviewers and respondents on unit and item nonresponse in Belgium. *Social Science Research, 67*, 229–238. https://doi.org/10.1016/j.ssresearch.2017.02.007.

Yan, T., Curtin, R., & Jans, M. (2010). Trends in income nonresponse over two decades. *Journal of Official Statistics, 26*(1), 145–164. https://www.scb.se/contentassets/ca21efb41fee47d293bbee5bf7be7fb3/trends-in-income-nonresponse-over-two-decades.pdf.

Chapter 9
The Measurement of Sexual Attraction and Gender Expression: Cognitive Interviews with Queer Women

Dana Garbarski and Dana LaVergne

Introduction

The measurement of sexual orientation and gender identity (SOGI) in surveys has gained increasing interest among survey practitioners and academic researchers, in order to reliably and validly measure the full scope of human experience as well as to enumerate and account for the range of issues surrounding some of the more vulnerable and marginalized populations in society. Best practices for asking SOGI questions have been collected and reported by a variety of working groups and researchers. In each of these sets of materials, the general consensus is that the best practice recommendations are preliminary and incomplete, requiring rigorous empirical examination across a range of populations and survey conditions. Importantly, much of the previous research focuses on the measurement of gender identity and sexual identity in surveys, with comparably little focus on best practices for the measurement of other dimensions gender and sexuality in surveys, such as gender expression and sexual attraction.

This study examines what underlies participants' answers to questions about gender expression and sexual attraction. We used cognitive interviewing, a method used by survey researchers to understand how respondents think about survey questions, to elicit this information, and followed a process of grounded theory coding (an inductive, iterative, and systematic procedure) to analyze what underlies participants' answers to these questions.

D. Garbarski (✉) · D. LaVergne
Loyola University Chicago, Chicago, IL, USA
e-mail: dgarbarski@luc.edu

Background

Survey Measurement of Sexual Orientation

Sexual orientation, like many of the axes of identity, is socially constructed, varying over time and across groups. Sexual orientation is conceived by researchers as a constellation of factors: most commonly identity, attraction, and behavior (Laumann et al. 1994; SMART 2009), but also factors such as contextual disclosure of sexual identity (Bulgar-Medina 2018) and various thoughts and feelings (Gordon and Silva 2015; van Anders 2015). Much of the focus in recent survey data collection efforts is on incorporating questions about *sexual identity*, e.g., "Do you consider yourself to be heterosexual, that is, straight, lesbian or gay, or bisexual?" Current research efforts seek to determine whether to allow respondents to choose just one option, have a forced choice set of response options, or a check-all-that-apply format (e.g., Brenner and Bulgar-Medina 2018). There is comparably little focus on *sexual attraction* and *sexual behavior*, which are also each key features of sexual orientation, related to yet distinct from sexual identity. Sexual attraction refers to physiological, sexual, or romantic desires and attachments to others. In surveys, questions on sexual attraction are asked in terms of the genders of persons to whom one is attracted, e.g., "People are different in their sexual attraction to other people. Which best describes your feelings? I am only attracted to females, mostly attracted to females, equally attracted to females and males, mostly attracted to males, only attracted to males, or I am not sure?" These are different from questions on sexual behavior, which refer to concrete sexual actions. In surveys the question is asked in terms of the types of person with whom one engages in sexual activity (which may be specific or broadly defined) within a particular point in time (ever, past year, past 5 years), e.g., "During your life with whom have you had sexual contact? I have never had sexual contact, females, males, females and males" (Federal Interagency Working Group 2016a). Clearly the gender binary is infused in these sexual orientation questions (as is the conflation between sex and gender), but these are current "best practice" versions used in large scale data collection efforts.

Sexual orientation is multifaceted at any given time as well as over the life course. The discrete facets of sexual orientation—identity, attraction, behavior—can be construed as separate continua on which individuals may be situated at a given point in the life course (van Anders 2015). The tension among capturing the complexity of lived experience at one point in time proliferates when wanting to capture it over the life course, e.g., someone can identify as bisexual who in the past 5 years has only had sexual encounters with a partner of another gender. When large scale data collection efforts minimize the dimensions sexuality, this may lead to undercounting and erasing segments of the population from the data. Furthermore, understanding of real risks to health may be obscured. For example, increasing evidence suggests that although sexual minorities are at increased risks for certain health outcomes, sexual identity may not be the best predictor of health disparities for sexual minorities (Brewster and Tillman 2012; Wolff et al. 2017), suggesting that data collection efforts must include a multifaceted understanding of sexual orientation in order to elucidate the pathways through which sexual minorities face increased health risks.

Survey Measurement of Gender

Research on the measurement of gender in survey research tends to be limited by the strong adherence to the gender binary, in which surveys conflate the concepts of sex and gender and assume gender can be easily determined by others, such as an interviewer (Westbrook and Saperstein 2015). Yet gender is more accurately understood as socially constructed: at a macro-level, gender is relational, a system of stratification that shapes interactions, resources, status, privilege, and power (Connell 2005; Courtenay 2000; Risman 2018); at a meso-level, "doing gender" indicates that the meanings and expressions of gender in myriad forms are performed, shaping and shaped by the structure in which they are embedded (Lorber 1994; Martin 2003; West and Zimmerman 1987). Although theoretical and analytic approaches may vary, the consensus among social scientists that study gender is that sex and gender are distinct and nonbinary. Moreover, how people identify in terms of sex or gender may not match the perception of others (Westbrook and Saperstein 2015).

The best-practice version for determining gender identity in surveys is a version that asks in two parts one's current gender identity, that is, their internal sense of gender (with response categories such as man, woman, trans man, trans woman, genderqueer, something else) and their assigned sex at birth ("What sex were you assigned at birth on your original birth certificate?") (The GenIUSS Group 2014). However, another key feature of the variation with which gender is lived, experienced, and has implications for one's everyday life is in terms of one's gender expression. Gender expression is the presentational dimension of gender, that is, how gender identity is displayed through appearance and enacted through behavior (Lorber 1994; Spence 2011; The GenIUSS Group 2014). For example, measuring gender expression that differs from societal expectations for one's ascribed gender in terms of "nonconformity" is associated with mental health and health risk behaviors for adolescents (Lowry et al. 2018).[1] Gender expression has mainly been measured in surveys in terms of how it is perceived by others, although recent research considers one's own perception of their gender expression (Magliozzi et al. 2016; Moore 2006; Smyth and Olson 2020). Overall, although gender expression is a distinct facet of gender, likely useful for understanding a range of inequalities in

---

[1] Others have argued (The GenIUSS Group 2014; Lowry et al. 2018) that this concept may be particularly useful for adolescents and young adults who have not formed an explicit gender identity—although we might argue that young adults are the agents of emergent identity formation and understandings thereof.

well-being by gender and sexual orientation, survey measurement of gender expression has received comparably little research focus.

Cognitive Interviewing and Grounded Theory

This study seeks to contribute the literature on the measurement of SOGI in surveys by examining what underlies participants' answers to questions about gender expression and sexual attraction: explanations of how the survey questions and different facets of gender expression and sexual attraction are experienced, conceptualized, interpreted, and integrated to formulate answers to the questions. We used cognitive interviewing to elicit this information from our participants and followed a process of grounded theory coding to analyze what underlies participants' answers to these questions.

In cognitive interviewing, the respondent answers a survey question while also providing the interviewer information about what they are thinking about (concurrent think aloud) or were thinking about (retrospective) when they answer the question; additional probes might ask respondents how they define key words or phrases from the survey question, why they chose one answer over another, how difficult it was to use the response options, and so forth. Cognitive interviewing is often used to discover problems with and repair survey questions, although it is increasingly used with the goal toward understanding how a given question measures a construct of interest; many studies, such as ours, do both (Willis 2015).

Although the cognitive interviewing protocol is structured, the synthesis and reduction of data into an interpretable form requires the use of one or more of the many methods that social scientists use to analyze qualitative data (Willis 2015). One common approach is thematic coding that derives from the grounded theory paradigm. In general, grounded theory refers to an approach to research in which theory is the result of the project, and the full range of themes underlying the data and their relationship emerge from the data in an inductive, iterative, and systematic process that includes processes such as theoretical sampling and inductive coding through constant comparison, such that the researcher does not begin with a predisposed theoretical framework in mind.[2] Our application of grounded theory methodology extends to coding, in which analytic codes and themes are identified during an inductive, iterative, and systematic coding process.

As noted by Willis (2015), the main benefit of a bottom-up thematic coding approach for analyzing cognitive interview data is its close fit to the data and description of full question function (as opposed to more top-down coding with pre-existing coding schemes, which may focus on more reparative codes and do not

---

[2]Note that distinct perspectives and applications of grounded theory emerged from the work that started with Glaser and Strauss (1967) then branched to Glaser (1978) and Strauss and Corbin (1998), with other distinct applications emerging (e.g., Charmaz 2006).

foresee what might emerge in that set of data). Its strength is its weakness, though, in the lack of generalizability—what is observed in one context may not emerge in others—and the loss of information through coding, which occurs with most data reduction strategies that summarize data. Overall, the process of grounded theory coding represents an important component of the survey researcher's toolkit to allow for a fuller understanding of social phenomena and ultimately better measurement thereof.

Methods

Data

The term "queer" has many meanings in discourse including the reclaimed use to describe either or both gender and sexual identities (Glick et al. 2018). We used "queer" in our recruitment tool as an umbrella grouping for sexual and gender minority women, as participants for this study were recruited as part of a broader study on the use of contraception among queer women. In the current study, we performed cognitive interviews with 16 self-identified queer women, as we expected that by using this broad framing from which to draw a sample ("queer women"), participants would show variability and nuance in considering dimensions of gender expression and sexual attraction. Participants were recruited with flyers on social media platforms such as Facebook's Chicago Queer Exchange, Chicago Intersectional Queer Exchange, and Chicago Queer Friendship. Interviews were conducted in a semi-public location of the participant's choice. Fourteen of the sixteen interviews were conducted in person, and two interviews were conducted via Skype with participants who had seen the recruitment online but were no longer living in the Chicago area. At the conclusion of the interview, participants received a $30 Amazon gift card.

During cognitive interviews, the interviewer (DL) read a series of survey questions measuring facets of sexual orientation and gender identity. After participants responded to a survey question, they were asked a series of probes on what they were thinking about when answering the question, why they chose their answer compared to answers in close proximity, and what key phrases meant to them, before moving on to the next survey item (Willis 2015). At the time of the interview, participants were given a packet with the questions (but not corresponding response scales) and were instructed to read if they forgot the question (the two participants interviewed on Skype were not given the questions). Each page of the packet corresponded to the question being posed, so that participants could not read ahead to the next question.

During the in-depth interview, participants were asked to describe in their own words their sexuality and gender identity as well as what labels they use to describe each of these. Of the sixteen participants, ten were cisgender women, while six were genderqueer or nonbinary (Table 9.1). In terms of sexual identity, seven participants expressed attraction to multiple genders (bisexual or pansexual), eight participants

Table 9.1 Participants' case identification and answers to question 3 and question 4 by gender identity

	Question 3: Gender expression in appearance, style, and dress		Question 4: Gender expression in mannerisms: (walk, talk, and gesture)	
	Cisgender women	Genderqueer or nonbinary	Cisgender women	Genderqueer or nonbinary
Mostly masculine			1	13
Somewhat or mostly masculine[a]		7		
Somewhat masculine	1	4, 13	14	8
Semi masculine[a]		6		
Equal	2	8	5	4
Slightly feminine[a]		15		
Somewhat feminine	5, 9, 14, 16		3, 9, 11, 12, 16	15
Feminine[a]				6
Mostly feminine	3, 10, 12		10	7
Very feminine	11			
Don't know			2	

[a]Answer participant provided is not one of the response options from the survey question

indicated they were queer, and two were lesbian (Table 9.2).[3] All but one participant was white, limiting our ability to draw conclusions about how these survey questions and the concepts underlying them might operate in racial/ethnic minority populations (Bulgar-Medina 2018; Moore 2006; Wolff et al. 2017). The participants were young adults, very much part of the Millennial and later generation with different understandings about gender and sexual identity compared to prior generations (Risman 2018).[4] Finally, these participants lived in or were tied to the city of Chicago, which might influence how they think about issues of identity and attraction (e.g., Silva 2017).

---

[3]Although some respondents indicated multiple sexual identity categories during the in-depth interview, we categorized them with one group for the purposes of analysis based on information they discussed during the in-depth interview and the cognitive interview. Participant 4 indicated an overarching alignment with the queer community and consistently noted academic considerations of queer politics, thus we placed them with "queer" in categorizing sexual identity. Participants 9, 10, and 16 all noted both queer and bisexual sexual identity. We characterize each as "bisexual" in terms of their sexual identity, as they each seem to use bisexual to specifically refer to their own identity and queer when speaking about community membership. Participant 4 indicated both cisgender and genderqueer identities.

[4]Participants ranged in age from 19 to 35 but were mainly in their twenties, with a median age of 24 and mean age of 24.75.

Table 9.2 Participants' case identification and answers to question 6 by sexual identity

	Bisexual or pansexual	Queer	Lesbian
Mostly attracted to males	10		
Equally attracted to males and females	1, 3, 12, 16	6, 15	
Mostly attracted to females	8	2, 4	11
Mostly attracted to females and not sure[a]	9		
Only attracted to females		14	5
Not sure		13	
Don't know[a]		7	

[a]Answer participant provided is not one of the response options from the survey question

Analytic Strategy

The cognitive interviews were transcribed in Microsoft Excel, with each cell comprising a turn of talk, which is one uninterrupted stream of talk from a participant. Our coding of the transcripts was iterative. Consistent with the constant comparative method in grounded theory (Glaser and Strauss 1967; Willis 2015), we deployed a bottom-up process of identifying the codes and the underlying concepts (i.e., themes) as they emerged from the data (that is, not relying on preconceived notions and coding schemes). We examined whether existing codes fit or needed to be revised with the addition of new data (new data being cases that had been previously interviewed and transcribed but had not yet been coded). Our coding focused both on the content of the answers (i.e., the substantive answers to the survey questions and probes) as well as the sequential structure and features of the interaction (Garbarski et al. 2016). We each independently developed codes for the text included in each turn of talk. We then built our coding scheme inductively through negotiated agreement as we considered a few cases at a time. This group consensus approach was particularly useful in examining phrases with multiple meanings and allowed us to vet inferences about what participants might have meant by something they said. As we made changes to our coding scheme, we returned to previously coded cases and compared them with the evolving coding scheme, recoding as needed. After following this process with each of the three questions for all 16 cases, we reconciled and revised both the coding scheme and coded cases to arrive at finalized versions of each.[5]

---

[5]We do not follow another approach common within grounded theory methodology and the constant comparative method: theoretical sampling, in which participants are purposively selected as indicated by the emerging conceptual codes in the data (Glaser and Strauss 1967).With theoretical sampling, data collection and analysis are confounded in that some analysis has occurred that indicates who should be interviewed next (as well as potential revisions to the interview script) (Willis 2015); this is not a problem with the method but something to be accounted for in analysis. Since our respondents were interviewed prior to data analysis, we did not follow the theoretical sampling that can be part of the iterative process of sampling and analysis in the grounded theory methodology. In this way, we are similar to other analyses of cognitive interviews that use the constant comparative method for coding but not sampling [see Willis (2015) for examples].

Results

Gender Expression: Appearance, Style, and Dress

Question 3: *A person's appearance, style, and dress may affect the way people think of them. Overall, how do you think people would describe your appearance, style, and dress?*

Very feminine, mostly feminine, somewhat feminine, equally feminine and masculine, somewhat masculine, mostly masculine, very masculine?

The participants ranged in their answers to Question 3, and although we cannot discern a statistical difference, cisgender women appear more likely to be on the feminine side of the scale, and those who are genderqueer or nonbinary tend to be on the masculine side of the scale (Table 9.1).

When participants report what they are thinking about when answering this question, all but two focus on features of their self-presentation, in which participants describe how they present themselves to the world. These features of self-presentation take myriad forms spanning clothing, accessories, and hair.[6] When participants describe what they are thinking about when they rate their appearance, style, and dress on this scale, however, they move beyond simply listing these aspects of gendered self-presentation and integrate them, particularly the components that are seemingly in opposition. We define *integrated* aspects of self-presentation as when two features of self-presentation are presented in opposition to one another, either based on societal expectations or based on the way in which the participant is describing it. Participants often describe this integration occurring (1) across contexts, (2) across time, and (3) within a given context or point in time. Over one third of participants mention integration of self-presentation across contexts; all of these participants were cisgender women. Participant 5 said "sometimes I look pretty ugly and like I look kind of butch a lot of time cause of my oh the way I put myself together sometimes um but other times you know I'm taking into account like wha like you know at Christmas dinner I looked very feminine it's like I have you know taken the average tally of every single time I get dressed yeah." She describes fluidity or variation in her gendered self-presentation across social settings and describes her estimation strategy in answering the question. Distinct but related, two participants discussed how their gender presentation changes across time, that is, "by day." Finally, integration of gendered self-presentation is described as occurring simultaneously, that is, *within* a given context or point in time: "my clothes are men's clothes and I dress like a man my nails are painted and I don't know I'm

---

[6]Gender presentation varies for and is interpreted through the lens of particular audiences and contexts in previous research on sexual minorities. In some cases, certain presentations take on a particular gendered meaning based on the audience and context (Luzzatto and Gvion 2004; Moore 2006); in others, presentation is used to communicate or disclose one's sexual identity (Bulgar-Medina 2018; Hebl et al. 2002). Indeed, distinctive looks to communicate queer identities have increasingly become both more diverse and mainstream.

wearing more earrings than I think is masculine to be wearing" (Participant 13). One quarter of participants described presentation as integrated within a given time period or context in terms of masculine and feminine (or feminine and "less than feminine" for two participants) and used language to present it as such. Overall, rather than just listing features of self-presentation, participants made it clear how these features were related in their self-presentation, integrating seemingly disparate components with respect to their appearance across and within context and time.

The response dimension is quantification of masculine or feminine gender presentation (in this version of the question, others' perceptions of one's gender presentation). "Feminine" and "masculine" are set up as bipolar opposites along the same unidimensional continuum (Bem 1993; Connell 2005; Constantinople 1973; Lorber 1994; Risman 2018) and the response options indicate the amount of masculinity or femininity with the midpoint signaling equal amounts of each. However, the response scale need not be constructed to reify the duality in which masculine and feminine are defined in opposition as relational statuses (e.g., dominance and subordination). Indeed, psychology has long studied masculine and feminine personality traits as two distinct dimensions, albeit not necessarily divorced from one's sex characteristics or gender identity (Constantinople 1973; Bem 1993; Risman 2018; Zucker et al. 2006). Our participants show that at an individual level, gender expression via appearance may integrate components of masculine and feminine presentation (relying on commonsense understandings of a given time and place) beyond the limited range of an "equal" response option. Some participants indicated high levels of both masculine and feminine presentation simultaneously, and some varied these presentations by context. It is an empirical question whether depolarizing masculine and feminine from the same response dimension may allow for respondents to more fully locate their gender presentation in a survey (see also Smyth and Olson 2020), but one that is worth exploring for both conceptual and empirical reasons.

In addition to the temporal fluidity of self-presentation noted above, temporality figures into what participants described when rating how others perceive their appearance, style, and dress. In particular, participants used words that mark the time frame they considered when answering the question as the present, such as "lately." They also signaled more specific time frames such as "past six months" and broader swaths of time such as "in the past." For example, Participant 9 said, "um this is something I have been thinking about a lot recently and I just like don't know um but my hair is long like I wear dresses and stuff but I also feel like I don't dress like very hyper-feminine enough like not as much as I did when I was younger um," indicating a change in presentation over some period of the life course from when they were younger to the present. Participant 1 linked the present to the past through a narrative of socialization: "I have never been overly feminine with things even though my parents spent years and years making me wear pink lacy frilly stuff," drawing on information from childhood to situate their answer within the current survey question.

The questions about gender expression are explicitly asking about others' perceptions, yet only one third of participants explicitly mentioned evidence of others' perceptions while answering. When they did, participants often shared examples of others' perceptions in terms of being perceived, viewed, or read as a man or a woman. Participant 7, who is genderqueer, noted "some people just like assume that I'm a man when they see me like out in public which is like a little safer feeling than if they were to assume that I was like a woman." The issue of safety voiced by this participant is important in terms of the queer community being a target for violence (Corteen 2002). Participant 12 answered the question as "mostly feminine" and was thinking "um mostly how like people have perceived me in the past...um just because I think that it's not really a question when someone looks at me"—for her, her gender expression was obvious and should be perceived by others as such. Participant 15, who is genderqueer, highlighted the complexity of a question that asks about appearance, style, and dress with respect to inferring the perceptions of others, an issue we turn to below: "usually no matter how masculine I dress I still get read as a woman." Our participants did not mention explicitly who the audience or "other" is that is judging their appearance, and the referent could be general or specific, public or private, in certain spaces, particular to one's community, coworkers, family members, or friends, among others—we have no way to discern this from the information provided, an important omission that needs to be assessed in future research (Bulgar-Medina 2018; Moore 2006).

Furthermore, these explicit mentions of others' perceptions were in terms of whether the participant was perceived to be a man or a woman and not in terms of variation in femininity or masculinity, the latter of which is what the question is asking. This highlights a potential difficulty in the task that is unique to these questions about gender expression that center on the perceptions of others—not only is the evidence of the perceptions of others far less than the evidence participants have for the things they do to present themselves as feminine or masculine, but the evidence participants do have speaks to perceptions of kind rather than variation in degrees of gender expression.

Although some previous research tends to treat gender expression as a broader concept (Clark et al. 2005; Lorber 1994; Moore 2006), Wylie et al. (2010) suggested that gender expression consists of at least two dimensions: gender expression of appearance and mannerisms. Our participants indicated further distinctions in the definitions of each of these defined subtopics, with implications for how they answered each question. All but two participants were asked what "appearance, style, and dress" meant to them.[7] In all but two of these cases, participants reported clothing and accessories. In addition, most participants reported more than one additional feature they considered, such as hair, makeup, and features of one's physical body. For example, Participant 8 reports "um style and dress meant like haircuts and what outfits you wear appearance was more face structures to me um yeah more like bone structure." Indeed, conceptual precision on the definition of each term—appearance, style, and dress—or whether each term is used to introduce

---

[7]Sometimes probes were skipped if the interviewer thought the participant had answered the probe in another part of their answer.

an overarching definition of how people are visually gendered would clarify for respondents and researchers what is actually being measured. It is interesting to note that almost all participants who are genderqueer, nonbinary, or describe their sexual identity as queer identify hair as a defining feature of appearance, style, and dress.

At the end of this first series of probes, participants were asked what "feminine" and then "masculine" means to them. About half of participants offered definitions of feminine or masculine in concrete terms using specific examples of types of clothing, makeup, and hair ("oh long hair makeup heels dresses," Participant 1), while about half redefined the meanings of feminine or masculine in more abstract terms, such as "um female presenting" (Participant 8). In most of their definitions of feminine or masculine, participants invoked the term "stereotype" or related terms, such as "traditionally masculine clothes" (Participant 4) and "um things that are normally associated with more male-centric fashion" (Participant 14). Overall, participants used commonsense typologies of gender expression in order to use the response options (Connell 2005; Constantinople 1973), and the more abstract definitions indicated that participants understood feminine (masculine) in this question to mean something along the lines of "having qualities or appearance traditionally associated with women (men)."

Defining masculine compared to feminine stems from the order of the probes in which feminine is presented first. About one third of participants defined masculine with a comparative statement that explicitly or implicitly referred to how they defined feminine, and about one third made reference to the content of a prior answer more abstractly. For example: "the same a more like boyish look" (Participant 6) had both a reference to the answer to the prior question ("the same") and a comparative statement "more boyish" compared to Participant 1, in which the participant made just comparative statements ("uh maybe more uh shorter hair um pants less jewelry") of "shorter" and "less."

Finally, with this first question on gender expression, the few issues explicitly raised by participants concerned the response options, in terms of the number ("I think very feminine was that one of them? Sorry there were a lot of choices" Participant 11) and the modifiers of the response dimension ("I don't even know what would mostly or very I don't I just picked somewhat" Participant 4). Participants 1 and 2 indicated that their choices were somewhat arbitrary. In addition, requests for clarification and repetition on the response options existed for Questions 3 and 4 (gender expression of mannerisms), indicating that the response scale might need to be clarified for survey respondents. The few comments on the difficulty or complexity of the task in the transcripts occurred with Questions 3 and 4. Taken together, these results indicate some difficulty with the question in general and with using the response scale in particular, suggesting modifications are needed to improve the measurement properties of survey questions on gender expression.

Suggestions Based on the above analysis, we propose a series of considerations for improving the measurement of gender expression in appearance, style, and dress. The goal of these refinements is to increase the consistency in how respondents understand all parts of the question (Fowler 1995) so that variation in answers reflects variation in respondents' perceptions of their gender expression through their appearance. In other words, the question should communicate the same thing to respondents as much as possible.

1. A summative question that asks respondents to consider something "overall" or "on average" does not fit when one's gender expression displayed by their appearance varies depending on temporality, context, or audience.[8] Adding a reference period (e.g., "in the last year," "currently") holds constant one aspect of potential fluidity (longer-term temporality, not when it varies by day) but not the others. Depolarizing the response options (discussed next) should improve measurement for respondents who vary their presentation across and within contexts and time, as they will not have to "choose" just one side of the scale, although it does not completely mitigate the issue. However, that this one question likely summarizes over various aspects of fluidity is not necessarily a bug in the question but rather a feature to be aware of, particularly if researchers want to explore holding constant one or more of these aspects.

2. As noted above, we suggest that the response continuum be depolarized into two unipolar response dimensions, one for masculine presentation and one for feminine presentation, for both conceptual and empirical reasons. These could be two separate questions (Wilson et al. 2014), or one question with both response scale presented together with the question (Magliozzi et al. 2016)—underneath the question when visual, or letting respondents know both are going to be presented when aural.

3. Participants indicated response processing issues when using the response options. Vague quantifiers such as these specify relative positions within ordinal response sets (Schaeffer 1991), and we as the authors think that the end of the scale is not well distinguished from second, as "mostly" and "very" are synonyms.[9] We suggest the following response options based on research on scaling of quantifiers (Beckstead 2014; Dobson and Mothersill 1979): "not at all feminine," "a little feminine," "somewhat feminine," "very feminine" (and the same for "masculine").[10]

---

[8]Wylie et al. (2010) propose using the phrase "on average" in gender expression questions to aid in respondents' cognitive averaging and integration of their perceived gender expression across these different domains. We used the term "overall" so as not to predispose respondents to a particular estimation strategy; another option could be "in general" to be even less specific. Other sorts of response strategies include signaling a modal response, such as "most of the time," or typicality, such as "on a typical day," and each of these might lead to different considerations among respondents for whom their appearance varies depending on context, time, or audience.

[9]Although "mostly" and "very" are considered synonyms that indicate a higher values of what is being measured, participants also could have had trouble with the scale because the verbal quantifiers mix dimensions: "mostly" is a quantifier denoting the amount of a whole, whereas "very" is a qualifier denoting value.

[10]The English language has a decided lack of adverbial quantifiers between "somewhat" and "very." "Pretty" and "quite" are two alternatives, although "pretty" may be complicated given that the question asks about appearance and "quite" sounds formal. Based on theory and research in

4. Although we did not empirically examine an option for "not sure" in Questions 3 and 4, its use in Question 6 indicates that "not sure" could be added in order to parse in part uncertainty from other potential causes of item nonresponse (Clark et al. 2005).
5. We suggest in visual presentations that the response scale start with "not at all" (Bradburn et al. 2004; Garbarski et al. 2019), yet it is an empirical question whether to randomly assign which scale is presented first or keep with the common practice of starting with the end of the scale that matches the respondent's gender in terms of the level and types of errors in measurement that might be introduced (see Discussion section).[11] In terms of response scale orientation, we suggest horizontal for paper and web administration so respondents can perceive the response options as a continuum, although we note that web administration may optimize with vertical layouts for smartphones and tablets.
6. Respondents do not attend to the "others' perceptions" component of the question; rather, they seem more likely to convey what they are doing to present themselves. We suggest that the "others' perceptions" component adds a layer of comprehension and processing difficulties and thus variability in terms of what respondents are attending to when answering the question. Since others' perceptions of gender expression is a focus of research, we argue that it could be included as a separate question asked after a question that first asks respondents to report their self-perception of their gender expression, since this is the information that respondents appear to report on both first and most often.
7. We suggest a definition of gender expression that does not speak to its effects, and thus removing the phrase "may affect the way people think of them." As some research shows that those who are visibly nonconforming are at an increased risk for poor health and discriminatory treatment by others (The GenIUSS Group 2014; Lowry et al. 2018), priming respondents to think of negative treatment due to their gender expression might influence answers to the question and thus its distribution and association with outcomes of interest. (Note this does not derive from the data but is based on the authors' review of the question.)
8. Defining "feminine" and "masculine" for respondents has been suggested (Wilson et al. 2014), although our participants seem to use commonsense definitions of masculine or feminine presentation or do so by example.
9. The question could clarify whether "appearance, style, and dress" is meant to be a conceptual umbrella of mutually defining synonyms or conceptually distinct

---

survey methodology (Kronsick and Presser 2010), we do not recommend rating scales with only endpoint labels and numbers for the intermediate response options (c.f. Magliozzi et al. 2016; Wilson et al. 2014).

[11]One common practice with the bipolar scale is to present the feminine side of the scale first if the respondent is presumed a woman and the masculine side if the respondent is presumed a man. Another practice is to present the same side of the scale to everyone regardless of gender in a paper-administered survey (e.g., Youth Risk Behavior Survey).

terms. This could be done by listing examples after the phrase as a whole, using the more general "appearance" followed by examples (omitting "style and dress" but including examples of these things), or including examples after each word.

Gender Expression—Mannerisms (Walk, Talk, and Gesture)

Question 4: *A person's mannerisms (such as the way they walk, talk, and gesture) may affect the way people think of them. Overall, how do you think people would describe your mannerisms?*

Very feminine, mostly feminine, somewhat feminine, equally feminine and masculine, somewhat masculine, mostly masculine, very masculine?

Participants' answers to Question 4 spanned more of the range of response options (for both gender identity groups) compared to Question 3 (Table 9.1). This is interesting to consider in terms of how some participants discuss the topics in Question 4 as unconscious and immutable, while facets of appearance, style, and dress in Question 3 are discussed as modifiable forms of self-presentation.

One issue that participants raised with Question 4 is how mannerisms are not just gendered but also linked to queerness in myriad ways. This highlights the heteronormativity underlying the commonsense understandings of "masculinity" and "femininity" (Bem 1981; Connell 2005; Constantinople 1973). Predicated on the gender binary, heteronormativity is the assumption that heterosexuality is the default societal standard. Here, heteronormativity added complexity to the notion of answering questions about "masculinity" and "femininity" in "walking, talking, and gesturing" among participants—notably, in a way that answering questions about appearance, style, and dress did not. One third of our participants discussed this in terms of thinking about "gay men," either in abstract terms as an example of something that complicated the notion of masculine and feminine, or in concrete terms in which the participant described their presentation as aligned with that of gay men or perceived by others to be as such. Participant 4, who is both cisgender and genderqueer, highlighted the complexity of the issue: "I don't know I mean I understand that there are like gender mannerism right? Like people manspreading on the train or like women not taking up a lot of space or I don't know I even think of some masculine mannerisms like uh things that can be like attributed to gay men even though those are feminine mannerisms um but yeah I don't know it's like I mean certainly there are gender mannerism but like that's a mixed bag and I don't think I'm doing any of those particularly." With Question 4 then, the taken-for-granted understandings of gender are depolarized, queered, or at least starting to be grappled with in a multidimensional way. It is interesting to note that half of the participant who are genderqueer or nonbinary brought this up, and fewer cisgender women raised the issue.

About one third of participants—all but one were cisgender women—mentioned how at least some of their or others' mannerisms might be unconscious or learned from others around them: "I don't try to outwardly be feminine you know but I feel like just in who I am it just comes out like that...I don't try to change anything" (Participant 12).[12] Related to walking, talking, and gesturing as being unconscious, Participant 2, a cisgender woman, highlights the complexity of understanding gendered mannerisms in terms of the dimensionality linked to queerness and socialization: "I don't even think about like what men like cisman or ciswomen like what straight people do because it's like to them it's so I guess for me it's so natural for what they should be doing their mannerisms whereas like um queer men or women or transman or women are growing into that and so like what they see as femme or masc um and what they feel in that direction is really like where I perceive um the femininity or masculinity of manner mannerism." In other words, what is a masculine or feminine mannerism is defined by those for whom the mannerism might not have been engrained through socialization starting from (before) birth. About one third of participants described socialization as figuring into how they or others might learn to walk, talk, or gesture a certain way when they describe what they were thinking about when answering the question: "oh everyone's been telling me since I was very little that I do not behave in a way that is ladylike" (Participant 1). It is interesting to note that three of these four participants chose "mostly masculine" or "somewhat masculine" for their answer.

Participants were asked what "walk, talk, and gesture" meant to them, and over half provided separate definitions of these components of mannerisms rather than one definition of mannerisms more generally: "I mean walk would be like you know gait the way the hips and feet are moving talk both the vocabulary choices and um the like inflections and the tone um and gesture is like mostly like hand and arm movements or like way people the way people might say it or move around" (Participant 7). This indicates that participants saw each of these as separate components, and the integration of answering how "masculine" or "feminine" each of these is could be further complicated when summarizing across one's life course and understandings of each. About half the participants who were asked to describe what "walk, talk, and gesture" meant defined "talk" in terms of vocal characteristics (Participant 7's quote above), while slightly fewer—all of whom were cisgender women—considered interactions with others: "um kind of like how you like come off and carry yourself and uh yeah like how you interact with other people" (Participant 9); Participant 14 noted both voice and interaction. This shows that participants were making distinctions within the concept of "talk," indicating it may require further specification in its definition. Overall, participants indicated that with respect to walking, talking, and gesturing, there may be distinctions in the definitions of each, with implications for how respondents answer Question 4.

---

[12]Only one participant discussed consciously modifying their mannerisms: Participant 11, a cisgender woman, stated, "um when I was younger I tried to be very masculine and very like sort of aggressive way like masculine in the sense of being uh not just physically aggressive but like like aggressive in the way I talked and uh sort of taking up a lot of space that sort of thing. But at the same time I always sort of walked and moved in a way that a lot of women do and then like actively tried not to and then it's just a mess I guess."

Participants were again asked what "feminine" and "masculine" meant to them with Question 4. Over half of participants offered definitions of "feminine" and "masculine" in concrete terms using examples of types of mannerisms ("um it's like hard to explain um like higher a slightly higher voice um inflections that are I don't know tend to be nicer um words going up at the end like that," Participant 7), while about one third redefined the meaning of feminine or masculine in more abstract terms. As with Question 3, participants invoked the term "stereotype" or related terms in many of their definitions of feminine or masculine for Question 4, in this case for about one third of participants.

"Taking up space" was a phrase used by one quarter of participants when describing their mannerisms or defining mannerisms as feminine or masculine in the context of this question: "[women] not taking up that much space" (Participant 4); "the guy on the train who's taking up three seats and who's playing music out loud on his phone" (Participant 11). Men's entitlement in social spaces has long been acknowledged in academic research (Henley 1977) and the phrase "taking up space" in particular has increasingly crept into popular culture to refer to stance, proximity to others, and body size. This sort of "presence" may not necessarily be invoked in behaviors such as walking, talking, or gesturing, but rather in sitting, standing, and body positioning as described by our participants. Thus, some of our participants considered gendered nonverbal gestures beyond those listed in the question when answering, which aligns with the recommendation for conceptual precision outlined below.

Suggestions In addition to the recommendations listed for Question 3 (gender expression in appearance), one additional recommendation arises for Question 4 (gender expression in mannerisms) with respect to defining the key concepts.

1. "Mannerisms" is used as the conceptual umbrella in Question 4, which is then further defined by the examples "walk, talk, and gesture." However, "mannerisms" potentially restricts and confounds the concepts considered, since it is a synonym for "gesture" and its varying definitions includes phrases such as "habitual" and "idiosyncrasy." The current conceptualization appears to signal more than simply walking, talking, and gesturing, encompassing presence within interactional spaces ("taking up space" while "standing" and "sitting"). We propose that the intent and understanding of the question may be more broadly construed as "body language," but can be communicated by explicitly listing the dimensions as is done here without the use of a conceptual umbrella term. In addition, we see at least two interpretations of "talk" that may need further refinement: vocal characteristics and how one interacts with others. Considering what participants indicated about what this question means to them in terms of gendered components of body language, we propose to communicate the intent of the question by defining through example, that is, listing each component of body language separately so all respondents consider them when answering the question: "Overall, how would you (how would others) describe how you walk, talk, sit, stand, and gesture?" Furthermore, one could add "interact with others" to this list depending on whether investigators are interested in further distinguishing from what talking and gesturing may communicate to respondents.

Sexual Attraction

Question 6: *People are different in their sexual attraction to other people. Which best describes your feelings?*

Are you only attracted to males, mostly attracted to males, equally attracted to males and females, mostly attracted to females, only attracted to females, or are you not sure?

Like the questions on gender expression in appearance and mannerisms, the response options for the question on sexual attraction are presented as a bipolar scale in which male and female are at opposite ends of the spectrum (Table 9.2). The response dimension is quantification of the amount sexual attraction to males and females, posed as a unidimensional construct on a bipolar scale in which attraction spans from only being attracted to males on one end, only being attracted to females on the other, and the midpoint signals equal attraction to males and females. When answering Question 6 and its first probe, participants described features of their attraction as well as issues with the question, how they chose among response options, and their response processing more generally.

Unlike the questions on gender expression, several participants (almost half) indicated issues with the subject of the sexual attraction questions in terms of the gender binary. This occurred both in terms of more abstract problems raised, e.g., "I feel like there are other genders that are left out of that question" (Participant 16), as well as an issue for how the participant's lived experience mapped onto the question, e.g., "um I want to say like not sure just because I feel like a lot of my attraction is to people who are like outside of the gender binary so I don't really know how to define it there" (Participant 7, who had indicated their sexual identity was "queer" during the in-depth interview). Similarly, the use of the terms "males" and "females" conflates understandings of "gender" and "sex," an issue raised by one quarter of participants: "I wanna know what you mean by males versus females I guess cause it could just be like body parts that sort of thing which to me doesn't really make the gender of a person versus like I'm attracted to women who tend to be more feminine more fitting that idea of feminine that I have" (Participant 11). How the response options are formatted sets up attraction up as relative to only two objects of attraction (male/man or female/woman), which does not allow for one to place themselves in terms of attraction to persons with other identities and reifies reductive understandings of sex/gender and the gender binary.

When we coded for markers of uncertainty during the answering of each survey question, only two participants expressed uncertainty while answer Question 6, compared to six participants each while answering Questions 3 and 4.[13] Thus, although

---

[13] We coded for the presence of the following features of the interaction that may indicate various forms of processing and difficulties in answering the survey questions. These each may indicate grappling with the task at hand or the mismatch of the task with one's lived experience: disfluencies tokens ("um," "uh") and markers of uncertainty: mitigating phrases ("probably," "I think") and "don't know" as an answer or mitigating phrase.

participants provided us with information and feedback on the underlying purpose of the sexual attraction question and how to clarify the scope of the question, they did not express verbal markers of uncertainty on where to situate themselves. Almost one third of participants did reference the parameters of the question, in which participants indicated needing to fit their responses to the question at hand, rather than the question fitting their life as written. For example, Participant 14 says "um in that phrasing only attracted to females." In contrast, referencing the parameters of the question happened only once with Questions 3 and 4.

Two participants noted that the "only" on the ends of the scales were extreme, for example, "I mean sure um only attracted to females seemed like a little extreme because like I can't like rule like it's not outside the realm of possibility that I may find uh men or people who identify as men attractive uh so that's why I picked mostly" (Participant 4). Although less so than with gender expression, temporal fluidity came up a few times such that the question was complicated for respondents for whom attraction is fluid: "um I mean it changes it's not always the same and like I don't know how I feel today even so" (Participant 13).

"Sex" as an action is ambiguous and its meaning varies across individuals and systematically across groups (Wolff et al. 2017). Similarly, "sexual attraction" is never defined in the question, and in at least one survey using this question, no follow up definition is for interviewers to use is shown in the documentation (NSDUH 2018). Thus, there could be measurement error to the extent that respondents define "sexual attraction" differently. All but one participant were asked to describe what sexual attraction meant to them, and over half answered in terms of describing desired behavior, e.g., reporting with whom someone *wants to* engage in certain types of activities, "oh you know like people that create like what desire that I might want to have sex with" (Participant 4) (Clark et al. 2005). Distinct from desired behavior, almost one third of participants defined sexual attraction in terms of actual experiences. With less frequency, participants also defined sexual attraction in terms of more general descriptions of feelings, features of the person (appearance, personality, body parts), and more general recapitulations of emotional, physical, and sexual attraction. Another facet of attraction that was discussed among one third of participants had to do with attraction to more "distal" others: "just looking at somebody definitely both" (Participant 6), "walking down the street I'd be like mostly notice the girls" and "Robert Downey Jr. um because I'm attracted to him he's cute" (Participant 8), and "sexual attraction is more so like um I see it as when I am approached or wanting to approach someone" (Participant 10).

Suggestions
1. We first want to note that one of the positive aspects of the sexual attraction question is the use of a generalized "other" to reduce social desirability bias: "People are different in their sexual attraction to other people" explicitly acknowledges that various types of sexual attraction are acceptable forms of human variation.
2. As noted by one participant, this question captures a snapshot and does not account for temporal fluidity. A reference period could aid respondents in

answering and communicate that attraction may not be fixed across the life course. Other options (filter+follow-up format) could be used depending on the scope of the project and level of detail needed (e.g., "have you ever been sexually attracted to men?").

3. The response options should refer to categories of gender (e.g., women, men) rather than sex. Furthermore, the response options for sexual attraction do not have a category that allows respondents specify attraction to genders other than women or men, restricting the choices of those who might have different attractions as well as reifying normative understandings of what sexual attraction is. In order to allow for respondents who have attraction to persons outside the gender binary, all respondents could be asked a filter question "Are you sexually attracted to persons with any other gender identities?" and if the respondent says "yes," they could fill in (or report in aural modes) those identities and then be given the response scale (up to a certain number of identities). We had three participants choose "not sure" in their answer to this question, and for two of the participants, this was due at least in part to not having a place to put attraction to genderqueer or nonbinary individuals, which would then be addressed by allowing for this slightly more expansive set of questions. Since we would already have separate attraction to women and men, adding attraction to other gender identities for respondents who choose this only adds one filter for everyone and possibly a few more scales for those to whom it applies.

4. In subjecting this question and its variants[14] to closer scrutiny, the sexual attraction question seems to conflate two different dimensions: quantifying the types of people one finds attractive (e.g., "most of the people you find attractive"), and quantifying strength of attraction to different types of people (e.g., "what is your level of attraction to certain types of people"). Depolarizing the current set of response options (which we recommend in order to consider one gender identity at a time) shows the issue with the response options "mostly" and "only": these quantify the types of people respondents find sexually attractive, yet respondents may not experience sexual attraction as an enumeration of people. We propose that the depolarized version of the question could focus on strength of attraction to types of people, e.g., "not at all, a little, somewhat, very attracted to men," "not at all, a little, somewhat, very attracted to women," and followed by a filter question as noted above that would also ask about other gender identities.

5. As with the gender expression questions, we suggest in visual presentation that the response scale be presented horizontally and start with "not at all," and we suggest it is an empirical question whether to randomly assign which scale is presented first or keep with the current practice of starting with the end of the

---

[14] The US PATH data uses the response dimensions "mostly to females and at least once to a male" (Federal Interagency Working Group 2016a). Rust (1992) measures strength of attraction as a percentage for one gender at the exclusion of others, e.g., 90% for women, 10% for men.

scale that matches the respondent's gender in terms of the level and types of errors in measurement that might be introduced (see Discussion).[15]

6. Continuing to include "not sure" should allow researchers to be able to parse in part this form of uncertainty in sexual attraction from other potential causes of item nonresponse.
7. Our participants show some consistency in the definition of the phrase "sexual attraction" as well as some important conceptual distinctions. In terms of the consistency, over half the participants understood "sexual attraction" to indicate those with whom they desire or want to engage in certain types of activity. However, in the absence of questions that allow respondents to report about other types of attraction that they feel, we did hear reports of other feelings of attraction beyond sexual.
8. Some participants defined sexual attraction in terms past behavior—not what they desire but what has been done. Of course, past behavior may be a data point that respondents will consider but should not substitute for attraction, and this could be communicated to respondents by a more precise definition or defined by prior questions in surveys that include questions about sexual behavior.
9. One definition that might be helpful would be to communicate to respondents whom they are to consider in their feelings of attraction: distal persons, more proximate friends, current relationships, or all of these. We posit that the notion of "attraction" as potentially the first step in an interaction, encounter, or relationship is being invoked for some participants and researchers should consider whether to add precision in their version of the measure.
10. Single questions that conflate identity and attraction are problematic for some respondents to answer (Federal Interagency Working Group 2016b). Although sensible for multiple measures of sexual orientation to be grouped together within a survey, no research exists to make a recommendation as to the ordering of questions on sexual identity, attraction, and behavior (Federal Interagency Working Group 2016b; SMART 2009). In our study, sexual identity is intertwined with how participants consider their answers to the sexual attraction question, as sexual identity is discussed in detail as part of the in-depth interview and a survey question on sexual identity directly precedes the question on sexual attraction in the cognitive interview. Research should examine whether and how answers to each influence answers to the others, and whether these effects are assimilating or contrasting (Tourangeau et al. 2000). This is an area of research for which there have been calls for future studies but little uptake.

---

[15]The current practice with the bipolar scale is to present the "only attracted to males" side of the scale first if the respondent is presumed a woman and the reverse if the respondent is presumed a man.

Discussion

The results of this study suggest certain considerations and possible refinements for measuring gender expression and sexual attraction in surveys, with implications for practitioners and researchers who are interested in measuring gender and sexual orientation to focus on the full scope in which gender and sexuality are experienced. While targeted projects could ask more specific sets of questions, measurement in large scale surveys—both based in the general population as well as focused on particular communities—require different considerations in terms of the number and content of items. Yet it is precisely because general population surveys serve a range of purposes for which all research questions cannot be predicted a priori that the multifaceted nature of gender and sexual orientation should be measured beyond just the most commonly reported measures (Wolff et al. 2017). Thus, it is imperative that if researchers are going to ask questions about gender expression and sexual attraction in large scale data collection efforts, we analyze and evaluate how to best measure what it is we are going to measure, the same way we have done and continue to do—and rightly so—for gender identity and sexual identity. This study is another step in this direction.

Our analytic approach is an important contribution to the analysis of cognitive interviews and transcribed talk more generally. We coded participants' cognitive interviews in an inductive, iterative, and systematic process, and include in our analysis all parts of their answers to the probes following the two questions on gender expression and one question on sexual attraction. This study focused on a small sample of participants, generous with their time and sharing of their thoughts. Their deep dive allowed us to do the same in considering how these questions might better fit the conceptual and operational goals of measurement not just for specific sexual and gender minority populations but everyone who partakes in answering these survey questions. Indeed, gender expression and sexual attraction are arguably more salient and considered topics for queer women compared to a random sample of the general population. By analyzing how this group of participants understands these questions, this should serve to improve the ability for everyone to answer these survey questions. Balancing the multidimensionality of gender and sexuality with the concision needed in a general population survey will always require future research, but this study provides concrete, actionable steps to improve the questions that have received less attention in SOGI measurement for future researchers to examine, contest, and change as they see fit and their data allow. Features of survey measurement such as whether multiple questions can measure a concept and question order effects must be considered, as well as mode, sample size, age range, location, periodicity, longitudinal or cross-sectional design, analysis plan, and many other factors playing a role in how any one question might eventually be asked. Even still, we expect these steps will improve measurement of gender expression and sexual attraction, refining our understanding of nuanced lived experience beyond the current landscape of presumed dualities and categorical differences.

How the gender expression and sexual attraction questions are administered in general population surveys further reifies heteronormativity, as the order of the response option is changed depending on the gender of the respondent with the current bipolar version of the question (e.g., starting with "only attracted to males" when respondents report they are women and the reverse when they are men for sexual attraction). This decision is likely based on the assumption that the errors driven by response option order will be roughly the same in both directions (e.g., no difference in whether presenting only women first to men and only men first to women), although we might expect any errors to be even more prominent among straight men given overriding cultural norms of heteronormative masculinity. Yet two complicating factors arise. First, the presumed order for presentation might change when the question is being used outside of a more "general population survey." For example, following the logic from general population surveys, a presentation that privileges attraction to women first would be sensible in a study of queer women. The second complicating factor is more fundamental to survey methodology in terms of starting with the most "desirable" set of response options. Indeed, starting with the least desirable response options first allows for respondents to be more likely to consider the range of responses before selecting an answer (Bradburn et al. 2004; Garbarski et al. 2015). This recommendation presumes that the underlying population considers the response options to be uniformly applicable; in studying questions about gender expression and sexual attraction, that presumption should be broadened to ask "desirable for whom?" Response option order (since we suggest here starting with "not at all") and heuristics like "up means good" (Tourangeau et al. 2013) might intersect in ways that are specific to the question at hand in terms of its content and how it is considered by groups of respondents rather than leading to an overarching axiom of how questions with this structure ought to be presented regardless of their content. We suggest it is an empirical question whether to randomly assign which scale is presented first (feminine or masculine, attraction to women or men) or keep with a practice of starting with the "most" or "least" desirable scale in terms of how it aligns with respondents' gender (from a heteronormative perspective) in terms of the level and types of errors in measurement that might be introduced, and whether this will vary depending on the type of data being collected (general population versus population-specific survey).

The bidirectional relationship between survey research and how it both reflects and shapes the population is highlighted when discussing sexual and gender minorities. Routine collection in surveys could serve the latter capacity to normalize the diversity of gender and sexuality and nuanced understandings of each in the general public. In addition, given the emergent understandings of gender and sexual orientation beyond existing categories, labels, and definitions, what works well for survey research now may be irrelevant within a span of time (Glick et al. 2018; Harrison-Quintana et al. 2015). This raises questions with how to proceed in the enumeration of statistical minority populations given the tension that might exist in further marginalization should researchers do it wrong from the individual and community perspective, and increasing measurement error should researchers get it wrong from the measurement perspective. Thus, the issues of reliability and validity have different standpoints—from the point of view of the individual, communities, and groups of scientific researchers, each of whom are not monolithic. The balance must consider the possibility of measurement error, as even small numbers of misclassification can lead to large errors in measurement in small sexual minority populations (SMART 2009) as well as errors in validity driven by researchers when processing data (such as the research on the health outcomes of "sexual minority" monolithic groups). Systems of data collection like large scale surveys should continue to work toward understanding the world as it exists at that moment and be amenable to changing questions so as not to fit people into the same obsolete categories by working with the members of the communities who may be measured (e.g., Harrison-Quintana et al. 2015). The process must be iterative and driven by mutuality on the part of those who are experts in their lives and experts in survey measurement to make sure resources and research remain timely as language, concepts, and communities evolve.

References

Beckstead, J. W. (2014). On measurements and their quality. Paper 4: Verbal anchors and the number of response options in rating scales. *International Journal of Nursing Studies, 51*(5), 807–814.

Bem, S. L. (1993). *The lenses of gender: Transforming the debate on sexual inequality*. New Haven and London: Yale University Press.

Bem, S. L. (1981) Gender schema theory: A cognitive account of sex typing. *Psychological Review, 88*(4):354–364.

Bulgar-Medina, J. (2018). Surveying sexual orientation disclosure. Paper presented at the annual meeting of the American Association for Public Opinion Research (AAPOR), Denver, CO.

Bradburn, N. M., Sudman, S., & Wansink, B. (2004). *Asking questions: The definitive guide to questionnaire design—for market research, political polls, and social and health questionnaires*. San Francisco: Wiley.

Brenner, P. S., & Bulgar-Medina, J. (2018). Testing mark-all-that-apply measures of sexual orientation and gender identity. *Field Methods, 30*(4), 357–370.

Brewster, K. L., & Tillman, K. H. (2012). Sexual orientation and substance use among adolescents and young adults. *American Journal of Public Health, 102*(6), 1168–1176.

Charmaz, K. (2006). *Constructing grounded theory: A practical guide through qualitative analysis*. Thousand Oaks, CA: Sage.

Clark, M. A., Armstrong, G., & Bonacore, L. (2005). Measuring sexual orientation and gender expression among middle-aged and older women in a Cancer screening study. *Journal of Cancer Education, 20*(2), 108–112.

Connell, R. W. (2005). *Masculinities*. Cambridge: Polity.

Constantinople, A. (1973). Masculinity-femininity: An exception to a famous dictum? *Psychological Bulletin, 80*(5), 389–407.

Corteen, K. (2002). Lesbian safety talk: Problematizing definitions and experiences of violence, sexuality and space. *Sexualities, 5*(3), 259–280.

Courtenay, W. H. (2000). Constructions of masculinity and their influence on Men's Well-being: A theory of gender and health. *Social Science & Medicine, 50*(10), 1385–1401.

Dobson, K. S., & Mothersill, K. J. (1979). Equidistant categorical labels for construction of Likert-type scales. *Perceptual and Motor Skills, 49*(2), 575–580.

Federal Interagency Working Group on Improving Measurement of Sexual Orientation and Gender Identity (SOGI). (2016a). *Current measures of sexual orientation and gender identity in federal surveys*. Accessed December 22, 2018, from https://nces.ed.gov/FCSM/pdf/current_measures_20160812.pdf.

Federal Interagency Working Group on Improving Measurement of Sexual Orientation and Gender Identity (SOGI). (2016b). Evaluations of *sexual orientation and gender identity survey measures: What have we learned?* Accessed December 22, 2018, from https://nces.ed.gov/FCSM/pdf/Evaluations_of_SOGI_Questions_20160923.pdf.

Fowler, F. J. (1995). Improving survey questions. Thousand Oaks, CA: Sage.

Garbarski, D., Schaeffer, N. C., & Dykema, J. (2015). The effects of response option order and question order on self-rated health. *Quality of Life Research, 24*(6), 1443–1453. https://doi.org/10.1007/s11136-014-0861-y.

Garbarski, D., Schaeffer, N. C., & Dykema, J. (2016). Interviewing practices, conversational practices, and rapport: Responsiveness and engagement in the standardized survey interview. *Sociological Methodology, 46*, 1–38. https://doi.org/10.1177/0081175016637890.

Garbarski, D., Schaeffer, N. C., & Dykema, J. (2019). The effects of features of survey measurement on self-rated health: Response option order and scale orientation. *Applied Research in Quality of Life, 14*(2), 545–560. https://ecommons.luc.edu/soc_facpubs/18/.

Glaser, B. G. (1978). *Theoretical sensitivity: Advances in the methodology of grounded theory*. Mill Valley, CA: Sociology Press.

Glaser, B. G., & Strauss, A. (1967). *The discovery of grounded theory: Strategies for qualitative research*. Chicago, IL: Aldine.

Glick, J. L., Theall, K., Andrinopoulos, K., & Kendall, C. (2018). For Data's sake: Dilemmas in the measurement of gender minorities. *Culture, Health & Sexuality, 20*, 1–16. https://doi.org/10.1080/13691058.2018.1437220.

Gordon, L. E., & Silva, T. J. (2015). Inhabiting the sexual landscape: Toward an interpretive theory of the development of sexual orientation and identity. *Journal of homosexuality., 62*(4), 95–530.

Harrison-Quintana, J., Grant, J. M., & Rivera, I. G. (2015). Boxes of our own creation a trans data collection Wo/manifesto. *TSQ: Transgender Studies Quarterly, 2*(1), 166–174.

Hebl, M. R., Foster, J. B., Mannix, L. M., & Dovidio, J. F. (2002). Formal and interpersonal discrimination: A field study of Bias toward homosexual applicants. *Personality and Social Psychology Bulletin, 28*(6), 815–825.

Henley, N. M. (1977). *Body politics. Power, sex, and nonverbal communication*. Englewood Cliffs, NJ: Prentice Hall.

Krosnick, J. A., & Presser, S. (2010). Question and questionnaire design. In P. V. Marsden & J. D. Wright (Eds.), *Handbook of survey research* (pp. 263–314). Bingley, UK: Emerald Group Publishing.

Laumann, E. O., Gagnon, J. H., Michael, R. T., & Michaels, S. (1994). *The social organization of sexuality: Sexual practices in the United States*. Chicago: University of Chicago press.

Lorber, J. (1994). *Paradoxes of gender*. New Haven and London: Yale University Press.

Lowry, R., Johns, M. M., Gordon, A. R., Austin, S., Robin, L. E., & Kann, L. K. (2018). Nonconforming gender expression and associated mental distress and substance use among high school students. *JAMA Pediatrics, 172*, 1020–1028. https://doi.org/10.1001/jamapediatrics.2018.2140.

Luzzatto, D., & Gvion, L. (2004). Feminine but not femme: The dual lesbian body. *Journal of Homosexuality, 48*(1), 43–77.

Magliozzi, D., Saperstein, A., & Westbrook, L. (2016). Scaling up: Representing gender diversity in survey research. *Socius, 2*, 237802311666435. https://doi.org/10.1177/2378023116664352.

Martin, P. Y. (2003). "Said and done" versus "saying and doing" gendering practices, practicing gender at work. *Gender & Society, 17*(3), 342–366.

Moore, M. R. (2006). Lipstick or timberlands? Meanings of gender presentation in black lesbian communities. *Signs: Journal of Women in Culture and Society, 32*(1), 113–139.

National Survey on Drug Use and Health (NSDUH). (2018). Accessed December 19, 2018, from https://nsduhweb.rti.org/respweb/homepage.cfm.

Risman, B. J. (2018). *Where the Millennials will take us: A new generation wrestles with the gender structure*. Oxford: Oxford University Press.

Rust, P. C. (1992). The politics of sexual identity: Sexual attraction and behavior among lesbian and bisexual women. *Social Problems, 39*(4), 366–386.

Schaeffer, N. C. (1991). Hardly ever or constantly? Group comparisons using vague quantifiers. *Public Opinion Quarterly, 55*(3), 395–423.

Silva, T. (2017). Bud-sex: Constructing normative masculinity among rural straight men that have sex with men. *Gender and Society, 31*(1), 51–73.

SMART. (2009). *Best practices for asking questions about sexual orientation on surveys. Created by the sexual minority assessment research team (SMART)*. L. Badgett and N. Goldberg (Eds.). Los Angeles, CA: The Williams Institute. Accessed December 19, 2018, from http://williamsinstitute.law.ucla.edu/wp-content/uploads/SMART-FINAL-Nov-2009.pdf.

Smyth, J. D., & Olson, K. (2020). Male/Female is not enough: Adding measures of masculinity and femininity to general population surveys. *Understanding Survey Methodology: Sociological Theory and Applications*, edited by P. Brenner. Springer.

Spence, J. T. (2011). Off with the old, on with the new. *Psychology of Women Quarterly, 35*(3), 504–509. https://doi.org/10.1177/0361684311414826.

Strauss, A., & Corbin, J. (1998). *Basics of qualitative research: Techniques and procedures for developing grounded theory* (2nd ed.). Thousand Oaks, CA: Sage.

The GenIUSS Group. (2014). *Best practices for asking questions to identify transgender and other gender minority respondents on population-based surveys (Created by the Gender Identity in U.S. Surveillance (GenIUSS) Group)*. J. L. Herman (Ed.). Los Angeles, CA: The Williams Institute. Accessed December 22, 2018, from https://williamsinstitute.law.ucla.edu/wp-content/uploads/geniuss-report-sep-2014.pdf.

Tourangeau, R., Rips, L. J., & Rasinski, K. A. (2000). *The psychology of survey response*. Cambridge: Cambridge University Press.

Tourangeau, R., Couper, M. P., & Conrad, F. G. (2013). "Up means good": The effect of screen position on evaluative ratings in web surveys. *Public Opinion Quarterly, 77*(S1), 69–88. https://doi.org/10.1093/poq/nfs063.

Van Anders, S. M. (2015). Beyond sexual orientation: Integrating gender/sex and diverse sexualities via sexual configurations theory. *Archives of Sexual Behavior, 44*(5), 1177–1213.

West, C., & Zimmerman, D. H. (1987). Doing Gender. *Gender and Society, 1*(2), 25–51.

Westbrook, L., & Saperstein, A. (2015). New categories are not enough: Rethinking the measurement of sex and gender in social surveys. *Gender and Society, 29*(4), 534–560. https://doi.org/10.1177/0891243215584758.

Willis, G. B. (2015). *Analysis of the cognitive interview in questionnaire design*. Oxford: Oxford University Press.

Wilson, B. D. M., Cooper, K., Kastanis, A., & Nezhad, S. (2014). *Sexual and gender minority youth in Foster Care: Assessing disproportionality and disparities in Los Angeles*. Los Angeles: The Williams Institute, UCLA School of Law. Accessed September 17, 2019, from https://escholarship.org/uc/item/6mg3n153.

Wolff, M., Wells, B., Ventura-DiPersia, C., Renson, A., & Grov, C. (2017). Measuring sexual orientation: A review and critique of U.S. data collection efforts and implications for health policy. *The Journal of Sex Research, 54*(4–5), 507–531. https://doi.org/10.1080/00224499.2016.1255872.

Wylie, S. A., Corliss, H. L., Boulanger, V., Prokop, L. A., & Austin, S. B. (2010). Socially assigned gender nonconformity: A brief measure for use in surveillance and investigation of health disparities. *Sex Roles, 63*(3–4), 264–276.

Zucker, K. J., Mitchell, J. N., Bradley, S. J., Tkachuk, J., Cantor, J. M., & Allin, S. M. (2006). The recalled childhood gender identity/gender role questionnaire: Psychometric properties. *Sex Roles, 54*(7), 469–483. https://doi.org/10.1007/s11199-006-9019-x.

Chapter 10
How Do Interviewers and Respondents Navigate Sexual Identity Questions in a CATI Survey?

Jerry Timbrook, Jolene D. Smyth, and Kristen Olson

Background

Survey-based research has demonstrated that sexual minority individuals experience unique outcomes in areas such as physical and mental health (Boehmer et al. 2007; Hatzenbuehler 2014, 2017), crime (Herek 2009), public education (Kosciw et al. 2015), same-sex romantic relationships and family (Powell and Downey 1997; Umberson et al. 2015), and economics (Black et al. 2007). Having a reliable and valid measure of sexual identity (i.e., the way in which an individual self-describes their sexual orientation) (Gagnon and Simon 1973) is essential for conducting research on sexual minorities. Indeed, many national surveys such as the General Social Survey, the National Health Interview Survey, and the National Survey of Family Growth ask survey respondents about their sexual identity.

The percentage of US adults identifying as a sexual minority has increased from 3.5% (8.3 million) in December 2012 to 4.1% (10.05 million) in December 2016 (Gates 2017). As the prevalence of sexual minorities is still low, inaccurate answers or item nonresponse to sexual identity questions (SIQs) may result in large distortions of estimates of sexual minorities. In a meta-analysis, Ridolfo et al. (2012) demonstrate that item nonresponse rates for SIQs range from 1.6% to 4.3%, with an average of approximately 2%. For context, this places item nonresponse for SIQs higher than education questions (1.1%), but below income questions (11.2%) (Conron et al. 2008). The threat of item nonresponse due to concerns over question sensitivity has led many researchers to advocate against the use of interviewers to administer SIQs (SMART 2009; Ridolfo et al. 2012). Instead, they recommend that survey researchers ask SIQs using only self-administered modes of data collection

---

J. Timbrook (✉) · J. D. Smyth · K. Olson
University of Nebraska-Lincoln, Lincoln, NE, USA
e-mail: jtimbrook2@huskers.unl.edu; jsmyth2@unl.edu; kolson5@unl.edu

(i.e., using mail surveys, web surveys, or Computer-Assisted Self-Interview [CASI] devices for face-to-face surveys) (SMART 2009; Ridolfo et al. 2012).

Yet asking SIQs exclusively in a self-administered context may not be a feasible approach. First, self-administered modes are not without drawbacks of their own: mail surveys are time consuming, face-to-face surveys using CASI are time consuming and expensive, and web surveys do not have a sampling frame with adequate coverage of the US population (Dillman et al. 2014). In contrast, researchers using telephone surveys can collect nationally representative data quickly. Second, while SIQs provide important demographic information, they are often not the primary focus of a survey. Many private survey companies (e.g., Pew, Gallup, Abt Associates) and government surveys (e.g., the Behavioral Risk Factor Surveillance System) rely on telephone surveys to achieve a variety of cost, quality, and timeliness objectives; these organizations are not likely to switch modes to improve data quality for a single demographic question like sexual identity. Thus, understanding the implications of administering SIQs in all modes, including telephone, is of continued interest.

Previous research on SIQs in telephone surveys has been limited to examinations of data quality indicators such as "Don't Know" or refusal answers (e.g., VanKim et al. 2010; Ridolfo et al. 2012; Fredriksen-Goldsen and Kim 2015). These studies do not consider interactional problems between the interviewer and the respondent that may occur prior to negotiating an answer. Yet investigating when and why the interaction between interviewers and respondents deviates from a paradigmatic "question asked/question answered" sequence can provide researchers with an in-depth understanding of problems with questions in interviewer-administered surveys (Schaeffer and Maynard 1996).

In this study, we explore interactional difficulties that result from telephone administration of an SIQ to gain insight into the problems associated with this question. Specifically, we focus on two potential sources of strain: (1) the sensitivity of the question and (2) the construction of the question. For example, the stigma associated with having a sexual minority status may lead some respondents to provide intentionally inaccurate answers or refuse to answer the question entirely (Sylva et al. 2010; Stange 2014). Issues with the question's construction may similarly lead some respondents to unintentionally misclassify their sexual identity (e.g., if they are unfamiliar was words like "heterosexual") (Miller and Ryan 2011; Ridolfo et al. 2011). Additionally, telephone surveys are a cognitively taxing aural medium (de Leeuw 2005; Dillman et al. 2014) in which respondents may experience problems with complex questions, requiring extra help to complete these items.

The construction of the SIQ we use in this study (Fig. 10.1) was recommended by the Sexual Minority Assessment Research Team (SMART 2009). This SIQ contains wording that is similar to many SIQs used in federal surveys.[1] Using this SIQ, we examine the following research questions:

---

[1] For an overview of these measures, see the Federal Interagency Working Group on Improving Measurement of SOGI 2016 report.

Do you consider yourself to be heterosexual or straight, gay or lesbian, or bisexual?
1   HETEROSEXUAL OR STRAIGHT
2   GAY OR LESBIAN
3   BISEXUAL
4   OTHER (SPECIFY)
8   DK
9   REF

Fig. 10.1 Sexual Identity Question

RQ1: Do respondents express concerns with the sensitivity of the sexual identity question? In what ways do they express sensitivity concerns?

RQ2: Do respondents express concerns with the construction of the sexual identity question? In what ways do they express question construction concerns?

RQ3: How do interviewers react to concerns over sensitivity and question construction?

RQ4: What respondent and interviewer characteristics are associated with problems with the sensitivity and construction of the sexual identity question?

Below, we consider how the sensitivity and the construction of the SIQ may differentially affect three classes of actors involved in administering an SIQ: (1) lesbian, gay, and bisexual (LGB) respondents,[2] (2) heterosexual respondents, and (3) interviewers.

Question Sensitivity

LGB respondents. LGB respondents may experience *stigma* when being asked about their sexual identity. Stigma is a sense of shame associated with an identity, condition, or status that is viewed as undesirable by society (Goffman 1963). More specifically, LGB respondents may fear experiencing sexual stigma if they associate themselves with a non-heterosexual identity (Herek 2009, 2011). As the social presence of another individual can activate concerns over stigma, interviewer-administered telephone surveys may trigger an LGB respondent's fear of being stigmatized (Goffman 1963; de Leeuw 2005).

Nearly a quarter of US adults believe that homosexuality should be discouraged (Pew Research Center 2017), making it reasonable for sexual minority respondents to expect some degree of disapproval if they disclose their identity to an interviewer. Fear of sexual stigmatization may be signaled when LGB respondents express reluctance before selecting "gay or lesbian" or "bisexual" as their sexual identity.

---

[2]We recognize that not all sexual minorities have a lesbian, gay, or bisexual identity. However, for the sake of brevity, we use the phrase "LGB respondents" to refer to all respondents with a minority sexual identity. We also do not examine transgender respondents or responses to questions about gender identity.

Reluctance may take the form of explicit comments about discomfort with or the intrusiveness of the SIQ (e.g., "That's a personal question."), or paralinguistic expressions of discomfort such as stuttering, disfluencies, or laughing (e.g., Lavin and Maynard 2001, 2002).

Instead of answering the SIQ honestly, LGB respondents may instead choose to conceal[3] their identity, potentially to avoid discrimination that may result from disclosing a stigmatized sexual identity (Goffman 1959, 1963; Sylva et al. 2010; Stange 2014). This may take the form of intentional misclassification, where LGB respondents select "heterosexual or straight" (the non-stigmatized identity) as their answer to the SIQ. Alternatively, LGB respondents may conceal their LGB identity by refusing to answer the SIQ altogether.

Finally, LGB respondents may be *unaffected* by the sensitivity of the SIQ. Assuming that they do not have issues with the construction of the SIQ, these respondents would answer the question paradigmatically using the "gay or lesbian" or "bisexual" response options.

Heterosexual respondents. Unlike LGB respondents, heterosexual respondents are not likely to consider their sexual identity stigmatized, as it reflects the majority (Goffman 1963; Herek 2009, 2011). However, these respondents may still consider the SIQ to be *intrusive* as it asks about sexual or romantic attraction to others, a topic that many consider private (Tourangeau et al. 2000). Similar to LGB respondents, heterosexual respondents may signal their discomfort with the question's sensitivity through explicit comments about the private nature of the question or with paralinguistic cues. These respondents may ultimately answer the question truthfully, or they may conceal their sexual identity by refusing to answer the question due to its sensitive nature (Tourangeau and Yan 2007).

Heterosexual respondents who are uncomfortable with the concept of homosexuality or bisexuality may express *backlash* when faced with an LGB-inclusive context (Hooten et al. 2009; Stange 2014; Stange et al. 2018). This backlash may take the form of explicit anti-LGB comments when asked to indicate their sexual orientation. For example, religious beliefs play an important role in the formation of individuals' opinions about homosexuality (Olson et al. 2006; Adamczyk and Pitt 2009), with major religious texts providing the basis for societal disapproval of homosexuality (Yip 2005). Thus, backlash may be expressed as religious-based disapproval of homosexuality (e.g., "The bible says that's wrong.").

Respondents may also express backlash to the SIQ if they fear being associated with the stigmatized LGB identity. This experience, known as homohysteria (Anderson 2009), may cause heterosexual respondents to dis-identify from being LGB rather than selecting the appropriate "heterosexual or straight" response option. These respondents may instead dis-identify from an LGB identity by providing answers such as "I'm not gay," "I'm normal," or "I'm 100% straight."

---

[3]We note that identity concealment cannot be observed in an observational dataset such as ours. We mention this here to describe what *may* happen when an SIQ is administered.

Some respondents who express backlash, despite their disapproval, may ultimately provide an accurate and acceptable answer. Other backlash respondents may refuse to answer the question in protest. Finally, it is also possible that in light of increasing rates of acceptance of homosexuality (Pew Research Center 2017), heterosexual respondents will have no issue with the sensitivity of the SIQ. These *unaffected* respondents will provide honest, acceptable answers to the question with no additional commentary.

Interviewers. An essential part of an interviewer's job is to ensure that respondents provide acceptable answers to each question in a survey, and continue to participate (Fowler and Mangione 1990; Schaeffer et al. 2010). Interviewers who demonstrate responsiveness to respondents' concerns during the survey interview cultivate a sense of rapport that can motivate respondents to provide accurate and thoughtful answers (Cannell et al. 1981; Dijkstra 1987; Garbarski et al. 2016). However, sensitive questions like the SIQ may represent a threat to rapport with the potential to derail respondents' continued and optimal participation in a survey.

To contend with the intrusive nature of sensitive questions, interviewers may engage in a variety of *rapport-building* behaviors to foster continued interaction with their respondents (Japec 2008; Garbarski et al. 2016). First, interviewers may attempt to minimize disruption to rapport by distancing themselves from the researcher. This can manifest through explicit comments such as "they make me ask these questions" (Houtkoop-Steenstra 2000) or when interviewers apologize to respondents for the topic (e.g., "I'm so sorry about this question") (Garbarski et al. 2016). Second, interviewers may seek to minimize the time spent on the SIQ. In such cases, interviewers may tell respondents they do not have to answer the question (e.g., offering the Don't know/Refusal response options) (Japec 2008). Similarly, interviewers may choose not to probe unacceptable answers to the SIQ (e.g., "I'm not gay") in an effort to move on to the next question as quickly as possible. These interviewers may incorrectly (but intentionally) code unacceptable answers as actual answers to avoid negotiating an acceptable response (Ridolfo et al. 2012). Finally, interviewers may skip asking the SIQ entirely to avoid an uncomfortable interaction, and falsify the respondent's answer to the question.

Interviewer behaviors change as they gain more experience with a particular survey (van der Zouwen et al. 1991; Olson and Peytchev 2007; Olson and Bilgen 2011). When administering the SIQ, interviewers may find that certain rapport-building strategies are more useful than others, making within-survey experience of interest. It is also possible that interviewers with more years on the job have more experience administering SIQs. Thus, these interviewers may have already cultivated strategies for coping with the sensitive and complex nature of the SIQ.

We also note that interviewers themselves are a component of the survey context. Thus, different characteristics of the interviewer may be perceived as more or less accepting of an LGB sexual identity. Accordingly, these characteristics may make LGB respondents more or less likely to accurately disclose their identity, or may increase or decrease the amount of backlash expressed by heterosexual respondents. For example, women are generally more supportive of homosexuality than men (Herek 2002). Thus, LGB respondents may be more likely to disclose their identity to female interviewers, while backlash respondents may feel more comfortable expressing their anti-LGB opinions to male interviewers. In addition, although we cannot assess it with the data from our study, because men are more likely to report anti-LGB attitudes to interviewers they perceive as being heterosexual (Kemph and Kasser 1996) backlash may be more common from male respondents when they believe their interviewer is heterosexual. Conversely, LGB respondents may be more comfortable discussing issues related to their sexual minority status with LGB interviewers (Rotheram-Borus et al. 1994) and may therefore be more apt to report being a sexual minority to interviewers they perceive as being LGB.

Construction of the SIQ

LGB respondents. The construct of sexual identity is more complex than straight, gay, lesbian, and bisexual. Many individuals possess sexual identities that do not easily conform to categorization, identities that may be fluid depending on time and place (Gamson 1995; Diamond 2008). For example, Ridolfo et al. (2012) describe a transitioning transgender respondent who preferred the sexual identity of "queer" to describe their simultaneous status as a homosexual man and a heterosexual woman. Respondents with these minority sexual identities may find that the response options to the SIQ are *inapplicable* to them (Ridolfo et al. 2012).

Respondents who do not self-identify as possessing any of the sexual identities expressed by the SIQ's response options may instead choose to endorse "Other" (Ridolfo et al. 2012; Eliason et al. 2016). However, in telephone surveys, this response option is not always offered as a part of the question stem; these respondents must reveal that their sexual identity does not conform to any of the response options provided, and the interviewer would then offer the "Other" response option. Thus, some respondents may intentionally misclassify their sexual identity or skip the question to avoid further interaction.

Heterosexual respondents. Fears of stigmatization stemming from having a minority status means that sexual identity is often salient for LGB individuals. However, individuals who occupy majority positions across social identities (e.g., gender, race, sexuality, class) rarely consider their identities due to their assumed normality (e.g., Perry 2001). Thus, heterosexual respondents without a salient sexual identity may find the SIQ's response options to be unfamiliar (Miller and Ryan 2011; Ridolfo et al. 2012).

Confusion over definitions in the question may prevent some respondents from providing an accurate answer, thereby compromising data integrity (Fowler 1995; Tourangeau et al. 2000). For example, cognitive interviews of SIQs have demonstrated that the words "gay," "lesbian," and "straight" are well understood by English-speaking respondents, but the word "heterosexual" is not (Miller and Ryan 2011). This may lead some respondents to express confusion with the SIQ's response options (Ridolfo et al. 2012). These respondents may unintentionally misclassify themselves as having a sexual identity of "Other," or skip the SIQ altogether (Ridolfo et al. 2012). Miller and Ryan (2011) also find that some heterosexual respondents may misunderstand the "bisexual" response option, believing that it expresses "one man and one woman." In the same study, some respondents conflated their sexual and gender identities (e.g., answering "I'm female"). Respondents who are older and less educated may be most likely to be unfamiliar with these terms (Ridolfo et al. 2012).

Respondents for whom sexual identity is not salient may, instead of endorsing an unfamiliar response option, answer the SIQ by dis-identifying from an LGB identity (Miller and Ryan 2011). In these cases, heterosexual respondents may indicate that they are "normal" or "not gay." Thus, dis-identification may not exclusively indicate distancing oneself from LGB due to homohysteria (as discussed above). Instead, dis-identification may also characterize respondents who wish to indicate that they do not have a minority sexual identity, but also do not understand the response options.

Words commonly used in SIQs may not have an equivalent meaning across different languages and cultures. For example, Spanish-speaking respondents in cognitive interviews have reported difficulty understanding translations of the words "gay," "lesbian," "bisexual," "homosexual," and "heterosexual" (Ridolfo and Schoua-Glusberg 2009; Miller and Ryan 2011; Michaels et al. 2017). Additionally, the vocabulary that members of the LGB community use to identify their sexual minority status differs across cultures (Kulick 2000). For instance, the word "gay" in Japanese conflates same-sex attraction and gender identity, referring to men who dress in women's clothing *and* are attracted to other men (Valentine 1997; McLelland 2000). Misunderstandings due to cultural/linguistic differences may lead respondents to unintentionally misclassify their sexual identity, or skip the SIQ (Miller and Ryan 2011; Ridolfo et al. 2012; Michaels et al. 2017). Although the present study uses only interviews conducted in English, this body of literature highlights the importance of pretesting translations of SIQs before administering them across cultures and languages.

Aural administration of the SIQ. Questions with complex syntax (e.g., questions with multiple clauses) can impair respondents' understanding of a question (Tourangeau et al. 2000). The SIQ in this study contains three main response options (clauses): (1) heterosexual or straight, (2) gay or lesbian, or (3) bisexual. Two of these clauses are further subdivided by the conjunction "or" (i.e., "heterosexual *or* straight" and "gay *or* lesbian"). This complex syntax may result in confusion that negatively impacts the accuracy of data collected using the SIQ (Ridolfo et al. 2011). Additionally, issues of question construction can disproportionately affect respondents with lower working memory capacity, such as those with lower educational attainment (Ceci 1991) and older adults (Salthouse 1991). Thus, the SIQ may be particularly taxing to respondents in these subgroups.

Asking questions in the aural channel of telephone surveys can magnify issues of complex syntax (de Leeuw 2005; Dillman et al. 2014). For example, respondents in a telephone survey may hear the clause "heterosexual or straight" and assume that heterosexual and straight are different response options as they are separated by the conjunction "or" (Ridolfo et al. 2011). Respondents may then think they are subsequently being asked if they are gay "or" lesbian, which can add additional confusion. This may lead some respondents to answer the SIQ before the full stem has been read by the interviewer (Dillman et al. 2014). For example, upon hearing "Do you consider yourself heterosexual or straight," respondents may prematurely answer with either "heterosexual" or "straight", or "yes" or "no".

Interviewers. Interviewers are often required to read questions exactly as worded in order to reduce variable interviewer effects on data (Fowler and Mangione 1990). However, interviewers sometimes make changes to questions that they feel are difficult for respondents to understand (Japec 2008; Dykema et al. 2020). Thus, changes when reading the SIQ to respondents may indicate an interviewer's attempt to repair the complexity of the question. These changes can be minor (i.e., changes that do not affect question meaning), or they can be major (i.e., changes that do affect question meaning). As an example, interviewers may add numbers to response options in the question stem to delimit them for respondents (e.g., "Do you consider yourself to be *one* heterosexual or straight, *two* gay or lesbian, or *three* bisexual?") (Haan et al. 2013). Changes in question reading may be more prevalent for experienced interviewers who are less likely to read questions exactly as worded (Fowler and Mangione 1990).

Measuring Problems with Sensitivity and Question Construction of the SIQ

Previous research has investigated construction issues with the SIQ in both lab and field studies. Miller and Ryan (2011) and Ridolfo et al. (2009, 2011, 2012) use cognitive interviewing, a qualitative lab-based technique (Willis 2005), to explore how lesbian, gay, bisexual, transgender, and heterosexual respondents interpret SIQs. To ensure representation, these studies oversampled minority sexual respondents.

Although these studies provide rich detail on how respondents interpret the question, cognitive interviews do not replicate the questing asking and answering experience that occurs in a field study. Additionally, sexual minority respondents were generally recruited from LGBT community centers, likely communicating an LGB-inclusive context to respondents. This also means that LGB respondents who may be more concerned with sexual stigma were likely excluded from these studies. Similarly, these studies used purposive recruitment and were sponsored by the federal government. Thus, these studies may have attracted heterosexual respondents who were more accepting of LGB identities or were generally unlikely to express backlash over the SIQs.

Ridolfo et al. (2012) and Fredriksen-Goldsen and Kim (2015) explore respondent reactions to SIQs in field studies by examining patterns of response (i.e., item nonresponse, and selecting "Other" response options). These results come from a naturalistic interviewer/respondent interaction, overcoming a criticism of cognitive interviews. In their analysis, the authors focus mainly on issues of question construction that lead to these patterns of response. As respondents are likely to skip questions that are confusing, researchers often use rates of item nonresponse to proxy for respondent difficulty with question construction (Krosnick 1991). However, respondents may also skip a question they find sensitive (Tourangeau and Yan 2007). Thus, investigating patterns of response alone does not enable researchers to disentangle issues of question construction and sensitivity.

In this study, we attempt to remedy the lack of representativeness in cognitive interviews and lack of in-depth understanding from the item nonresponse analyses by using behavior coding to explore the interaction between respondents and interviewers during telephone administration of the SIQ in a random sample national survey (Schaeffer and Maynard 1996). We identify when the interaction between interviewers and respondents deviates from a paradigmatic sequence, and classify the problem that caused the deviation (i.e., question sensitivity, construction, or both).

Data and Methods

Sample

The data for this study come from the Work and Leisure Today 2 (WLT2) survey, a dual-frame random-digit dial telephone survey of U.S. adults conducted by Abt SRBI during August and September of 2015. The survey consisted of 58 questions asking about respondents' use of leisure time, use of technology, and demographics. The survey had 902 respondents (AAPOR RR3 = 7.8%), but three cases were eliminated from analysis due to call quality issues. Further, in four cases, interviewers did not administer the SIQ to respondents. This leaves $n = 895$ cases for analysis.

After transcribing each interview, we extract all conversational turns[4] related to the SIQ. Our unit of analysis is the full administration of this item (i.e., all conversational turns related to the asking and answering of this item). Notably, the SIQ was administered directly after respondents were asked about their marital/partner status. If they were married or partnered, respondents were also asked if that was to someone of the same sex or the opposite sex.

---

[4]We define conversational turns as a period of uninterrupted speech by a single actor, with turns ending when an actor finished speaking or was interrupted by another actor. Instances of overlapping speech were counted as their own turns.

Behavior Codes

The majority of our measures for this study come from behavior coding the interaction between interviewers and respondents during administration of the SIQ. The behavior coding method is used to objectively and reliably identify when interviewers and respondents deviate from a paradigmatic "question asked/question answered" sequence (Fowler and Cannell 1996; Schaeffer and Maynard 1996). This allows us to identify when an interaction problem occurred during administration of the SIQ and classify the problem as an indicator of difficulty with question sensitivity, construction, or both. With the exception of interviewer question asking behaviors, codes in our dataset are not mutually exclusive. Thus, each behavior code is assigned independently of all other codes.

Our first set of behavior codes proxy for respondent issues with the sensitivity of the SIQ (Table 10.1). For each case, we code whether or not (no = 0; yes = 1) the respondent ever refuses to answer the SIQ during the interaction, regardless of whether this was the final answer in the data set. As a measure of *intrusiveness*, we code whether or not the respondent ever makes an explicit comment that the SIQ asks about a sensitive/personal topic or is generally off-topic (e.g., that the question deviated from the survey topic of leisure activities). *Backlash* is represented by two codes: whether or not the respondent makes a comment about their religious beliefs in connection to homosexuality, or expresses discomfort or anger over homosexuality. We also create a summary variable of whether a respondent ever expresses any of these four indicators of sensitivity (=1) or not (=0).

Next, we code interviewer *rapport-building* behaviors that indicate reactions to the sensitive nature of the SIQ for each case. We code whether or not the interviewer ever (1) blames the researcher for having to administer the SIQ, (2) apologizes for having to ask the SIQ, (3) offers the Don't Know/Refusal (DK/REF) response options, or (4) neglects to probe an unacceptable answer (i.e., does not probe when they should have). Again we create a summary variable of whether an interviewer ever engages in any of these four sensitivity behaviors or not.

Our third set of codes proxy for respondent confusion with the SIQ's construction. First, we code whether or not (no = 0; yes = 1) respondents ever commented that they answered this question in a previous question (e.g., because the previous question asks about the gender of the respondent's marital partner). Next, we create variables for four respondent behaviors that indicate difficulty with the *definitions* of words in the question. We code whether or not respondents expressed confusion about (1) the difference between the words "heterosexual" and "straight", (2) the difference between sexual identity and sexual behavior (e.g., if a respondent indicates they are asexual because they are too old to engage in sexual behavior), (3) the difference between sexual identity and gender (e.g., answering with one's gender), or (4) the definition of any other words in the question. Our final two codes for construction problems indicate whether or not the respondent confused the SIQ's *response options* for yes/no rather than multiple choice. We code for whether or not respondents give a positive answer (e.g., "yes") or a negation (e.g., "no" or "nope")

Table 10.1 Proportions, Kappas, and Percent Agreement for Each Behavioral Indicator

Code	Mean	(SE)	Kappa	% Agreement
Indicators of question sensitivity				
Respondent behaviors				
Refused to answer	1.8%	(0.4%)	1.00	100.0%
Intrusiveness				
Comments about question being sensitive/off topic	3.4%	(0.5%)	1.00	100.0%
Backlash				
Comments about religion	0.7%	(0.2%)	–	–
Comments about discomfort with homosexuality	1.2%	(0.4%)	–	–
Any respondent indicator of question sensitivity	5.1%	(0.6%)		
Interviewer behaviors				
Rapport-building				
Blames the researcher for the question topic	0.7%	(0.3%)	–	–
Apologizes for the question topic	0.3%	(0.2%)	–	–
Offers the DK/REF response options	0.4%	(0.2%)	1.00	100.0%
Should have probed, but did not	4.5%	(0.8%)	1.00	100.0%
Any interviewer indicator of question sensitivity	5.3%	(0.8%)		
Indicators of question construction problems				
Respondent behaviors				
Comments answer was given in a previous question	0.2%	(0.2%)	–	–
Definition confusion				
Heterosexual vs. straight	2.1%	(0.6%)	1.00	100.0%
Sexual identity vs. sexual behavior	0.6%	(0.4%)	1.00	100.0%
Sexual identity vs. gender	0.8%	(0.3%)	–	–
Confusion with any other word in the question	1.2%	(0.3%)	–	–
Response option confusion				
Positive answer (e.g., "yes")	1.9%	(0.5%)	–	–
Negation (e.g., "no")	4.2%	(0.7%)	0.66	98.8%
Any respondent indicator of construction problems	9.8%	(1.0%)		
Interviewer behaviors				
Question asking				
Asked exactly as worded	88.9%	(3.1%)	0.64[a]	82.7%
Asked with a minor change	7.2%	(1.5%)		
Asked with a major change	3.9%	(1.9%)		
Read numbers with response options	4.8%	(3.4%)	1.00	100.0%
Any interviewer indicator of construction problems	11.8%	(3.7%)		
Behaviors indicating question sensitivity or construction problems				
Comments with uncertainty of answer	2.9%	(0.5%)	–	–
Dis-identification				
Answers what is not (e.g., "I'm not gay")	0.9%	(0.3%)	1.00	100.0%
Comments about degree of own sexuality	4.2%	(0.5%)	0.75	96.8%
Comments about heterosexual as normative	1.5%	(0.4%)	1.00	100.0%

(continued)

Table 10.1 (continued)

Code	Mean	(SE)	Kappa	% Agreement
Respondent paralinguistic expressions				
Stuttering	5.0%	(0.7%)	0.86	97.9%
Disfluencies	15.2%	(1.3%)	0.97	98.9%
Laughter	12.5%	(1.8%)	0.94	98.9%
Interviewer paralinguistic expressions				
Stuttering	3.5%	(0.7%)	0.86	97.9%
Disfluencies	12.7%	(2.8%)	1.00	100.0%
Laughter	9.1%	(2.2%)	1.00	100.0%
Any construction or sensitivity indicator by any actor	31.6%	(3.1%)		

[a]One kappa value was created to assess the question asking codes as they are dependent upon one another

as a final response. We conclude by creating a summary measure indicating whether or not any of the seven indicators of respondent construction confusion were present during the SIQ's administration.

We also code three variables indicating interviewer reactions to the confusing construction of the SIQ. If an interviewer's reading of the SIQ deviated from the questionnaire's wording, we coded whether or not that was a minor change (i.e., a change not affecting question meaning) or a major change (i.e., a change affecting question meaning). We also code whether or not interviewers added numbers to each response option when reading the question stem (e.g., "*one* heterosexual or straight, *two* gay or lesbian, or *three* bisexual."). Again we create an overall indicator of any interviewer problems with question construction.

Our final collection of behavior codes represents variables that could indicate problems with the sensitivity *or* the construction of the question. First, we code whether or not respondents made comments about the uncertainty of their answer. Next, we code for the absence or presence of three respondent indicators of dis-identification from an LGB identity: (1) answering the question in terms of what is *not* their sexual orientation (e.g., "I'm not gay"), (2) commenting that the degree of their sexuality is fully heterosexual (e.g., "I'm 100% straight"), or (3) referring to heterosexual or straight as being "normal". We also create variables for the three paralinguistic expressions for both respondents and interviewers. We code whether or not each actor ever stuttered, made a filler disfluency (e.g., "uh" or "um"), or laughed during administration of the SIQ. We conclude by creating an overall indicator of any problem with the SIQ's sensitivity or construction made by either the respondent or the interviewer. This indicator includes respondent uncertainty and dis-identification, but excludes paralinguistic expressions (as they may indicate behaviors other than problems with the SIQ's sensitivity/construction).

Inter-Coder Reliability

Two individuals with extensive experience coding interviewer-respondent interactions (the first author and a research assistant) coded the same 10% random subset of the full sample ($n = 94$ cases) on each variable. Kappa values and percent agreement for each variable were calculated in Stata version 14.2 using the kap command (third and fourth column of Table 10.1). Behaviors that have "–" instead of a kappa value did not occur in the 10% subsample, making it impossible for Stata to calculate kappa values. All variables had kappa values greater than .60. We note that three variables had kappa values <.8, but in these cases, this does not indicate low agreement. For example, the code indicating whether or not a respondent answered with a negation had a kappa of .66 (bordering moderate agreement) but had a percent agreement of 98.8%; the coders only disagreed on negation codes for 2 of 94 cases. Therefore, we also report percent agreement, an alternative to kappa for rare events, for each variable (Viera and Garrett 2005). Percent agreement exceeds 80% for each variable.

Respondent and Interviewer Characteristics

Our final set of variables are used to explore the association between respondent and interviewer characteristics (Table 10.2). Respondent measures come from the survey dataset itself. For our respondent characteristics, we code the respondent's: (1) age overall ($M = 54.1$) and by the categories 18–35 (18.7%), 36–55 (52.5%), and 66+ (28.8%); (2) level of education as high school graduate or less (31.2%), some college (26.2%), college graduate or higher (42.6%); and (3) gender as male (47.5%) or female (52.5%). Missing values to these variables were imputed to the mean/mode (percent missing <4%). We also code each respondent's sexual identity using their answer to the SIQ from the interview transcript (i.e., we do not use the answers recorded by interviewers). The majority of our sample was heterosexual or straight (90.6%), with 0.6% identifying as gay or lesbian, 2.4% identifying as bisexual, 0.1% identifying as "Other," 1.8% providing DK or REF answers, and 4.5% of respondents providing uncodable answers (i.e., answers that did not fit one of the response options).

Interviewer characteristics were obtained from the survey organization's administrative records. We code each of our $n = 27$ interviewers' tenure on the job as 1 year or less (70.4%) or more than 1 year (29.6%), and code each interviewer's gender as male (59.3%) or female (40.7%). Finally, we code interviewers' within-survey experience at the respondent level: each interview was coded as occurring within the first half of each interviewer's WLT2 cases, or the second half.

Table 10.2 Respondent and Interviewer Characteristics

Respondent Characteristics	
Number of respondents	895
Age	
18–35	18.7%
36–65	52.5%
66+	28.8%
Mean (in years)	54.1
Education	
High school graduate or less	31.2%
Some college	26.2%
College graduate or more	42.6%
Sex	
Male	47.5%
Female	52.5%
Sexual identity (coded from transcripts)	
Heterosexual or straight	90.6%
Gay or lesbian	0.6%
Bisexual	2.4%
Other	0.1%
Don't know/refused	1.8%
Uncodable answer	4.5%
Interviewer characteristics	
Number of interviewers	27
Interviewer tenure	
One year or less	70.4%
More than one year	29.6%
Sex	
Male	59.3%
Female	40.7%
Average # of R per I'wer	34

Analysis Methods

In telephone surveys, respondents are nested within interviewers (Hox 1994; Olson and Peytchev 2007; Olson and Bilgen 2011). Thus, the analyses in this study use the complex survey design procedures (svy procedures) in Stata 14.2 to account for the clustering of respondents within interviewers.

We start by computing proportions for each of our behavior coded variables of interest to explore the frequency with which each behavior occurs. Then, we compare our overall rates of problems with question sensitivity to overall rates of problems with question construction separately for respondents and interviewers using dependent tests of proportions.

Next, we use a logistic regression framework to examine the bivariate relationship between respondent's age and each of our four overall indicators (i.e., overall indicators of question sensitivity and construction problems for both respondents and interviewers). We analyze respondent age first as a categorical predictor (i.e., 18–35, 36–65, and 65+), and then as a continuous, mean-centered variable. We then use a logistic regression framework to examine the bivariate relationship between each of our four overall indicators and respondent education, interviewer tenure, interviewer sex, and interviewer within-survey experience. Finally, we estimate four multivariate logistic regression models, each one predicting whether or not one of our four overall indicators occurred. In these multivariate models, we include all respondent and interviewer characteristics as predictors. With one exception (footnoted in the Results section), none of our bivariate results change in these multivariate models.

Results

Indicators of Question Sensitivity

The first two columns of Table 10.1 present overall proportions of occurrence and standard errors for each behavior-coded variable in this study. The top path of Fig. 10.2 displays a tree diagram of respondent behaviors indicating problems with the SIQ's sensitivity. First, 1.8% of respondents refused to answer the SIQ at some point during the interaction, even if they ultimately provided an answer. For indicators that respondents perceived the SIQ to be *intrusive*, 3.4% of respondents commented that the question was sensitive (e.g., "Wow. We're getting personal now huh?") or off-topic ("Like, what does that have to do with leisure?"). The majority of these comments were made by heterosexual respondents (63.3% of the comments), however, 16.7% of these comments were made by respondents who ultimately refused to answer the question, and 16.7% were made by respondents who never provided an acceptable answer due to the interviewer's failure to probe. Only 1 respondent who self-identified as bisexual (3.3% of the comments) commented that the question was intrusive, while no respondents self-identifying as gay or lesbian made such a comment. This indicates that respondents who identify as LGB generally have no trouble with the intrusiveness of the SIQ.

Only a small proportion of respondents expressed *backlash* to the SIQ. Few respondents (0.7%) made references to religion in connection with the SIQ, with some indicating that they are "what the good Lord made [them] to be." 1.2% of respondents made explicit comments about being uncomfortable with homosexuality (e.g., "[I'm] not involved in all this gay activities. I don't even want to hear none about that."). Overall, these backlash comments were made exclusively by heterosexual respondents (53.8% of the comments) and respondents who never provided an acceptable answer (46.2%). None of the respondents expressing backlash refused to answer the SIQ. Overall, 5.1% of respondents expressed at least one of our three indicators of question sensitivity (i.e., refusal to answer, intrusiveness, or backlash).

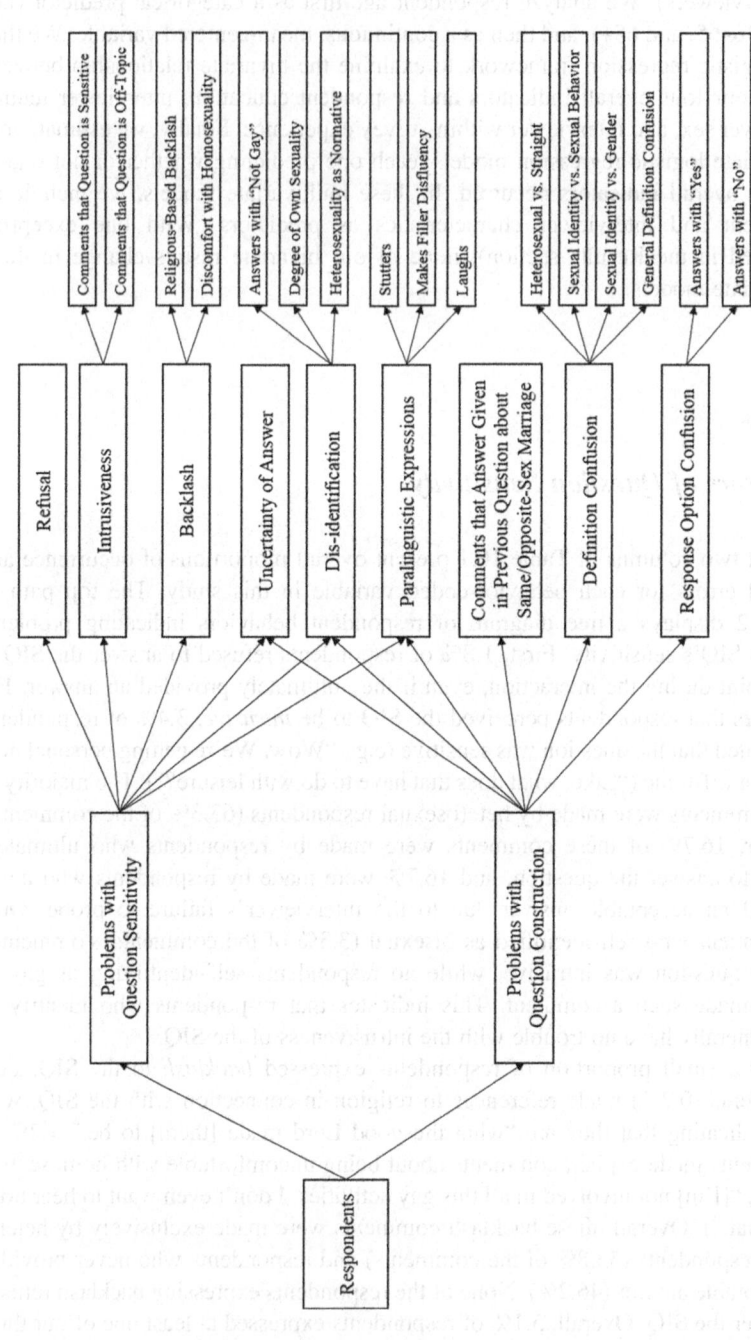

Fig. 10.2 Tree Diagram of Coded Respondent Behaviors

We find that interviewers express some indication of sensitivity (i.e, *rapport-building* behaviors) in 5.3% of the cases. These behaviors are displayed graphically in the top path of Fig. 10.3. In a few cases (0.7%) interviewers blame the researcher for having to ask the question (e.g., "They make us. I have to hear you say it."). In only 0.3% of cases, interviewers apologized for the question topic. Next, in 0.4% of cases, interviewers offered the DK/REF response option to the respondent (e.g., "All you have to do is say skip it, I can move on.").

The most common indicator of interviewers' sensitivity to the SIQ was a failure to probe unacceptable answers, occurring in 40 cases (4.5%). For example, after a respondent answered "I'm normal," the interviewer replied with "What uh, what, what uh, your, your uh, uh [laughter] uh never mind let me just skip this one here," and moved on to the next question. This finding implies that for these 40 cases that were not properly probed, interviewers should not have been able to code respondents' answers, but still did. Of these 40 cases, interviewers classified 20 respondents as heterosexual, 1 as bisexual, 3 as "Other", and 16 as DK/REF. As mentioned in the Data AND Methods section, we also find that interviewers failed to administer the SIQ in four cases (not included in our main analysis). In each of these four cases, the respondent expressed backlash in the question preceding the SIQ, which asked the respondent about the sex of their spouse or partner.

Indicators of Question Construction

As shown in Table 10.1, in 9.8% of our cases, respondents exhibited at least one indicator of difficulty with the construction of the SIQ (bottom path of Fig. 10.2). These expressions generally came from heterosexual respondents (67.1% of the comments) or respondents who never provided an acceptable answer (29.6%), though a small proportion came from respondents who refused to answer the SIQ (2.2%) or bisexual respondents (1.1%). Respondents self-identifying as gay or lesbian did not express any trouble with the SIQ's construction.

Few respondents (0.2%) expressed concern that they had answered this question in the previous item about marriage. This indicates that respondents generally had no trouble with the placement of the SIQ after a question asking about relationship status and the gender of their partner. When examining respondents' *confusion with the definition* of words in the SIQ, we find that 2.1% of respondents expressed confusion about the difference between heterosexual and straight. Few respondents (0.6%) confused sexual identity with sexual behavior. For example, these individuals sometimes expressed a lack of sexual desire at older ages (e.g., "At this point, I'm non-sexual at my...old age."). Other respondents (0.8%) confused sexual identity and gender (e.g., "I'm all woman, sweetheart."), and 1.2% of respondents expressed confusion about the definition of any word in the question (e.g., "There's so many different meanings on anything"). We also find that several respondents were *confused about the appropriate response option*. 1.9% of respondents

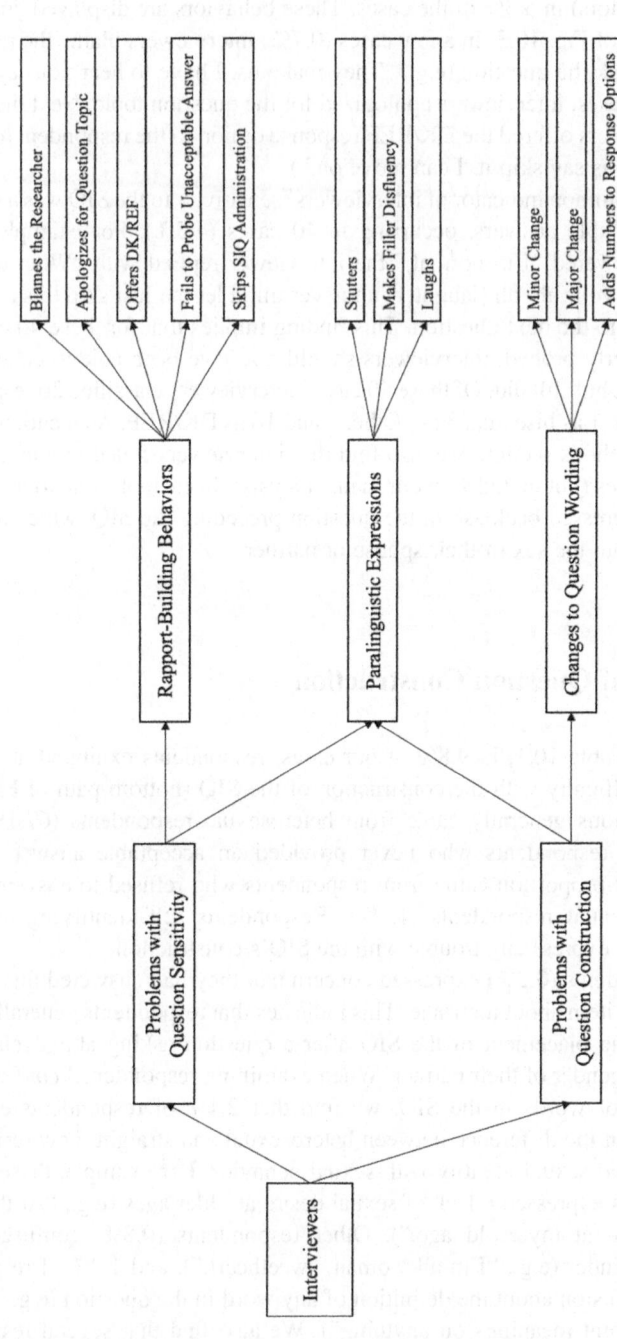

Fig. 10.3 Tree Diagram of Coded Interviewer Behaviors

answered with a positive answer (e.g., "yes") instead of a response option, and 4.2% of respondents answered this question with a negation (e.g., "no").

Overall, indicators of respondent problems with question construction ($M = 9.8\%$) occur 4.7 percentage points more often than indicators of problems with question sensitivity ($M = 5.1\%$), a statistically significant difference ($z = -3.77; p < .001$). This indicates that although some respondents do find the SIQ sensitive, more deviations from paradigmatic interactions are caused by the SIQ's construction.

Finally, when examining interviewers' *question asking* behaviors (bottom path of Fig. 10.3), we find that interviewers make minor changes to question wording for 7.2% of respondents, and make major changes for 3.9% of respondents. Additionally, for 4.8% of respondents (43 cases), interviewers added numbers to each of the response options in the question stem. When interviewers added these numbers, respondents always gave an acceptable answer, indicating that this addition may increase respondents' understanding of the SIQ. Of the 43 respondents who received numbers with the SIQ's response options, 35 (81.4%) answered using the words of the response option (e.g., "heterosexual or straight"); all 35 of these respondents self-identified as heterosexual. The remaining eight respondents (18.6%) answered using the number of the response option (e.g., "I'm one"). One of these eight respondents self-identified as a sexual minority, and the rest indicated that they were heterosexual.

Similar to respondents, interviewers' indicators of problems with question construction ($M = 11.8\%$) occur 6.5 percentage points more often than indicators of problems with question sensitivity ($M = 5.3\%$), a statistically significant difference ($z = -4.99; p < .001$). We see that interviewers' interaction problems on the SIQ caused by question wording outnumber those caused by sensitivity. We do note, however, that these interviewer question construction behaviors (e.g., adding numbers to the SIQ's response options) may have improved data quality by helping respondents to provide accurate, codable answers. Interviewer behaviors indicating problems with question sensitivity (e.g., failure to probe unacceptable answers), while less prevalent, are more likely to harm data quality.

Indicators of Question Sensitivity or Construction

Several of our indicators do not uniquely signal problems with the SIQ's sensitivity or construction. First, 2.9% of respondents indicated that they were uncertain of their answer. It is unclear if these expressions of uncertainty are due to confusion with question construction or because respondents are uncertain of their own sexuality. For example, many respondents indicated that their answer was "probably heterosexual" or "straight, I guess." One interpretation of these answers is that respondents are sure of their own sexual identity, but they are unsure that they have mapped that identity onto the correct response option. Another interpretation is that respondents are unsure of their own sexuality. Hedging phrases such as "probably" or "I guess" may be expressing some degree of uncertainty or sexual fluidity not being captured by the question's response options.

Among the indicators of dis-identification, we find that a small percentage of respondents (0.9%) answered the question in terms of what they or not (e.g., "I'm not gay."). The most prominent indicator of dis-identification was respondents expressing that they were fully straight (4.2%). Respondents used phrases that ranged from "I'm definitely straight" to "Strictly dickly here." 1.5% of respondents answered using heteronormative language, with most saying "I'm normal" to indicate straight.

Respondents' and interviewers' paralinguistic expressions may indicate either discomfort with the topic of the SIQ, or trouble understanding and responding to the question. Overall, 5.0% of respondents stuttered, 15.2% made filler disfluencies such as "uh" or "um", and 12.5% laughed. Interviewers stuttered for 3.5% of respondents, made filler disfluencies for 12.7% of respondents, and laughed for 9.1% of respondents.

Overall, we find that in 31.6% of cases, the respondent or the interviewer expressed some behavior indicating problems with the SIQ's sensitivity or construction (excluding paralinguistic expressions). This summary statistic demonstrates that when aggregating our individual indicators, sensitivity and construction issues with the SIQ may affect measurement of sexual identity for nearly one-third of respondents.

Associations Between Respondent and Interviewer Characteristics and Problems with the SIQ

We begin our bivariate analyses by examining the relationship between respondent age[5] and indicators of sensitivity and construction problems with the SIQ (Table 10.3). We find a significant linear effect for three of our indicator groups: older respondents are more likely to express indicators of sensitivity ($t = 2.69$, $p < .05$) and construction problems ($t = 3.94$, $p < .01$), and have interviewer indicators of sensitivity ($t = 3.04$, $p < .01$). This indicates that, as hypothesized, older respondents are less likely to be comfortable answering questions about their sexuality and less likely to be familiar with the terms used in an SIQ. Additionally, interviewers likely react to older respondents' sensitivity by engaging in additional rapport-building behaviors. Respondent age is not significantly associated with interviewers' reactions to the SIQ's construction.

Next, interviewers are more likely to exhibit question sensitivity behaviors when respondents are less educated ($F = 4.96, p < .05$): these interviewer behaviors occur for 7.5% of respondents with a high school education or less, 6.4% of respondents

---

[5]Questions asking respondents about their age and education were administered before the SIQ in our questionnaire. Thus, interviewers knew these respondent characteristics when asking the SIQ.

Table 10.3 Indicators of Sensitivity and Construction Problems by Respondent and Interviewer Characteristics

	Sensitivity: R			Sensitivity: I'wer			Construction: R			Construction: I'wer		
	Mean	(SE)	F/t	Mean	(SE)	F/t	Mean	(SE)	F/t	Mean	(SE)	F/t
R characteristics												
R age												
18–35	1.2%	(0.9%)		1.8%	(1.0%)		3.0%	(1.2%)		15.0%	(4.2%)	
36–65	6.4%	(0.9%)		4.9%	(1.0%)		8.9%	(1.6%)		11.5%	(3.7%)	
66+	5.4%	(1.4%)	2.55	8.1%	(2.0%)	2.81	15.9%	(2.8%)	6.68**	10.5%	(4.0%)	1.61
Linear effect			2.69*			3.04**			3.94**			−1.22
R education												
HS or less	4.3%	(1.1%)		7.5%	(1.4%)		13.6%	(1.8%)		12.2%	(3.7%)	
Some college	3.4%	(1.4%)		6.4%	(1.7%)		9.0%	(1.9%)		9.8%	(3.5%)	
College+	6.8%	(1.1%)	1.81	2.9%	(0.9%)	4.96*	7.6%	(1.3%)	5.12*	12.9%	(4.5%)	0.36
I'wer characteristics												
I'wer tenure												
<= 1 year	5.6%	(0.6%)		4.5%	(0.8%)		10.0%	(1.1%)		6.6%	(1.7%)	
> 1 year	3.9%	(1.1%)	1.39	7.3%	(2.0%)	2.08	9.5%	(2.1%)	0.04	26.7%	(11.3%)	6.58*
I'wer sex												
Male	5.4%	(0.8%)		6.0%	(1.3%)		10.9%	(1.5%)		12.1%	(5.9%)	
Female	4.7%	(0.8%)	0.40	4.2%	(0.8%)	1.58	8.4%	(1.3%)	−1.28	11.5%	(3.3%)	−0.08
Within-survey experience												
First half	4.1%	(0.8%)		4.3%	(1.0%)		9.5%	(1.4%)		10.9%	(3.6%)	
Second half	6.2%	(0.9%)	1.67	6.2%	(1.0%)	1.61	10.1%	(1.1%)	0.40	12.8%	(4.4%)	0.60

Note: $*p < .05$, $**p < .01$, $***p < .001$

with some college, but for only 2.9% of respondents with at least a college degree. Respondent indicators of sensitivity were not significantly associated with respondent education. These results indicate that interviewers are more likely to attempt to salvage rapport with less educated respondents when administering the SIQ, even though respondents' sensitivity behavior is not associated with their education levels. We also find that respondents with more education are less likely to have trouble with question construction ($F = 5.12, p < .05$). 13.6% of respondents with a high school education or less express issues with construction, compared to 9.0% of respondents with some college, and 7.6% of respondents with at least a college degree. Interestingly, interviewer construction-related behaviors were not associated with respondent education.

When examining interviewer characteristics (second half of Table 10.3), we find that experienced interviewers exhibit more problems with the SIQ's construction (e.g., changes to question wording) (26.7%) compared to inexperienced interviewers (6.6%; $F = 6.58, p < .05$). This difference indicates that more experienced interviewers may be more likely to repair the wording of the SIQ to make it more understandable. We also find that interviewer sex and within-survey experience[6] were not significantly related to respondent or interviewer expressions regarding the SIQ's sensitivity or construction.

Discussion

In this study, we perform interaction-based behavior coding on a telephone administration of a question asking about respondents' sexual identity. This is the first study to our knowledge that explores the interaction between respondents and interviewers on an SIQ in a field study. We have four main takeaway points.

First, we find that some respondents conveyed concerns about the sensitivity of the SIQ. These concerns generally took the form of comments about the intrusive/ sensitive nature of the question. Such behaviors may signal respondents' uneasiness with being asked about a personal topic, but these comments might also be driven by an underlying discomfort with homosexuality and bisexuality (i.e., a form of backlash). Further research is needed to disentangle the possible motivations behind these comments about intrusiveness. Other respondents explicitly expressed anti-LGB backlash in the form of comments about their discomfort with homosexuality. Overall, 1.8% of our respondents refused to answer the question, a rate comparable to Ridolfo et al. (2012). These indicators of problems with the SIQ's sensitivity generally came from older respondents; thus, these behaviors may reflect

---

[6]These results change in a multivariate context. Using a logistic regression model to control for all other respondent and interviewer characteristics, we find that interviewers administering the second half of their WLT2 cases are more likely to engage in rapport-building, sensitivity behaviors than those administering the first half (coef. $= .527, p < .05$).

generational differences in attitudes towards LGB individuals that might disappear over time.

Second, we find behaviors indicating that some interviewers also experience the SIQ as sensitive. This sensitivity was rarely expressed in the form of explicit comments about the SIQ (e.g., apologizing to the respondent for having to administer the SIQ). Rather, interviewers engaged in actions that limited the amount of time they spent interacting with the respondent on the SIQ. In 4.5% of cases, interviewers did not probe unacceptable respondent answers, but still coded final answers (i.e., interviewers potentially recorded incorrect sexual identities in these cases). A further four survey respondents were omitted from our analysis altogether because the interviewer skipped administration of the SIQ, but still coded a final answer for these respondents. Although these interviewer behaviors occurred in a relatively small number of cases, sexual minority individuals represent a small proportion of the population. Thus, interviewers intentionally misclassifying respondents in these ways may have serious implications for sample estimates of LGB respondents in telephone surveys.

We recommend that survey administrators better train interviewers to administer SIQs. Specifically, these results provide a collection of respondent behaviors that interviewers can expect to encounter when administering an SIQ. Interviewers can be trained to properly react to each of these behaviors in a way that continues the survey interview. For example, when respondents comment that a question is off-topic or sensitive, or refuse to answer the question, interviewers can inform respondents that the question is for demographic purposes, and reinforce the survey agency's promise of privacy and/or confidentiality. Armed with this knowledge, interviewers may be less likely to avoid interacting with respondents on this question. Future work is needed to test whether such a strategy improves measurement with a telephone-administered SIQ.

Third, we find that respondent and interviewer behaviors indicating problems with the SIQ's construction were more prevalent than behaviors indicating concern over sensitivity. For example, some respondents expressed confusion over definitions of the response options in the SIQ, especially the difference between heterosexual and straight. Thus, we provide field evidence in support of previous researchers' calls to remove "heterosexual" from the response options of SIQs (e.g., Miller and Ryan 2011).

We also find that respondents sometimes interpret the SIQ as a yes/no question. To combat this confusion, it seems that interviewers sometimes change the wording of the SIQ by speaking numeric labels before each response option. In our survey, this change ensured that all respondents gave an acceptable answer. Interviewers with more time on the job were more likely to change their reading of the SIQ from the wording in the questionnaire. Thus, these interviewers may be relying on their experience administering the SIQ to help respondents better understand the question.

Fourth and finally, we identify several indicators that do not uniquely identify problems with the SIQ's sensitivity or construction. Several respondents elaborate on their answer to the SIQ with some degree of uncertainty (e.g., "I'm straight, I guess.") Additionally, respondent indicators of dis-identification could signal that respondents are either distancing themselves from the LGB identity, or dis-identifying from the LGB identity because being "not gay" is more salient than their heterosexual identity. Future research on this topic should ask interviewers to probe these responses to help disentangle the substantive meaning of these comments.

Based on this collection of evidence and previous research (e.g., Miller & Ryan 2011; Ridolfo et al. 2011, 2012; Dahlhamer et al. 2014), we propose a new interviewer-administered SIQ for testing: *"Do you consider yourself to be one, lesbian or gay, two, straight, that is not lesbian or gay, three, bisexual, or four, something else?"* We believe that this will reduce respondent confusion over differences between the response options, may prevent respondents from prematurely answering with unacceptable positive (e.g., "yes") or negative (e.g., "no") answers, and may also reduce unacceptable dis-identification answers (e.g., "I'm not gay"). However, future research is needed to examine the measurement and data quality implications of this new SIQ construction.

This study is not without limitations. We have no benchmark data against which our present findings might be compared. These results would be strengthened by analyzing similar variables for non-sensitive questions (e.g., do interviewers incorrectly code respondent answers to non-sensitive questions at the same rate as the SIQ?). Additionally, we did not have access to several respondent and interviewer characteristics that may have been associated with our variables of interest. Variables such as respondents' religion or political affiliation, or interviewers' age should be investigated in future studies to better understand why respondents and interviewers might be exhibiting these behaviors.

Overall, this study presents several insights into the administration of an SIQ that would not have been possible using traditional methods that analyze patterns of response (e.g., item nonresponse rates) or use cognitive interviews. We find that nearly one-third of our respondents experience problems with the sensitivity or construction of the SIQ, and these problems come from both the interviewers and the respondents themselves. Administrators of telephone surveys can use these results to prepare their interviewers for respondent concerns about the SIQ's sensitivity. Questionnaire designers can use respondent and interviewer behaviors regarding question construction to revise the SIQ. Application of these findings will ensure that collection of sexual identity information via telephone surveys is not only feasible, but efficient and effective.

References

Anderson, E. (2009). *Inclusive masculinity: The changing nature of masculinities*. Oxford, UK: Routledge.

Adamczyk, A., & Pitt, C. (2009). Shaping attitudes about homosexuality: The role of religion and cultural context. *Social Science Research, 38*(2), 338–351.

Black, D. A., Sanders, S. G., & Taylor, L. J. (2007). The economics of lesbian and gay families. *Journal of Economic Perspectives, 21*(2), 53–70.

Boehmer, U., Bowen, D. J., & Bauer, G. R. (2007). Overweight and obesity in sexual-minority women: Evidence from population-based data. *American Journal of Public Health, 97*(6), 1134–1140.

Cannell, C. F., Miller, P. V., & Oksenberg, L. (1981). Research on interviewing techniques. *Sociological Methodology, 12*, 389–437.

Ceci, S. J. (1991). How much does schooling influence general intelligence and its cognitive components? A reassessment of the evidence. *Developmental Psychology, 27*, 703.

Conron, K. J., Mimiaga, M. J., & Landers, S. J. (2008). *A health profile of Massachusetts adults by sexual orientation identity: Results from the 2001–2006 Behavioral Risk Factor Surveillance System surveys*. Commonwealth of Massachusetts, Dept. of Public Health.

Dahlhamer, J. M., Galinsky, A. M. Joestl, S. S. & Ward, B. W. (2014). Sexual orientation in the 2013 national health interview survey: A quality assessment. *Vital and Health Statistics, 2*(169), 1–32.

de Leeuw, E. D. (2005). To mix or not to mix data collection modes in surveys. *Journal of Official Statistics, 21*(2), 233–255.

Diamond, L. M. (2008). *Sexual fluidity*. Cambridge: Harvard University Press.

Dillman, D. A., Smyth, J. D., & Christian, L. M. (2014). *Internet, phone, mail, and mixed-mode surveys: The tailored design method*. Hoboken: Wiley.

Dijkstra, W. (1987). Interviewing style and respondent behavior: An experimental study of the survey-interview. *Sociological Methods & Research, 16*(2), 309–334.

Dykema, J., Schaeffer, N. C., Garbarski, D., & Hout, M. (2020). The role of question characteristics in designing and evaluating survey questions. In P. Beatty et al. (Eds.), *Advances in questionnaire design, development, evaluation, and testing* (pp. 117-152). Hoboken: Wiley.

Eliason, M. J., Radix, A., McElroy, J. A., Garbers, S., & Haynes, S. G. (2016). The 'something else' of sexual orientation: Measuring sexual identities of older lesbian and bisexual women using National Health Interview survey questions. *Women's Health Issues, 26*, S71–S80.

Fowler, F. J., & Cannell, C. F. (1996). Using behavioral coding to identify cognitive problems with survey questions. In N. Schwarz & S. Sudman (Eds.), *Answering questions: Methodology for determining cognitive and communicative processes in survey research* (pp. 15–36). San Francisco: Jossey-Bass.

Fowler, F. J., & Mangione, T. W. (1990). *Standardized survey interviewing: Minimizing interviewer-related error*. Sage.

Fowler, F. J. (1995). *Improving survey questions: Design and evaluation*. Thousand Oaks: Sage.

Fredriksen-Goldsen, K. I., & Kim, H.-J. (2015). Count me in: Response to sexual orientation measures among older adults. *Research on Aging, 37*(5), 464–480.

Gagnon, J. H., & Simon, W. (1973). *Sexual conduct: The social origins of human sexuality*. Chicago: Aldine.

Gamson, J. (1995). Must identity movements self-destruct? A queer dilemma. *Social Problems, 42*(3), 390–407.

Garbarski, D., Schaeffer, N. C., & Dykema, J. (2016). Interviewing practices, conversational practices, and rapport: Responsiveness and engagement in the standardized survey interview. *Sociological Methodology, 46*(1), 1–38.

Gates, G. J. (2017). *In U.S., more adults identifying as LGBT*. Available from http://news.gallup.com/poll/201731/lgbt-identification-rises.aspx

Goffman, E. (1959). *The presentation of self in everyday life*. New York: Doubleday Anchor Books.

Goffman, E. (1963). *Stigma: Notes on the management of spoiled identity*. New York: Simon and Schuster.

Haan, M., Ongena, Y., & Huiskes, M. (2013). Interviewers' question rewording: Not always a bad thing. In P. Winker, N. Menold, R. Porst, & D. Peter Lang (Eds.), *Interviewers' deviations in surveys* (pp. 173–193).

Hatzenbuehler, M. L. (2014). Structural stigma and the health of lesbian, gay, and bisexual populations. *Current Directions in Psychological Science, 23*(2), 127–132.

Hatzenbuehler, M. L. (2017). The influence of state laws on the mental health of sexual minority youth. *JAMA Pediatrics, 171*(4), 322–324.

Herek, G. M. (2002). Gender gaps in public opinion about lesbians and gay men. *Public Opinion Quarterly, 66*(1), 40–66.

Herek, G. M. (2009). Hate crimes and stigma-related experiences among sexual minority adults in the United States: Prevalence estimates from a national probability sample. *Journal of Interpersonal Violence, 24*(1), 54–74.

Herek, G. M. (2011). Anti-equality marriage amendments and sexual stigma. *Journal of Social Issues, 67*(2), 413–426.

Hooten, M. A., Noeva, K., & Hammonds, F. (2009). The effects of homosexual imagery in advertisements on brand perception and purchase intention. *Social Behavior and Personality: An International Journal, 37*(9), 1231–1238.

Houtkoop-Steenstra, H. (2000). *Interaction and the standardized survey interview: The living questionnaire*. Cambridge: Cambridge University Press.

Hox, J. J. (1994). Hierarchical regression models for interviewer and respondent effects. *Sociological Methods & Research, 22*(3), 300–318.

Japec, L. (2008). Interviewer error and interviewer burden. In J. M. Lepkowski et al. (Eds.), *Advances in telephone survey methodology* (pp. 187–211). Hoboken: Wiley.

Kemph, B. T., & Kasser, T. (1996). Effects of sexual orientation of interviewer on expressed attitudes toward male homosexuality. *The Journal of Social Psychology, 136*(3), 401–403.

Kosciw, J. G., Palmer, N. A., & Kull, R. M. (2015). Reflecting resiliency: Openness about sexual orientation and/or gender identity and its relationship to well-being and educational outcomes for LGBT students. *American Journal of Community Psychology, 55*(1–2), 167–178.

Krosnick, J. A. (1991). Response strategies for coping with the cognitive demands of attitude measures in surveys. *Applied Cognitive Psychology, 5*(3), 213–236.

Kulick, D. (2000). Gay and lesbian language. *Annual Review of Anthropology, 29*(1), 243–285.

Lavin, D., & Maynard, D. W. (2001). Standardization vs. rapport: Respondent laughter and interviewer reaction during telephone surveys. *American Sociological Review, 66*(3), 453.

Lavin, D., & Maynard, D. W. (2002). Standardization vs. rapport: How interviewers handle the laughter of respondents during telephone surveys. In D. W. Maynard, H. Houtkoop-Steenstra, N. C. Schaeffer, & J. van der Zouwen (Eds.), *Standardization and tacit knowledge: Interaction and practice in the survey interview* (pp. 335–364). New York: Wiley.

McLelland, M. (2000). Is there a Japanese 'Gay Identity'? *Culture, Health & Sexuality, 2*(4), 459–472.

Michaels, S., et al. (2017). Improving measures of sexual and gender identity in English and Spanish to identify LGBT older adults in surveys. *LGBT Health, 4*(6), 412–418.

Miller, K., & Ryan, J. M. (2011). *Design, development and testing of the NHIS sexual identity question*. Hyattsville, MD: National Center for Health Statistics.

Olson, K., & Bilgen, I. (2011). The role of interviewer experience on acquiescence. *Public Opinion Quarterly, 75*(1), 99–114.

Olson, K., & Peytchev, A. (2007). Effect of interviewer experience on interview pace and interviewer attitudes. *Public Opinion Quarterly, 71*(2), 273–286.

Olson, L. R., Cadge, W., & Harrison, J. T. (2006). Religion and public opinion about same-sex marriage. *Social Science Quarterly, 87*(2), 340–360.

Perry, P. (2001). White means never having to say you're ethnic: White youth and the construction of "cultureless" identities. *Journal of Contemporary Ethnography, 30*(1), 56–91.

Pew Research Center. (2017). *The partisan divide on political values grows even wider*. Available from http://www.people-press.org/2017/10/05/5-homosexuality-gender-and-religion/

Powell, B., & Downey, D. B. (1997). Living in single-parent households: An investigation of the same-sex hypothesis. *American Sociological Review*, 521–539.

Ridolfo, H., & Schoua-Glusberg, A. (2009). Testing of NHANES A-CASI sexual behavior questions: Results of interviews conducted November 2008-February 2009. *Q-Bank*. Retrieved from http://www.cdc.gov/qbank.

Ridolfo, H., Miller, K., & Maitland, A. (2012). Measuring sexual identity using survey questionnaires: How valid are our measures? *Sexuality Research and Social Policy, 9*(2), 113–124.
Ridolfo, H., Perez, K., & Miller, K. (2011). *Testing of sexual identity and health related questions, results of interviews conducted May–July 2005.* Hyattsville, MD: National Center for Health Statistics.
Rotheram-Borus, M. J., et al. (1994). Sexual and substance use acts of gay and bisexual male adolescents in New York City. *Journal of Sex Research, 31*(1), 47–57.
Salthouse, T. A. (1991). Mediation of adult age differences in cognition by reductions in working memory and speed of processing. *Psychological Science, 2*(3), 179–183.
Schaeffer, N. C., Dykema, J., & Maynard, D. W. (2010). Interviewers and interviewing. In P. V. Marsden & J. D. Wright (Eds.), *Handbook of survey research* (pp. 437–470). Bingley, UK: Academic.
Schaeffer, N. C., & Maynard, D. W. (1996). From paradigm to prototype and back again: Interactive aspects of cognitive processing in standardized survey interviews. In N. Schwarz & S. Sudman (Eds.), *Answering questions: Methodology for determining cognitive and communicative processes in survey research* (pp. 65–88). Jossey-Bass: San Francisco.
SMART (2009). *Best practices for asking questions about sexual orientation on surveys.* Available from: https://williamsinstitute.law.ucla.edu/wp-content/uploads/SMART-FINAL-Nov-2009.pdf
Stange, M. (2014). *Tailoring general population surveys to address participation and measurement challenges of surveying lesbian, gay, and bisexual people.* Doctoral dissertation, University of Nebraska-Lincoln.
Stange, M., Smyth, J. D., & Olson, K. (2018). Drawing on LGB identity to encourage participation and disclosure of sexual orientation in surveys. *The Sociological Quarterly*, 1–21.
Sylva, D., Rieger, G., Linsenmeier, J. A., & Bailey, J. M. (2010). Concealment of sexual orientation. *Archives of Sexual Behavior, 39*(1), 141–152.
Tourangeau, R., Rips, L. J., & Rasinski, K. (2000). *The psychology of survey response.* Cambridge: Cambridge University Press.
Tourangeau, R., & Yan, T. (2007). Sensitive questions in surveys. *Psychological Bulletin, 133*(5), 859.
Umberson, D., Thomeer, M. B., Kroeger, R. A., Lodge, A. C., & Xu, M. (2015). Challenges and opportunities for research on same-sex relationships. *Journal of Marriage and the Family, 77*(1), 96–111.
Valentine, J. (1997). Pots and pans: Identification of queer Japanese in terms of discrimination. In A. Livia & K. Hall (Eds.), *Queerly phrased: Language, gender, and sexuality* (pp. 95–114). Oxford: Oxford University Press.
van der Zouwen, J., Dijkstra, W., & Smit, J. H. (1991). Studying respondent interviewer interaction: The relationship between interviewing style, interviewer behavior, and response behavior. In P. P. Biemer, R. M. Groves, L. E. Lyberg, N. A. Mathiowetz, & S. Sudman (Eds.), Measurement errors in surveys (pp. 419–437). New York: Wiley.
VanKim, N. A., Padilla, J. L., Lee, J. G., & Goldstein, A. O. (2010). Adding sexual orientation questions to statewide public health surveillance: New Mexico's experience. *American Journal of Public Health, 100*(12), 2392–2396.
Viera, A. J., & Garrett, J. M. (2005). Understanding interobserver agreement: The kappa statistic. *Family Medicine, 37,* 360–363.
Willis, G. B. (2005). *Cognitive interviewing: A tool for improving questionnaire design.* Thousand Oaks: Sage Publications.
Yip, A. K. (2005). Queering religious texts: An exploration of British non-heterosexual Christians' and Muslims' strategy of constructing sexuality-affirming hermeneutics. *Sociology, 39*(1), 47–65.

Chapter 11
Male/Female Is Not Enough: Adding Measures of Masculinity and Femininity to General Population Surveys

Jolene D. Smyth and Kristen Olson

Introduction

Survey research and sociological theory each provide insights into how and why people and groups act, think, and feel. Sociological theories identify what concepts are important for understanding and representing the social world. That is, sociological theories inform what to measure in surveys, and, to a certain extent, how to measure it. Survey research permits sociologists to carefully specify what is to be measured *vis a vis* sociological theory, setting surveys apart as a social research tool. It is this level of specification of concepts and measures that allow surveys to provide continued value at a time when "big data" proliferate. High quality survey measurement and estimation is necessary for sociologists to evaluate sociological theory among generalizable samples with well-developed questions, leading to further refinement and improvement of the theory and improved understanding of the social world. High quality surveys also provide insights into where sociological theories fail and where they must be adjusted for different subgroups, as well as basic insights into the prevalence of outcomes of interest. Together, sociological theory and survey methods produce insights about society that can inform decision-making and social policy.

This mutually reinforcing relationship between sociological theory and survey methods requires sociological theory to evolve from insights obtained using survey methods and survey measurement to evolve with advances in in sociological theory. The measurement of sex and gender in surveys is one area where the development of survey measures has not kept pace with sociological theory and empirical, largely qualitative, findings. Contemporary gender theory sees sex and gender as separate concepts, both of which are important for understanding behaviors and outcomes.

J. D. Smyth (✉) · K. Olson
University of Nebraska-Lincoln, NE, Lincoln, USA
e-mail: Jsmyth2@unl.edu; Kolson5@unl.edu

Yet, virtually all contemporary surveys measure sex as a binary "male" versus "female" categorization and fail to measure gender, ignoring important heterogeneity in gender identification that may exist within sex categories and any overlap that may occur across categories.

Both gender scholars and survey researchers are potentially affected by this shortcoming of modern survey measurement. Gender scholars lose an important tool for assessing gender theories, especially on generalizable samples, risking conclusions that are specific to a small group of individuals rather than the population at large. Survey researchers risk producing theoretically obsolete data, limiting the utility of the data or potentially generating misleading conclusions. Survey data that fail to capture and reflect modern and complex understandings of our social realities also face increased risk of being replaced by "big data" such as administrative and social media data. Survey data that do reflect modern and complex understandings can bring value not available in administrative or other data and are therefore unlikely to be replaced.

This paper is part of a growing chorus advocating for updates to how modern surveys measure sex and gender. We argue that the reliance on a single binary measure of sex (male or female) is out of step with current sociological understandings of sex and gender. In response, we propose and test a new theoretically-informed gradational measure of gender identification in a nationally representative mail survey. We evaluate whether respondents answer the gender measure and examine the reliability and predictive validity of the measure. In particular, we examine whether measuring gender gradationally adds explanatory value beyond sex on important social outcomes such as sexuality, childcare, grocery shopping, housework, working for pay, and military service. We also examine whether sex moderates the effect of gender identification in the ways that sociological theory would suggest on these outcomes.

Background

Sociologists have pointed out that many people understand and thus organize their social worlds around the "sex and gender binary," or the belief that there are only two types of people, male-bodied masculine and female-bodied feminine (Lorber 1996; Wade and Ferree 2019). In this popular view, sex and gender are conflated. Men are masculine and women are feminine. In contrast, modern Sociologists understand sex and gender as separate social phenomena (Lorber 1996; Lucal 1999). Sex generally refers to biological sex, which is commonly determined during the social processes of sex categorization (i.e., usually determined at birth by a medical professional using socially-derived criteria) (Kessler 1990; Kessler and

McKenna 1978).[1] Gender is separate from sex and exists at multiple societal levels, including as deep-seated ideologies that structure institutions and social lives at the macro level (Acker 1990, 1992; Britton 1997; Connell 1987; Hall 1993; Price 2008; Risman 2004) and as identities at the individual level and expressions of those identities at the interactional level (Ridgeway and Smith-Lovin 1999; West and Zimmerman 1987). Social behaviors are enabled and/or constrained by macro-level gender ideologies and structures and reflect micro-level identities (Burke 1991; Ridgeway and Smith-Lovin 1999). Because sex and gender are separate, sociologists understand that people of any sex can have masculine and/or feminine gender identification (Connell 1995; Lucal 1999), that gender identification can vary within sex categories (i.e., some men [women] may feel more masculine or feminine than other men [women]—Connell 1995; Geist et al. 2017), and that there can be overlap in gender identification between the sexes (i.e., some women [men] may identify as just as masculine [feminine] as some men [women]—Magliozzi et al. 2016). Further, sociologists believe that both sex and gender relate in complex and often interacting ways to affect important social, economic, and health outcomes (Annandale and Hunt 1990; Geist et al. 2017; Hyde 2005; Saugeres 2002).

The gender binary is reflected strongly in the nearly ubiquitous survey practice of asking respondents or interviewers (e.g., the General Social Survey) to report respondent sex using only two categories, male or female, as a single demographic measure of sex/gender. The binary sex measure has allowed researchers to identify differences between men and women in types of paid and unpaid labor (Bianchi et al. 2000; Padavic and Reskin 2002); pay rates (Padavic and Reskin 2002); propensities and pathways to commit different types of crimes (Kruttschnitt 2013); health behaviors and outcomes (Verbrugge 1985); and in many other important domains, but fails to reflect current, more complex sociological understandings of sex and gender. Binary sex measures conflate sex and gender, as illustrated by the common interchange of the terms "sex" and "gender" in these questions, and obscure the variation in gender within and across sex categories that sociologists find of central importance. As a result, sociologists have increasingly critiqued survey research's heavy reliance on binary measures, calling instead for the addition of non-binary categories (e.g., "transgender"), measurement of both sex at birth and current sex to better reflect the sociological understanding that sex can change over the life course (Federal Committee on Statistical Methodology 2016a, b, c; Fraser 2018; The GenIUSS Group 2014), and measurement of individuals' gender identity and expression separate from sex (Magliozzi et al. 2016; Westbrook and Saperstein 2015; Geist and Ruppanner 2018; Geist et al. 2017).[2]

---

[1]Work on the case management of intersex babies reveals the extent to which sex categorization is a social process (Epstein 1990, cited in Lorber 1996; Kessler 1990).

[2]"Gender identity" is sometimes used to refer to cisgender versus transgender (i.e., one's sense of oneself of male or female regardless of sex), but in this paper we use it to refer to self-perceived masculinity/femininity.

Psychologists have developed a handful of gender identification measures, most measuring femininity and masculinity, but these have not been widely adopted by population-based surveys because they are impractical (containing anywhere from 24 to 144 items [Bem 1974; Mahalik et al. 2005; Spence et al. 1974] or multiple vignettes [Kroska 2000]), rely heavily on stereotypically masculine or feminine traits that change over time (e.g., Bem 1974; Egen and Perry 2001; Mahalik et al. 2005; Spence et al. 1974), or have been developed using convenience samples of limited subpopulations (e.g., adolescent males, Oransky and Fischer 2009). These measures are costly for inclusion in a wide range of surveys, and may not be suitable for contemporary general adult populations. As a result, survey-based empirical gender literature, with its reliance on binary sex measures, has focused almost entirely on cisgender individuals, failing to capture gender diversity and its consequences (Geist and Ruppanner 2018) and undermining the use of surveys as a tool to study this fundamental organizing feature of society.

However, if measures that capture gender diversity can be developed and deployed alongside measures of sex, surveys should be reasonable tools for examining both sex and gender variation and their social correlates. This point has been made by the Federal Committee on Statistical Methodology, which has joined sociologists in pushing for more inclusive measures of sexual orientation and gender identification in surveys (FCSM 2016a, b, c). In a review of existing measures, only two studies (one an unpublished report) examined continuous measurements of masculinity and femininity (Correll et al. 2014 as cited in FCSM 2016b; Magliozzi et al. 2016), both of which use separate seven-point unipolar scales. The Magliozzi et al. (2016) measure asked respondents to rate how feminine and masculine they see themselves on unipolar endpoint-labeled scales ("not at all" to "very"). Consistent with sociological theory, they find considerable variability in gender identification within men and women, overlap in gender identification between men and women, and an association between gender identification and marital status such that higher gender polarization (i.e., high femininity and low masculinity or vice versa) is associated with being married. The Magliozzi et al. (2016) scales are practical from a survey standpoint because they take up far less space and respondent effort than prior multi-item or multi-vignette masculinity/femininity scales, making it more affordable to measure gender identification in surveys on a wide variety of topics and when respondent burden is a concern. However, these measures were evaluated on an unrepresentative, convenience sample (Amazon Mechanical Turk) using only one predictive validity outcome (marital status). In addition, Magliozzi and colleagues' gender polarization operationalization failed to reveal how each gender identification is directly associated with marital status, whether this association is moderated by sex, how gender non-conforming polarizations are related to marital status, and they did not examine theoretically informed interactions between sex and gender.

In addition to these studies, Smyth (2007) and Smyth et al. (2018) introduced a gender self-perception measurement in which respondents placed marks representing themselves on a horizontal line labeled "completely feminine" at one end and "completely masculine" at the other. Using a ruler, they measured the number of millimeters from the completely feminine endpoint to the respondents' mark. Using this measure, they showed that gender self-perception is associated with women's involvement in farm and ranch work, with more involved women perceiving themselves as more masculine. However, while capturing the continuum of gender identification, this measure is unlikely to be widely adopted due to labor-intensive data entry. For a gradational gender identification scale to be useful and transportable enough to be widely adopted by population-based surveys, it needs to (1) be parsimonious to administer and process, (2) be a measure respondents are willing and able to answer, (3) exhibit high reliability, and (4) exhibit high validity.

In this paper, we test a new gradational measure of gender identification in which respondents are asked to report how masculine or feminine they are on a 21-point scale labeled "Completely Feminine" at one end and "Completely Masculine" at the other. By virtue of being only one item with explicit response options (i.e., no ruler needed), our measure of gender identification meets criteria #1 above. We assess the measure on the remaining three criteria.

We assess whether it meets criteria #2 by examining item nonresponse, which is a commonly used tool to evaluate survey item quality (e.g., Beatty and Herrmann 2002; Krosnick 2002). Item nonresponse rates that are higher than other commonly-asked items (in this case, sex) indicate respondent difficulty with the item while similar or lower item nonresponse rates indicate no such difficulty. An additional desired outcome is that item missingness is not related to any of the variables that are of interest in the survey—that is, that nonresponse is missing completely at random (e.g., Little and Rubin 2002). Empirically, older respondents and respondents with lower levels of education often have higher item nonresponse rates than their younger and more educated counterparts (see review in de Leeuw et al. 2003). Other demographic characteristics of respondents (i.e., sex and race) are less consistently related to item missing data rates.

Criteria #3, reliability, will be assessed in two ways. First, we will examine the association between gender identification and other demographic variables, the most important of which is sex. Given that most of the U.S. population is cisgender, we expect considerable overlap between these two measures. However, we do not expect complete overlap because gender diversity within sex categories (Connell 1995; Geist et al. 2017) is what we are trying to capture with this measure. In addition to sex, we also examine other common demographics, following Magliozzi, et al. As a second assessment of reliability, we test whether responses to the gender identification item are influenced by questionnaire context. It is well established that the context of survey items can affect responses to these items by influencing how respondents understand questions, what information they use in responding, and how they incorporate that information into their responses (Tourangeau and Rasinski 1988; Sudman et al. 1996; Tourangeau et al. 2000). For example, context effects can occur when information from surrounding questions triggers social comparisons in the domain of interest (Schwarz and Strack 1999). To the extent that individuals have a well-formed gender identification, the context of surrounding questions will not change their gender identification ratings, indicating high reliability. However, asking about society's ideal man or woman before asking about one's self-placement may trigger important comparisons between themselves and this ideal, leading to different answers (e.g., "I don't meet this ideal, so I am going to answer differently from my answer there") and indicating lower reliability.

We use a series of predictive validity assessments based on sociological gender theory to examine criteria #4. The theory of "doing gender" says that individuals produce gender through everyday interactions with others (West and Zimmerman 1987). Individuals are expected to - and expect others to - act in accordance with macro-level gender ideologies. When individuals act as expected by these societal norms, they are rewarded (i.e., socially accepted, complimented, etc.). When an individual's behavior challenges gender norms, they are held accountable (i.e., judged, devalued, and/or treated negatively) (Lucal 1999). Interactional behaviors that support gender norms or hold others accountable for doing so reproduce macro gender ideologies and sustain existing gender identities.

We may see this distinction between reward and accountability when examining sexuality. Individuals deploy gender displays strategically to try to manage their social experiences related to sexuality. Appearing straight (independent from one's sexuality) requires doing gender in a way that closely aligns with one's sex. Likewise, to be visible as a sexual minority (e.g., when dating or to challenge social norms) requires doing gender non-normatively (Wade and Ferree 2019; West and Zimmerman 1987; Frye 1983 as cited in West and Zimmerman 1987, p. 145). We do not expect the likelihood of being heterosexual or GLB to differ by sex alone or by gender identification alone, but because doing sexuality requires masculine or feminine gender presentation *relative to a sex category*, we do expect the relationship between gender identification and sexuality to differ for men and women. In particular, while there is undoubtedly variation in gender identities within sexuality categories, overall, we expect women who identify as more masculine to be more likely to self-identify as lesbian or bisexual and less likely to self-identify as straight and men who identify as more feminine to be more likely to self-identify as gay or bisexual.

Beyond this important social identity, a number of studies have uncovered interactional behaviors through which people commonly produce gender such as through the household division of labor (Berk 1985; South and Spitze 1994). One explanation for the fact that women do more housework on average than men (Bianchi et al. 2000; Bianchi et al. 2012) is that housework is a means for doing gender. Doing cooking, cleaning, and laundry is doing femininity for women (Berk 1985). Likewise, doing household repairs, mowing the lawn, and grilling meat are means for producing masculinity for men (Berk 1985; Sobal 2005). Even avoiding opposite-gendered tasks can be a way of doing gender, as is the case for U.S. men who contribute less to housework to bolster their masculinity when they lose their status as primary provider (Bittman et al. 2003; Brines 1994; Greenstein 2000). Consistent with much previous research, we expect sex to predict who sees themselves as the primary person in the household who does different types of tasks (housekeeping, household repairs, etc.) and how many hours they spend on tasks, but we also expect an association between these outcomes and gender identification. Moreover, we expect the association between gender identification and these outcomes to be moderated by sex (i.e., femininity will be associated with the likelihood claiming to be the primary housekeeper differently for women than men).

The division of labor in childcare is also a means through which men and women do gender (Dalton and Bielby 2000; Hays 1996; McMahon 1995; Walzer 1998). In trying to achieve ideological gendered standards of parenthood (or simply to function as a parent in a world that expects them), men and women parent in gendered ways, even when they desire otherwise (Walzer 1998). Women mother and men father (nobody is simply a parent), leading them to reproduce gendered parenting ideology and influence their own identities as parents and as women or men. Thus, we expect that women will be more likely to say that they are the primary person involved in childcare and spend more hours on care work than men. Gender identification may also be related to these tasks in that individuals who perceive themselves as more feminine may be more likely to engage in this kind of care work. Alternatively, engaging in care work may lead all respondents to perceive themselves as more feminine. While we cannot disentangle causal order on this issue, we do expect an association between gender identification and care work and we expect it to differ for men and women.

Paid employment also provides an arena for doing gender. To the extent that men are more likely to work for pay (Bureau of Labor Statistics 2018) and to hold full-time work (Bureau of Labor Statistics 2014), they are doing masculine gender (Bittman et al. 2003). Thus, we expect men and those who report more masculine gender identification to report more hours working for pay than women and those reporting feminine gender identifications. Performing sex-typed work (i.e., driving a truck or teaching school) is another means for doing gender (England 1992; Padavic and Reskin 2002). Doing farm work, for example, leads women to be perceived by others and to perceive themselves as more masculine (Brandth 2006; Smyth et al. 2018). Women in male-typed occupations commonly have to perform the "feminine apologetic" (i.e., put extra emphasis on feminine appearance and behaviors - Felshin 1974) to offset these perceptions. Women in the military have been shown to go to fairly extreme measures to do femininity to offset their masculine military jobs (Herbert 1998). Given that the military is largely a male/masculine domain and associated with masculine work (Enloe 2004), we expect men and those who are more masculine to be more likely to report having ever served.

In sum, based on theory and previous literature, we expect both sex and gender identification to be associated with each of these outcomes, and in some cases we expect sex to moderate the effect of gender identification. To the extent that gender identification explains variation in these outcomes above and beyond sex alone, or provides a more nuanced understanding of the joint roles of sex and gender, then we have evidence that our gender identification scale has predictive validity.

Methods

The data for this paper come from the National Health, Wellbeing, and Perspectives Survey (NHWPS; AAPOR RR1 = 16.7%, n = 1002; AAPOR 2016), a 12-page (77-item) mail survey conducted between April and August 2015. NHWPS was designed to examine mechanisms underlying sex differences in mental and physical wellbeing and to test methodological features of surveys. The design included a fully crossed 3×3×2 experiment with three within-household selection instruction treatments (instruction in the cover letter alone, in the cover letter and questionnaire, in the cover letter and questionnaire with a verification question; Olson and Smyth 2017), three incentive treatments (no incentive, $1 cash at first mailing, and $1 cash at third mailing; Smyth et al. 2019), and two versions of the questionnaire.[3] A simple random sample of 6000 addresses was selected from the USPS Delivery Sequence File by Survey Sampling International, and randomly assigned to one of the resulting 18 experimental treatments. The next birthday within-household selection procedure was used to sample an adult from each household (Gaziano 2005). Sampled households were contacted by postal mail up to four times (initial invitation, postcard reminder, and two full-packet reminders).

When examining item nonresponse, our analytic data set is n = 1002. Four questionnaires were returned with their identification numbers torn off, making it impossible to know their geographic region (a control variable, described below) or incentive treatment. Thus, when examining the other outcomes, our analytic data set is n = 922 cases with full data on sex and gender identification and intact questionnaire ID numbers. Although our imputation and missing data indicators (described below) ensure that no cases are dropped due to independent variables, we allow casewise deletion for missing data on dependent variables, resulting in some variation in sample size for the predictive validity analyses.

Measures

Independent Variables

Sex was measured with the categories "male" (coded 0) and "female" (coded 1) within a household roster that asked for information for up to six household members. Missing data (8.48%, unweighted estimate) on sex was logically imputed using information on sexuality, partnerships, sex of partners, the gender scale, and household tasks. 1.5% of missing cases could not be imputed. *Gender identification* was measured using a continuum with 21 unnumbered scale points ranging from "Completely Feminine" to "Completely Masculine" (See Fig. 11.1). Respondents

---

[3] Each had the same questions, but design features within questions differed.

Version 1

75. Whether male or female, people often differ in how masculine or feminine they feel. How masculine or feminine are each of the following?

	Completely Feminine — Completely Masculine
Yourself	○○○○○○○○○○○○○○○○○○○○○
Society's ideal man	○○○○○○○○○○○○○○○○○○○○○
Society's ideal woman	○○○○○○○○○○○○○○○○○○○○○

Version 2

75. Whether male or female, people often differ in how masculine or feminine they feel. How masculine or feminine are each of the following?

	Completely Feminine — Completely Masculine
Society's ideal man	○○○○○○○○○○○○○○○○○○○○○
Society's ideal woman	○○○○○○○○○○○○○○○○○○○○○
Yourself	○○○○○○○○○○○○○○○○○○○○○

Fig. 11.1 NHWPS Survey Item Measuring Masculinity/Femininity

were asked to rate the femininity/masculinity of themselves, society's ideal man, and society's ideal woman and were randomly assigned to receive the items with the "yourself" scale first or last. Gender identification is a continuous measure ranging from 1 to 21 with higher numbers denoting more masculinity and less femininity. No imputation was used for this variable.

Dependent Variables for Predictive Validity Models

Sexuality was measured by an item asking, "Do you consider yourself to be: Heterosexual or straight, Gay or lesbian, Bisexual." An indicator variable coded 1 for those who reported being heterosexual or straight (92.85%) and 0 for those reporting being gay or lesbian or bisexual (GLB; 7.15%) was created (See Table 11.1). Logical imputation using information from the household roster was used to fill in missing data where possible. Remaining missing cases are casewise deleted when sexuality is used as a dependent variable and represented by a missing indicator to avoid the loss of cases when it is used as an independent variable, yielding 91.42% straight, 7.04% GLB, and 1.53% missing.

The next set of dependent variables capture whether respondents see themselves as the primary person in the household to do childcare, grocery shopping, housekeeping, and household repairs. After completing the household roster, respondents

Table 11.1 Descriptive Statistics for Dependent Variables (n = 922)

	Unweighted Frequency	Weighted Mean or Percent	Standard Deviation	Minimum	Maximum
Sexuality					
Straight	870	92.85			
GLB	38	7.15			
Missing	14				
Respondent is most likely person in the household to do...					
Childcare					
No	538	67.12			
Yes	274	32.88			
Missing	110				
Grocery shopping					
No	229	32.36			
Yes	666	67.64			
Missing	27				
Housekeeping					
No	232	35.78			
Yes	645	64.22			
Missing	45				
Household repairs					
No	367	44.52			
Yes	510	55.48			
Missing	45				
In a typical week, hours spent on...					
Working for pay					
Mean # hours		27.41	22.78	0	168
Missing	97				
Housework					
Mean # hours		9.28	10.56	0	112
Missing	81				
Caring for family					
Mean # hours		13.39	28.59	0	168
Missing	116				
Military service					
No	764	89.11			
Yes	114	10.89			
Missing	44				

Note: When sexuality is used as a dependent variable, cases that remain missing after logical imputation are casewise deleted. When it is used as a control variable, a missing data indicator for these cases is included

were asked, "Thinking about the people you listed in question #48, who is most likely to do each of the following tasks?" For each task, respondents who selected themselves are coded 1 and those who did not are coded 0.

Three continuous variables capture the number of hours spent weekly on care work, housework, and working for pay, as measured by the question, "Thinking about how you spend your time in a typical week, how many hours do you spend on each of the following?" One version of the questionnaire also included the instruction, "your best estimate is fine," which did not change responses (Timbrook et al. 2016). The items included, "Working for pay at all jobs, including overtime," "On household work, not including childcare and leisure time activities," and "Looking after family members (children, elderly, ill, or disabled family members)." Items on leisure time and sleep are not examined here. Responses to these items are top coded at 168 hours (24 hours × 7 days).

The final dependent variable is an indicator of having ever served in the military (1 = yes, 0 = no). This item was part of a separate experiment to examine full versus quasi-filters (Olson et al. 2018). Version 1 utilized a full filter asking, "Are you a veteran or currently serving in the military?" followed by items asking when the respondent served and if they served in a combat zone. Respondents were coded as having served if they answered affirmatively to the filter question or skipped the filter question but subsequently indicated a service time period or having served in a combat zone. In version 2, there was no filter question; rather the service dates and combat zone questions included the quasi-filter response option "Never served in the military." Respondents were coded as having served in the military if they reported any time period of service or having served in a combat zone, and coded as not having served if they selected "Never served in the military".

Control Variables

To account for other factors that may be associated with the outcomes and reduce the likelihood of spurious associations, we control for age, education, race, ethnicity, sexuality (when not the dependent variable), political affiliation, having dependents under age 18 living in the household, and region in all models. We also control for the experimental design factors. Missing data is accounted for with probabilistic single imputation and missing category indicators for the categorical variables and with group mean imputation for age. Descriptive statistics for these variables are shown in Table 11.2.

A continuous measure of age was calculated using reports of respondents' date of birth. Education was measured by a nominal item asking for highest degree. Indicator variables were created for high school or less, some college, a four-year degree or more (BA+), and missing data.

Race was measured with a check-all-that-apply question asking, "What is your race? White, Black or African American, American Indian or Alaska Native, Asian, Native Hawaiian or Other Pacific Islander, Other." Ethnicity was measured by an item asking, "Are you Spanish, Hispanic, or Latino?". The race and ethnicity measures were combined to produce a set of five indicator variables for combinations of race and ethnicity (non-Hispanic white, Hispanic white, non-Hispanic black,

Table 11.2 Descriptive Statistics for Control Variables (n = 922)

	Unweighted Frequency	Weighted Mean or Percent	Standard Deviation	Minimum	Maximum
Age					
Mean		49.09	17.65	17.63	99.27
Education					
HS or less	172	34.04			
Some college	302	34.35			
Ba+	441	30.91			
Missing	7	0.71			
Race and ethnicity					
Non-Hispanic white	713	64.73			
Hispanic white	31	7.41			
Non-Hispanic black	65	11.21			
Non-Hispanic other	63	8.70			
Hispanic other	16	4.92			
Missing	34	3.03			
Sexuality					
GLB	38	7.04			
Straight	870	91.42			
Missing	14	1.53			
Political party affiliation					
Democrat	318	35.72			
Independent	302	34.56			
Republican	259	24.94			
Missing	43	4.77			
Region					
South	316	40.02			
Northeast	175	17.31			
Midwest	246	22.62			
West	185	20.05			
Dependents under age 18					
No	650	62.10			
Yes	207	31.83			
Missing	65	6.06			
Experimental treatments					
Questionnaire version					
Version 1	485	52.16			
Version 2	437	47.84			
Within household selection					
Instruction in letter only	332	37.47			
Inst. In letter & questionnaire	301	30.52			

(continued)

Table 11.2 (continued)

	Unweighted Frequency	Weighted Mean or Percent	Standard Deviation	Minimum	Maximum
Inst. In Letter & Questionnaire w/ verification question	289	32.01			
Incentives					
No incentive	242	23.61			
$1 with first mailing	358	38.54			
$1 with third mailing	322	37.85			

Note: N = 922 cases where both sex and gender had values and all experimental treatments were known

non-Hispanic other, and Hispanic-other) plus a final missing data indicator for remaining missing cases.

Political party affiliation was measured by a question asking, "In politics today, do you consider yourself a...Republican, Democrat, Independent." Indicator variables for Republican, Democrat, and Independent, and missing, were created.

Respondents were asked how many dependents from five age groups (under 1, 1–5, 6–11, 12–17, and 18 or older) were living with them. Responses were used to generate a dichotomous variable coded 0 for those with no dependents in the first four categories (i.e., under age 18) and 1 for those with dependents in these categories.

Geographic region, obtained from the sample file, is represented by a series of indicator variables for Northeast, Midwest, South, and West based on census regions. Indicator variables were also created to represent the experimental factors to account for any effects of the experimental design.

Analyses

Item nonresponse. We examine the item nonresponse rate for gender identification overall, for men versus women, and compared to that of the sex question using dependent t-tests. We then use logistic regression to evaluate whether certain subgroups (using the control variables described above) are more or less likely to fail to answer the gender identification question.

Reliability. Next, we examine response distributions for sex and gender identification and the response distribution for gender identification by sex category to determine how much variation in gender identification there is within and between sex categories. We determine how much variance in gender identification is shared with sex and how much is unique by regressing (OLS) the gender scale on sex. The resulting R^2 value reflects shared variance with sex, and $1 - R^2$ reflects unique gender identification variance. Next, we examine whether the gender identification ratings change over different measurement contexts by comparing responses across the two question orders (yourself reported before or after society's ideals, Fig. 11.1). We look at the effect of this experiment on the mean gender identification ratings overall and separately for men and women using OLS regression. We then use OLS regression to examine whether the demographic variables described above predict gender identification ratings, and how much variation in the gender identification scale is explained by these demographic variables.

Predictive Validity. Finally, we examine the association between each of our dependent variables and sex and gender identification by estimating a series of logistic (for dichotomous outcomes) and negative binomial (for count outcomes with overdispersion) regression models using STATA 15.1. For each dependent variable, we estimate four models: sex alone, gender alone, sex with gender, and an interaction model. All models include the control variables.

All analyses account for the survey design using STATA's *svy* command and are weighted.

Findings

Item Nonresponse

Overall, 8.6% of respondents did not answer the gender identification question; in comparison, 7.6% did not answer the sex question.[4] These dependent proportions are not statistically different from each other (F(1, 1001) = 0.37, p = 0.541). Men and women were equally likely to answer the gender identification item (men 91%, women 93%, t = -0.88; p = 0.381), and those who skipped the sex question also were more likely to skip the gender identification question (42% of those who were missing on sex answered the gender identification question; t = 2.78, p = 0.006).

Next we examine whether item missing data on the gender identification measure was related to age, education, race/ethnicity, sexual orientation, political ideology, region of the country, having any dependents, and the experimental variation in question order, selection instructions, and incentive (results available from authors on request).[5] Across all of these characteristics, failing to answer the sex, education, political affiliation, and dependents questions were all the strongest predictors of failing to answer the gender identification question (p < .03 for all items). This makes sense as these items were all located in the same section of the questionnaire. Substantively, individuals with higher education levels were less likely to omit the item relative to those with a high school degree or less (F(2,995) = 8.09, p < .0001) and respondents whose race/ethnicity is Hispanic White were more likely to fail to

---

[4]Weighted estimates.

[5]n = 998. Four cases were excluded because of missing questionnaire ID numbers, making it impossible to know experimental treatment and region (n = 998).

answer this item compared to non-Hispanic White respondents (OR = 4.56, t = 2.72, p = 0.007). Additionally, those who received a questionnaire with the instructions on the front of it were more likely to omit answering this item compared to those who received the instructions in a cover letter (OR = 3.64, t = 2.60, p = 0.009). There was no association between item missing data rates on the gender identification question and age, sexual orientation, political affiliation, region of the country, having dependents, the question order experiment, or incentives.

Reliability

In this study, 46.7% of adults identified as male and 53.3% identified as female. Figure 11.2 shows the percent of men and women selecting each point on the gender scale. As expected, the scale skews heavily masculine for men (42.6% chose "completely masculine") and heavily feminine for women (36.8% chose "completely feminine") (Design adjusted $F(16.36, 15099.08) = 20.65$, $p = 0.0000$). The average gender rating on the scale was 4.5 (SD = 4.05, IQR = 6) for women and 18 (SD = 3.38, IQR = 4) for men. Both sexes used almost the entire range of the gender scale (women 1 to 21; men 2 to 21). Thus, there is considerable range in gender identification within each sex category and considerable overlap between them.

Regressing the gender scale on sex reveals that sex is a significant predictor of gender ($t = -36.21$, $p < 0.000$) and explains 76.4% of the variance in the gender identification scale, leaving 23.6% of the variance not shared by sex. Some of this unexplained variation is explained by the experimental variation in question order. Although there is no difference in gender identification by question order overall

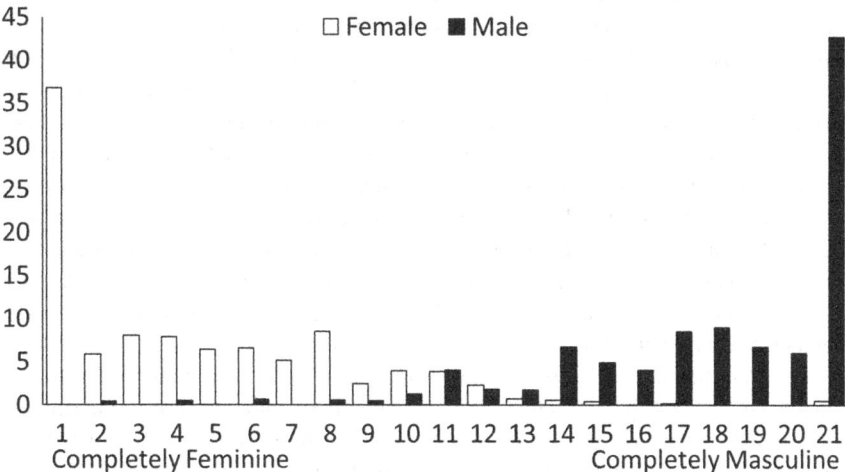

Fig. 11.2 Percent selecting each point on the gender identification scale by sex

Table. 11.3 Mean reported gender self-identification by question order and sex of respondent

	Overall	Men	Women
Self-perception asked first	10.35	18.26	3.31
Society's ideal asked first	11.27	17.69	5.73
Difference in responses (society ideal-self-perception)	0.92	−0.57	2.42
P-value	0.207	0.33	< .0001
N	922	359	563

Note: There are 5 people with a missing value for sex who answered the gender question. There is no difference in reports of gender identification across the questionnaire versions for these 5 people ($p = 0.412$)

($t = 1.26$, $p = 0.207$), there are important sex differences (see Table 11.3). Men evaluate their gender identification similarly regardless of whether they evaluate themselves first or after society's ideals ($t = -1.00$, $p = 0.319$). Women, on the other hand, evaluate themselves as 2.42 points *more masculine* ($t = 5.39$, $p < .0001$) when they are asked to evaluate society's ideal man and woman first versus when they evaluate themselves first. Thus, asking about society's ideals first creates a significant anchoring effect for women but not men. Adding the indicator for the question order experiment and the interaction between sex and the order experiment to the regression of the gender scale on sex explains an additional 1.4% of variance in gender identification, leaving 22.2% of the variance in gender unexplained.

We now examine demographic predictors of gender identification. Notably, none of the demographic predictors (age, education, race/ethnicity, political affiliation, region of the country, presence of dependents, the selection experiment, or the incentive experiment) other than sex are associated with gender identification at the $p < .05$ level when men and women are included in the same model, likely because masculinity and femininity operate in opposite directions on the scale.

However, there are significant associations in self-perceived gender identification with many of these demographic variables when examining men and women separately (Table 11.4). For instance, older men rate themselves as more masculine and older women rate themselves as more feminine than their younger counterparts. Overall, education is not associated with gender identification for men ($F = 0.44$, $p = 0.722$) or women ($F = 1.58$, $p = 0.193$). Race/ethnicity is associated with evaluations of gender identification for both men ($F = 8.24$, $p < .0001$) and women ($F = 4.81$, $p = 0.0002$)—Hispanic white men and women and non-Hispanic black men and women evaluate themselves as more gender normatively polarized than their non-Hispanic white counterparts. Republican men evaluate themselves as more masculine and Republican women evaluate themselves more feminine than their Democrat counterparts (men: $F = 9.96$, $p < .0001$; women: $F = 2.36$, $p = 0.070$). Gender identification varies by region for men ($F = 4.74$, $p = 0.0027$), but not for women ($F = 0.14$, $p = 0.936$). Having dependents and the other experimental conditions are not associated with gender identification for either men or women. These results mirror many of the associations between gender polarization and a similar set of demographic variables examined by Magliozzi et al. (2016), indicating

Table 11.4 Linear Regression Coefficients Predicting Gender Identification for Men and Women

	Men		Women	
	Coef.	SE	Coef.	SE
Question order experiment				
Self-perception asked first	–		–	
Society's ideal asked first	−0.81+	0.449	2.29***	0.399
Age	0.08***	0.012	−0.05***	0.012
Education				
HS or less	–		–	
Some college	−0.55	0.593	0.61	0.563
Ba+	−0.12	0.549	1.06*	0.526
Missing	−0.50	1.859	−0.40	1.819
Race/ethnicity				
Non-Hispanic white	–		–	
Hispanic white	2.76***	0.612	−1.40+	0.753
Non-Hispanic black	1.78*	0.843	−2.82***	0.627
Non-Hispanic other	−1.28	1.160	0.76	0.934
Hispanic other	−2.00	2.864	−1.63*	0.768
Missing race & ethnicity	5.68*	2.376	0.86	1.307
Political affiliation				
Democrat	–		–	
Independent	0.90	0.613	0.06	0.510
Republican	1.15+	0.626	−0.98+	0.550
Missing	−5.98***	1.664	−1.73	1.089
Region				
South	–		–	
Northeast	−2.75***	0.773	−0.23	0.612
Midwest	−0.33	0.622	−0.03	0.510
West	−0.92+	0.536	0.16	0.615
Any dependents				
No	–		–	
Yes	0.49	0.540	−0.39	0.507
Missing	0.85	1.307	−0.55	0.652
Cover experiment				
Letter only	–		–	
Instructions	0.15	0.448	0.49	0.461
Verification question	0.49	0.560	0.32	0.501
Incentive experiment				
No incentive	–		–	
Pre-paid incentive	−0.44	0.631	−0.04	0.510
Incentive with reminder	−0.89	0.667	0.16	0.520
Intercept	14.70***	1.410	5.70***	1.149
N	359		563	
Model F	6.55***		8.07***	
R^2	29.14%		29.04%	

+$p < .10$, *$p < .05$, **$p < .01$, ***$p < .001$

that gender identification is socially contingent (p. 5). This collection of demographic variables explains about 29% of the variation in gender identification for both men and women.

Predictive Validity

The first set of associations we examine are between sex, gender identification, and sexuality (Table 11.5—full models in online supplement). As expected, neither sex nor gender identification on their own (Models 1 and 2) nor the two of them together (Model 3) are significantly associated with the likelihood of reporting being heterosexual. However, there is a significant interaction effect between sex and gender identification ($t = -2.25$, $p = 0.025$), graphed in Fig. 11.3. As men report higher masculinity, the likelihood of them reporting being heterosexual increases, but as

Table 11.5 Odds Ratios Predicting Heterosexual Sexuality (n = 902)

	Model 1	Model 2	Model 3	Model 4
Female	1.33		1.59	22.70*
Gender identification		0.99	1.02	1.15*
Female * gender identification				0.79*

Notes: All models controlled for age, education, race, ethnicity, political affiliation, region, dependents under 18 in the household, and experimental treatments. + $p \leq 0.100$, * $p \leq 0.050$, ** $p \leq 0.010$, *** $p \leq 0.001$

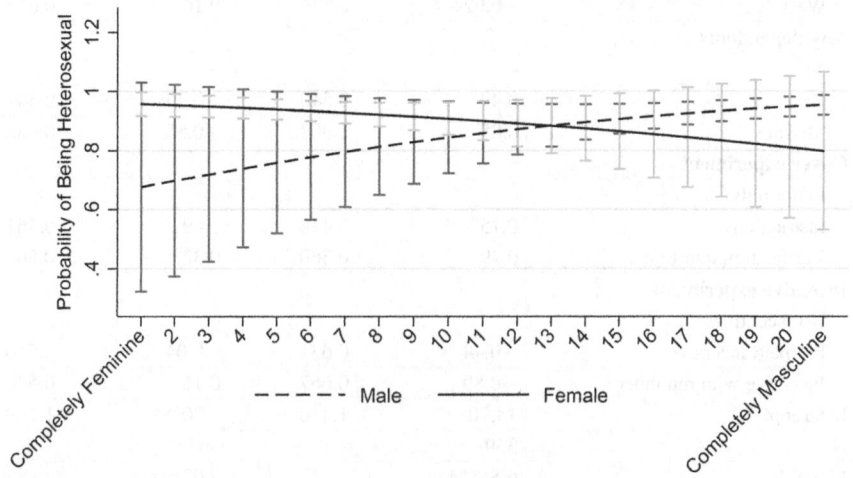

Fig. 11.3 Predicted Probability of being Heterosexual by Sex and Gender Identification

Table 11.6 Odds Ratios Predicting Reporting Self as the Person in the Household Most Likely to Do Tasks

	Model 1	Model 2	Model 3	Model 4
Childcare (n = 812)				
Female	4.78***		3.34*	1.51
Gender identification		0.91***	0.97	0.94
Female * gender identification				1.07
Grocery shopping (n = 895)				
Female	9.04***		5.20***	9.75*
Gender identification		0.87***	0.96	0.98
Female * gender identification				0.94
Housekeeping (n = 865)				
Female	13.80***		3.87**	14.95**
Gender identification		0.83***	0.90**	0.95
Female * gender identification				0.89+
Household repairs (n = 877)				
Female	0.09***		0.33*	1.89
Gender identification		1.19***	1.12***	1.22**
Female * gender identification				0.86+

Notes: All models controlled for age, education, race, ethnicity, sexuality, political affiliation, region, dependents under 18 in the household, and experimental treatments. + p ≤ 0.100, * p ≤ 0.050, ** p ≤ 0.010, *** p ≤ 0.001

women report higher masculinity, the likelihood of them reporting being heterosexual decreases.[6] Thus, the effect of gender identification depends on sex.

Table 11.6 shows the association of sex and gender identification with the likelihood of reporting oneself as the household member most likely to do childcare, grocery shopping, housekeeping, and household repairs. Women are significantly (p = 0.023 and p = 0.001) and substantively (OR from 3.34 to 5.20) more likely to report being the primary person to do childcare and the primary grocery shopper. Gender identification is not associated with either of these reports above and beyond sex (Model 3, childcare t = −0.74, p = 0.458, groceries t = −1.33, p = 0.184), nor is there a significant interaction between gender identification and sex for either outcome (Model 4, childcare t = 0.90, p = 0.369, groceries t = −0.92, p = 0.357).

For housekeeping, Model 3 shows that women are more likely than men to report being the primary housekeeper (t = 2.66, p = 0.008) and those who rate themselves as more masculine, net of sex, are less likely to do so (t = −3.13, p = 0.002). Additionally, there is a marginally statistically significant interaction between sex and gender identification (Model 4, t = −1.80, p = 0.073, see Fig. 11.4). Both men and women are less likely to report being the primary person to do housekeeping as

---

[6]This is not to imply that all sexual minority males are feminine or that all sexual minority females are masculine. Gender identity ratings varied within these groups, from 10 to 21 for sexual minority men and from 1 to 13 for sexual minority women. In this survey, the most feminine men and masculine women were heterosexual, counter stereotypes.

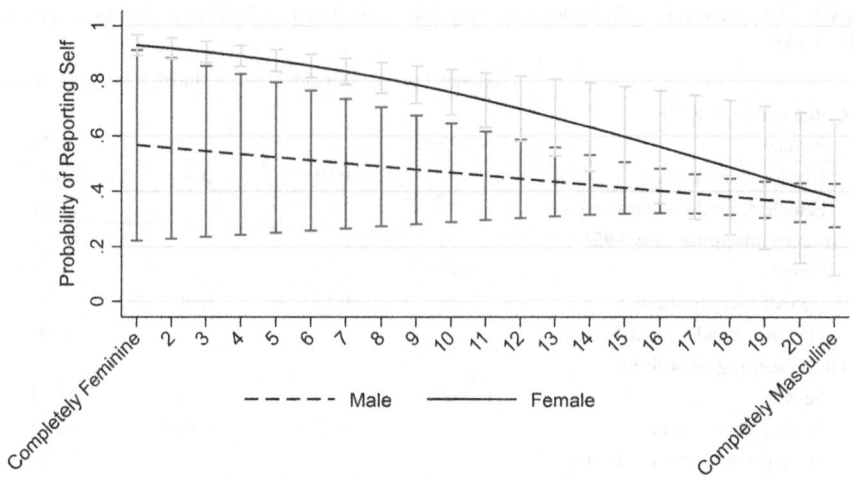

Fig. 11.4 Predicted Probability of Reporting Oneself as the Person in the Household Most Likely to do Housekeeping

they rate themselves more masculine, but the decline is steeper for women and gap between men and women closes as women approach the masculine side of the gender identification scale.

The results for household repairs also indicate that both sex and gender identification matter. Net of gender identification, women are less likely than men to report this status (Model 3, t = −2.26, p = 0.024), and net of sex, those who rate themselves as more masculine are more likely to report this status (Model 3, t = 3.29, p = 0.001). However, as Model 4 shows, there is a moderately statistically significant interaction between sex and gender (t = −1.94, p = 0.052, see Fig. 11.5). On the feminine end of the scale, the probability of claiming to be the primary person to do household repairs is similarly low for males and females. As both sexes rate themselves more masculine, the likelihood of reporting this status increases, but at a faster rate for men than women, resulting in the largest differences between the sexes at the completely masculine endpoint of the scale.

Table 11.7 shows how sex and gender identification predict hours spent working for pay, on housework, and on family care work. For all three outcomes, sex and gender identification individually are statistically significant (Models 1 and 2). Women report fewer hours working for pay (t = −3.32, p = 0.001) and more hours on housework (t = 4.38, p = 0.000) and care work (t = 4.62, p = 0.000) than men. More masculine ratings on the gender identification scale are associated with more hours working for pay (t = 2.95, p = 0.003) and fewer hours on housework (t = −3.73, p = 0.000) and care work (t = −4.40, p = 0.000). However, these effects appear to be due to the overlap (i.e., shared variance) between these two measures. When they are entered into the model simultaneously (Model 3) the

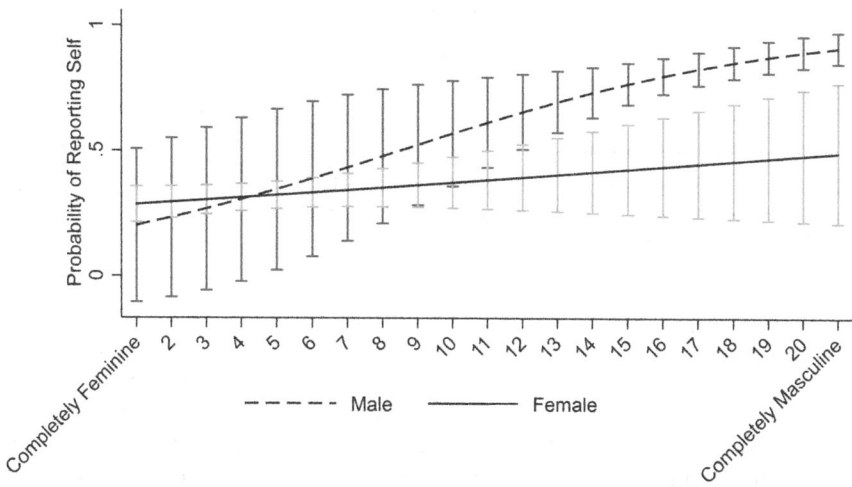

Fig. 11.5 Predicted Probability of Reporting Oneself as the Person in the Household Most Likely to do Household Repairs

Table 11.7 Coefficients from Negative Binomial Regression of Number of Hours Spent on Tasks on Sex and Gender Identification

	Model 1	Model 2	Model 3	Model 4
Hours working for pay (n = 825)				
Female	−0.31***		−0.29	0.18
Gender identification		0.02**	0.00	0.02
Female * gender identification				−0.04
Hours on housework (n = 841)				
Female	0.43***		0.36+	0.68+
Gender identification		−0.03***	−0.01	0.01
Female * gender identification				−0.03
Hours caring for family (n = 806)				
Female	0.91***		0.53	−0.10
Gender identification		−0.06***	−0.03	−0.06
Female * gender identification				0.05

Notes: All models controlled for age, education, race, ethnicity, sexuality, political affiliation, region, dependents under 18 in the household, and experimental treatments. + p ≤ 0.100, * p ≤ 0.050, ** p ≤ 0.010, *** p ≤ 0.001

effects of sex and gender are virtually eliminated, and there are no statistically significant interactions for any outcome.

Table 11.8 shows results for military service. Both sex and gender identification, entered individually (Models 1 and 2), are significantly associated with having ever served in the military. Women are less likely to have served than men and increases in masculinity ratings are associated with increased likelihood of having served. However, Model 3 shows that when sex and gender identification are both accounted

Table 11.8 Odds Ratios Predicting Having Ever Served in the Military (n = 849)

	Model 1	Model 2	Model 3	Model 4
Female	0.14***		1.26	0.40
Gender identification		1.16***	1.17**	1.12
Female * gender identification				1.09

Notes: All models controlled for age, education, race, ethnicity, sexuality, political affiliation, region, dependents under 18 in the household, and experimental treatments. + $p \leq 0.100$, * $p \leq 0.050$, ** $p \leq 0.010$, *** $p \leq 0.001$

for, only gender identification remains significant. Net of sex, each additional point toward the masculine end of the gender identification scale increases the odds of having served by 17 percent. There is no significant interaction between sex and gender identification. Thus, apparent sex differences in military service may in fact be gender differences. Including a gender measure in longitudinal studies would help reveal whether more masculine identifying people are more likely to enlist, the experience of military service leads people to identify as more masculine, or perhaps both.

Discussion and Conclusions

While binary sex measures have helped reveal inequalities between men and women in many domains, the heavy reliance on binary measures is out of step with contemporary sociological understanding and theorizing of sex and gender. The lack of good gender measurement, separate from sex, inhibits the ability to understand how this concept shapes peoples' lives, above and beyond sex. To overcome this glaring limitation, measures of gender that can practically be included in population based surveys need to be developed. In this paper, we examine one such measure that asks respondents to rate their femininity/masculinity on a 21-point scale. Our criteria for assessing the measure is that (1) it must be parsimonious, (2) respondents must be able and willing to answer it, (3) it must exhibit measurement reliability, and (4) it must exhibit validity and have explanatory value above and beyond traditional binary measures of sex.

Our short one-item measure meets all of these criteria. Respondents are just as likely to answer it as they are to answer the binary sex measure, and the predictors of item nonresponse are what is seen in other studies examining item nonresponse more generally in mail surveys (e.g., low education). The strongest predictors of item nonresponse on this measure were item nonresponse on other demographic measures, suggesting a general tendency for people to skip demographic items and no specific problems with the gender identification measure. This is noteworthy, given that the gender identification question was the third to last question in a 12-page questionnaire.

The gender identification item also exhibits reasonable reliability. As expected, we found considerable (although not complete) overlap between this measure and the binary sex measure. In addition, many demographic characteristics were significantly associated in the same direction with gender identification here as in Magliozzi et al. (2016). Thus, while the two scales are operationalized differently, they seem to be reliably tapping into the same underlying construct. Our gender identification measure was subject to measurement context effects, particularly for women, who rated themselves more masculine when asked about society's ideal man and woman before themselves. This context effect only accounts for 1.4% of the variance in the gender identification scale. Nevertheless, future research should examine why the comparison to the ideals affects women's responses but not men's.

The predictive validity analyses illustrate the contributions of both sex and gender to many important outcomes. For example, the results showed that gender identification has different effects for men and women on the probability of reporting being heterosexual versus a sexual minority. Consistent with expectations, higher ratings of masculinity were associated with increased likelihood of men but decreased likelihood of women identifying as heterosexual. This is consistent with the theory that people "do heterosexuality" by "doing gender" in a way that is consistent with their biological sex. We also found significant interactions between sex and gender on the likelihood of identifying as the person in the household most likely to do housekeeping and household repairs. These findings add considerable nuance to previous research focusing on sex differences in these types of labor and are consistent with the notion that the labor one does is intricately linked to gender.

In contrast to housekeeping and household repairs, the outcomes of being the person most likely to do childcare or grocery shopping and hours working for pay, doing housework, and doing care work did not see added explanatory value from gender identification. It seems the shared variance between the sex and gender identification measures is what is associated with these outcomes. Finally, our data suggest that gender identification is more important than sex in explaining military service. Future research could examine whether this gender effect is caused by serving in the military or by more masculine individuals selecting into the military (and other similar occupations).

Taken together, our results confirm the findings of Magliozzi et al. (2016) that measures of gender identification add considerable explanatory value beyond measures of binary sex. In addition, our one-item measure is parsimonious, answerable, and reliable and valid. Our results also extend the work of Magliozzi et al. (2016) by evaluating the gender identification scale in a national probability sample survey and with considerably more outcomes motivated by contemporary gender theory. In addition, we were able to examine the moderating effect of gender identification on existing sex differences findings.

There are several notable differences between our measure and that of Magliozzi et al. (2016). Whereas Magliozzi and colleagues utilized separate scales for masculinity and femininity, we utilized only one scale, placing masculinity and femininity in contrast to one another. The use of a single bipolar scale for gender identification has been critiqued for treating masculinity and femininity as mutually exclusive and opposites (Constantinople 1973), but these critiques were developed in the context of multi-item, domain- or trait-specific batteries that were largely designed to discriminate between males and females. In essence, these early bipolar masculinity/femininity scales were designed to be social/psychological proxies for biological sex, not to capture gender as something separate from (or in addition to) sex. The new gradational measures of gender identification proposed here do not rely on specific domains or traits. Instead, they are "more comprehensive" (Magliozzi et al. 2016:7) measures. Thus, it is unclear the extent to which old critiques apply to these new measures.

Certainly separate masculinity and femininity scales can capture more nuance than a single scale and more closely match sociological theory about masculinity and femininity. However, it is unclear whether these sociological ideas make sense to general population members who will be asked to answer surveys. General understanding of a construct has direct bearing on how people answer the questions, what the questions are actually measuring, and how much measurement error they produce. Several researchers have demonstrated through qualitative work that gender nonconforming people understand and find utility in separate feminine and masculine scales (Kasabian 2015; Magliozzi et al. 2016; Garbarski and LaVergne, Chap. 9 this volume), but little research has examined how cisgender individuals understand and answer them. These are unsettled questions that will need to be addressed in order to move gradational gender measures into wide-scale general population survey use.

In addition to the theoretical debate about one versus two scales, this choice has practical implications for data collection, processing, and analyses that should be considered. Two scales require more space in the questionnaire and data entry time, which have direct cost implications. Respondents' ability and willingness to answer may also differ. A direct comparison of item nonresponse rates across one and two-item measures should be made, and item-nonresponse rates should be compared across the items in the two-item format (higher item nonresponse rates to the second item would indicate respondent difficulty understanding masculinity and femininity as separate concepts).[7,8] Since the goal is to be able to use these measures in general population surveys, these tests should be conducted in general population surveys.

As gender identification measures continue to be developed and refined, thought should also be given to whether and how they can be administered in different survey modes, especially in telephone surveys with no visual cues. An open question is how respondents understand these scales when they cannot see them. Whether

---

[7]Magliozzi, et al. did not report item nonresponse rates. Even so, the rates are not comparable across the two studies because of other design differences such as sample type and survey mode (web surveys typically have lower item nonresponse than mail – see *Survey Practice* 2012, volume 5, issue 2).

[8]That Magliozzi, et al. included an instruction to "Please answer on both scales below" to prompt responses to both the feminine and masculine scales suggests respondents may not understand these concepts as separate in the way gender scholars do.

placing the two concepts on a single continuum or separating them into two scales helps or hinders this process is also an open question.

Measuring gender identification with one versus two items also has implications for the operationalization of variables for analyses. Given that most people in the general population are cisgender, we would expect a high correlation between the separate masculinity and femininity scales, making it difficult to use them in their original form in analyses because of multicollinearity. Magliozzi, et al. do not report correlations between their two scales or discuss multicollinearity, but they also do not include the two separate items in their predictive validity regression model, opting instead to combine them into a single measure of gender polarization. Using this measure, they find that more polarized people (i.e., high masculinity and low femininity or high femininity and low masculinity) are more likely to be married, but we don't know from their analysis the effect of gender identification in and of itself on marital status (i.e., are femininity and masculinity associated with marital status net of sex?) or if it varies by sex. We also do not know whether the reported association is the same for polarized masculine versus polarized feminine people or whether this depends on sex (i.e., are women who are polarized masculine more likely to be married, or just those who are polarized feminine?). Essentially, this choice to combined the two measures, which may have been driven by multicollinearity challenges, has the effect of eliminating the explanatory power that motivated asking about masculinity and femininity separately in the first place. This is a direct result of the heavily skewed (by sex) distribution of gender identification in the population at large. In less gender-conforming subpopulations, the masculinity and femininity scales may be less correlated, eliminating this challenge (see Garbarski and LaVergne, Chap. 9, this volume, for example), but it is a problem that will likely persist in general population usage. Using a single, bipolar scale eliminates these challenges in general population usage, allowing for a direct assessment of the association between gender identification and outcomes of interest. It also eliminates the potential for people to report being high on both femininity and masculinity, and thus may not fully capture existing gender variation. A direct experimental comparison between the two scales in a general population survey would help illuminate how many and what types of people might be affected by this omission.

A second difference between the two scales that raises important questions for future research is the number of scale points used. Whereas Magliozzi and colleagues used seven-point scales for each measure of masculinity and femininity, we used a 21-point scale to capture both, allowing for finer gradation in reports. How much gradation is needed to accurately capture gender variation is another open question.

While many empirical questions remain about how best to measure gender identification in general population surveys, this paper has demonstrated that it can be done in practical and affordable ways with reasonable reliability and validity, and that doing so adds considerable explanatory value. It is no longer sufficient to rely solely on binary measures of sex.

References

AAPOR. (2016). *Standard definitions: Final dispositions of case codes and outcome rates for surveys*. American Association for Public Opinion Research. Retrieved November 29, 2018, from www.aapor.org.
Acker, J. (1990). Hierarchies, jobs, bodies: A theory of gendered organizations. *Gender & Society, 4*(2), 139–158.
Acker, J. (1992). From sex roles to gendered institutions. *Contemporary Sociology, 21*, 565–569.
Annandale, E., & Hunt, K. (1990). Masculinity, femininity, and sex: An exploration of their relative contribution to explaining gender differences in health. *Sociology of Health and Illness, 12*(1), 24–46.
Beatty, P., & Herrmann, D. (2002). To answer or not to answer: Decision processes related to survey item nonresponse. In R. Groves, D. Dillman, J. Eltinge, & R. Little (Eds.), *Survey nonresponse* (pp. 71–69). New York, NY: Wiley.
Bem, S. L. (1974). The measurement of psychological androgyny. *Journal of Consulting and Clinical Psychology, 42*(2), 155–162.
Berk, S. F. (1985). *Gender factory: The apportionment of work in American households*. New York: Plenum Press.
Bianchi, S. M., Milkie, M. A., Sayer, L. C., & Robinson, J. P. (2000). Is anyone doing the housework? Trends in the gender division of household labor. *Social Forces, 79*(1), 191–228.
Bianchi, S. M., Sayer, L. C., Milkie, M. A., & Robinson, J. P. (2012). Housework: Who did, does or will do it, and how much does it matter? *Social Forces, 91*(1), 55–63.
Bittman, M., England, P., Sayer, L., Folbre, N., & Matheson, G. (2003). When does gender trump money? Bargaining and time in household work. *American Journal of Sociology, 109*(1), 186–214.
Brandth, B. (2006). Agricultural body-building: Incorporations of gender, body and work. *Journal of Rural Studies, 22*(1), 17–27.
Brines, J. (1994). Economic dependency, gender, and the division of labor at home. *American Journal of Sociology, 100*(3), 652–688.
Britton, D. M. (1997). Gendered organizational logic: Policy and practice in Men's and Women's prisons. *Gender & Society, 11*, 796–818.
Bureau of Labor Statistics. (2014). *Women in in the labor force: A Databook*. U.S. Bureau of Labor Statistics Report 1052, Washington DC. Retrieved November 9, 2018, from https://www.bls.gov/opub/reports/womens-databook/archive/women-in-the-labor-force-a-databook-2014.pdf
Bureau of Labor Statistics. (2018). *Employment status of the civilian noninstitutional population 16 years and over by sex, 1970s to date*. U.S. Bureau of Labor Statistics, Washington DC. Retrieved November 9, 2018, from https://www.bls.gov/cps/tables.htm#empstat
Burke, P. J. (1991). Identity processes and social stress. *American Sociological Review, 56*(6), 836–849.
Connell, R. W. (1987). *Gender and power: Society, the person, and sexual politics*. Stanford, CA: Stanford University Press.
Connell, R. W. (1995). *Masculinities: Knowledge, power and social change*. Berkeley, CA: University of California Press.
Correll, S., Ridgeway, C., Saperstein, A., & Westbrook, L. (2014). *Gender Identity and Diversity: Revision and Updates*. (unpublished report)
Dalton, S. E., & Bielby, D. D. (2000). 'That's our kind of constellation': Lesbian mothers negotiate institutionalized understandings of gender within the family. *Gender & Society, 14*(1), 36–61.
de Leeuw, E. D., Hox, J., & Huisman, M. (2003). Prevention and treatment of item nonresponse. *Journal of Official Statistics, 19*(2), 153–176.
Egen, S. K., & Perry, D. G. (2001). Gender identity: A multidimensional analysis with implications for psychosocial adjustment. *Developmental Psychology, 37*(4), 451–463.
England, P. (1992). *Comparable worth: Theories and evidence*. New York: Aldine de Gruyter.

Enloe, C. (2004). Wielding masculinity inside Abu Ghraib: Making feminist sense of an American military scandal. *Asian Journal of Women's Studies, 10*(3), 89–102.

Epstein, J. (1990). Either/or-neither/both: Sexual ambiguity and the ideology of gender. *Genders, 7*, 100–142.

Federal Committee on Statistical Methodology. (2016a). *Current measures of sexual orientation and gender identity in federal surveys.* August 2016. Retrieved December 10, 2018 from https://nces.ed.gov/FCSM/interagency_reports.asp

Federal Committee on Statistical Methodology. (2016b). *Evaluations of sexual orientation and gender identity survey measures: What have we learned?* September 2016. Retrieved December 10, 2018, from https://nces.ed.gov/FCSM/interagency_reports.asp

Federal Committee on Statistical Methodology. (2016c). *Toward a research agenda for measuring sexual orientation and gender identity in federal surveys: Findings, recommendations, and next steps.* October 2016. Retrieved December 10, 2018, from https://nces.ed.gov/FCSM/interagency_reports.asp

Felshin, J. (1974). The triple option for women in sport. *Quest, 21,* 36–40.

Fraser, G. (2018). Evaluating inclusive gender identification measures for use in quantitative psychological research. *Psychology & Sexuality, 9*(4), 343–357.

Frye, M. (1983). *The Politics of Reality: Essays in Feminist Theory.* Trumansburg, NY: The Crossing Press.

Gaziano, C. (2005). Comparative analysis of within-household respondent selection techniques. *Public Opinion Quarterly, 69*(1), 124–157.

Geist, C., Reynolds, M. M., & Gaytán, M. S. (2017). Unfinished business: Disentangling sex, gender, and sexuality in sociological research on gender stratification. *Sociology Compass, 11*(4), e12470.

Geist, C., & Ruppanner, L. (2018). Mission impossible? New housework theories for changing families. *Journal of Family Theory and Review, 10,* 242–262.

Greenstein, T. N. (2000). Economic dependence, gender, and the division of labor in the home: A replication and extension. *Journal of Marriage and the Family, 62,* 322–335.

Hall, E. J. (1993). Waitering/waitressing: Engendering the work of table servers. *Gender & Society, 7,* 329–346.

Hays, S. (1996). *The cultural contradictions of motherhood.* New Haven, CT: Yale University Press.

Herbert, M. S. (1998). *Camouflage Isn't only for combat: Gender, sexuality, and women in the military.* New York, NY: New York University Press.

Hyde, J. (2005). The gender similarities hypothesis. *American Psychologist, 60*(6), 581–592.

Kasabian, A. (2015). *Capturing the Gendiverse: A test of the gender self-perception scale, with implications for survey data and labor market measures.* Unpublished doctoral dissertation. Lincoln, NE: University of Nebraska-Lincoln.

Kessler, S. J. (1990). The medical construction of gender: Case Management of Intersexed Infants. *Signs, 16*(1), 3–26.

Kessler, S. J., & McKenna, W. (1978). *Gender: An Ethnomethodological approach.* New York: Wiley.

Kroska, A. (2000). Conceptualizing and measuring gender ideology as an identity. *Gender & Society, 14,* 368–394.

Krosnick, J. A. (2002). The causes of no-opinion responses to attitude measures in surveys: They rarely are what they appear to be. In R. M. Groves, D. A. Dillman, J. L. Eltinge, & R. J. A. Little (Eds.), *Survey nonresponse* (pp. 88–100). New York: Wiley.

Kruttschnitt, C. (2013). Gender and crime. *Annual Review of Sociology, 39,* 291–308.

Little, R. J. A., & Rubin, D. B. (2002). *Statistical analysis with missing data.* Hoboken, NJ: Wiley.

Lorber, J. (1996). Beyond the binaries: Depolarizing the categories of sex, sexuality, and gender. *Sociological Inquiry, 66,* 143–159.

Lucal, B. (1999). What it means to be gendered me: Life on the boundaries of a dichotomous gender system. *Gender & Society, 13,* 781–797.

Magliozzi, D., Saperstein, A., & Westbrook, L. (2016). Scaling up: Representing gender diversity in survey research. *Socius, 2*, 1–11.

Mahalik, J. R., Morray, E. B., Coonerty-Femiano, A., Ludlow, L. H., Slattery, S. M., & Smiler, A. (2005). Development of the conformity to feminine norms inventory. *Sex Roles, 52*, 417–435.

McMahon, M. (1995). *Engendering motherhood: Identity and self-transformation in Women's lives*. New York: Guilford Press.

Olson, K., & Smyth, J. D. (2017). Within-household selection in mail surveys explicit questions are better than cover letter instructions. *Public Opinion Quarterly, 81*(3), 688–713.

Olson, K., Watanabe, M., & Smyth, J. D. (2018). A comparison of full and quasi-filters for autobiographical questions. *Field Methods, 30*(4), 371–385.

Oransky, M., & Fischer, C. (2009). The development and validation of the meanings of adolescent masculinity scale. *Psychology of Men and Masculinity, 10*(1), 57–72.

Padavic, I., & Reskin, B. (2002). *Women and men at work*. Thousand Oaks, CA: Sage.

Price, K. (2008). Keeping the dancers in check: The gendered Organization of Stripping Work in the Lion's Den. *Gender & Society, 22*, 367–389.

Ridgeway, C. L., & Smith-Lovin, L. (1999). The gender system and interaction. *Annual Review of Sociology, 25*, 191–216.

Risman, B. J. (2004). Gender as social structure: Theory wrestling with activism. *Gender & Society, 18*, 429–450.

Saugeres, L. (2002). 'She's not really a woman, She's half a man': Gendered discourses of embodiment in a French farming community. *Women's Studies International Forum, 25*(6), 641–650.

Schwarz, N., & Strack, F. (1999). Reports of subjective Well-being: Judgmental processes and their methodological implications. In D. Kahneman, E. Diener, & N. Schwarz (Eds.), *Well-being: The foundations of hedonic psychology* (pp. 61–84). New York, NY: Russell Sage Foundation.

Smyth, J. D. (2007). *Doing gender when home and work are blurred: Women and sex-atypical tasks in family farming. Unpublished dissertation*. Pullman, Washington: Washington State University.

Smyth, J., Olson, K., & Stange, M. (2019). Within-household selection methods: A critical review and experimental examination. Chapter 2. In P. J. Lavrakas, M. W. Traugott, C. Kennedy, A. L. Holbrook, E. D. de Leeuw, & B. T. West (Eds.), *Experimental methods in survey research: Techniques that combine random sampling with random assignment* (pp. 23–46). Hoboken, NJ: Wiley.

Smyth, J. D., Swendener, A., & Kazyak, E. (2018). Women's work? The relationship between Farmwork and gender self-perception. *Rural Sociology, 83*(3), 654–676.

Sobal, J. (2005). Men, meat, and marriage: Models of masculinity. *Food and Foodways, 13*, 135–158.

South, S. J., & Spitze, G. (1994). Housework in marital and NonMarital households. *American Sociological Review, 59*, 327–347.

Spence, J. T., Helmreich, R., & Stapp, J. (1974). The personal attributes questionnaire: A measure of sex-role stereotypes and masculinity and femininity. *JSAS: Catalog of Selected Documents in Psychology, 4*, 43–44.

Sudman, S., Bradburn, N. M., & Schwarz, N. (1996). *Thinking about answers: The application of cognitive processes to survey methodology*. San Francisco, CA: Jossey-Bass.

The GenIUSS Group. (2014). *Best practices for asking questions to identify transgender and other gender minority respondents on population-based surveys*. Los Angeles, CA: The Williams Institute. Retrieved December 10, 2018, from https://williamsinstitute.law.ucla.edu/wp-content/uploads/geniuss-report-sep-2014.pdf

Timbrook, Jerry, Jolene D. Smyth, and Kristen Olson. (2016). *Does Adding 'Your Best Estimate is Fine' Affect Data Quality?* Paper presented at the International Conference on Questionnaire Design, Development, Evaluation, and Testing, Miami, FL, November 9–13, 2016.

Tourangeau, R., & Rasinski, K. A. (1988). Cognitive processes underlying context effects in attitude measurement. *Psychological Bulletin, 103*(3), 299–314.
Tourangeau, R., Rips, L., & Rasinski, K. (2000). *The psychology of survey response.* Cambridge, MA: Cambridge University Press.
Verbrugge, L. M. (1985). Gender and health: An update on hypotheses and evidence. *Journal of Health and Social Behavior, 26*(3), 156–182.
Wade, L., & Ferree, M. M. (2019). *Gender: Ideas, interactions, institutions* (2nd ed.). New York: W. W. Norton & Company.
Walzer, S. (1998). *Thinking about the baby: Gender and transitions into parenthood.* Philadelphia, PA: Temple University Press.
West, C., & Zimmerman, D. H. (1987). Doing Gender. *Gender & Society, 1*, 125–151.
Westbrook, L., & Saperstein, A. (2015). New categories are not enough: Rethinking the measurement of sex and gender in social surveys. *Gender & Society, 29*(4), 534–560.

Chapter 12
Correlates of Differences in Interactional Patterns among Black and White Respondents

Jennifer Dykema, Dana Garbarski, Nora Cate Schaeffer, Isabel Anadon, and Dorothy Farrar Edwards

Introduction

While survey research remains one of the most important methodologies through which researchers collect data about key characteristics of populations, fundamental features of the survey interview may increase variable error, decreasing the precision of estimates. These features can also lead to systematic differences in respondents' answers across the spectrum of racial, ethnic, or other socially defined cultural groups, compromising researchers' ability to make group comparisons. In this chapter, we describe patterns of how answers to standardized survey questions about participating in medical research, some of which focus on race-related topics, occur during interviews with members from different racial groups, whose distinctive experiences with the topics of the questions may differentially affect how they cognitively process the items. We use interviewer-respondent interaction as a vehicle to examine and understand this processing.

J. Dykema (✉) · N. C. Schaeffer · I. Anadon · D. F. Edwards
University of Wisconsin-Madison, Madison, WI, USA
e-mail: dykema@ssc.wisc.edu

D. Garbarski
Loyola University Chicago, Chicago, IL, USA

Participation in Medical Research: A Legacy of Mistrust among African Americans

Despite a mandate from the National Institutes of Health (NIH) to improve the inclusion of women and racial/ethnic minorities in research (NIH 2008), African Americans and other underrepresented groups continue to have very low rates of participation in medical research studies (Brown and Topcu 2003; George et al. 2014; Luebbert and Perez 2016). A growing body of literature specifically addresses the problems of recruitment and retention of minority participants in health-related research (Branson et al. 2007). The results of both qualitative and quantitative studies have identified many common barriers to participation, as well as issues unique to specific communities. The majority of these studies have focused on Black and African Americans, with fewer publications describing the attitudes and beliefs of Latinos and American Indians; however, the same themes consistently emerge across the groups. One of the most commonly cited factors includes a fear and mistrust of medical researchers based on episodes of unethical treatment by such investigators or discrimination associated with government sponsored programs.

The impact of unethical research practices has left a lingering sense of mistrust of biomedical research in the African American community in particular (Corbie-Smith 1999, Corbie-Smith et al. 1999, Corbie-Smith 2004). Mistrust of academic and research institutions are the most significant attitudinal barriers to research participation reported by African Americans and other groups underrepresented in biomedical research (George et al. 2014; Hoyo et al. 2003; Luebbert and Perez 2016). The etiology of mistrust is complex and multifaceted. One of the most frequently cited reasons for negative attitudes towards research are the historic violations of research ethics best exemplified by the Tuskegee Syphilis Trials (Bates et al. 2005; Gamble 1993; Shavers-Hornaday et al. 1997; Thomas and Quinn 1991). The negative consequences and resulting perceptions that followed Tuskegee and other well-known studies continues to influence research participation today; however, some researchers argue that awareness of Tuskegee alone does not predict mistrust of the medical care system (Branson et al. 2007; Scharff et al. 2010; Shavers et al. 2001).

One common consequence of the Tuskegee study is concern by subjects that they will be denied treatment for the health conditions under investigation. The belief expressed by some African Americans that HIV/AIDS was created in a laboratory and deliberately released in the Black community is plausibly a long-term consequence of that community's knowledge about the Tuskegee study (Washington 2006). Attitudinal studies suggest that mistrust of clinical investigators is highly influenced by perceived racial disparities in health, limited access to health care, and negative encounters with health care providers (Boulware et al. 2003; Halbert et al. 2006). Several investigators have found that Blacks are more likely than age-, education-, and gender-matched Whites to believe that research findings will be used to reinforce negative stereotypes about their racial/ethnic group (Goldman et al. 2008; Schulz et al. 2003), or will expose them to unnecessary risks (Branson et al.

2007; Corbie-Smith et al. 1999). For example, Corbie-Smith and colleagues worked with the Roper polling organization to collect survey data from a nationally representative sample of African Americans and White Americans. They reported that 79% of the African American respondents believed that they (or people like them) might be used as guinea pigs without consent and 63% of African Americans believe that they actually have been used in medical studies without consent.

It is within this social and historical context that we designed and administered the Voices Heard Survey, a standardized survey interview developed to identify barriers and facilitators to participating in medical studies designed to identify genetic, physiological, behavioral, environmental, or lifestyle markers of disease or disease risk.

Standardized Interviewing and Interviewer-Respondent Interaction

Survey data are overwhelmingly gathered using standardized interviewing, which aims to control interviewer variability (Hyman 1975 [1954]; O'Muircheartaigh and Campanelli 1998; Schaeffer 1991; Schaeffer et al. 2010; West and Blom 2017). The rules of standardization most commonly referred to are those offered by Fowler and Mangione (1990): read questions as written; probe inadequate answers non-directively; record answers without discretion; and be interpersonally nonjudgmental regarding the substance of answers. If survey questions are clearly written and fit the target population, standardized interviews should consist of a series of "paradigmatic" question-answer sequences (Schaeffer and Maynard 1996, 2008), in which the interviewer reads the question as scripted and the respondent provides an answer to the question that is codable (e.g., "yes" or "no" for a yes/no question); optionally, the interviewer may acknowledge the respondent's answer (e.g., "thank you") before moving on to the next question. However, answers to survey questions are interactional accomplishments, and nonparadigmatic question-answer sequences arise for many reasons. These include respondents' displays of problems comprehending the meanings of questions and the terms they contain, difficulties respondents encounter mapping responses that summarize their attitudes and experiences onto the response categories provided, and a poor fit between the content of questions and respondents' knowledge or past experiences (Dykema et al. 1997; Holbrook et al. 2006).

Motivation for examining interviewer-respondent interaction is provided by the interactional model of the question-answer sequence that we developed in prior work (see Fig. 12.1; Dykema et al. 2020). The model summarizes paths that link the practices of standardization and conversation, characteristics of questions, respondents, and interviewers, cognitive processing of the survey participants, and the production of survey answers. The model is informed by a variety of sources: evidence of interviewer variance, which motivates the practices of standardization;

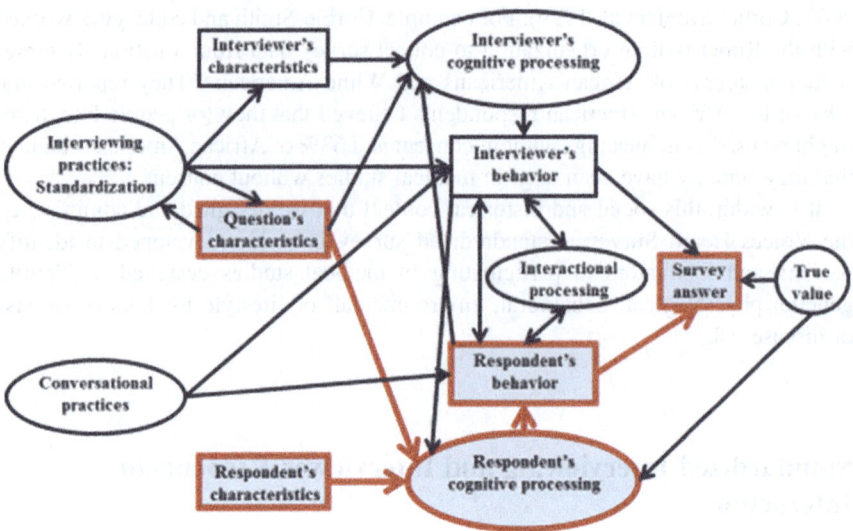

Fig. 12.1 International model of the question-answer sequence adpted from Dykema et al. 2020

evidence that features of interaction such as response latency are associated with cognitive processing (Schaeffer and Dykema 2011a); and ways in which conversational practices affect standardized measurement (Garbarski et al. 2011, 2016; Schaeffer et al. 2010; Schaeffer and Maynard 2002; Schwarz 1996).

In Fig. 12.1, we highlight features of the model that are particularly relevant for this chapter. The model posits that for a given survey question, a respondent's cognitive processing is directly influenced by the question's characteristics, such as its topic, sensitivity, format, and complexity, and the respondent's characteristics, such as their past experiences and socio-demographic attributes including race and ethnicity. A respondent's cognitive processing, in turn, affects their behavior including how they respond, what they say, and what they offer as an answer. Data obtained in the survey interview are thus accomplished through the interplay of the instrument, respondent, and interviewer (Krosnick 2011; Schaeffer and Dykema 2011b; van der Zouwen and Smit 2004). Interviewer-respondent interaction is the vehicle through which the various characteristics of questions, respondents, and interviewers affect cognitive processing and data quality, with the verbal and nonverbal behavioral displays produced during the interaction providing inferences about the quality of the data generated (Dykema et al. 1997; Fowler 2011; Fowler and Cannell 1996; Ongena and Dijkstra 2007; Schaeffer and Dykema 2011a, b).

During the course of answering survey questions, respondents produce several distinct categories of talk including codable answers, uncodable answers, requests for repetition or clarification, and conversational elements (see Table 12.1). As noted previously, the survey interview is designed to obtain a codable answer. To be codable, an answer must occur after the respondent has heard the entire question,

Table 12.1 Examples of units-of-talk provided by respondents during the course of answering the selection questions included in the current study

Unit-of-talk	Definition	Examples
Codable answers		
Exact repetition	Answer that is an exact repetition of one of the response categories	"extremely hard" for question 34
Kernel	Answer that is a "kernel" of a category (i.e., a word or phrase that uniquely and unambiguously identifies a single category)	"extremely" for "extremely hard" for question 34
Category reference	Answer that references a specific category based on the location of the category relative to the other categories	"the last one" for "extremely" for question 34
Uncodable answers		
Hypothetical response category	Answer is a response option that could hypothetically be included along the response dimension but is not included as one of the response categories offered	"little likely" for question 1, "pretty often" for question 40
Repeat or paraphrase part of the question	Answer repeats part of the question verbatim or paraphrases part of question in a way that does not provide new information	"I would answer the questions" for question 1
Repeat response dimension	Answer repeats some part or all of the response dimension but without the intensifier and so does not uniquely identify a single response category	"likely" for question 1, "often" for question 39
Report	Answer does not only repeat or paraphrase part of the question but provides relevant information that is stated as an answer but is not codable	"they seem like they care when I've done them" for question 35, "everybody's just a number when they are doing it they aren't thinking about them as people" for question 41
Requests		
Request repetition or clarification	Comment or question requesting repetition or clarification of a term, phrase, or some part of the question or response categories	"can you read/repeat that," "what are the five options," "are we talking about researchers in the United States" for question 32
Conversational elements		
Apology	Word or phrase that conveys the act of being sorry	"I apologize," "excuse me," "I'm sorry"
Comment	Unscripted talk, often evaluative in nature, about the question, respondent, interviewer, or interviewing situation	"it's hard to answer that," "that's a good question," "I'm losing my focus"
Elaboration	Additional information offered along with a codable answer to explain the answer provided and	"because I can't stand blood" for question 3, "depends on the

(continued)

Table 12.1 (continued)

Unit-of-talk	Definition	Examples
	sometimes preceded by "because," "depends" or "if"	medication they're testing for" for question 6
Exclamation	Word or phrase that expresses sudden surprise, anger, excitement, happiness, or other emotion	"boy," "dear," "geez," "gosh," "shoot," "wow"
Laughter	Freestanding laughter (laughter that occurs between words) or laugh tokens (particles of laughter that occur within words or phrases)	
Mitigator	Word or phrase that reduces the exactness, precision, or certainty of another utterance or that itself expresses uncertainty	"about," "just," "kind of," "I would say," "I don't know," "maybe"
Token	Particles of speech that indicate a delay or disruption in the actor's cognitive processing	"ah," "aw," "eh," "er," "hm," "huh," "mm," "uh," "um"

adequately answer the question, and match the response format of the question (e.g., one of the response categories or the format on the screen or paper) (Schaeffer et al. 2020).

All of the questions in the current study have a similar response format consisting of a set of ordered categories, commonly referred to as a rating scale (see Appendix A). For this type of response format, an answer is codable if it is an exact repetition of one of the response categories (e.g., "extremely hard" when the response categories are "not at all hard, a little hard, somewhat hard, very hard, extremely hard"), a "kernel" of a response category, a word that uniquely and unambiguously identifies a single category (e.g., "extremely" uniquely and unambiguously identifies the category "extremely hard"), or a category reference, a reference to a specific category based on the positioning of the category relative to the other categories (e.g., "the last one" as a reference to "extremely hard").

In lieu of providing a codable answer, respondents may offer an uncodable answer, an answer that is provided in an attempt to respond to the survey question, but that cannot be coded using the response format or response categories offered. As described in more depth in Table 12.1, uncodable answers in this study take many forms including hypothetical response categories, repetitions or paraphrases of the question, repeating the response dimension without indicating a unique response category, and reports. Alternatively, because they did not hear or did not understand some part or all of a question or the response categories, respondents may refrain from answering a question and instead request repetition or clarification. Finally, respondents may provide different kinds of conversational elements along with codable answers, uncodable answers, and requests (Garbarski et al. 2016). These conversational elements include such varied behaviors as apologies, comments, elaborations, exclamations, laughter, mitigators, and tokens.

The presence (or absence) of any of these categories of talk likely varies based primarily on characteristics of questions but also on characteristics of respondents and to a lesser extent, because they are trained to be standardized, characteristics of interviewers (e.g., Olson and Smyth 2015). While uncodable answers, requests, and conversational elements arise for many reasons, including everyday conversational practices, they frequently occur when respondents encounter difficulty answering questions and may signal a problem with cognitive processing. For example, interactional behaviors that evince uncertainty (e.g., mitigators) or problems with response processing (e.g., reports) appear to increase when respondents must integrate conflicting information about their health, such as the presence of disease but high physical functioning, when answering a question on self-rated health (Garbarski et al. 2011). Because many of these behaviors are often associated with survey data that are of lower quality as indicated by being less reliable or valid (Dykema et al. 1997; Schaeffer and Dykema 2011b) or with response patterns that are undesirable, studying these behaviors may tell us something about the quality of the data we are collecting.

Racial/Ethnic Variation in Survey Response Processing

Coding interaction between survey participants to study cultural variation in how respondents behave is a "relatively new innovation" (Johnson et al. 2019, p. 272). Although research is limited, some evidence suggests intensive study of interviewer-respondent interaction may index differences across racial/ethnic groups in how respondents process survey concepts or how they exhibit comprehension or mapping difficulties. For example, Holbrook et al. (2006) evaluated questions about health events and behaviors used in federal population surveys and found certain racial and ethnic minority groups showed more interactional behaviors associated with comprehension problems—such as requests for clarification—than did non-Hispanic Whites. These differences suggest the meaning of concepts may vary across groups in such a way that respondents from minority groups have difficulty comprehending questions when the language or concepts are fitted to the dominant group; however, this study found no differences across groups in behaviors that indicate mapping difficulties such as providing inadequate or imprecise answers.

Johnson et al. (2015) examined levels of interactional indicators of possible measurement problems, such as interruptions, requests for clarification, and problems answering, displayed by respondents during the administration of questions about self-reported racial and ethnic discrimination. The questions studied used two different approaches to measuring discrimination: a one-stage approach in which questions directly focused on discrimination based on race/ethnicity (e.g., "... how often have you been treated with less respect than other people because you are RACE/ETHNICITY") versus a two-stage approach in which questions asked about non-race-related treatment first (e.g., "how often have you been treated with less respect than other people") followed by a list of reasons including race/ethnicity (e.g., "because of your race or skin color"). Overall, results indicated that while the two-stage approach was associated with lower odds of respondent problems than the one-stage form, the interactional indicators did not vary by race/ethnicity with the exception that the odds of exhibiting problems answering were lower among Latino than White respondents.

More recently, Johnson et al. (2019) sought to determine whether respondents from diverse racial and ethnic backgrounds and interviewed in multiple languages would display similar levels of comprehension and mapping difficulties when responding to questions deliberately designed to evoke such difficulties. For example, questions posed comprehension problems by asking about nonexistent objects (e.g., "how frequently have you visited a serrerium") and presented mapping challenges by mismatching the response format projected by the question (e.g., "Does it ever snow at the equator?" which projects a yes/no response) and response options (e.g., "never, occasionally, sometimes, or frequently?"). Overall, findings indicated that the levels of behaviors indicating difficulties demonstrated by the groups were remarkably consistent. An exception was that in contrast to non-Hispanic Whites, Korean-Americans interviewed in English produced lower levels of mapping problems for questions written to elicit such difficulties.

Current Study

We use interaction coding to examine differences between Black and White respondents answering sets of questions on varied topics including the likelihood of participating in medical research studies that collect different kinds of measures (e.g., blood, saliva) and questions about trust in medical researchers that are or are not focused on race. Trust is a central concept in many disciplines including sociology, survey methodology, and medicine (e.g., Dillman et al. 2014). Past research demonstrates that trust in medical researchers varies across racial and ethnic groups. For African Americans this distrust is rooted in the legacy of historical atrocities that have been perpetrated against them and that make up the collective memory of many African Americans. Distrust also stems from knowledge of and experience with a system of health research and health care that produces and reproduces unequal access, experiences, and treatment of individuals in that group (Corbie-Smith et al. 2002; Feagin and Bennefield 2014; Scharff et al. 2010). Consequently, we posit the questions on trust in medical research that focus on race are a better cultural fit for the Black respondents, in that they will be more likely to have had experiences and knowledge that align with what the questions are asking. We predict White respondents will be more likely to display behavioral indicators of problems for the race-focused questions about trust because they ask about concepts and use language that is less familiar for this group. We predict the other question sets—used here as controls for comparison to some extent—will be associated with similar levels of indicators of problems with cognitive processing for both racial groups.

Methods

Sample

The Voices Heard computer-assisted telephone survey sought to interview a total of 400 individuals from Wisconsin, equally distributed among the following racial and ethnic groups: White, Black, Latino, and American Indian. We employed a quota sampling strategy for the study because the costs of screening to identify members in the non-White groups would have been prohibitively expensive. The quota sample consisted primarily of volunteers; however, to supplement the volunteer sample, a targeted list containing names was provided by a vendor of consumer data (see Appendix B for more detail on the sample). Interviewers conducted 410 usable interviews (in English only) between October 2013 and March 2014 with respondents in the four subgroups defined by their race and ethnicity.

Respondents were categorized into the four racial/ethnic groups based on self-reports to a series of questions about their perceived racial and ethnic identities. The series began with a yes/no question asking respondents if they are "Hispanic or Latino." Respondents answering "yes" to this question were classified as "Latino" regardless of how they answered a follow-up question about their race. To assess race, respondents were asked, "Which one or more of the following would you say is your race: White, Black or African American, American Indian, Alaska Native, Asian, or Native Hawaiian or Other Pacific Islander?" Interviewers were instructed to record all of the categories offered by the respondent; respondents provided up to three categories. Respondents were classified as: "White," if they answered "no" to the question on Hispanic origin and reported no other racial categories; "Black," if they answered "no" to the question on Hispanic origin and reported "Black" only or "Black" and "White" as their race; or "American Indian" if they answered "no" to the question on Hispanic origin and reported "American Indian" alone or in combination with one or more other racial categories. In addition, one respondent who failed to answer the question on Hispanic origin, but reported "American Indian" as their race, was classified as "American Indian."

The average time to complete the interview was 25.21 minutes. We produced digital recordings for 371 interviews; 24 interviews were not recorded because the respondent refused and 15 were lost due to poor quality or recording errors. We limit our analysis to a comparison between the Black (n = 90) and White (n = 94) respondents because of the well-documented differences between these two groups in their experiences with, attitudes toward, and knowledge about the health care system.

Questionnaire and Items

The primary objective of the survey was to measure respondents' perceptions of the barriers and facilitators to participating in medical research studies that collect biomarkers, such as saliva, blood and tissue, and to document whether there were important differences among groups defined by their race and ethnicity. The telephone interview was part of a larger research effort that involved key informant and cognitive interviews with members of populations underrepresented in biomedical research. Questions covered the following topics: ratings of the likelihood to participate in specific types of medical research studies such as those that collect biomarkers; ratings of the likelihood to participate in medical research studies depending on the characteristics of the person making the request (e.g., "a member of your community"); evaluation of things medical researchers do to encourage participation (e.g., provide results or incentives); evaluation of things that sometimes concern people about participating in medical research; views toward medical researchers (e.g. how much trust or mistrust respondents have); measures of general health status, health-related quality of life, health behaviors, chronic conditions, and health care utilization; general knowledge of research procedures; and sociodemographic characteristics.

The current analysis focuses on three sets of questions (see Appendix A). The first set of questions is from a battery of items that uses the same response categories for each question and asks respondents to rate their self-assessed likelihood of participating in medical research studies that involve answering questions, giving samples of saliva, blood, tissue, or cerebrospinal fluid, or participating in a clinical trial. The second and third set of questions are from a twelve-item scale about trust in medical researchers adapted from previously administered instruments (Dykema et al. 2019). The response categories for these questions vary depending on the underlying dimension in the question (e.g., "never" to "extremely often" for frequency-based questions versus "not at all" to "extremely" for intensity-based questions). Within this twelve-item scale about trust in medical researchers, we make a further distinction about whether the questions focus on race or not. Thus, the second set of questions are race-focused trust in medical research questions, and the third set of questions are non-race-focused trust in medical research questions.

Systematic Transcriptions and Interaction Coding

Three transcribers listened to the audio recordings and created systematic transcriptions based on procedures we developed in previous work and which we describe in some detail here. Transcribers recorded all of the interaction that occurred between the interviewer and respondent for a given question. Within a question, interaction was segmented into turns, a unit-of-talk from one actor—the interviewer or respondent—that was not broken up by talk from the other actor. A turn-of-talk reached

Table 12.2 Example of systematic transcription for Questions 36 and 37, Case 10032, White male

ID	Question	Actor	Turn	Interruption	Overlap	Laugh Token
10032	36	i	when selecting participants for their most risky studies how likely are medical researchers to select minorities not at all likely a little likely somewhat likely very likely or extremely likely?			
		r	I I I I think that's a really weird question I'm just going to say not likely		1	
		i	{L} ok um not at all likely or a little likely I guess I have to ask you		1	
		r	not at all likely		1	
		i	ok			
	37	i	how often do medical researchers hide information about the possible risks of participating in medical research studies never rarely sometimes very often or extremely often?			
		r	well I mean a as as an express eh obviously I'd had no answer I mean I would hope it's never but I don't know			
		i	ok don't know			

Notes: "i" = interviewer, "r" = respondent, {L} = freestanding laughter

completion when the other actor began talking either because the original actor's talk concluded or the current actor interrupted the original actor.

For each interview, transcribers began with a template formatted in Excel containing a row that displayed the exact wording of each question (see Table 12.2). Transcribers listened to the audio and recorded any departures interviewers made in administering the question exactly as worded. In subsequent rows of the Excel sheet, transcribers recorded talk produced by the interviewer or respondent before the interviewer moved on to the next question. In addition to recording talk verbatim, transcribers also wrote out tokens (e.g., "ah"), coded whether the respondent interrupted the interviewer's initial reading of the question, and recorded whether the turn contained overlapping talk, freestanding laughter (laughter that occurs between words), or laugh tokens (particles of laughter that occur within words or phrases).

Coding the turns-of-talk was done in Stata using the electronic transcripts by a member of the project team in consultation with other members of the team. Using commands to read string variables, the primary coder identified strings of text capturing different units of talk, such as those described in Table 12.1. These string functions allowed us to parse talk into discrete coding units. As an example, in response to the race-focused Question 36, "When selecting participants for their most risky studies, how likely are medical researchers to select minorities: not at all likely, a little likely, somewhat likely, very likely, or extremely likely?", a respondent answered "that's a tricky one cause it depends what they're studying ah I would say a little likely." We coded this respondent's turn into categories representing a comment on the question ("that's a tricky one"), an elaboration ("cause it depends what they're studying"), a token ("ah"), a mitigator ("I would say"), and a codable answer ("a little likely").

Measures

We examine five outcomes previous research has found to be associated with lower data quality and that are hypothesized to be indicators of potential cognitive problems respondents have when processing a survey question. Note that these are not mutually exclusive indicators of processing difficulties but different ways to conceptualize separate but related features of the response process and potential breakdowns in cognitive processing (Garbarski et al. 2011). Our first outcome indicated whether the question-answer sequence contained more than three turns, a sign the respondent may have had difficulty answering the question and the interviewer intervened by following up in order to obtain a codable answer. Second, we examine whether the respondent failed to provide a codable answer during their first turn of talk. As noted, respondents routinely include other non-standardized talk with a codable answer, particularly in the course of thinking out loud and formulating a response. As long as this talk did not contradict the respondent's final answer, it was included as part of a codable answer. Third, we code whether the respondent requested to have all or part of the question or response categories repeated or requested clarification of a term or phrase in their first turn. These requests happened in sequences with a codable answer, but were more likely to occur in lieu of providing a codable answer. Our fourth outcome marked whether the respondent's talk included an affective element such as laughter, a laugh token, or an exclamation (e.g., "gosh," "oh boy," or "wow") during their first turn of talk. Finally, we examine whether the respondent's initial turn of talk included a token, such as "ah," "er," "uh," or "um." These particles likely indicate a delay or disruption in the actor's cognitive processing (e.g., Bortfeld et al. 2016).

Although the primary respondent characteristic of interest is the respondent's race, we also include gender, age, and education (high school education or less, some college, college or more) as control variables in the multivariate models.

Analytic Strategy

Our unit of analysis is the question-answer sequence. A question-answer sequence began with the interviewer's administration of the question and ended with the last utterance spoken before the next question was read, typically the respondent's final answer or a statement by the interviewer acknowledging the respondent's answer (e.g., "ok"). The analysis examines 3301 question-answer sequences produced by the 184 respondents answering the 18 questions; ten question-answer sequences are omitted because the recording for the question was not audible.

To account for the complicated crossed and nested structure of the data, we implement a mixed-effects model with a variance structure that uses crossed random effects. Initial models included random effects for interviewers, questions, and respondents (nested within interviewers and crossed with questions). However, results indicated that including all three random effects resulted in the models being overfitted and the estimate of the interviewer effect being close to zero, and so we removed the random intercept for the interviewer. Respondent characteristics and question set (i.e., trust in medical research questions that are race-focused, those that are not race-focused, and likelihood to participate in medical research questions) are modeled as fixed effects which are nested within and crossed with the random effects. Each of the dependent variables are binary; logit models were computed in Stata using the meqrlogit function. Because of our relatively small sample of respondents, we describe results with a p-value of less than .10 as marginally significant and .05 or less as statistically significant.

Results

Descriptive statistics are shown in Table 12.3. Approximately 23% of the question-answer sequences contained more than three turns. Respondents did not provide a codable answer in their first turn in 19% of the sequences. They requested a repetition or clarification in nearly 8% of all of their first turns, and their response included an affective element in the first turn in 5% of the question administrations. Tokens were fairly common, occurring in the first turn in 25% of the sequences. The quota sample yielded approximately equal numbers of Black and White respondents, slightly more women than men, and a roughly equal distribution of respondents in the three educational categories.

In a series of bivariate analyses, we examine whether there was a difference between Black and White respondents in the likelihood of producing the outcomes of interest for each of the question sets. Table 12.4 presents results from separate multilevel logistic regression models in which the interactional outcome is regressed on the respondents' race, separately for each question set.

For the models predicting question-answer sequences with more than three turns, no codable answer, and requests for repetition or clarification, results indicate that

Table 12.3 Descriptive statistics for interactional outcomes, respondent characteristics, and question sets

	Mean or Percent	Standard Deviation	Minimum	Maximum	n
Interactional outcomes					
More than 3 turns (vs. less)	23.21		0	1	3301
No codable answer (vs. codable answer)	19.21		0	1	3301
Any request for repetition or clarification (vs. none)	7.66		0	1	3301
Affective response (vs. not)	4.85		0	1	3301
Token (vs. none)	25.05		0	1	3301
Respondent characteristics					
Race					
Black	48.91				90
White	51.09				94
Gender					
Male	44.02				81
Female	55.98				103
Education					
High school or less	35.87				66
Some college	28.26				52
College or more	35.87				66
Age (in years)	44.70	16.74	18.00	90.00	184
Question sets					
Trust questions: Race-focused	27.78				5
Trust questions: Non-race-focused	38.89				7
Likelihood to participate	33.33				6

when answering the race-focused trust questions, White respondents were significantly (or marginally so for requests) more likely to produce longer sequences, uncodable answers, and marginally more likely to produce requests than Black respondents. In contrast, the levels of these outcomes did not differ between White and Black respondents for the non-race-focused trust questions or the likelihood-to-participate questions.

The pattern of results for affective elements and tokens was slightly different (Table 12.4). White respondents were (marginally) more likely to display an affective element than Black respondents for both the race- and non-race-focused trust questions, while levels were the same for the likelihood-to-participate questions. The only question set to show a difference between White and Black respondents for tokens was for the non-race-focused trust questions, for which White respondents were more likely to produce one or more tokens while answering.

Next, we examine whether the levels of differences for the Black and White respondents in the bivariate models are statistically significant across the question

Table 12.4 Bivariate, multilevel logistic regression analyses of interactional outcomes on respondents' race within question set

	More than 3 turns						No codable answer						Request repetition or clarification					
	Trust race-focused		Trust non-race-focused		Likelihood to participate		Trust race-focused		Trust non-race-focused		Likelihood to participate		Trust race-focused		Trust non-race-focused		Likelihood to participate	
Variables	Coef	SE	Coef	SE	Coef	SE	Coef	SE	Coef	SE	Coef	SE	Coef	SE	Coef	SE	Coef	SE
Respondent characteristics																		
White (vs. Black)	0.462*	0.228	−0.073	0.218	0.071	0.144	0.904***	0.282	0.090	0.243	−0.025	0.874	0.665+	0.345	0.203	0.243	−0.062	0.234
Intercept	−1.956***	0.258	−2.015***	0.230	−0.631***	0.107	−2.415***	0.294	−2.341***	0.232	−1.067***	0.149	−3.430***	0.388	−3.045***	0.232	−2.571***	0.268
Random-effects parameters																		
Question-level variance	0.157	0.124	0.166	0.110	0.003	0.016	0.141	0.118	0.112	0.081	0.053	0.048	0.133	0.130	0.263	0.180	0.162	0.133
Respondent-level variance	0.768	0.280	0.814	0.258	0.186	0.106	1.540	0.435	1.089	0.321	0.205	0.123	1.644	0.664	0.601	0.333	0.045	0.297
Model fit statistics																		
N	918		1288		1095		918		1288		1095		918		1288		1095	
Wald chi-square	4.11*		0.11		0.24		10.25**		0.14		0.03		3.72+		0.62		0.07	
Log likelihood	−432.18		−525.81		−714.17		−412.52		−481.10		−628.82		−254.65		−320.94		−287.86	

(continued)

Table 12.4 (continued)

	Affective element						Token					
	Trust race-focused		Trust non-race-focused		Likelihood to participate		Trust race-focused		Trust non-race-focused		Likelihood to participate	
Variables	Coef	SE	Coef	SE	Coef	SE	Coef	SE	Coef	SE	Coef	SE
Respondent characteristics												
White (vs. Black)	1.039+	0.563	0.830+	0.428	0.416	0.329	0.394	0.242	0.533*	0.214	0.347	0.221
Intercept	−5.342***	0.838	−4.680***	0.519	−3.426***	0.357	−1.738***	0.191	−1.778***	0.196	−1.244***	0.179
Random-effects parameters												
Question-level variance	0.020	0.080	0.023	0.082	0.125	0.113	0.000	0.000	0.075	0.059	0.029	0.035
Respondent-level variance	4.437	2.693	1.908	1.068	1.526	0.593	1.150	0.324	1.020	0.251	1.176	0.284
Model fit statistics												
N	918		1288		1095		918		1288		1095	
Wald chi-square	3.40+		3.75+		3.29		2.65		6.19*		2.46	
Log likelihood	−141.58		−178.40		−307.69		−468.85		−655.76		−635.64	

sets. Table 12.5 presents results from multivariate models that include interaction terms for race by question set; the models also control for respondents' sociodemographic characteristics. To facilitate interpretation of the results, Fig. 12.2 provides the estimated marginal predicted probability of each outcome by race and question set. For the model predicting question-answer sequences with more than three turns, we find that White respondents answering the race-focused trust questions are more likely to require more than three turns to answer the question compared to Black respondents (b = 0.355, p < .10; coefficient for "White" because the reference group is Black respondents answering the race-focused trust questions), although the effect is attenuated compared to the results in Table 12.4 by controlling for respondents' sociodemographic characteristics. Further, the interaction between race and question set is significant for non-race-focused trust questions (b = −0.492, p < .05), indicating that the effect of race in the race-focused trust questions is significantly different from the effect of race in the non-race-focused trust questions. The interaction of race with the likelihood-to-participate questions is not significant, indicating that the effect of race in the race-focused trust questions is not different from the effect of race in the likelihood-to-participate questions.

A similar but stronger pattern of results is shown for question-answer sequences that fail to result in a codable answer in the first turn. White respondents are significantly more likely not to provide a codable answer than Black respondents to race-focused trust questions (b = 0.643, p < .01). Both of the interaction terms are significant, indicating that the effect of race in the race-focused trust questions is significantly different from the effect of race in the non-race-focused trust questions and the likelihood-to-participate questions.

Requests for repetition or clarification mirror the previous results but are not as strong, likely due to the fact that such requests rarely occur. The effect of race for the race-focused trust questions is marginally significant (b = 0.537, p < .10) as is the interaction term for race by the non-race-focused trust questions (b = −0.651, p < .10).

Turning to the results predicting the presence of an affective element in the first term, while the effect of race for the race-focused trust questions is marginally significant (b = 0.537, p < .10), the effect of race in the race-focused trust questions is not different from the effect of race in the non-race-focused trust questions or the likelihood-to-participate questions. Finally, net of other respondent characteristics, race is no longer a significant predictor of tokens.

Discussion

Overall, we find that non-Hispanic Whites display more interactional behaviors and patterns that may indicate comprehension and mapping difficulties than do Black respondents for questions about trust in medical researchers that invoke race. In bivariate analyses, this pattern holds for the indicators of multiple turns of talk, uncodable answers, requests for repetition or clarification, and the presence of

Table 12.5 Multivariate, multilevel logistic regression analyses of interactional outcomes on respondent characteristics, question sets, and interaction terms

	More than 3 turns		No codable answer		Request repetition or clarification		Affective element		Token	
	Coef	SE	Coef	SE	Coef	SE	Coef	SE	Coef	SE
Respondent characteristics										
White (vs. Black)	0.355+	0.214	0.643**	0.229	0.537+	0.306	0.785+	0.430	0.329	0.248
Female (vs. male)	0.093	0.137	0.067	0.154	0.260	0.208	0.402	0.251	−0.139	0.183
Education										
High school or less	–	–	–	–	–	–	–	–	–	–
Some college	−0.105	0.167	0.234	0.186	0.476+	0.254	0.182	0.317	0.463*	0.226
College or more	−0.119	0.160	−0.111	0.181	0.344	0.242	0.320	0.290	0.413	0.217
Age	0.009*	0.004	0.011*	0.005	0.004	0.006	0.015+	0.008	−0.007	0.006
Question sets										
Trust questions: race-focused	–	–	–	–	–	–	–	–	–	–
Trust questions: non-race-focused	−0.054	0.275	−0.099	0.268	−0.017	0.383	−0.180	0.472	−0.072	0.204
Likelihood to participate	1.155***	0.271	0.921***	0.263	0.203	0.390	1.011*	0.424	0.487*	0.205
Interaction terms										
White × non-race-focused trust questions	−0.492*	0.240	−0.666**	0.252	−0.388	0.339	−0.077	0.510	0.157	0.227
White × likelihood-to-participate questions	−0.336	0.222	−0.778***	0.235	−0.651+	0.348	−0.520	0.449	−0.027	0.226
Intercept	−2.242***	0.322	−2.656***	0.353	−3.705***	0.497	−5.347***	0.612	−1.526***	0.376
Random-effects parameters										
Question-level variance	0.102	0.047	0.103	0.408	0.223	0.099	0.125	0.082	0.038	0.025
Respondent-level variance	0.415	0.088	0.544	0.108	0.757	0.203	0.791	0.275	1.010	0.167
Model fit statistics										
N	3301		3301		3301		3301		3301	
Wald chi-square	51.63***		43.24***		10.72		25.77**		26.11**	
Log likelihood	−1657.98		−1506.86		−851.90		−590.69		−1705.65	

+p < 0.10, *p < 0.05, **p < 0.01, ***p < 0.001

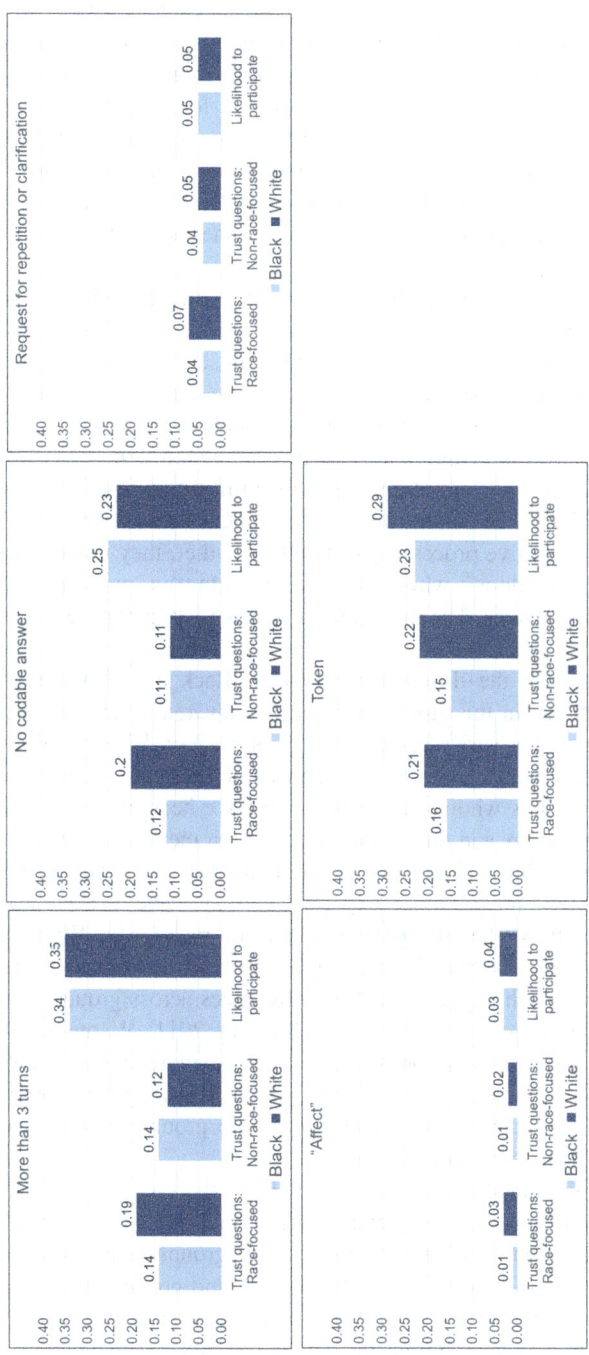

Fig. 12.2 Estimated marginal predicted probability of interactional outcome by race and question set

affective elements. In multivariate analyses that include interaction terms for race by question set and control for other socio-demographic characteristics, we find that the difference between Blacks and Whites answering the race-focused trust questions is significantly different from the race effect (1) for the non-race-focused questions for the model predicting more than three turns; (2) for both the non-race-focused questions and likelihood-to-participate questions for the model predicting no codable answer in the first turn; and (3) for the likelihood-to-participate questions for the model predicting requests in the first turn. For affective elements, neither of the interaction terms are significant, possibly due to the fact that these are very infrequent behaviors.

Tokens occur relatively frequently—respondents utter them in their first turn in a quarter of the question-answer sequences examined—and they are associated with a different interactional trajectory. In bivariate analyses, tokens are more commonly produced by White respondents for the non-race-focused trust questions (Table 12.5), but this effect is no longer significant when other characteristics of respondents are controlled and neither of the interaction terms is significant in the multivariate models. Interestingly, there is a significant association between education and tokens. It may be that the delay and disfluency tokens analyzed here are not associated with cognitive processing difficulties; rather, they reflect ways in which speakers "hold the floor" while they are thinking in ways that vary across sociodemographic groups. The implications of this finding require future theorizing and research.

We speculate that the differences between Black and White respondents in interactional patterns in this study arise because awareness of the concept of trust in medical researchers varies across these groups. Non-Hispanic Whites are less familiar with the concept of (dis)trust in medical researchers compared to racial/ ethnic minority groups who are more likely to have been exposed to such considerations both personally and during interactions with members of their communities (Corbie-Smith et al. 2002; Feagin and Bennefield 2014; Scharff et al. 2010). Lack of general familiarity and personal experiences may have exacerbated cognitive processing difficulties when the questions focus on race for the White respondents. Although the evidence is limited and the findings somewhat mixed, these results and some previous research suggest potential differences across groups in the response processing of survey questions (Schoua-Glusberg 2011; Warnecke et al. 1997). These findings add to a small body of work that explores whether the interaction that unfolds between interviewers and respondents in standardized interviews varies across respondents from different racial or ethnic groups (Holbrook et al. 2006; Johnson et al. 2015; Johnson et al. 2019).

Our study was limited in several regards. First, the sample sizes for each of the groups under study was relatively small and may have decreased our ability to detect statistically significant differences between the groups, especially for the rarer behaviors of requesting repetition or clarification and providing affective elements as part of one's response. Second, due to cost constraints, respondents were not recruited randomly, which limits the generalizability of our sample to a larger population. Third, the questions we examine were not randomly sampled from a population of questions that focus on race versus not, and so the conclusions we draw may be limited to the comparisons tested in this study. Fourth, the five outcomes we examine were selected because they have been shown to be associated with lower data quality in previous research and they feature characteristic types of talk that respondents display when answering survey questions. However, we may have overlooked behaviors characteristics of Black respondents that have not been described in the literature. Furthermore, our indicators of problems in cognitive processing are not independent of each other. For example, when respondents fail to produce a codable answer or request clarification, interviewers are trained to follow up, with the result that the question-answer sequence will by necessity contain more than three turns.

Fifth, we use interaction coding as a vehicle to study differences in how respondents from different racial groups process surveys items. As a criterion that indexes data quality, behavior from interviewer-respondent interaction has the advantages that it can be observed and coded for all questions from any interviewer-administered instrument and provides information about the performance of individual items in actual operational setting. Further, the rich quantitative and qualitative data produced during the question-answer sequences can be coded reliably from transcriptions, particularly using the methodology advanced in the current study of systematically coding strings of text. In addition, although recording, transcribing, and coding interactions is not inexpensive, it may be less expensive than other designs for assessing data quality, although we are not aware of studies that compare question-testing methodologies in terms of costs.

There are, of course, disadvantages to the methodology. Some response processing problems may be internal to the participants and leave no trace in the interaction. As Johnson et al. (2019, p. 274) document "respondents may in some instances elect to answer difficult or unclear questions without revealing any misunderstandings or other confusion about them." While research is limited, it does appear, however, that respondents from different racial and ethnic backgrounds demonstrate similar levels of problem indicators when responding to questions intentionally written to evoke comprehension and mapping difficulties (Johnson et al. 2019). Although past research demonstrates they are often associated with measures of validity and reliability (Schaeffer and Dykema 2011b), the behavioral outcomes we examine are only proxy measures of response error, and we lack external criteria to determine whether the behaviors we examine predict measurement error. It is possible that the behaviors we examine may be influenced by factors that are not direct influences on data quality (see Palmieri 2016).

The requirements of standardized measurement may pose challenges for respondents from different social and cultural backgrounds—and these challenges may affect measurement differently for these groups, compromising the use of surveys as a tool for comparative research. In so far as the differential rate of problematic behaviors is associated with measurement error, this error complicates estimates of differences across groups and may lead to incorrect conclusions about the overall levels of and differences in an outcome of interest among groups, such as apparent differences in health across groups even though true differences do not exist or apparent similarities when true differences exist, using health as an example. Previous research on interviewer-respondent interaction during the standardized survey interview has focused on documenting what features of this interaction reveal about response processing and data quality. A new generation of research has begun exploring what a detailed analysis of interaction may tell us about how respondents from various cultural groups, including those that differ based on their race and ethnicity, respond to questions that vary in their topics and characteristics. Products of this research have important implications for the practice of survey research. A detailed analysis of interviewer-respondent interaction can: (1) inform best practices for writing survey questions and designing survey forms for respondents with varying backgrounds and characteristics, (2) identify features of interaction, such as those that indicate uncertainty, to use as control variables to augment analysis, and (3) highlight techniques to improve interviewer training, for example, by using evidence of what participants actually do to inform decisions about when and how interviewers should intervene in the question-answer process to obtain codable answers (Garbarski et al. 2016; Schaeffer et al. 2016).

Acknowledgements The collection of survey data for the Voices Heard Survey was funded by NIMHD grant P60MD003428 (PD: A. Adams). Project: Increasing Participation of Underrepresented Minorities in Biomarker Research (PI: D. Farrar Edwards). This study is based upon work supported by the National Science Foundation (grant number SES-1853094 to J. Dykema and D. Garbarski]. Project: Effects of Interviewers, Respondents, and Questions on Survey Measurement. Additional support was provided by the University of Wisconsin-Madison Office of the Vice Chancellor for Research and Graduate Education with funding from the Wisconsin Alumni Research Foundation, the Charles Cannell Fund in Survey Methodology at the University of Michigan, the University of Wisconsin Survey Center (UWSC), which receives support from the College of Letters and Science at the University of Wisconsin-Madison, and the facilities of the Social Science Computing Cooperative and the Center for Demography and Ecology (NICHD core grant P2C HD047873). The authors thank Steven Blixt for comments on earlier drafts and Russell Diamond for advice on the analysis. Opinions expressed here are those of the authors and do not necessarily reflect those of the sponsors or related organizations.

Appendix A: Exact Question Wordings by Topic

Question Number	Question Stem	Response Categories
Likelihood to participate in medical research		
1	If a medical researcher asked you to participate in a medical research study by **answering questions about yourself**, how likely would you be to participate	very likely, somewhat likely, neither likely nor unlikely, somewhat unlikely, or very unlikely
2	If a medical researcher asked you to participate in a medical research study by **giving a sample of your saliva**, how likely would you be to participate	very likely, somewhat likely, neither likely nor unlikely, somewhat unlikely, or very unlikely

(continued)

Question Number	Question Stem	Response Categories
3	If a medical researcher asked you to participate in a medical research study by **giving a sample of your blood**, how likely would you be to participate	(very likely, somewhat likely, neither likely nor unlikely, somewhat unlikely, or very unlikely)
4	Tissue is located in the human body and is made up of cells. Small pieces of tissue can be taken from the body by a health care professional. If a medical researcher asked you to participate in a medical research study by **giving a sample of your tissue**, how likely would you be to participate	very likely, somewhat likely, neither likely nor unlikely, somewhat unlikely, or very unlikely
5	Cerebrospinal fluid is a fluid that surrounds your brain. It can be collected by inserting a small needle into your lower back, a procedure called a lumbar puncture or spinal tap. If a medical researcher asked you to participate in a medical research study by **giving a sample of your cerebrospinal fluid**, how likely would you be to participate	(very likely, somewhat likely, neither likely nor unlikely, somewhat unlikely, or very unlikely)
6	A clinical trial is a study that tests new drugs or treatments. If a medical researcher asked you to participate in a **clinical trial**, how likely would you be to participate	(very likely, somewhat likely, neither likely nor unlikely, somewhat unlikely, or very unlikely)
Trust in medical research: Non-race-focused		
32	All things considered, how much do you trust medical researchers	none, a little, some, quite a bit, or a great deal
34	How hard do medical researchers work to make sure that the participants in their studies are safe	not at all hard, a little hard, somewhat hard, very hard, or extremely hard
35	To what extent do medical researchers care more about the findings of their research than they do about their participants	not at all, a little, somewhat, quite a bit, or a great deal
37	How often do medical researchers hide information about the possible risks of participating in medical research studies	never, rarely, sometimes, very often, or extremely often
39	How often do medical researchers tell participants everything they need to know about the risks of participating in their studies	never, rarely, sometimes, very often, or extremely often
41	How hard do medical researchers work to make sure they keep information from participants private and secure	not at all hard, a little hard, somewhat hard, very hard, or extremely hard
43	How often do medical researchers want to know more than they need to know	never, rarely, sometimes, very often, or extremely often

(continued)

Question Number	Question Stem	Response Categories
Trust in medical research: Race-focused		
33	When they are conducting research, how often do medical researchers have the best interests of participants from your racial or ethnic group in mind	never, rarely, sometimes, very often, or extremely often
36	When selecting participants for their most risky studies, how likely are medical researchers to select minorities	not at all likely, a little likely, somewhat likely, very likely, or extremely likely
38	How often do medical researchers treat participants from your racial or ethnic group like guinea pigs in their studies	never, rarely, sometimes, very often, or extremely often
40	How often do medical researchers treat participants from your racial or ethnic group the same as participants from other racial or ethnic groups	never, rarely, sometimes, very often, or always
42	How concerned are you that the information collected in medical research studies could be used to confirm or promote stereotypes	not at all concerned, a little concerned, somewhat concerned, very concerned, or extremely concerned

Appendix B: Sample Description

The following table shows the distribution of completed interviews by race/ethnicity for the volunteer and vendor lists.

Volunteer list. For the volunteer sample, members of the project team recruited 471 (n = 46 White, n = 137 Black, n = 144 Latino, and n = 144 American Indian) individuals through connections they built with leaders in specific racial and ethnic communities, by visiting churches and community centers, by attending events sponsored by specific racial or ethnic groups (e.g., pow-wows), and by posting flyers at targeted locations in communities. Project staff collected names, demographic data (e.g., race and ethnicity), and contact information (e.g., phone numbers) for these potential respondents, and all individuals identified through these channels were contacted and asked to participate in the study.

Vendor list. A total of 8075 records were purchased from Infogroup, a business and consumer data provider. Infogroup filtered data from their databases based on a surname algorithm and geo-coding that would supposedly help target individuals living in diverse communities in Wisconsin. In addition, Infogroup filtered records to accrue only those with high-deliverability for direct mail and those with active telephone numbers. From the list of records, a total of 700 cases (7 replicates of 100 cases each, consisting overall of 100 White, 200 Black, 200 Latino, and 200 American Indian targeted individuals) were fielded for calling.

Number of Completed Cases by Race/Ethnicity of List Source

Race/Ethnicity	Volunteer List	Vendor List
White	29	73
Black	103	3
Latino	93	7
American Indian	101	1
Total	326	84

References

Bates, B. R., Lynch, J. A., Bevan, J. L., & Condit, C. M. (2005). Warranted concerns, warranted outlooks: A focus group study of public understandings of genetic research. *Social Science & Medicine, 60*(2), 331–344. https://doi.org/10.1016/j.socscimed.2004.05.012

Bortfeld, H., Leon, S. D., Bloom, J. E., Schober, M. F., & Brennan, S. E. (2016). Disfluency rates in conversation: Effects of age, relationship, topic, role, and gender. *Language and Speech, 44*(2), 123–147. https://doi.org/10.1177/00238309010440020101.

Boulware, L. E., Cooper, L. A., Ratner, L. E., LaVeist, T. A., & Powe, N. R. (2003). Race and trust in the health care system. *Public Health Reports, 118*(4), 358–365. https://doi.org/10.1093/phr/118.4.358.

Branson, R. D., Davis, K., & Butler, K. L. (2007). African Americans' participation in clinical research: Importance, barriers, and solutions. *The American Journal of Surgery, 193*(1), 32–39. https://doi.org/10.1016/j.amjsurg.2005.11.007.

Brown, D. R., & Topcu, M. (2003). Willingness to participate in clinical treatment research among older African Americans and Whites. *The Gerontologist, 43*(1), 62–72. https://doi.org/10.1093/geront/43.1.62.

Corbie-Smith, G. (1999). The continuing legacy of the Tuskegee Syphilis Study: Considerations for clinical investigation. *The American Journal of the Medical Sciences, 317*(1), 5–8. https://doi.org/10.1016/S0002-9629(15)40464-1.

Corbie-Smith, G. (2004). Minority recruitment and participation in health research. *North Carolina Medical Journal, 165*(6), 385–387.

Corbie-Smith, G., Thomas, S. B., & St. George, D. M. M. (2002). Distrust, race, and research. *Archives of Internal Medicine, 162*(21), 2458–2463. https://doi.org/10.1001/archinte.162.21.2458.

Corbie-Smith, G., Thomas, S. B., Williams, M. V., & Moody-Ayers, S. (1999). Attitudes and beliefs of African Americans toward participation in medical research. *Journal of General Internal Medicine, 14*(9), 537–546. https://doi.org/10.1046/j.1525-1497.1999.07048.x.

Dillman, D. A., Smyth, J. D., & Christian, L. M. (2014). *Internet, phone, mail, and mixed-mode surveys: The tailored design method* (4th ed.). Hoboken, NJ: Wiley.

Dykema, J., Garbarski, D., Wall, I. F., & Edwards, D. F. (2019). Measuring trust in medical researchers: Adding insights from cognitive interviews to examine agree-disagree and construct-specific survey questions. *Journal of Official Statistics, 35*(2), 353-386. https://doi.org/10.2478/jos-2019-0017.

Dykema, J., Lepkowski, J. M., & Blixt, S. (1997). The effect of interviewer and respondent behavior on data quality: Analysis of interaction coding in a validation study. In L. Lyberg, P. Biemer, M. Collins, E. de Leeuw, C. Dippo, N. Schwarz, & D. Trewin (Eds.), *Survey measurement and process quality* (pp. 287–310). New York, NY: Wiley. https://doi.org/10.1002/9781118490013.ch12.

Dykema, J., Schaeffer, N. C., Garbarski, D., & Hout, M. (2020). The role of question characteristics in designing and evaluating survey questions. In P. Beatty, D. Collins, L. Kaye, J. Padilla, G. Willis, & A. Wilmot (Eds.), *Advances in questionnaire design, development, evaluation, and testing* (pp. 449–470). Hoboken, NJ: Wiley. https://doi.org/10.1002/9781119263685.ch6.

Feagin, J., & Bennefield, Z. (2014). Systemic racism and U.S. health care. *Social Science & Medicine, 103*, 7–14. https://doi.org/10.1016/j.socscimed.2013.09.006.

Fowler, F. J., Jr. & Cannell, C. F. (1996). Using behavioral coding to identify cognitive problems with survey questions. In N. Schwarz & S. Sudman (Eds.), *Answering questions: Methodology for determining cognitive and communicative processes in survey research* (pp. 15–36). San Francisco, CA: Jossey-Bass.

Fowler, F. J., Jr. & Mangione, T. W. (1990). *Standardized survey interviewing: Minimizing interviewer-related error*. Newbury Park: Sage.

Fowler, F. J., Jr. (2011). Coding the behavior of interviewers and respondents to evaluate survey questions. In J. Madans, K. Miller, A. Maitland, & G. Willis (Eds.), *Question evaluation methods: Contributing to the science of data quality* (pp. 5–21). Hoboken, NJ: Wiley. https://doi.org/10.1002/9781118037003.ch2.

Gamble, V. N. (1993). A legacy of distrust: African Americans and medical research. *American Journal of Preventive Medicine, 9*(6), 35–38.

Garbarski, D., Schaeffer, N. C., & Dykema, J. (2011). Are interactional behaviors exhibited when the self-reported health question is asked associated with health status? *Social Science Research, 40*(4), 1025–1036. https://doi.org/10.1016/j.ssresearch.2011.04.002.

Garbarski, D., Schaeffer, N. C., & Dykema, J. (2016). Interviewing practices, conversational practices, and rapport: Responsiveness and engagement in the standardized survey interview. *Sociological Methodology, 46*(1), 1–38. https://doi.org/10.1177/0081175016637890.

George, S., Duran, N., & Norris, K. (2014). A systematic review of barriers and facilitators to minority research participation among African Americans, Latinos, Asian Americans, and Pacific Islanders. *American Journal of Public Health, 104*(2), e16–e31. https://doi.org/10.2105/ajph.2013.301706.

Goldman, R. E., Kingdon, C., Wasser, J., Clark, M. A., Goldberg, R., Papandonatos, G. D., et al. (2008). Rhode Islanders' attitudes towards the development of a statewide genetic biobank. *Personalized Medicine, 5*(4), 339–359. https://doi.org/10.2217/17410541.5.4.339.

Halbert, C. H., Armstrong, K., Gandy, O. H., Jr., & Shaker, L. (2006). Racial differences in trust in health care providers. *Archives of Internal Medicine, 166*(8), 896–901. https://doi.org/10.1001/archinte.166.8.896.

Holbrook, A., Cho, Y. I., & Johnson, T. (2006). The impact of question and respondent characteristics on comprehension and mapping difficulties. *Public Opinion Quarterly, 70*(4), 565–595. https://doi.org/10.1093/poq/nfl027.

Hoyo, C., Reid, M. L., Godley, P. A., Parrish, T., Smith, L., & Gammon, M. (2003). Barriers and strategies for sustained participation of African-American men in cohort studies. *Ethnicity & Disease, 13*(4), 470–476.

Hyman, H. H. (1975 [1954]). *Interviewing in social research*. Chicago, IL: The University of Chicago.

Johnson, T. P., Holbrook, A., Cho, Y. I., Shavitt, S., Chavez, N., & Weiner, S. (2019). Examining the comparability of behavior coding across cultures. In T. P. Johnson, B. Pennell, I. A. L. Stoop, & B. Dorer (Eds.), *Advances in comparative survey methods: Multinational, multiregional, and multicultural contexts (3MC)* (pp. 271–291). Hoboken, NJ: Wiley. https://doi.org/10.1002/9781118884997.ch13.

Johnson, T. P., Shariff-Marco, S., Willis, G. B., Cho, Y. I., Breen, N., Gee, G. C., et al. (2015). Sources of interactional problems in a survey of racial/ethnic discrimination. *International Journal of Public Opinion Research, 27*(2), 244–263. https://doi.org/10.1093/ijpor/edu024.

Krosnick, J. A. (2011). Experiments for evaluating survey questions. In J. Madans, K. Miller, A. Maitland, & G. Willis (Eds.), *Question evaluation methods: Contributing to the science of data quality* (pp. 215–238). Hoboken, NJ: Wiley. https://doi.org/10.1002/9781118037003. ch14.

Luebbert, R., & Perez, A. (2016). Barriers to clinical research participation among African Americans. *Journal of Transcultural Nursing, 27*(5), 456–463. https://doi.org/10.1177/1043659615575578.

NIH. (2008). Guidelines on the inclusion of women and minorities as subjects in clinical research–Amended, October, 2001.

Olson, K., & Smyth, J. D. (2015). The effect of CATI questions, respondents, and interviewers on response time. *Journal of Survey Statistics and Methodology, 3*(3), 361–396. https://doi.org/10.1093/jssam/smv021.

O'Muircheartaigh, C., & Campanelli, P. (1998). The relative impact of interviewer effects and sample design effects on survey precision. *Journal of the Royal Statistical Society, Series A, 161*, 63–77. https://doi.org/10.1111/1467-985X.00090.

Ongena, Y. P., & Dijkstra, W. (2007). A model of cognitive processes and conversational principles in survey interview interaction. *Applied Cognitive Psychology, 21*(2), 145–163. https://doi.org/10.1002/acp.1334.

Palmieri, M. (2016). Is verbal interaction coding a reliable pretesting technique? *Bulletin of Sociological Methodology/Bulletin de Méthodologie Sociologique, 129*(1), 64–77. https://doi.org/10.1177/0759106315615512.

Schaeffer, N. C. (1991). Conversation with a purpose–or conversation? Interaction in the standardized interview. In P. P. Biemer, R. M. Groves, L. E. Lyberg, N. A. Mathiowetz, & S. Sudman (Eds.), *Measurement errors in surveys* (pp. 367–392). New York: Wiley. https://doi.org/10.1002/9781118150382.ch19.

Schaeffer, N. C., & Dykema, J. (2011a). Questions for surveys: Current trends and future directions. *Public Opinion Quarterly, 75*(5), 909–961. https://doi.org/10.1093/poq/nfr048.

Schaeffer, N. C., & Dykema, J. (2011b). Response 1 to Fowler's chapter: Coding the behavior of interviewers and respondents to evaluate survey questions. In J. Madans, K. Miller, A. Maitland, & G. Willis (Eds.), *Question evaluation methods: Contributing to the science of data quality* (1st ed., pp. 23–39). Hoboken, NJ: Wiley. https://doi.org/10.1002/9781118037003.ch3.

Schaeffer, N. C., Dykema, J., Coombs, S. M., Schultz, R. K., Holland, L., & Hudson, M. L. (2020). General interviewing techniques: Developing evidence-based practices for standardized interviewing. In K. Olson, J. D. Smyth, J. Dykema, A. Holbrook, F. Kreuter, & B. T. West (Eds.), *Interviewer effects from a total survey error perspective* (pp. 33-46). Boca Raton, FL: CRC Press Taylor & Francis Group.

Schaeffer, N. C., Dykema, J., & Garbarski, D. (2016). Answers to standardized questions: Recognizing "codable" answers and maintaining standardization and rapport. Paper presented at the International Conference on Survey Methods in Multinational, Multiregional and Multicultural Contexts (3MC), July, Chicago, IL.

Schaeffer, N. C., Dykema, J., & Maynard, D. W. (2010). Interviewers and interviewing. In P. V. Marsden & J. D. Wright (Eds.), *Handbook of survey research* (2nd ed., pp. 437–470). Bingley, UK: Emerald Group Publishing Limited.

Schaeffer, N. C., & Maynard, D. W. (1996). From paradigm to prototype and back again: Interactive aspects of cognitive processing in survey interviews. In N. Schwarz & S. Sudman (Eds.), *Answering questions: Methodology for determining cognitive and communicative processes in survey research* (pp. 65–88). San Francisco, CA: Jossey-Bass.

Schaeffer, N. C., & Maynard, D. W. (2002). Standardization and interaction in the survey interview. In J. Holstein & J. Gubrium (Eds.), *Handbook of Interviewing* (pp. 577–601). Thousand Oaks, CA: Sage.

Schaeffer, N. C., & Maynard, D. W. (2008). The contemporary standardized survey interview for social research. In F. G. Conrad & M. F. Schober (Eds.), *Envisioning the survey interview of the future* (pp. 31–57). Hoboken, NJ: Wiley. https://doi.org/10.1002/9780470183373.ch2.

Scharff, D. P., Mathews, K. J., Jackson, P., Hoffsuemmer, J., Martin, E., & Edwards, D. (2010). More than Tuskegee: Understanding mistrust about research participation. *Journal of Health Care for the Poor and Underserved, 21*(3), 879–897. https://doi.org/10.1353/hpu.0.0323.

Schoua-Glusberg, A. (2011). Response 2 to Fowler's chapter: Coding the behavior of interviewers and respondents to evaluate survey questions. In J. Madans, K. Miller, A. Maitland, & G. Willis (Eds.), *Question evaluation methods: Contributing to the science of data quality* (pp. 41–48). Hoboken, NJ: Wiley. https://doi.org/10.1002/9781118037003.ch4.

Schulz, A., Caldwell, C., & Foster, S. (2003). "What are they going to do with the information?" Latino/Latina and African American perspectives on the human genome project. *Health Education & Behavior, 30*(2), 151–169. https://doi.org/10.1177/1090198102251026.

Schwarz, N. (1996). *Cognition and communication: Judgmental biases, research methods, and the logic of conversation.* New York, NY: Psychology Press.

Shavers, V. L., Lynch, C. F., & Burmeister, L. F. (2001). Factors that influence African-Americans' willingness to participate in medical research studies. *Cancer, 91*(S1), 233–236. https://doi.org/10.1002/1097-0142(20010101)91:1+<233::Aid-cncr10>3.0.Co;2-8.

Shavers-Hornaday, V. L., Lynch, C. F., Burmeister, L. F., & Torner, J. C. (1997). Why are African Americans under-represented in medical research studies? Impediments to participation. *Ethnicity & Health, 2*(1-2), 31–45. https://doi.org/10.1080/13557858.1997.9961813.

Thomas, S. B., & Quinn, S. C. (1991). The Tuskegee Syphilis Study, 1932 to 1972: Implications for HIV education and AIDS risk education programs in the Black community. *American Journal of Public Health, 81*(11), 1498–1505. https://doi.org/10.2105/ajph.81.11.1498.

van der Zouwen, J., & Smit, J. H. (2004). Evaluating survey questions by analyzing patterns of behavior codes and question-answer sequences: A diagnostic approach. In S. Presser, J. M. Rothgeb, M. P. Couper, J. T. Lessler, E. Martin, J. Martin, & E. Singer (Eds.), *Methods for testing and evaluating survey questionnaires* (pp. 109–130). New York: Wiley. https://doi.org/10.1002/0471654728.ch6.

Warnecke, R. B., Johnson, T. P., Chávez, N., Sudman, S., O'Rourke, D. P., Lacey, L., & Horm, J. (1997). Improving question wording in surveys of culturally diverse populations. *Annals of Epidemiology, 7*(5), 334–342. https://doi.org/10.1016/S1047-2797(97)00030-6.

Washington, H. A. (2006). *Medical apartheid: The dark history of medical experimentation on black Americans from colonial times to the present.* New York: Random House.

West, B. T., & Blom, A. G. (2017). Explaining interviewer effects: A research synthesis. *Journal of Survey Statistics and Methodology, 5*(2), 175–211. https://doi.org/10.1093/jssam/smw024.

Chapter 13
Theories of Public Opinion Change Versus Stability and their Implications for Null Findings

Kevin H. Wozniak, Kevin M. Drakulich, and Brian R. Calfano

The Study of Opinion Change and the Problem of Null Findings

There is more or less a consensus agreement among pollsters and scholars that measures of public opinion are influenced by factors such as question wording or order, interviewer-respondent dynamics, or other features of the context in which the survey takes places (Dillman et al. 2009; Groves et al. 2009; Lepkowski et al. 2007; Tourangeau et al. 2004; Tourangeau and Smith 1996). However, scholars who work in different social science disciplines tend to interpret the *meaning* of public opinion's mutability in different ways. A primary paradigm in survey research, the "total survey error" perspective (TSE), rests upon an implicit positivist assumption that people possess "true" opinions about social, political, and economic issues, and it is the researcher's job to design a survey that minimizes exogenous influences so as to maximize the likelihood of measuring the respondent's true response (Groves 2004). According to a strict reading of the TSE perspective, changes in measured opinions that are attributable to survey design or method are *errors*; they interfere with a researcher's ability to gather a valid measure of the respondent's opinion. Researchers who work within the "cognitive aspects of survey methodology" paradigm (CASM) built upon the principles of TSE in order to better understand the features of human cognition that explain *why* survey design can influence respondents' answers to the survey. Numerous CASM studies elucidate a wide range of

---

K. H. Wozniak (✉)
University of Massachusetts Boston, Boston, MA, USA
e-mail: kevin.wozniak@umb.edu

K. M. Drakulich
Northeastern University, Boston, MA, USA

B. R. Calfano
University of Cincinnati, Cincinnati, OH, USA

cognitive heuristics that people use (consciously and subconsciously) to understand survey questions, and proper understanding of the cognition of survey response empowers researchers to minimize survey error through design (Tourangeau et al. 2000). However, while the TSE and CASM paradigms have much to teach researchers about ways to minimize exogenous influences on survey response so as to garner valid measures of people's opinions, they shed relatively little theoretical light on the reasons *why* people hold the opinions that they do in the first place.

In contrast, sociologists and political scientists typically devote more attention to studying exogenous influences not as sources of *error*, but rather as integral components of the process of opinion formation. Sociologists emphasize the social context of communication and argue that people's expressed opinions are a function of the "audience" with whom they are communicating at a given time (Goffman 2009; Gorden 1952; Steiner 1954). Variance in response may not be disingenuousness, but rather a reflection of the fact that people "perform" different identities in different spheres of their lives with different people (Brenner and DeLamater 2016; Stryker 1980). Political scientists are perhaps the most explicitly interested in public opinion change. They have theorized that expressed opinions are a function of the cognitive considerations about an issue that are most salient at the moment a person is queried by a pollster (Zaller 1992). The salience and accessibility of considerations are themselves shaped by the way that politicians and the media "frame" debates about issues (Chong and Druckman 2007). Framing theory compliments the CASM paradigm in that it provides theoretical guidance to better understand how and when exogenous forces influence the cognitive heuristics people use to form opinions (Kahneman 2011).

What these different theoretical paradigms share in common is a focus on *opinion change*. Survey methodologists study the causes of response variability so as better to isolate and prevent them through design (Groves et al. 2009). Sociologists seek to understand the ways that issue framing and intergroup interactions can mobilize groups into collective action (Benford and Snow 2000). Political scientists study how framing can shift individual and mass policy preferences, which often leads to electoral turnover and/or policy change (Baumgartner and Jones 2009; Chong and Druckman 2007). Across disciplines, many scholars of public opinion employ survey experiments to test how methodological design differences and/or exposure to alternative frames and information affects expressed opinion (Druckman et al. 2006). These literatures are built upon empirical evidence that exposure to systematic variation in survey instruments causes variation in measured opinion.

However, what is the researcher to do if the experimental treatment causes no significant differences between participants in different groups? Null results are generally considered to be the most dreaded of all outcomes of primary data collection, for we know that studies in which the researcher cannot reject the null hypothesis are more likely to remain unpublished than those that support hypotheses of change (i.e., significant effects) (Franco et al. 2014; Gerber and Malhotra 2008a, b). However, we argue that the absence of change is potentially just as interesting and meaningful as a significant treatment effect if the null results are compatible with theories of opinion *stability*.

Theorizing Opinion Stability: Finding Meaning in the Null

To consider opinion stability, we turn our attention away from the exogenous factors, like survey design characteristics or political messages, that may influence opinion and turn our attention toward the *nature of the opinions themselves* that we seek to measure. In a seminal work, Converse (1964) posited that many people possess "nonattitudes" about social and political issues; they possess little information and care even less about many topics queried by pollsters. Many theories of opinion change hearken back to Converse's theory because they specify the conditions under which weakly-held opinions are vulnerable to outside influence. However, following Converse, many scholars sought to "redeem" the average citizen and determine whether or not people ever hold strong, stable opinions about public issues.

As one example, the political scientists Edward Carmines and James Stimson (1980) differentiated between "easy" and "hard" issues. They argued that hard issues deal with complicated, technical issues frequently related to public policies about which the average citizen knows little. Due to their complexity, it is relatively challenging for citizens to form opinions about hard issues, and those opinions are weaker and more vulnerable to influence by framing. Easy issues, in contrast, are largely symbolic in nature, and they address topics that are familiar to most people. Whereas people have to draw upon new, unfamiliar information to form an opinion about hard issues, they only need to rely upon their emotions, personal beliefs, and "gut responses" to form opinions about easy issues (Carmines and Stimson 1980, pg. 78). As such, opinions about easy issues tend to be more strongly-held, which makes them more resistant to manipulation. Likewise, survey methodologists have tested whether attitude strength moderates survey design effects. Though results are not uniform (Krosnick and Schuman 1988), the bulk of the evidence indicates that people's strongly-held opinions are more stable and less vulnerable to influence than weakly-held opinions (Howe and Krosnick 2017). This includes evidence that strongly-held opinions are relatively resistant to the types of stimuli of interest to political scientists (Druckman and Nelson 2003; Haider-Markel and Joslyn 2001; Lecheler et al. 2009).

Viewed in light of these studies, null experimental results may indicate not a failed hypothesis, but rather plausible evidence that the issue under study is one about which it is easy for people to form opinions, and possibly one about which they feel strongly. Under such conditions, people's resistance to influence is just as theoretically meaningful as the discovery of cues that can shift their opinions through a significant treatment effect. However, without the proper use of theory, null results provide no clarity. Survey methodologists have devoted significant attention to understanding how best to measure attitude strength; they have discovered that it is not a single construct. Rather, "strength" encompasses many different attitude dimensions, such as importance, certainty, and accessibility (Howe and Krosnick 2017). But this body of knowledge largely fits within the CASM paradigm. It teaches us the *cognitive aspects* of strongly- versus weakly-held attitudes, but it provides somewhat less guidance as to *why* a person would perceive some issues to be more important than others, or why he or she would feel ambivalence.

In this chapter, we argue that sociological and political science theories provide guideposts to understand why people feel more strongly about some issues than others because these theories explain how people formulate their beliefs within social and political context. They remind survey researchers to consider the full social and political meaning of the questions they ask participants, and they could help researchers anticipate which questions might be most vulnerable versus resistant to treatments and survey design effects. Equipped with theories of both change and stability, a researcher should be prepared to find meaning in any set of empirical findings.

The Case: Media Coverage of Police-Civilian Interactions during an Era of Protest

To provide an example of the balanced use of theories of change and stability, we present the results of a survey experiment designed to test the effect of exposure to media images of police on public attitudes toward law enforcement. A series of recent, fatal encounters between police officers and people of color reignited long-simmering tensions between law enforcement and African American communities. First the 2014 death of Michael Brown in Ferguson, Missouri and then the 2015 death of Freddie Gray in Baltimore, Maryland sparked weeks of mass public protests and sporadic vandalism and violence in their respective cities (Cobbina 2019; Melley 2014; Sappenfield 2014). Many commentators drew parallels between the Ferguson and Baltimore protests and the "long, hot summers" of the 1960s that were likewise characterized by numerous urban uprisings sparked by perceived police mistreatment of African Americans (Kennedy and Schuessler 2014; National Advisory Commission on Civil Disorders and Kerner 1968; Yokley 2015), but the contemporary incidents received even more extensive media coverage due to the evolution of technology. Journalists and civilians used smart phone cameras to provide visual documentation of police confronting protesters in full riot gear, often with guns drawn, sometimes from atop armored vehicles (Gately and Stolberg 2015; Thorsen and Giegerich 2014). Walter Olson (2014) of the Cato Institute commented, "The dominant visual aspect of the [Ferguson] story...has been the sight of overpowering police forces confronting unarmed protesters who are seen waving signs or just their hands." Senator Rand Paul wrote in *Time Magazine* (2014), "When you couple this militarization of law enforcement with an erosion of civil liberties and due process that allows the police to become judge and jury...we begin to have a very serious problem on our hands. Given these developments, it is almost impossible for many Americans not to feel like their government is targeting them."

In so many words, Olson and Paul hypothesized that seeing pictures and video of heavily-armed police officers confronting unarmed, peaceful protesters would undermine people's trust in law enforcement and government. Their intuition was consistent with two bodies of theory that predict opinion change. First is framing theory; seeing images of hostile confrontations between police and civilians could activate people's cognitive considerations of police misconduct and biased treatment of people of color (Zaller 1992). Second is procedural justice theory; Tyler (2006) theorized that the legitimacy of legal authorities depends upon whether or not the public believes that those authorities act in a fair manner, consistent with due process and equal treatment under the law. According to both theories, triggering thoughts of police misconduct would cause a reduction in people's trust in the police, whereas triggering thoughts of fair, effective policing would cause an increase in people's trust. Prior empirical studies provide some support for these hypotheses. Scholars have found that news consumption is significantly related to public opinion about the police (Callanan and Rosenberger 2011; Dowler and Zawilski 2007), and specific coverage of police misconduct, brutality, or controversy is associated with decreased public satisfaction with and confidence in the police (Lasley 1994; Weitzer 2002; Weitzer and Tuch 2005).

In contrast, we argue that a third body of theory predicts that people's opinions about the police will be relatively stable and immune to influence, even when presented with cues about police misconduct and use of force. Jonathan Jackson and his colleagues (Jackson and Bradford 2009; Jackson and Sunshine 2007) argue that the police hold a symbolic role in society. They draw upon Durkheim to argue, "When people think about the police and their 'crime-fighting' activities, they also think about what 'crime' stands for (erosion of norms and social ties that underpin group life) and what 'policing' stands for (organized defense of the norms and social ties). Individuals who are concerned about long-term social change, who see the modern world as too individualized and too atomized, then look to the police to defend a sense of order...." (Jackson and Bradford 2009, pg. 499). In other words, people's attitudes toward the police are deeply intertwined with their beliefs about morals and the state of society because they view the police as symbolic guardians of morality and order. A few empirical studies confirm that a relationship exists between opinion about the police and opinions about morals and the state of society (e.g., Jackson and Bradford 2009; Jackson and Sunshine 2007; Wozniak 2016). Some aspects of contemporary events are consistent with this "neo-Durkheimian" perspective on policing. Many politically conservative commentators criticized the Black Lives Matter movement not by denying activists' right to demand equal protection under the law, but rather by arguing that BLM activists disrespect the police (Alcindor 2016; Holley 2016; Vitale 2016). The degree to which a person "supports the police" became the barometer by which a person's support for social order was judged.

Though the social, political, and economic affairs of nations are complicated, it is not difficult for people to assess how they *feel* about the state of society. If the police are a symbolic proxy for the moral stability of society, then it stands to reason that it would be easy for people to form opinions about the police—they need only assess how they feel about social order at the present time. According to the typology of Carmines and Stimson (1980), we would then expect that seeing pictures of police interactions with civilians would not change people's opinions about the police; they would only reinforce people's extant positive or negative evaluations of law enforcement.

Design of the Present Study

It is possible to categorize police tactics along a spectrum defined by the police-civilian relationship (Weisburd and Eck 2004). On one side of the spectrum is community policing, which encourages officers to develop collegial relationships and maintain close communication with civilians in the communities they service. Citizen satisfaction with the police is a primary concern in the community policing model. On the other side of the spectrum are crime control tactics that emphasize intense surveillance and frequent arrests for offenses. One example of these tactics is stop-and-frisk policing in which officers focus on catching large numbers of minor offenses in order to deter more serious crimes. The confrontations between police and protesters in Ferguson and Baltimore likely stand at the furthest point on the hostile side of the spectrum. Critics contend that aggressive crime control tactics create a contentious, "us vs. them" relationship between police and community members.

We designed a self-administered, online survey experiment to test whether exposure to images of police-civilian interactions affects public opinion about the police. We chose three pictures intended to represent the spectrum of police-civilian relations. The first picture was an image of two male police officers in riot gear atop an armored vehicle pointing a rifle at a group of protesters in the street with their hands raised; this was a picture taken during the 2014 protests in Ferguson, Missouri following the shooting of Michael Brown. We chose this image to represent hostile, "militarized" conflict between police and civilians. The second picture showed two smiling police officers (one male, one female), one of whom was giving a "high five" to a civilian seated on his porch. We chose this image to represent positive, "community policing-style" interaction between police and civilians. Finally, the third picture showed two male police officers patting down two male civilians who had their hands pressed against a wall. We chose this image to represent a confrontational, "stop-and-frisk-style" interaction between police and civilians.[1]

---

[1]The treatment images may be viewed on the following websites, which are the sources from which we copied the pictures for use in our survey experiment: militarized policing (Topaz 2014), community policing (Mirko 2013), stop and frisk (Post Editorial Board 2015). The original stop and frisk image actually depicted an officer training exercise, and the officers were carrying bright blue model side arms. We digitally altered the picture in order to color the handgun hilts black so that they would look like regular guns, thereby depicting a typical stop and frisk.

The experimental manipulations were embedded on the first, introductory page of the survey. Above the survey's title ("a study of public opinion about government and police"), participants who were randomly-assigned to an experimental condition saw a banner that contained three pictures. Two of the pictures were constant across all three groups; these were a picture of Members of the U.S. House of Representatives delivering remarks at a podium emblazoned with the House seal and a picture of members of the U.S. National Guard in camouflage fatigues handing out care packages to a mother and child. These constant images of government professionals were designed to slightly obscure the study's central focus on images of the police in order to minimize the possibility that respondents would guess the intent of the pictures and reply as they thought the surveyors desired. The third image, placed in the center of the banner, contained one of the three police-civilian interaction pictures. Respondents were randomly assigned to receive one of the three treatment pictures or to receive a control condition that contained only the title text, no pictures.

We chose actual pictures of police and civilians found through Google image searches. This means that the treatment stimuli reflect the kinds of pictures that people routinely see online and on the news. As such, the treatments possess a degree of external validity, but this comes at the cost of precision. Since the pictures each contain numerous elements, we cannot specify precisely which facet of the images may generate a framing effect on people's opinions about the police. Due to the complicated racial dynamics at the center of the policing debate (Peffley and Hurwitz 2010), we were careful to ensure that the pictures represented racial diversity as much as possible. No picture contained solely white people, and only the community policing treatment picture was racially-homogenous; both of the officers and the civilian in the picture were African American.

We ensured that participants were properly exposed to the treatment in two ways. First, the title screen was set on a 5 s delay before participants could proceed, so they could not immediately skip over the pictures. Second, following the title screen, participants were reshown each of the three images in the title banner, one by one, and asked to briefly describe what they saw in the picture; participants in the control group proceeded directly to the survey questions. Only about 1% of respondents in each experimental group provided no descriptions or wrote blatantly-inaccurate descriptions of the pictures they saw, indicating that respondents were successfully treated (Mutz 2011). Furthermore, evidence indicates that the random assignment to conditions was successful. There were no statistically significant differences across groups in regard to respondents' political party affiliation ($\chi^2[12, N = 1068] = 19.25, p = 0.08$), political ideology ($\chi^2[12, N = 1025] = 8.46, p = 0.75$), self-reported degree of attention they paid to the news in the previous 7 days ($\chi^2[6, N = 1078] = 6.82, p = 0.34$), or race ($\chi^2[12, N = 1100] = 5.73, p = 0.93$), which indicates that the random assignment to conditions was successful.

Hypotheses

According to the theories we identify as theories of change in relation to the present case (Tyler 2006; Zaller 1992), we hypothesize that respondents' confidence in the police will vary across the experimental conditions in the following manner:

H_{change}: *Community Policing > Control Group > Stop & Frisk > Militarized Policing.*

According to the theories we identify as theories of stability in relation to the present case (Carmines and Stimson 1980; Jackson and Bradford 2009; Jackson and Sunshine 2007), we hypothesize that exposure to different images of police-civilian interactions will not cause significant differences in respondents' confidence in the police across the experimental conditions

$H_{stability}$: *Community Policing = Control Group = Stop & Frisk = Militarized Policing.*

Data

We recruited respondents from Qualtrics' national, online panel to participate in a survey to "study people's opinions about how well the government and the police are addressing problems facing the nation." The survey contained a variety of questions measuring respondents' attitudes toward the police, their local government, and the federal government. These were original questions that we wrote for the purpose of this study. The survey was fielded in late April 2016. We procured responses from 1100 participants. Since this is a nonprobability sample, we do not claim that the point estimates of respondents' attitudes toward the police are generalizable to the national population (Baker et al. 2010). Rather, we were interested in the causal relationship between image exposure and expressed opinion, and studies find that experiments administered to opt-in panel samples generate results that are similar to experiments administered to randomly-selected samples (e.g., Weinberg et al. 2014; Yeager and Krosnick 2012).

Still, there is value in understanding who these participants were. Our sample was 70.6% white, 21.1% black, 4.6% Asian American, and 1.3% Pacific Islander. Twenty percent of the sample identified as Hispanic. The average age of participants was 45 years old with a standard deviation of 17 years. Males comprised 49.9% of the sample, females comprised 49.8%, and transgender individuals comprised 0.3%. In regard to education, 17.6% completed high school or less formal education, 58.5% possessed some college education or a bachelor's degree, and 23.9% possessed some graduate education or a graduate degree. In regard to annual household income, 30.4% of respondents made less than $35,000, 36.0% made between $35,000 and $75,000, and 33.7% made greater than $75,000. Republicans comprised 21.6% of the sample, Democrats 46.0%, Independents 23.9%, 0.9% identified with another party, and 7.9% said they had no partisanship preference.

Dependent Variables

The first two dependent variables were preceded by the prompt, "Now, we'd like to talk about your perceptions of the police. First, we'd like to talk about the police in your own community."

1. *Evaluation of Local Police*: This scale variable was comprised of the answers to four questions that shared a common root: "Do you think that your local police do a good job or a bad job in..." (1) "...dealing with problems that really concern people?" (2) "...preventing crime?" (3) "...responding to people after they have been victims of crime?" (4) "...maintaining order on the streets and sidewalks?" All four questions shared the same response scale: a very bad job, a somewhat bad job, a slightly bad job, a slightly good job, a somewhat good job, a very good job.[2] A factor analysis with orthogonal rotation revealed that these four items loaded onto a single factor with an Eigenvalue of 2.92. The factor loadings of the items were 0.86, 0.86, 0.85, and 0.84, respectively. We combined these items into an additive scale with a range of 4 to 24; higher values indicate stronger perception that the respondent's local police do a "good job" at their duties. This scale had a Cronbach's alpha of 0.92.
2. *Local Police Misconduct*: This scale variable was comprised of the answers to four questions, three of which shared a common root: "How often do you think your local police officers..." (1) "...stop people on the streets without good reason?" (2) "...when talking to people, use insulting language against them?" (3) "...use excessive force (more force than is necessary under the circumstances) against people?" The fourth question was, (4) "How common do you think corruption (such as taking bribes or involvement in the drug trade) is in your local department?" Questions one through three shared the same response scale: never, on occasion, fairly often, very often. The response options for the fourth question were very uncommon, somewhat uncommon, fairly common, very common. A factor analysis with orthogonal rotation revealed that these four items loaded onto a single factor with an Eigenvalue of 2.37. The factor loadings of the items were 0.77, 0.83, 0.84, and 0.61, respectively. We combined these items into an additive scale with a range of 4 to 16; higher values indicate stronger perception that the respondent's local police engage in improper behavior more frequently. This scale had a Cronbach's alpha of 0.87.

The next three dependent variables were preceded by the following prompt, "Now, we'd like to talk about your perceptions of the police in general across the country."

---

[2] All questions in this survey included a "prefer not to answer" response option. We dropped these responses prior to the present analyses. Only between 31 and 48 respondents chose this option in each of the dependent variable questions.

3. *Evaluation of National Police*: This scale variable was comprised of the answers to four questions that shared a common root: "Do you think that the police in general do a good job or a bad job in..." (1) "...dealing with problems that really concern people?" (2) "...preventing crime?" (3) "...responding to people after they have been victims of crime?" (4) "...maintaining order on the streets and sidewalks?" All four questions shared the same response scale: a very bad job, a somewhat bad job, a slightly bad job, a slightly good job, a somewhat good job, a very good job. A factor analysis with orthogonal rotation revealed that these four items loaded onto a single factor with an Eigenvalue of 2.94. The factor loadings of the items were 0.86, 0.85, 0.87, and 0.86, respectively. We combined these items into an additive scale with a range of 4 to 24; higher values indicate stronger perception that the police, in general, do a "good job" at their duties. This scale had a Cronbach's alpha of 0.92.
4. *National Police Misconduct*: This scale variable was comprised of the answers to five questions, four of which shared a common root: "How often do you think police in general..." (1) "...stop people on the streets without good reason?" (2) "...when talking to people, use insulting language against them?" (3) "...use excessive force (more force than is necessary under the circumstances) against people?" (4) "...stop and question or frisk people in communities across the country?" The fifth question was, (5) "How common do you think corruption (such as taking bribes or involvement in the drug trade) is in police departments across the country?" Questions one through four shared the same response scale: never, on occasion, fairly often, very often. The response options for the fifth question were very uncommon, somewhat uncommon, fairly common, very common. A factor analysis with orthogonal rotation revealed that these five items loaded onto a single factor with an Eigenvalue of 3.03. The factor loadings of the items were 0.83, 0.81, 0.82, 0.80, and 0.62, respectively. We combined these items into an additive scale with a range of 5 to 20; higher values indicate stronger perception that the police, in general, engage in improper behavior more frequently. This scale had a Cronbach's alpha of 0.89.
5. *National Police Bias*: This scale variable was comprised of the answers to four questions: (1) In general, do you think that police across the country treat wealthy people better, the same, or worse than poor people? (2) In general, do you think the police treat white people better, the same, or worse than black people? (3) In general, do you think the police treat white people better, the same, or worse than Hispanics? (4) In general, do you think the police treat English-speaking people better, the same, or worse than non-English speaking people? All four items shared variations of the same, five point response scale, which was, "Treat [Group A] much worse/somewhat worse/the same as/somewhat better than/much better than [Group B]." A factor analysis with orthogonal rotation revealed that these four items loaded onto a single factor with an Eigenvalue of 2.37. The factor loadings of the items were 0.65, 0.87, 0.86, and 0.69, respectively. We combined these items into an additive scale with a range of 4 to 20; higher values indicate stronger perception that the police, in general, treat a socially-advantaged group

in society better than a socially-disadvantaged group. This scale had a Cronbach's alpha of 0.85.

Data Quality Check

In order to verify the quality of these data, we created dummy variables that identified respondents who gave the same response to an entire string of questions that comprised each dependent variable, as described above. Straight-lined responses are problematic if they are an indication that respondents sped through the survey without truly paying attention or meaningfully answering the questions. The number of "straight-line" responses ranged from a low of 1 (a respondent who said that the police treat wealthy people, white people, and English-speakers "much worse" than poor people, black people, Hispanic people, and non-English speakers) to a high of 277 (respondents who said that "on occasion" police in general across the country engage in misconduct behaviors). Of the 25 possible response options across all the dependent variable questions, only 5 prompted more than 100 respondents to straight-line their responses.

Even though this analysis reveals that a majority of responses to the dependent variable questions were heterogeneous rather than straight-lined, to err on the side of caution, we also identified respondents who fell within the fifth (about 6 min) and ninety-fifth percentiles (about 34 min) of the completion time distribution (the mean completion time was about 20 min, and the median time was about 12 min). We assume that the most inattentive or distracted respondents were likely contained within these groups of the fastest and slowest respondents. We dropped these 105 respondents and reran all analyses. The substantive results were unchanged. All together, these sensitivity analyses give us greater confidence that our results are not a function of invalid responses in the data.

Results

Figure 13.1 presents the average of respondents' scores on each of the five dependent variable scales across the experimental groups. It clearly shows that the treatment had no significant impact on respondents' answers; the average values are nearly identical across groups. A series of one-way, between-subjects ANOVA tests confirm no significant differences between groups in regard to evaluation of local police [$F(3, 1044) = 1.20, p = 0.31$], local police misconduct [$F(3, 1025) = 0.30, p = 0.83$], evaluation of national police [$F(3, 1048) = 0.08, p = 0.97$], national police misconduct, [$F(3, 1041) = 0.24, p = 0.87$], or national police bias [$F(3, 1040) = 0.14, p = 0.94$]. We reiterate that virtually all respondents passed the manipulation check by providing accurate descriptions of the pictures to which they were exposed, which means that these results are not evidence of a failure to treat.

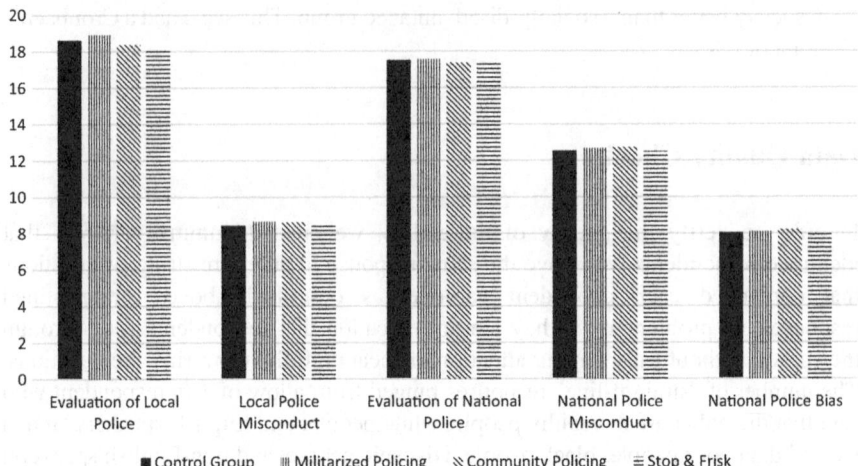

Fig. 13.1 Attitudes toward police across experimental image conditions. Note: The dependent variable scales are not standardized, so comparisons should only be made between groups within each dependent variable, not across dependent variables

Evidence also indicates that randomization was successful. The results genuinely indicate that exposure to these images of police-civilian interactions did not significantly influence respondents' attitudes toward local or national police. We cannot reject the null hypothesis.[3]

We also conducted a secondary analysis. As discussed earlier in this chapter, most controversies about policing in the United States center on the relationship between police and communities of color. Unsurprisingly, racial minorities express more critical opinions about police than do whites (Graziano and Gauthier 2019; Peck 2015; Peffley and Hurwitz 2010). As such, we tested whether the effect of image exposure varied across racial groups (full results available upon request). For the sake of parsimony, we restricted this analysis to non-Hispanic white, non-Hispanic black, and Hispanic respondents; these three racial/ethnic groups made up over 90% of the sample. We found no significant interactions between treatment condition and race in regard to local police evaluation, local police

---

[3]Two additional pieces of evidence strengthen our conclusion of null findings. First, we also conducted a series of two one-sided tests of equivalence for each of the dependent variables following the recommendations of Lakens (2017). Equivalence tests provide an additional check against the possibility that non-significant treatment effects are a Type II error; essentially, they test whether a difference between two groups is large enough to be meaningful according to a standard set by the researcher. This validity check confirmed that the differences in police attitudes across treatment groups are statistically equivalent; these results are available from the first author upon request. Second, in a separate analysis, we did find that the treatment caused significant differences in respondents' expressed presidential vote preference (Wozniak et al. 2019). This finding indicates that image exposure did affect some of the respondents' expressed preferences, just not their attitudes toward the police.

misconduct, national police evaluation, or national police misconduct. We found two significant interactions in regard to assessment of national police bias. Hispanic respondents who saw the image of the militarized police response in Ferguson or the image of a stop and frisk scored significantly higher on the scale of perceived police bias than Hispanic respondents in the control group ($p < .05$). However, this interaction effect was no longer significant once a Bonferroni correction for multiple comparisons was applied. Given the instability of this finding, and given the overall lack of interracial differences in treatment effects across the dependent variables, we still believe that the most valid and reliable interpretation of these findings is that image exposure did not substantively change people's expressed opinions about the dimensions of policing assessed in this study.

Opinion Stability: The Police as Symbols of Social Order

As quoted in the introduction to this chapter, Walter Olson and Rand Paul expressed concern that seeing images of the hostile, violent confrontations between police officers and peaceful protesters would shake people's confidence in law enforcement. Our results do not support their conjecture. The protests and confrontations received extensive media coverage and fueled heated rhetoric in the political sphere (Alcindor 2016; Arora et al. 2019). Some research suggests that people's attitudes toward the police and/or the Black Lives Matter movement polarized and mobilized voters to express even stronger support for Hillary Clinton or Donald Trump in the 2016 presidential election (Drakulich et al. 2017). The issue of police-community relations (especially with African Americans) certainly held emotional and political weight during the time period we gathered these data, yet seeing pictures designed to evoke the contemporary debate did not significantly alter our respondents' confidence in the police. Rather than supporting the theories of opinion change that were implicit in the concerns expressed by Olson and Paul, our results are consistent with the theoretical perspective that people's opinions about the police are intertwined with their opinions about morals, values, and the state of society—beliefs that are deep-rooted and resistant to easy change. Our results support the argument that opinions about the police should be classified as an easy issue according to Carmines and Stimson's (1980) typology.

Why are our findings inconsistent with prior evidence that news consumption, specifically coverage of cases of police brutality, is significantly related to variation in public opinion about the police (Callanan and Rosenberger 2011; Dowler and Zawilski 2007; Lasley 1994; Weitzer 2002; Weitzer and Tuch 2005)? To explain the discordance between these prior studies and our current findings, we posit that there may be a meaningful difference in the stimuli under study. Though many critics (predominantly of a liberal persuasion) alleged that the militarized police responses in Ferguson and Baltimore were examples of police misconduct, it is highly plausible that many Americans would disagree with that perspective. If one perceives mass protest (and, it must be acknowledged, some acts of vandalism and violence amidst predominantly peaceful protests) as acts of disorder that must be contained and suppressed, then one would consider the police's aggressive response to be entirely appropriate—not an example of *misconduct*, but rather an example of the *proper exercise of duty* under difficult circumstances.[4] *Collective* police response to protest is qualitatively different from the actions of *individual officers* that cause great *physical harm or death* to civilians. The latter cases fit more easily into the type of individualistic thinking that perpetuates systemic racism and white hegemony (Bonilla-Silva 2017); white people can condemn the actions of individual officers if they are clearly egregious while continuing to support the overall legitimacy of the police, thereby dismissing the more *systemic* concerns of Black Lives Matter. Even our treatment picture of the militarized police reaction in Ferguson may not have risen to the level of misconduct in our participants' minds. In that light, our null findings are less surprising. Thus, we cannot rule out the possibility that other types of cues designed to evoke considerations of police misconduct and wrongdoing would cause significant changes in people's confidence in the police. This would be a fruitful avenue of research to test in future framing experiments.

Implications for Survey Research

Given discussions of publication bias that favors significant results (Franco et al. 2014; Gerber and Malhotra 2008a, b), scholars dread few things more than completing a study only to discover that the evidence is insufficient to reject the null hypothesis. However, single-minded focus on discovering statistically-significant relationships implicitly favors theories of change. Theories of stability, in contrast, are supported precisely when a treatment fails to cause an effect and the null hypothesis cannot be rejected. If a scholar were to rely exclusively on the theories that emphasize mutability in public opinion (Converse 1964; Zaller 1992), she would be stumped by an experiment that failed to cause opinion differences between groups of participants. However, other scholars remind us that human beings are not *tabula rasa* (Haider-Markel and Joslyn 2001). Even though they do not spend a great deal of time thinking about many social or political issues, it is still true that most people *do* hold opinions about *some* issues that are meaningful or interesting to them. When scholars study public opinion about issues that are deeply intertwined with people's beliefs and values, they should expect to find that even "ignorant

---

[4]Moule et al. (2019) present evidence that supports this interpretation. They found that nearly 65% of respondents to their national survey expressed support for the use of police SWAT teams to respond to "instances of civil unrest." On the other hand, only about 7% of respondents supported the use of SWAT teams to respond to "peaceful protests." Their finding suggests that people judge the appropriateness of police tactics differently under different circumstances, but the nature of those circumstances may be in the eye of the beholder. See also Lockwood et al. (2018) for complimentary findings.

voters" are more resistant to outside influence than we might expect (Carmines and Stimson 1980; Druckman and Nelson 2003).

A deep consideration of Carmines and Stimson's typology of easy versus hard issues calls on us to recognize that not all public opinion is equal. We often think of public opinion as the dependent variable—something that is subject to influence by social and psychological forces that interest us. Carmines and Stimson reminded us that some opinions are less subject to influence than others—an insight for which survey researchers have produced empirical support (Howe and Krosnick 2017). However, properly incorporating the insight that attitude strength matters into survey design is more complicated. As discussed earlier, methodologists have shown that attitude strength is a multi-dimensional concept, which means that a researcher could be faced with the daunting task of writing numerous questions for each construct in the survey: one question to measure an opinion and several follow-up questions to measure the various dimensions of the strength with which the respondent holds that opinion. Such an approach would very quickly consume the limited number of questions surveyors can reasonably expect respondents to answer in a single sitting. There is a tradeoff between quality versus quantity in regard to the measurement of constructs in a survey.

It is here that sociological and political science theories may be useful. A careful use of theory can help researchers plausibly classify survey topics as easy or hard (or strong vs. weak) *a priori*. With theoretical guidance, a researcher could either selectively target *which* constructs most need additional questions to *measure* attitude strength, or she could save the space consumed by strength questions by making a *theory-based* argument as to why a particular construct should be assumed to be strongly- or weakly-held. As we showed in our case study, we think that Durkheim is particularly useful in this regard since he postulated a link between morals, values, and social structure. If a researcher can make the case that a particular construct is likely a proxy for a person's deeper feelings about the state of values in society, it is plausible to assume that said attitude will be strongly-held (for a similar psychological perspective, see Haidt 2012). A similar, compatible political science theory holds that people form opinions about policy proposals based upon an assessment of the moral and social value of the people in society who will most benefit or be most harmed by said proposal (Schneider and Ingram 1993). Regardless of the complexity of actual policy implementation, it is easy for people to judge that they want policies to benefit small business owners and harm pedophiles, for example; it would not be surprising to find that frames cannot sway these opinions all that much.

In conclusion, the TSE and CASM paradigms have made invaluable contributions to survey research methodology, but it would be a mistake for scholars to focus so much on the process of crafting valid measures that they neglect to thoroughly frame their whole research project around theory. By drawing upon public opinion theories of both stability and change from across the social sciences, scholars will be prepared to draw *substantive meaning* out of both statistically significant and statistically insignificant findings. Discovering the topics over which elites have little power to sway the opinions of the mass public is just as interesting as identifying frames that cause significant opinion change.

References

Alcindor, Y. (2016, August 16). *Trump, rallying white crowd for police, accuses democrats of exploiting blacks* (p. 9). The New York Times.

Arora, M., Phoenix, D. L., & Delshad, A. (2019). Framing police and protesters: Assessing volume and framing of news coverage post-Ferguson, and corresponding impacts on legislative activity. *Politics, Groups, and Identities, 7*(1), 151–164. https://doi.org/10.1080/21565503.2018.1518782.

Baker, R., Blumberg, S. J., Brick, J. M., Couper, M. P., Courtright, M., Dennis, J. M., et al. (2010). AAPOR report on online panels. *Public Opinion Quarterly, 74*(4), 711–781. https://doi.org/10.1093/poq/nfq048.

Baumgartner, F. R., & Jones, B. D. (2009). *Agendas and instability in American politics* (2nd ed.). Chicago: University of Chicago Press.

Benford, R. D., & Snow, D. A. (2000). Framing processes and social movements: An overview and assessment. *Annual Review of Sociology, 26*(1), 611–639. https://doi.org/10.1146/annurev.soc.26.1.611.

Bonilla-Silva, E. (2017). *Racism without racists: Color-blind racism and the persistence of racial inequality in America* (5th ed.). Lanham, MD: Rowman & Littlefield Publishers.

Brenner, P. S., & DeLamater, J. (2016). Lies, damned lies, and survey self-reports? Identity as a cause of measurement bias. *Social Psychology Quarterly, 79*(4), 333–354. https://doi.org/10.1177/0190272516628298.

Callanan, V. J., & Rosenberger, J. S. (2011). Media and public perceptions of the police: Examining the impact of race and personal experience. *Policing and Society, 21*(2), 167–189. https://doi.org/10.1080/10439463.2010.540655.

Carmines, E. G., & Stimson, J. A. (1980). The two faces of issue voting. *American Political Science Review, 74*(1), 78–91.

Chong, D., & Druckman, J. N. (2007). Framing theory. *Annual Review of Political Science, 10*, 103–126.

Cobbina, J. E. (2019). *Hands up, Don't shoot: Why the protests in Ferguson and Baltimore matter, and how they changed America*. New York: New York University Press.

Converse, P. E. (1964). The nature of belief systems in mass publics. In D. E. Apter (Ed.), *Ideology and discontent* (pp. 206–261). New York: Free Press.

Dillman, D. A., Phelps, G., Tortora, R., Swift, K., Kohrell, J., Berck, J., & Messer, B. L. (2009). Response rate and measurement differences in mixed-mode surveys using mail, telephone, interactive voice response (IVR) and the internet. *Social Science Research, 38*(1), 1–18. https://doi.org/10.1016/j.ssresearch.2008.03.007.

Dowler, K., & Zawilski, V. (2007). Public perceptions of police misconduct and discrimination: Examining the impact of media consumption. *Journal of Criminal Justice, 35*(2), 193–203. https://doi.org/10.1016/j.jcrimjus.2007.01.006.

Drakulich, K., Hagan, J., Johnson, D., & Wozniak, K. H. (2017). Race, justice, policing, and the 2016 American presidential election. *Du Bois Review: Social Science Research on Race, 14*(1), 7–33. https://doi.org/10.1017/S1742058X1600031X.

Druckman, J. N., Green, D. P., Kuklinski, J. H., & Lupia, A. (2006). The growth and development of experimental research in political science. *American Political Science Review, 100*(4), 627–635. https://doi.org/10.1017/S0003055406062514.

Druckman, J. N., & Nelson, K. R. (2003). Framing and deliberation: How citizens' conversations limit elite influence. *American Journal of Political Science, 47*(4), 729–745.

Franco, A., Malhotra, N., & Simonovits, G. (2014). Publication bias in the social sciences: Unlocking the file drawer. *Science, 345*(6203), 1502–1505. https://doi.org/10.1126/science.1255484.
Gately, G., & Stolberg, S. G. (2015, November 16). Baltimore police assailed for response after Freddie Gray's death. *The New York Times*. Retrieved from https://www.nytimes.com/2015/11/17/us/baltimore-police-assailed-for-response-after-freddie-grays-death.html
Gerber, A., & Malhotra, N. (2008a). Do statistical reporting standards affect what is published? Publication bias in two leading political science journals. *Quarterly Journal of Political Science, 3*(3), 313–326. https://doi.org/10.1561/100.00008024.
Gerber, A., & Malhotra, N. (2008b). Publication bias in empirical sociological research: Do arbitrary significance levels distort published results? *Sociological Methods & Research, 37*(1), 3–30. https://doi.org/10.1177/0049124108318973.
Goffman, E. (2009). *Stigma: Notes on the management of spoiled identity*. Simon and Schuster.
Gorden, R. L. (1952). Interaction between attitude and the definition of the situation in the expression of opinion. *American Sociological Review, 17*, 50–58. https://doi.org/10.2307/2088359.
Graziano, L. M., & Gauthier, J. F. (2019). Examining the racial-ethnic continuum and perceptions of police misconduct. *Policing and Society, 29*(6), 657–672. https://doi.org/10.1080/10439463.2017.1310859.
Groves, R. M. (2004). *Survey errors and survey costs*. Hoboken, NJ: Wiley.
Groves, R. M., Fowler, F. J., Jr., Couper, M. P., Lepkowski, J. M., Singer, E., & Tourangeau, R. (2009). *Survey methodology* (2nd ed.). Wiley.
Haider-Markel, D. P., & Joslyn, M. R. (2001). Gun policy, tragedy, and blame attribution: The conditional influence of issue frames. *Journal of Politics, 63*(2), 520–543.
Haidt, J. (2012). *The righteous mind: Why good people are divided by politics and religion*. Knopf Doubleday Publishing Group.
Holley, P. (2016, July 18). Wisconsin sheriff: Black lives Matter's 'hateful ideology' caused police killings. *Washington Post.*. Retrieved from https://www.washingtonpost.com/news/post-nation/wp/2016/07/18/sheriff-black-lives-matters-hateful-ideology-caused-police-killings/.
Howe, L. C., & Krosnick, J. A. (2017). Attitude strength. *Annual Review of Psychology, 68*(1), 327–351. https://doi.org/10.1146/annurev-psych-122414-033600.
Jackson, J., & Bradford, B. (2009). Crime, policing and social order: On the expressive nature of public confidence in policing. *The British Journal of Sociology, 60*(3), 493–521. https://doi.org/10.1111/j.1468-4446.2009.01253.x.
Jackson, J., & Sunshine, J. (2007). Public confidence in policing: A neo-Durkheimian perspective. *The British Journal of Criminology, 47*(2), 214–233. https://doi.org/10.1093/bjc/azl031.
Kahneman, D. (2011). *Thinking, fast and slow*. New York. Farrar, Straus and Giroux.
Kennedy, R., & Schuessler, J. (2014, August 14). *Ferguson images evoke civil rights era and changing visual perceptions* (p. A14). The New York Times.
Krosnick, J. A., & Schuman, H. (1988). Attitude intensity, importance, and certainty and susceptibility to response effects. *Journal of Personality and Social Psychology, 54*(6), 940–952. https://doi.org/10.1037/0022-3514.54.6.940.
Lakens, D. (2017). Equivalence tests: A practical primer for t-tests, correlations, and meta-analyses. *Social Psychological and Personality Science, 8*(4), 355–362. https://doi.org/10.1177/1948550617697177.
Lasley, J. R. (1994). The impact of the Rodney king incident on citizen attitudes toward police. *Policing and Society, 3*(4), 245–255. https://doi.org/10.1080/10439463.1994.9964673.
Lecheler, S., de Vreese, C., & Slothuus, R. (2009). Issue importance as a moderator of framing effects. *Communication Research, 36*(3), 400–425.
Lepkowski, J. M., Tucker, N. C., Brick, J. M., de Leeuw, E. D., Japec, L., Lavrakas, P. J., et al. (2007). *Advances in telephone survey methodology*. Hoboken, NJ: Wiley.

Lockwood, B., Doyle, M. D., & Comiskey, J. G. (2018). Armed, but too dangerous? Factors associated with citizen support for the militarization of the police. *Criminal Justice Studies, 31* (2), 113–127. https://doi.org/10.1080/1478601X.2017.1420652.
Melley, B. (2014, August 31). Ferguson's flashpoint sparks national outrage. *Detroit News*. Retrieved from https://www.detroitnews.com/story/news/local/metro-state/2014/08/31/fergusons-flashpoint-sparks-national-outrage/14900625/
Mirko, M. (2013, July 3). Pictures: New Haven community policing. Retrieved October 1, 2019, from Courant.com website.: https://www.courant.com/news/connecticut/hc-new-haven-community-policing-20130703-photogallery.html
Moule, R. K., Parry, M. M., & Fox, B. (2019). Public support for police use of SWAT: Examining the relevance of legitimacy. *Journal of Crime and Justice, 42*(1), 45–59. https://doi.org/10.1080/0735648X.2018.1556862.
Mutz, D. C. (2011). *Population-based survey experiments*. Princeton, N.J: Princeton University Press.
National Advisory Commission on Civil Disorders, & Kerner, O. (1968). *Report of the National Advisory Commission on Civil Disorders*. Washington, DC: US Government Printing Office.
Olson, W. (2014, August 13). Police militarization in Ferguson—And your town. Retrieved October 17, 2019, from Cato institute website.: https://www.cato.org/blog/police-militarization-ferguson-nationwide
Paul, R. (2014, August 14). *We must demilitarize the police*. Time Magazine. Retrieved from https://time.com/3111474/rand-paul-ferguson-police/
Peck, J. H. (2015). Minority perceptions of the police: A state-of-the-art review. *Policing: An International Journal of Police Strategies & Management, 38*(1), 173–203. https://doi.org/10.1108/PIJPSM-01-2015-0001.
Peffley, M., & Hurwitz, J. (2010). *Justice in America: The separate realities of blacks and whites*. New York: Cambridge University Press.
Post Editorial Board. (2015, June 1). How many New Yorkers must die before the mayor brings back stop-and-frisk? Retrieved October 1, 2019, from https://nypost.com/2015/06/01/how-many-new-yorkers-must-die-before-the-mayor-brings-back-stop-and-frisk/
Sappenfield, M. (2014, November 30). *Can Ferguson spark new civil rights movement?* How times have changed. Christian Science Monitor. Retrieved from https://www.csmonitor.com/USA/Society/2014/1130/Can-Ferguson-spark-new-civil-rights-movement-How-times-have-changed
Schneider, A., & Ingram, H. (1993). Social construction of target populations: Implications for politics and policy. *American Political Science Review, 87*(2), 334–347. https://doi.org/10.2307/2939044.
Steiner, I. D. (1954). Primary group influences on public opinion. *American Sociological Review, 19*(3), 260–267. https://doi.org/10.2307/2087755.
Stryker, S. (1980). *Symbolic interactionism: A social structural version*. Caldwell, NJ: Blackburn.
Thorsen, L., & Giegerich, S. (2014, August 10). *Shooting of teen by Ferguson officer spurs angry backlash* (p. A1). St. Louis Post-Dispatch.
Topaz, J. (2014, August 14). Critics slam "militarization" of police. Retrieved October 1, 2019, from POLITICO website.: https://www.politico.com/story/2014/08/ferguson-critics-police-militarization-110017
Tourangeau, R., Couper, M. P., & Conrad, F. (2004). Spacing, position, and order: Interpretive heuristics for visual features of survey questions. *Public Opinion Quarterly, 68*(3), 368–393.
Tourangeau, R., Rips, L. J., & Rasinski, K. (2000). *The psychology of survey response*. New York: Cambridge University Press.
Tourangeau, R., & Smith, T. W. (1996). Asking sensitive questions: The impact of data collection mode, question format, and question context. *Public Opinion Quarterly, 60*(2), 275–304.
Tyler, T. R. (2006). *Why people obey the law* (2nd ed.). Princeton, N.J: Princeton University Press.
Vitale, A. S. (2016, July 19). *Giuliani's convention speech got everything wrong about policing*. The Nation. Retrieved from https://www.thenation.com/article/giulianis-convention-speech-got-everything-wrong-about-policing/

Weinberg, J., Freese, J., & McElhattan, D. (2014). Comparing data characteristics and results of an online factorial survey between a population-based and a crowdsource-recruited sample. *Sociological Science, 1*, 292–310. http://dx.doi.org.ezproxy.lib.umb.edu/10.15195/v1.a19.

Weisburd, D., & Eck, J. E. (2004). What can police do to reduce crime, disorder, and fear? *The Annals of the American Academy of Political and Social Science, 593*(1), 42–65.

Weitzer, R. (2002). Incidents of police misconduct and public opinion. *Journal of Criminal Justice, 30*(5), 397–408. https://doi.org/10.1016/S0047-2352(02)00150-2.

Weitzer, R., & Tuch, S. A. (2005). Racially biased policing: Determinants of citizen perceptions. *Social Forces, 83*(3), 1009–1030. https://doi.org/10.1353/sof.2005.0050.

Wozniak, K. H. (2016). Ontological insecurity, racial tension, and confidence in the police in the shadow of urban unrest. *Sociological Forum, 31*(4), 1063–1082. https://doi.org/10.1111/socf.12296.

Wozniak, K. H., Calfano, B. R., & Drakulich, K. M. (2019). A "Ferguson effect" on 2016 presidential vote preference? Findings from a framing experiment examining "shy voters" and cues related to policing and social unrest. *Social Science Quarterly, 100*(4), 1023–1038. https://doi.org/10.1111/ssqu.12622.

Yeager, D. S., & Krosnick, J. A. (2012). Does mentioning "some people" and "other people" in an opinion question improve measurement quality? *Public Opinion Quarterly, 76*(1), 131–141. https://doi.org/10.1093/poq/nfr066.

Yokley, E. (2015, January 18). In Ferguson, push for criminal justice reform draws comparisons to '60s fight for civil rights (p. A11). The New York Times.

Zaller, J. (1992). *The nature and origins of mass opinion.* New York: Cambridge University Press.

Chapter 14
Conclusions and Future Directions for Understanding Survey Methodology

Philip S. Brenner

The two primary goals for this volume were ambitious. The first goal was to illustrate the explanatory power of sociological theory to illuminate survey methodological phenomena. Four chapters highlighted multiple sociological paradigms and theories that may be used to understand survey methodological phenomena, including social exchange theory, modernization and secularization theories, symbolic interaction and identity theory, and status characteristics and expectation states theory. The application chapters took on this task as well, illustrating the usefulness of sociological approaches for the study of surveys, including gender theory, queer theory, grounded theory and others. Together, these theory and application chapters compliment and challenge the dominant cognitive paradigm used by survey methodologists, cognitive aspects of survey methodology (CASM) by adding a social and interactional dimension that frames and provides deeper meaning to the cognitive approach.

The second goal was to demonstrate that survey methodology could, as Paul Lazarsfeld challenged a previous generation of public opinion researchers, "become more aware of [survey research's] potentialities and more eager to develop them." (1950:617) Following Howard Schuman's advice, these chapters recognize survey artifacts as an outcome of social processes that are rooted in social interaction and, therefore, an "opportunity for understanding" human behavior (1982:23). To be sure, the improvement of survey techniques is still an intermediate goal of survey methodology, much in the same way that sociology, economics, political science, anthropology all have intermediate goals. While the ultimate goal of sociology and the other social sciences is understanding human society and interaction by way of a grand theory (Mills 1959), the day-to-day focus of social science is on intermediate problems and middle-range theory (Merton 1968). But with its ultimate focus shifted

---

P. S. Brenner (✉)
Department of Sociology, Center for Survey Research, University of Massachusetts Boston, Boston, MA, USA
e-mail: philip.brenner@umb.edu

to a higher level interest in interaction and society, survey methodology takes it place among the other social sciences.

This volume endeavors to expand the purview of survey methodology in line with this change in focus. To engage sociologists and other social scientists with an interest in survey methodology, this volume was organized primarily in two parts, theory and applications. Within the theory section, chapters highlight ways that survey methodology can benefit from a stronger program of theory building and testing. Within the applications section, chapters were arranged by substantive topics, including immigration, gender and sexuality, and race and ethnicity. However, an alternative organization more familiar to survey methodologists would offer a volume structured around methodological topics.[1] Three major methodological topics were investigated in the preceding chapters, theory and application chapters alike: item and unit nonresponse, socially desirable responding, and interaction and interactional problems in the survey interview. This final chapter is structured around these methodological foci to make connections between chapters and highlight areas in which future research could be fruitful and beneficial for both disciplines.

Item and Unit Nonresponse

Daniel Herda (Chap. 7) investigates the sources of item nonresponse to a question that asks respondents about the size of the immigrant population in their country. Respondents who fail to answer the question, reporting that they "don't know" the size of the immigrant population, hold similarly anti-immigrant views as those whose anti-immigrant views cause them to grossly overestimate the size of that population. The question remains as to whether ignorance about immigrant communities and demography cause anti-immigrant views or whether anti-immigrant attitudes reduce one's curiosity about immigrants and immigrant populations. Whichever way the causal arrow points, there is likely a connection between attitudes toward immigrants and an interest in or curiosity about the world.

How might one conceptualize such curiosity about our world? Walking in someone else's shoes in a more literal sense by visiting their country, sampling their cuisine, learning some simple phrases in their local tongue, learning about their past and how they live now can change one's understanding of oneself and one's place in the world. Holding a passport may be considered an indicator, albeit imperfect, of these experiences or a desire or willingness to have them. Analyses of the 2016 American National Election Study demonstrates that holding a passport is a significant predictor of more positive attitudes toward immigrants, even when

---

[1] See comment on usage of terms "substantive" and "methodological" in Chap. 1, *fn* 4.

controlling for political orientation, educational attainment, income, and other demographic characteristics that should moderate their relationship.[2]

Findings from Jerry Timbrook, Jolene Smyth, and Kristen Olson's (Chap. 10) investigation of interactional problems administering a sexual orientation question during a telephone interview can also be understood in terms of one's desire to understand and empathize with others. Respondents at the highest risk of encountering a problem answering the sexual orientation question and who are at the highest risk of item nonresponse are those who object to the content of the question. Where Herda finds xenophobia-caused item nonresponse, it may be that homophobia or biphobia is generating the potential for survey errors here. But what could be a predictor of acceptance or positive attitudes towards lesbians, gays, and bisexuals, analogous to holding a passport as a predictor of a curious view toward the world? An appropriate choice may be a characteristic that identifies the respondent as willing to walk in someone else's shoes in a more figurative sense by empathetically understanding and appreciating their viewpoints, troubles, and lives. Perhaps having a close friend or family member who is lesbian, gay, or bisexual would be a predictor of positive attitudes toward sexual minorities.

Katharina Meitinger and Timothy Johnson (Chap. 4) analyze cross-national survey data, focusing on the prevalence and causes of item nonresponse. They apply the theoretical frameworks used in cross-cultural research assessed by Henning Silber and Timothy Johnson in Chap. 4, testing cultural level as well as individual level variables in a multi-level model. Although Silber and Johnson's review highlighted a number of connections between cultural level variables and item nonreponse, Meitinger and Johnson find that their cultural level variables fail to predict the outcome. They do, however, find that a number of individual level variables have explanatory power. Notably, feelings of marginalization and powerlessness and related demographic characteristics are found to be significant predictors of item nonresponse. A lack of trust in the promise of social justice and equality—the belief that one will not be treated fairly in various situations because of one's race, ethnicity, gender or sexual identity—yields feelings of marginalization. As such, marginalized respondents may choose to refrain from offering information that they think may be ill-used. Thus, item nonresponse is linked to many of the same factors discussed by Bianca Manago in Chap. 5, in her introduction to status characteristics and expectation states theory.

Parallels can be drawn between Herda's, Timbrook, Smyth, and Olson's, chapters and that of Meitinger and Johnson. Both Europeans who hold anti-immigrant attitudes and Americans who hold anti-LGB attitudes may see themselves as stigmatized and marginalized for their beliefs and feel powerless to stem the tides of social change that have welcomed immigrants into their countries and welcomed

---

[2] Analysis is the author's own and available upon request. Of course, there's nothing magical about receiving a passport that leads one to automatically change one's attitudes about immigrants or change one's outlook on the people of other countries. Rather curiosity about the world is a likely a common cause of getting a passport and a positive view of immigrants.

lesbian, gay, and bisexual people to live openly in their communities. Indeed, many conservative religious groups and individuals in the US see themselves as stigmatized and even persecuted for their beliefs, including their beliefs in the sinfulness of lesbian, gay, and bisexual people and same-sex marriage (Castelli 2007; Hochschild 2016; Jones et al. 2017; McAlister 2019). Justified or not, their view that they are persecuted for their religious beliefs is clearly one that colors many conservative Christians' perspective and is likely to influence how they answer, or fail to answer, survey questions (Brenner 2019).

In each of these cases, survey methodology illuminates social phenomena. The presence of a survey artifact, item nonresponse, allows the investigation of perceptions of prejudice, marginalization, and stigmatization in a real-world context. Beyond just the answers respondents give, survey methodology allows us to understand *how* respondents answer questions and *why* they may fail to do so. Moreover, in both cases, survey methodology can be benefitted by a sociological understanding that can give insight into the meanings behind the interaction between interviewer and respondent. Thus, bringing together survey methods and sociology gives us insight into the survey artifact as well as a better understanding of the social forces behind it.

But feelings of powerlessness, marginalization, and persecution, like those discovered in these chapters, may instead yield a decision to not participate in the survey at all. Numerous research findings have linked the response decision to these same characteristics, some to higher response rates, some to lower. However, as Don Dillman suggests in Chap. 2, we need theory that more completely explains this phenomenon: a theory that fully accounts for the contexts of response and nonresponse across modes and every survey design decision.

Measurement and Social Desirability

Mathew Creighton (Chap. 6) investigates feelings of stigmatization and marginalization as a potential cause of measurement error. He focuses on socially desirable responding in answers to questions measuring attitudes toward immigrants, specifically Muslim immigrants in the Netherlands. Creighton argues that the threat of giving a socially undesirable answer may yield stigma. As such, respondents may opt to give socially desirable responses to questions about attitudes toward Muslim immigrants.

While this finding does sync with those of previous chapters investigating item nonresponse, it also raises an important question. How does the respondent, faced with a question to which their honest answer could be stigmatizing, decide what to do? With a few notable exceptions (e.g., the US Census), participating in surveys is voluntary; a fact not lost on those we sample, given our current difficulties with achieving adequate response rates. Moreover, respondents are typically told upfront that they can choose to skip any question that they would prefer not to answer. Thus, the decision to answer any individual survey question is voluntary; a choice that, given findings from chapters in this volume, respondents clearly understand and exercise as they see fit. Given this choice, how do respondents choose between three possible strategies for responding: giving a valid answer, giving an answer that is not valid, or refraining from giving an answer?

Philip Brenner attempts to answer this question in Chap. 3. Like Creighton, his interest is also in socially desirable responding, linking answers back to respondents' self-views. In short, respondents tend to tell us how they see themselves when questions ask about parts of themselves that are deeply important to their self-concepts. These types of questions have often been referred to as "sensitive questions." Timbrook, Smyth, and Olson use the term to describe the focus of their chapter: a question measuring sexual orientation. But Brenner separates these kinds of questions into three types: those focused on objects that could identify the respondent and threaten the guarantee of their confidentiality or anonymity; those focused on objects that engender repulsion or disgust in the respondent; and those focused on objects potentially linked to identities, which he argues comprise the largest share of these questions. He argues that the last of these generate measurement error, as Creighton suggests. For this type of question, respondents may see themselves as tolerant, empathetic, or charitable people and may report in a way that allows them to maintain that self-view. In essence, they create a fourth choice for responding: giving a valid answer to a pragmatic, rather than semantic, interpretation of the question.

The first two types of "sensitive questions," identification threats and repulsive objects, tend to generate item nonresponse. This does appear to explain the difference between the findings of Creighton and Timbrook et al. Where Creighton's respondents give an answer that may not match their "true value" as a result of a socially desirable responding process, Timbrook's respondents may fail to provide an answer given their disapproval of or disgust with the object of the question, although, notably, relatively few respondents fail to provide an answer. Herda's findings in Chap. 7 differ from these expectations unless one considers, as Herda does, that respondent's answering "don't know" to factual question is a legitimate, substantive, and valid answer.

Interaction and Measurement

Social identities such as gender, sexual orientation, and race, are the foci of status characteristics and expectation states theory introduced in Chap. 5 by Bianca Manago. The potential of a direct connection between the theory and survey methodology is substantial and promising. These social status characteristics influence interaction in novel interactional contexts, including survey interviews and other survey data collection procedures. Indeed, many of these social characteristics have long been included in the survey research programs on interviewer effects, focused on the influence of race (Finkel et al. 1991), ethnicity (Reese et al. 1986), and gender (Kane and Macaulay 1993) in survey interviews. This line of research specifies the scope conditions under which those characteristics can be expected to influence survey reports; when the question object is related to the characteristic differing between the interviewer and respondent. In this volume, in line with the findings of Meitinger and Johnson, survey reports of those with marginalized statuses are linked to survey artifacts.

Jennifer Dykema and her colleagues take on marginalization and powerlessness from a different perspective in Chap. 12, focusing on questions about trust in medical research. They examine how the lived experience of race can influence respondents' comprehension of and approach to answering survey questions. African Americans have good reason to be skeptical of the goodwill of medical science and research, given a long history of inhumane treatment that reaches back to the Tuskegee Syphilis Study and beyond (Thomas and Quinn 1991). Understanding this history, Dykema and colleagues investigate differences between White and Black respondents in their reported trust in medical science and research. They find that White respondents demonstrate problems understanding questions linked to race and have a higher rate of item nonresponse, as well as other measurement problems. Thus, where Meitinger and Johnson find that marginalization can harm data quality by increasing item nonresponse, Dykema and colleagues find that the relevance and salience of the question topic can change how respondents approach it.

Dana Garbarski and Dana LaVergne clearly understand this lesson on the benefits of topic salience. In Chap. 9, they approach the measurement of gender and sexual identity by hinging their work on the relevance of the questions for their respondents. They test novel measures of gender expression and sexual attraction with a convenience sample of self-identified queer women. They avoid the problem detailed by Dykema and colleagues by focusing their test with this specific population. Their assessment leads them to propose a series of strategies to hopefully avoid problems like those discussed in Dykema et al.

Like Garbarski and LaVergne, Jolene Smyth and Kristen Olson also assess measures of gender identity, testing the reliability and predictive validity of a measure that puts the respondents' self-view of their own gender into context with their view of society's ideal; essentially generating a reflected appraisal, as introduced in Brenner's Chap. 3. In so doing, they find that women are more likely influenced by question order than are men. By asking about society's ideal for women before asking women about their own view of themselves, the survey places women's self-views in the context of what they think society sees as the ideal for women. However, men are not influenced by the order of these questions: they report in the same way regardless of (their view of) society's ideal man. While not a laboratory experiment, as is common to much of the research on status characteristics that manipulates relevant traits, it does illuminate how the theory may be applied to survey methodology. The respondent is asked to imagine what others think that they should be; measured here as a general view of society's expectations. The respondent then interacts with that impression and negotiates how they see themselves as a result. That women, but not men, are influenced is a finding that gender and status characteristics theorists should investigate more closely.

Kevin Wozniak, Kevin Drakulich, and Brian Calfano, also investigate a context effect of a sort. This intentionally introduced context effect, typically called a framing experiment, uses a salient feature to potentially influence survey measurement. The authors use photographs of police performing their duties as a context for the survey questions that follow. These photographs include race as a salient feature and vary from benevolent (police helping members of the community) to confrontational (militarized police in conflict with citizens). These photographs were expected to frame the subsequent questions on attitudes toward police and influence respondents' answers. However, these frames did not work as expected. Similar to the male respondents from Smyth and Olson's context experiment on gender identity, Wozniak and his colleagues' respondents were unmoved by the context provided in the photographs. However, what both findings illustrate is stability—in either one's self-view as a man or in one's attitudes toward the police—in the face of contextual information manipulated in a survey experiment. This stability reflects the strength of the respondents' self-view and their connection to others vis-à-vis the characteristic, linking this finding back to identity theory as introduced in Chap. 3. Future research should investigate further the role that self-views play in attitude formation and strength.

Conclusion

Perceived inequalities—feelings of powerlessness, marginalization, and stigmatization—appear in these findings to be an important cause, or at least strongly associated with item nonresponse, measurement error, and perhaps other types of survey errors. Respondents who feel that their perspectives and life experiences are disvalued or disdained are less likely to share them with survey interviewers or on survey questionnaires, or, if they choose to participate in the survey and answer relevant questions, are more likely to report with error.

This finding is distressing. Paired with well-planned and well-executed probability-based sampling designs, surveys sample and measure from all echelons of society and can reflect the behaviors, attitudes, and opinions of the marginalized as well as the powerful; from the minority and majority alike. Indeed, this is the *raison d'être* of survey research. Surveys have been seen since their inception as crucial for democratic governments to function in the best interests of the people. They provide a conduit that allows—or even compels—those with political power to hear the voices of their constituents (Gallup and Rae 1940). Although high quality survey research is increasingly difficult, expensive, and criticized, it remains an important foundation for our representative democracy (Newport 2004). But if inequalities are reflected in individuals' decisions to participate in surveys, in the answers they give, and in the errors they include, then inequalities are also reflected in the voices heard, and those that go unheard, by those in power.

Inequality is a primary focus of sociological theory and research. No field is similarly equipped to investigate and understand it and phenomena related to it. Thus, the need for sociological understandings in survey methodology is great. Moreover, the survey artifacts uncovered in these chapters and elsewhere offer sociologists an opportunity to examine how social phenomena, like inequality and others, influence interactions. Therefore, these chapters plan and illustrate a path forward that is founded in sociological theory. In addition to those demonstrated in the theory and application chapters, I highlight here a few extensions and additional theories and perspectives that may be fruitfully applied to survey methodological problems.

Affect control theory may be used to inform problems of reliability and validity in attitudinal measures. The theory operationalizes measurement of an attitudinal object on three dimensions: virtue (good–bad), potency (powerful–weak), and activity (active–passive) (Heise 2010; MacKinnon and Robinson 2014). Importantly, objects may be rated differently across contexts and populations. For example, different groups in the United States, such as Whites and Blacks, may rate police officers similarly on potency (powerful) and activity (active), but may diverge in their ratings of officers' virtue (good v. bad). Similarly, political conservatives and liberals may rate immigrants similarly on potency (weak) and activity (active) but disagree on their virtue (bad v. good). Divergences may be intentionally manipulated by survey experiments, just as with different framing or priming perhaps identifying areas for political compromise or policymaking. Although not appropriate for every survey, this approach may be useful for understanding attitude stability and change, an important concern for survey methodologists and many other researchers using survey research to study public opinion.

In Chap. 2, Dillman highlights his previous work using social exchange theory to explain the causes of survey nonresponse and techniques to avoid it. The theory applies a rational choice approach to understanding human relationships, focusing on cost–benefit analysis as a prerequisite for behavior while taking social structure and power into account. Answering the critiques of utilitarian theories, social exchange posits that behavior may be focused on future favors, altruism, consistency with one's social position, competition with one's adversaries, and even influenced by emotion (Lawler and Thye 1999; Meeker 1971). In addition to testing nonresponse hypotheses founded in the most up-to-date version of social exchange theory, it may also be of use for understanding attitudinal measures, measures that rely on social comparisons, and other phenomena.

Survey methodologists and sociologists may revisit the findings of interviewer effects and context effects studies from the lens of status characteristics and expectation states theory. Such an approach may enhance our understanding of these phenomena and expand our understanding of similar phenomena from related research programs. Other theories introduced here, explicitly or implicitly, may also be more fully explicated and applied in future work. Identity theory and structural symbolic interactionism, gender theory, queer theory, critical race theory, conflict theories, and others may have purchase for understanding phenomena at various stages of the process, design, or quality perspectives of survey methodology.

These chapters, and the suggestions for future research throughout the volume, represent only a beginning to the potential for connections between sociological theory and survey methodology. Most importantly, a more complete and effective use of theory would begin with a theoretical explanation before moving on to hypothesis construction and testing with survey data, paradata, linked administrative record data, or survey experiments. It is my sincere hope, and I expect that of the authors of this volume's chapters as well, that future research will forge stronger connections between survey methodology and sociological theories and perspectives that will benefit both disciplines. Reintroducing social and interactional theory to survey methodology will both compliment and challenge the predominant cognitive approach (Bradburn 2016) while moving the field forward as it develops into a more comprehensive social science. The time has clearly arrived to bring survey methodology and sociological theory together again.

References

Bradburn, N. M. (2016). Surveys as social interactions. *Journal of Survey Statistics and Methodology, 4*, 94–109.

Brenner, P. S. (2019). Authenticity and the religious identity. In J. E. Stets & R. T. Serpe (Eds.), *Identities in everyday life* (pp. 75–92). New York: Oxford University Press.

Castelli, E. A. (2007). Persecution complexes: Identity politics and the "war on Christians.". *Differences, 18*, 152–180.

Finkel, S. E., Gutterbock, T. M., & Borg, M. J. (1991). Race-of-interviewer effects in a Preelection poll: Virginia 1989. *Public Opinion Quarterly, 55*, 313–330.

Gallup, G. H., & Rae, S. F. (1940). *The pulse of democracy: The public opinion poll and how it works*. New York: Simon & Schuster.

Heise, D. R. (2010). *Surveying cultures: Discovering shared conceptions and sentiments*. New York: Wiley.

Hochschild, A. R. (2016). *Strangers in their own land*. New York: New Press.

Jones, R. P., Cox, D., Cooper, B., & Lienesch, R. (2017). *Majority of Americans oppose transgender bathroom restrictions*. Washington, DC: Public Religion Research Institute. Retrieved March 10, 2017, from http://www.prri.org/research/lgbt-transgender-bathroom-discrimination-religious-liberty

Kane, E. W., & Macaulay, L. J. (1993). Interviewer Gender and Gender Attitudes. *Public Opinion Quarterly, 57*, 1–28.

Lawler, E. J., & Thye, S. R. (1999). Bringing emotions into social exchange theory. *Annual Review of Sociology, 25*, 217–244.

MacKinnon, N. J., & Robinson, D. T. (2014). Back to the future: 25 years of research in affect control theory. *Advances in Group Processes, 31*, 139–173.

McAlister, M. (2019). Evangelical populist internationalism and the politics of persecution. *The Review of Faith and International Affairs, 17*(3), 105–117.

Meeker, B. F. (1971). Decisions and exchange. *American Sociological Review, 36*(3), 485–492.

Merton, R. K. (1968). *Social theory and social structure*. New York: Free Press.

Mills, C. W. (1959). *The sociological imagination*. Oxford: Oxford University Press.

Newport, F. (2004). *Polling matters: Why leaders must listen to the wisdom of the people*. New York: Warner.

Reese, S. D., Danielson, W. A., Shoemaker, P. J., Chang, T. K., & Hsu, H. L. (1986). Ethnicity-of-interviewer effects among Mexican-Americans and Anglos. *Public Opinion Quarterly, 50*, 563–572.

Thomas, S. B., & Quinn, S. C. (1991). The Tuskegee syphilis study, 1932 to 1972: Implications for HIV education and AIDS risk education programs in the black community. *American Journal of Public Health, 81*(11), 1498–1505.

Correction to: Power, Culture and Item Nonresponse in Social Surveys

Katharina M. Meitinger and Timothy P. Johnson

Correction to:
Chapter 8 in: P. S. Brenner (ed.), *Understanding Survey Methodology*, Frontiers in Sociology and Social Research 4, https://doi.org/10.1007/978-3-030-47256-6_8

The original version of the chapter was inadvertently published with an error. The chapter has now been corrected.

In the final paragraph of the Results section (paragraph labeled *Country Level Variables*), the third and fourth sentences have been updated as follows: "In a similar vein, respondents from countries with higher values of uncertainty avoidance show higher risks of INR, a finding that is opposite of what H10 expected. Although, we could not find significant effects for individualism (H9) and power distance (H8), the directions of those effects each go in the hypothesized direction, respectively."

In the second paragraph of the Discussion section, the fifth sentence has been updated as follows: "However, in the analyses reported here, we only could find a significant effect for the dimension of uncertainty avoidance, and the direction of that association was the opposite of what we had hypothesized (H10)." In addition, the following sentence should be inserted after the sixth sentence: "This finding suggests that respondents embedded within uncertainty avoidant cultures might be more inclined to avoid answering, perhaps when confronted with ambiguous questions or topics."

The updated online version of this chapter can be found at
https://doi.org/10.1007/978-3-030-47256-6_8

In the final paragraph of the chapter (paragraph labeled *Future Research*), the following sentence has been inserted after the fifth sentence: "Relatedly, the contrary findings regarding the direction of uncertainty avoidance effects requires additional investigation, as questions that are structured ambiguously or that address ambiguous topics may be more likely to produce INR within uncertainty avoidant cultures."

Index

A
Academic disciplines, 1, 2
Academics, 1, 2, 9, 128, 193, 198, 208, 278
Acceptance, 53, 71, 129, 223, 327
Accuracy, 77, 99, 162, 225
Acquiescence, 73, 75, 76
Action opportunities, 70, 92
Activists, 309
Address-based sampling, 18
Administration, survey, 103
Adolescents, 195, 250
Adulthood, 71
Adult-to-Adult communication theory, 29
Affect, 2, 21, 24, 37, 88, 93, 94, 97, 99, 101–104, 106, 150, 160, 162, 200, 205, 206, 225, 226, 238, 249, 251, 277, 280, 297, 316
Affect control theory, 332
Affect heuristics, 150, 151
Affective response, 290
Affirmative action, 50, 155
Africa, 6, 118, 174
African, 155
African American, 51, 257, 278, 279, 284, 285, 308, 311, 317, 330
Agree/disagree items, 75
Alcohol, 59, 77, 95
Altruism, 332
American Association for Public Opinion Research (AAPOR), 1, 254
Americans, 1, 50, 105, 155, 171, 257, 278, 308, 330
Anchoring effect, 262
Answers, survey, 19, 279
Anonymity, 6, 45, 98, 115–117, 121–122, 125, 130–132, 138, 329
Anthropology, 325
Antipathy, 132
Armored vehicles, police use of, 310
Artifact, survey, 9, 48, 325, 328, 330
Asexual, 228
Asia, 6
Asian American, 312
Asians, 184
Assertiveness, 69
Asylum, 118
Atrocities, 284
Attention, 3, 4, 7, 9, 22, 23, 30–33, 39, 50, 95, 96, 105, 144, 164, 169, 213, 306, 307, 311, 315
Attention check, 96, 105–106
Attitude change, 9
Attitudes, 5, 25, 46, 101, 116, 156, 224, 278, 316, 331
    anti-immigrant, 5, 6, 326, 327
    anti-immigration, 326, 327
    anti-LGB, 224, 327
    anti-Muslim, 6, 131
    masked, 6, 115, 121, 122, 130–132
    weakly-held, 307
Attraction, sexual, 194, 196, 212, 213, 330
Attractiveness, 102, 106
Australia, 41
Austria, 147
Authoritarianism, 69, 173
Authority, 31, 37, 71
Autonomy, 70, 72, 173
Avoidance, 4, 75, 181
Axinn, W., 95

B

Backlash, respondent, 223, 224
Back-stage performance, 121
Balanced Inventory of Desirable Responding (BIDR), 77
Baltimore, Maryland, 308
Basic Human Values, theory of, 70
Behavior, 3, 15, 46, 67, 87, 117, 171, 194, 227, 247, 280, 313, 331
Behavior coding, 7, 227, 228, 240
Behavior, counternormative, 46, 47, 59
Behavior, normative, 46, 47, 59
Belgium, 146, 147
Beliefs, 25, 29, 31, 68, 91, 117, 119, 150, 222, 228, 278, 307–309, 317, 318, 327
Belonging, 178, 181, 183
Benefit-cost theory, 34, 35
Benevolence, 70
Berger, J., 52, 91, 93
Biemer, P.P., 67, 72
Bilingual, 183
Binary, 8, 124, 125, 127, 134, 176, 194, 209, 248–250, 268, 269, 271, 289
Biomarkers, 286
Biomedical, 278, 286
Biomedical research, 278, 286
Bipolar scale, 205, 209, 212, 271
Bisexual, 194, 197, 198, 221, 222, 224–226, 231, 233, 235, 242, 252, 255, 327, 328
Bisexuality, 222, 240
Black Lives Matter (BLM), 309, 317, 318
Black/African Americans, 278, 285
Blood samples, 286
Blumer, H., 52, 156
Bradburn, N.M., 72, 205, 214, 251
Brenner, P.S., 1–10, 45–61, 98, 100, 116, 117, 133, 194, 306, 325–333
Burden of proof, 92
Burke, P.J., 249

C

Calfano, B., 9, 305–319
Callbacks, 17, 22
Canada, 41, 145–147
Cannell, C.F., 223, 228, 280
Carmines, E.G., 307, 310, 312, 317, 319
Cash, 16, 21, 30, 33, 38, 254
Catholic, 55
Cato institute, 308
Ceiling effect, 123, 125, 139
Ceteris paribus, 94, 97
Characteristics, diffuse, 90, 91, 93, 94, 102–104

Characteristics, specific, 27, 90
Check-all-that-apply, 194, 257
Childcare, 248, 253, 255, 256, 265, 269
Childhood, 71, 201
Children, 29, 30, 58, 257
Chile, 175, 184
China, 70
Christianity, 81
Chronological data collection, 61
Church attendance, 60
Churches, 300
Cialdini, R., 30–32, 37, 40
Cisgender, 90, 93, 197, 198, 200, 206, 249, 251, 271
Citizens, 54, 58, 307, 331
Citrin, J., 120, 144, 145, 150, 156, 161
Civilians, 308–311, 318
Civil liberties, 308
Clarification, requests for, 203, 283, 297
Clinton, H., 317
Codable answers, 237, 280, 288, 289, 293, 297, 298
Coders, 231, 287
Coding, 7, 124, 176, 184, 193, 196, 199, 228, 231, 283, 284, 286, 288, 297, 300
Cognition, 305
Cognitive, 193
Cognitive approach, 325, 333
Cognitive aspects of survey methodology (CASM), 2, 97, 106, 305–307, 319, 325
Cognitive availability, 148, 151, 156, 157, 160, 163, 164
Cognitive dissonance theory, 3, 28
Cognitive interviewing, 7, 77, 196–197, 226
Cognitive psychology, 2
Cohesion, 173
Collectivism, 4, 69, 72, 75–80, 173
College, 6, 128–130, 132, 231, 240, 257, 288, 312
Communication, aural, 26, 204, 211, 220, 225
Communications, 20, 22, 24, 26, 29, 30, 35, 36, 39, 40, 310
Community policing, 310, 311
Competence, 90, 91, 102
Completion, survey, 155
Complexity, 61, 99, 125, 183, 194, 202, 203, 207, 226, 280, 307, 319
Compliance, 32
Comprehension, 60, 183, 205, 283, 284, 293, 297, 330
Computer-assisted self-interviewing (CASI), 220
Computer-assisted telephone survey, 285

Computer, 19, 24, 30, 220, 285
Conceptualization, 7, 30, 37, 68, 208
Conditions, research, 126
Confidence, 128–130, 136, 138, 151, 163, 315
Confidentiality, 23, 34, 38, 241, 329
Conflict theories, 332
Conformity, 70, 75–77, 173
Confrontations, police and civilian, 309
Confucian societies, 75
Conrad, F., 2, 305
Conservatism, 70, 75, 152
Conservatives, 50, 117, 120, 125
Constitution, 31
Contact, survey, 18, 22, 40
Conversation, 6, 38, 39, 54, 279
Conversational practices, 280, 283
Converse, P.E., 307, 318
Cooley, C.H., 51, 53
Cooperation, survey, 20, 33
Corporations, 80, 123
Correll, S.J., 90–92, 105
Cost, constraints of, 296
Costs, survey, 34, 35
Counternormative behavior, 46, 47, 59
Counter-roles, 56
Couper, M.P., 2, 31, 32, 305
Coverage, sampling, 220
Covert attitudes, 116
Creighton, M.J., 5, 115–132
Crime, 150, 219, 249, 309, 310, 313, 314
Crime-fighting, 309
Criterion validity, 60
Critical race theory, 332
Croatia, 175, 184
Cross-cultural research, 327
Cross-national research, 172
Crowne, D.P., 47, 76
Cultural frameworks, 68, 69, 71, 79, 80, 172
Cultural research, 327
Culture, 5, 50, 67, 105, 120, 146, 169–184, 208
Czech Republic, 147, 153, 157

D
Data collection, 7, 15, 17, 35, 38, 40, 46, 51, 67, 126, 172, 177, 181, 194, 213, 215, 219, 270, 306, 329
Data quality, 2, 9, 88, 95, 101–104, 170, 220, 237, 242, 280, 288, 297, 315, 330
Deference, 75, 94
DeLamater, J., 59, 61, 98, 99, 117, 306
de Leeuw, E.D., 220, 221, 225, 251
Democracy, 5, 331

Democrat, 55, 259, 312
Demography, 326
Denmark, 147, 177
Design effect, 125, 307, 308
Development, survey, 2, 247
Deviance, 69
Deviance Nations, 173
Dillman, D.A., 4, 15–41, 97, 169, 170, 220, 225, 284, 305, 328, 332
Disadvantaged, 182
Disadvantageous, 95
Discrimination, 96, 222, 278, 283
Disenfranchisement, 102
Disfluency, 230, 296
Disgust, feelings of, 60
Distrust, 183, 284
Diversity, 7, 119, 153, 157, 169, 173, 178, 182, 214, 250, 251
Diversity, neighborhood, 153, 155
Doctorates, 1
Doing gender, 195, 252, 253, 269
Don't know responses, 6, 143, 144, 147, 151, 160, 170
Drakulich, K., 9, 305–319, 330
Dramaturgy, 121
Durkheim, J., 309, 319
Drugs, 45–47, 59, 77, 95, 299, 313, 314
Durkheim, E, 309, 319
Dutch, 118, 122–124
Dykema, J., 8, 99, 199, 226, 277–300, 330

E
Economic, 71, 119–121, 173, 219, 249, 305, 309, 325
Education, 6, 24, 41, 56, 79, 90, 116, 151, 170, 231, 251, 288, 312
Effectiveness, 18, 23, 28, 29, 38
Egalitarianism, 4, 71
Election, 53, 54, 144, 145, 147, 151, 326
Email, 18, 19, 23–25, 37, 38, 99
Embeddedness, 4, 70, 72, 76
Emotions, 46, 52, 55, 59, 150, 151, 210, 282, 307, 317, 332
England, 253
English, 204, 224, 225, 284, 285, 314
English-speakers, 315
Environmental factors, 122, 279
Estonia, 41, 147
Ethics, 278
Ethnic groups, 151, 171, 178, 278, 283–285, 296, 300, 316

Ethnicity, 2, 5, 50, 67, 68, 105, 156, 170, 176, 257, 258, 260, 262, 263, 265, 267, 268, 280, 283, 285, 286, 298, 300, 327, 329
Europe, 6, 79, 120, 144–146, 155, 162
European, 76, 120, 145, 146, 327
European Social Survey (ESS), 6, 75, 124, 144, 145, 147, 148, 156
Eurostat, 118
Evaluation, question, 5, 7, 18, 35, 36, 51, 53, 54, 91, 94, 262, 286, 310, 313–317
Exclusion, 171, 182, 211
Expectation states, 5, 87–106, 325, 327, 332
Expenditure, 19, 30
Experiential sampling method (ESM), 61
Experiment, 6, 9, 33, 122, 123, 125, 127, 128, 130, 133, 134, 136, 138–139, 254, 257, 260–263, 308, 310, 318, 330, 331
Expertise, 104–106
Eysenck Personality Inventory, 77

F

Factual question, 6, 45, 329
Family, 30, 52, 58, 60, 71, 118, 150, 202, 219, 256, 257, 266, 267, 327
Father, 175, 253
Federal Committee on Statistical Methodology (FCSM), 249, 250
Federal government, 226, 312
Female, 51, 127, 147, 152, 163, 170, 203, 209, 224, 231, 232, 247–271, 290, 294, 310
Female-bodied, 248
Feminine orientations, 69
Femininity, 4, 72, 79, 206, 249, 250, 252, 253, 255, 262, 267–271
Ferguson, M., 308, 310, 317, 318
Festinger, L., 28, 31, 40
Filter questions, 211, 257
Finland, 147, 148, 153, 174
Floor, 125
Floor effect, 123, 138, 139
Focus groups, 87, 183
Follow-up survey, 33
Foreign-born, 118, 150
Foreigners, 150
Formalization, 87
Fowler, F.J., 46, 53, 54, 203, 223, 224, 226, 228
Fractionalization, 178, 180–182
Framing, 9, 59, 197, 306, 307, 309, 311, 318, 330, 332
Framing theory, 306, 309
France, 147, 148
Francophone, 147

Friendship, 149, 154, 157, 197
Front-stage performance, 121

G

Gallup Organization, 20
Gamification, 30, 36
Gamification theory, 30
Garbarski, D., 7, 8, 193, 199, 205, 214, 223, 270, 271, 277–300, 330
Gay, 194, 206, 221–226, 230–233, 235, 238, 242, 252, 255, 327, 328
Gender, 7, 193
Gender expression, 193, 330
Gender fluidity, 200
Gender nonconforming, 270
Gender presentation, 200, 201, 252
Genderqueer, 325, 332
Gender theory
Generalizability, 170, 172, 182, 296
General Social Survey (GSS), 144, 145, 183, 219, 249
Georgia, 181
Germany, 148, 171, 177
Gesture, 53, 206–208
Globalization, 80
Goffman, E., 47, 51, 52, 54, 55, 117, 118, 121, 221, 222, 306
Google, 311
Government, 17, 19, 23, 25, 26, 174, 177, 181, 183, 185, 220, 278, 308, 311, 312, 331
Gratification, 70
Gross domestic product (GDP), 177, 180, 181
Grounded theory, 7, 193, 196, 199, 325
Group-enhancement, 69
Group interactions, 88, 92, 93, 106
Group-level, 122, 123
Group-orientation, 94
Groves, R., 2, 16, 31–33, 48, 50, 58, 68, 72, 79, 101, 305, 306

H

Harkness, J., 67, 74
Harmony, 4, 70, 72, 74
Health, 5, 16, 52, 77, 79, 102, 177, 194, 195, 215, 219, 249, 254, 278, 283, 285, 297, 299
Hedonism, 70
Herda, D., 6, 143–164, 326, 327, 329
Herek, G., 219, 221–223
Herfindahl index
Heterogeneity, 178

Heteronormativity, 206, 214
Heterosexuality, 269
Heuristics, 2, 31, 32, 34, 37, 148, 150, 160, 214, 306
Hierarchy, 4, 5, 56, 57, 70, 72, 92
High-status, 52, 89, 93
Hispanic, 147, 171, 257, 258, 260, 262, 263, 285, 312, 314–317
HIV/AIDS, 278
Hofstede, G., 68–71, 75, 76, 78–80, 172, 173, 178, 181, 182
Homohysteria, 222, 225
Homosexual, 224, 225, 233
Homosexuality, 221–223, 228, 229, 240
House of Representatives, United States, 311
Household division of labor, 252
Households, 18, 19, 41, 126, 254
Housekeeping, 8, 252, 255, 256, 265, 266, 269
Housework, 58, 248, 252, 256, 257, 266, 267, 269
Hungary, 118, 146

I

Iceland, 175
Identities, 4, 16, 47, 90, 116, 219, 249, 285, 306, 325
  identity commitment, 56
  identity cybernetic model, 55
  identity discrepancy, 55
  identity prominence, 56–59
  identity salience, 56, 57
  identity theory, 4, 51–60, 331, 332
  identity verification, 55
Ignorance, 49, 143, 144, 147, 151, 155, 163, 164, 326
Immigrants, 144, 151, 156, 163, 326
Immigration, 5, 6, 117–122, 124, 125, 129–132, 138, 144, 151, 155–157, 326
Immigration restrictionism, 157, 160
Impression management, 4, 46–49, 51, 53, 76, 77
Incarceration, 102
Incentives, 3, 16, 21, 23–25, 27, 30, 33, 37, 38, 41, 254, 259–263, 286
Incentives, pre-paid, 263
Income, 27, 41, 45, 120, 126, 127, 130, 132–134, 136, 138, 147, 152, 154, 176, 177, 188, 219, 312, 327
Independence, 69, 173
Independents (political), 147, 151, 157, 312
In-depth interviewing, 198, 209, 212
India, 175, 184

Individualism, 4, 69, 72, 74, 76, 77, 173, 178, 180, 182
Individualistic, 81, 173, 318
Individual-level analysis, 7, 70, 75, 76, 98, 116, 122, 173, 177, 181, 183, 201, 249, 327
Inductive research, 7, 193, 196, 199, 213
Indulgence, 4, 70
Inequality, 2, 7, 76, 171, 177, 180–182, 331
Influences, exogenous, 306, 307
Influence theory, 30
Inglehart, R., 71, 80
In-group, 69, 79, 80, 87, 89, 93, 106, 183
Initial conditions, 93, 94, 100, 104–106
Initiative, 77, 183
Innumeracy, population, 6, 144, 145, 147, 151, 152, 156, 157, 160–162, 164
Institutional review board (IRB), 23, 46
Instructional manipulation check (IMC), 96, 97
Intelligence, 154
Interaction, 4, 20, 47, 68, 87, 122, 195, 237, 252, 293, 317, 325
Interactional research, 2, 3, 5, 7–9, 51, 52, 54–56, 103, 208, 220, 249, 252, 277–298, 325–327, 329, 333
Interaction coding, 284, 286, 288, 297
Interactive voice response (IVR), 48
Interdependence, 69
Intergroup contact, 149, 153–157, 164
International Social Survey Program (ISSP), 6, 76, 78, 174–178, 184, 185
Internet, 16, 18–21, 23, 25–27, 31, 32, 36, 40, 125
Interpersonal, 74, 148, 150, 156, 279
Interviewing, 22, 53, 77, 95, 145, 193, 196, 226, 279, 281
Interviewing, face-to-face, 16, 18, 33, 78, 147, 220
Interviewer-administered survey, 50, 78, 220
Interviewer-respondent interaction, 226, 231, 277, 279, 280, 283, 297, 298
Interviewers, 2, 18, 48, 75, 101, 145, 170, 196, 238, 249, 296, 328
Interviewer variability, 279
Interview, survey, 33, 36, 79, 219
Intolerance, 117, 119–122, 125, 129–132, 138
Intrusiveness, 222, 228, 229, 233, 240
Ipsos MORI, 144
Ireland, 147, 148
Islam, 119, 120
Islamophobia, 115–132
Israel, 145
Italy, 118, 146

J
Jackson, J., 309, 312
James, W., 51, 56
Japan, 41, 174
Johnson, T.P., 4, 6, 68, 169–184, 297, 327

K
Korean-Americans, 284
Krosnick, J.A., 48, 75, 95, 97, 147, 151, 251, 280, 307, 312, 319
Kuklinski, J.H., 117, 306

L
Labour-market, 119
Labour-market competition, 119
Language, 68, 120, 172, 173, 183, 201, 204, 208, 215, 225, 238, 283, 284, 313, 314
Latinos, 278
Latvia, 174
Law enforcement, 8, 308, 310, 317
Lazarsfeld, P.F., 1, 9, 95, 325
Legitimacy, survey, 19, 45
Length, survey, 20, 21, 27, 39, 97
Lesbian, 194, 198, 199, 221, 222, 224–226, 230–233, 235, 242, 252, 255, 327, 328
Lesbian, gay, bisexual/transgender (LGBT), 226
Lesbian, gay/bisexual (LGB), 221–226, 230, 233, 241, 242
Leverage-saliency theory, 4, 32, 34, 36, 40
Liking, 31
List experiment, 6, 122–125, 127, 128, 130, 133, 136, 138–139
Listwise deletion, 143, 144, 160, 161, 164
Longitudinal Internet Studies for the Social Sciences (LISS), 125, 126, 129, 136, 138, 183
Long-term orientations, 70
Loosveldt, G., 170–172, 174
Low-status, 89, 90, 92

M
Macro-level, 2, 4, 195, 249, 252
Magliozzi, D., 195, 204, 205, 249–251, 262, 269–271
Mailings, survey, 23
Mail surveys, 21, 22, 32, 48, 54, 79, 220, 248, 254, 268
Majority, 46, 103, 118, 128, 144, 147, 153, 156, 172, 181, 183, 184, 222, 224, 228, 231, 233, 278, 315, 331
Male, 51, 75, 126, 152, 181, 203, 209, 211, 224, 231, 261, 263, 287, 310, 331
Male-bodied, 248
Male-typed, 253
Malware, 16, 19
Manago, B., 5, 87–106, 327, 329
Manipulation check, 96, 315
Manipulations, 28, 96, 105, 106, 131, 139, 307, 311
Mannerisms, 22, 202, 203, 206–209
Marginalization, 7, 171, 182, 184, 214, 327, 328, 330, 331
Marginalized groups, 7, 171, 182, 183
Marital status, 250, 271
Marlowe, D., 47, 76, 77, 98
Marriage, 235
Masculine, 8, 69, 75, 78, 200–206, 214, 248–250, 252–254, 261, 262, 265, 266, 268–271
Masculine orientation, 69, 75
Masculinity, 4, 74, 75, 206, 214, 262
Masking, 121, 122, 130, 132
Mastery, 4, 70, 72
Materialist, 71
Maynard, D.W., 220, 222, 227, 228, 279
Mead, G.H., 51
Meaning, 6, 47, 51, 52, 54, 60, 115, 118, 132, 157, 195, 197, 200, 203, 208, 210, 225, 226, 230, 235, 242, 279, 283, 305, 307, 308, 319, 325, 328
Measurement, 2, 51, 72, 92, 116, 145, 220, 247, 280, 319, 328
Measurement and Experimentation in the Social Sciences (MESS), 125
Measurement bias, 5, 6, 58, 61
Measurement error, 57, 61, 72, 73, 116, 132, 210, 214, 270, 297, 328, 329, 331
Mechanical Turk, 250
Media coverage, 308–310, 317
Medical research, 8, 9, 277–279, 284, 286, 289, 298–300, 330
Medicine, 8, 52, 284
Memory, 148, 225, 284
Men, 8, 90, 96, 100–103, 152, 171, 203, 206, 211, 214, 223–225, 248–250, 252, 253, 259–269, 289, 330
Meso-level, 195
Messages, 10, 24, 32, 39, 40, 307
Meta-analysis, 16, 219

Methodologists, 1–3, 5, 9, 10, 15, 47, 57, 87, 88, 93–96, 100, 101, 104, 106, 107, 306, 307, 319, 326, 332
Methodology, 325
Methods, 1, 2, 16, 32, 41, 61, 95, 98, 115, 122, 174, 178, 193, 196, 199, 227–231, 235, 242, 247, 254, 285, 305, 328
Mexican, 105
Micro-level, 2
Middle East, 118
Migrants, 118, 176
Migration, 118, 172
Militarization, police, 308
Military, 248, 253, 257, 267–269
Miller, K., 220, 224–226, 242
Minority, 6, 143, 144, 172, 175, 176, 179, 181, 183, 184, 197, 213, 214, 219, 220, 224–226, 237, 241, 252, 269, 278, 283, 288, 296, 316, 327, 331
Misclassification, sexual identity, 215, 222
Misconduct, police, 309, 313–315, 317, 318
Missing completely at random (MCAR), 147, 160, 161, 164, 170
Missing data, 6, 147, 160, 170, 251, 254–257, 259–261
Missing at random (MAR), 161
Missingness, 161, 162, 251
Mitigator, conversational, 282, 288
Mixed-effects, 178, 179, 289
Mixed-mode, 16, 36, 38
Mobility, 69, 116, 132
Modernization, 4, 71, 325
Modernization theory, 4, 325
Moral, 70, 91, 309, 317, 319
Morality, 71, 309
Morocco, 118
Most people projective questioning (MMPQ), 98
Mother, 52, 253, 311
Multi-cultural, 72
Multi-ethnic, 67
Multiple imputation, 6, 143, 144, 152, 161, 163, 164
Multiple-mode, 16, 18, 19, 28
Muslim, 6, 116–124, 126, 128–132, 135–138, 156, 328

N
Nation, 68, 70, 71, 75, 77–79, 146, 177, 309, 312
National Guard, 311
National Institutes of Health (NIH), 278
National Research Council, 2, 19
Native American, 171
Nativism, 117
Negative affect, 149, 154, 160, 163
Netherlands, 5, 115–132, 135–138, 146, 147, 328
Networks, 148
New Zealand, 181
Non-answers, 183
Nonattitudes, 307
Non-binary, 88, 249
Non-directiveness, 53, 279
Non-Hispanic, 171, 257, 261–263, 283, 284, 293, 296, 316
Non-immigrants, 120, 126
Non-missing, 126, 143, 160
Non-Muslim, 120
Nonparadigmatic question-answer sequences, 279
Nonprobability sampling, 312
Non-random, 147, 160
Nonrespondents, 79, 155
Nonresponse, 2–4, 6, 7, 17, 19, 23, 25, 29, 36, 38, 67, 72, 73, 78, 151, 156, 219, 226, 242, 251, 259, 268, 270, 328, 332
Nonresponse, item (INR), 3, 5–7, 73, 78, 143, 153, 165, 169–184, 205, 212, 219, 227, 251, 254, 260, 261, 268, 270, 326–331
Nonresponse, unit (UNR), 6, 73, 79, 169, 170, 326
Nonsampling error, 72
Nonverbal gestures, 208
Normative attitudes, 48
Normative behaviors, 58
Norms, 4, 16, 20, 22, 29, 46, 48–50, 68–70, 75, 76, 98, 115, 117–119, 121, 131, 214, 252, 309
Norway, 145, 147, 174

O
Observable, 50, 92, 93, 103
Observable power, 89, 92
Observable power and prestige order (OPPO), 92, 103
Occupations, 127, 132–134, 136, 138, 253, 269
Old, 228, 235, 270, 312
Olson, K., 7, 8, 19, 33, 34, 219–242, 264, 283, 330
Olson, W., 308, 317, 329
Onerousness, survey, 20, 21, 26
Openness-to-change, 70

Operationalization, 250, 271
Operationalize, 38, 41, 67, 68, 116, 151, 152, 269, 332
Opinion change, 31, 305–320
Opinions, 1, 31, 47, 92, 115, 145, 183, 331
Opportunities, 3, 19, 22, 24, 31, 52, 58, 67, 69, 92, 169, 172, 325
Opt-in panel, 312
Organization for Economic Co-operation and Development (OECD), 178
Other-deception, 49, 60
Out-groups, 69, 79, 80, 156, 164
Overestimation, 147, 152, 155, 156, 162, 163
Over-report, 6, 130
Overreporting, 50, 58
Oversampling, 126, 226
Oversimplification, 176
Overstated, 117
Over-statement, 121
Overt attitudes, 116
Oyserman, D., 69, 71, 80

P
Pansexual, 197
Paradata, 333
Paradigmatic sequence, question-answer, 9
Paradigms, 3–5, 9, 71, 88, 106, 196, 220, 222, 227, 228, 237, 279, 305–307, 319, 325
Paralinguistic cues, 222
Paralinguistic expressions, 222, 230, 238
Parenthood, 253
Parenting, 253
Parents, 149, 150, 154, 155, 157, 158, 201, 253
Participant, research, 5, 94, 101
Participation, 278
Participation, likelihood of, 8, 284, 286
Participation, survey, 7, 79, 94, 97, 279, 283
Partisanship, 312
Party for Freedom (PVV), 119, 121
Passport, 326, 327
Paul, R., 317
Payments, 15, 19, 21
Perceptions, 29, 34, 53, 88, 91, 100, 102, 120, 121, 124, 126, 131, 145, 150, 153, 155, 161, 163, 195, 201, 202, 204, 205, 250, 253, 286, 313, 314, 328
Performance expectations, 88–90
Performance outputs, 92
Persecution, 328
Personality, 4, 47, 49, 51, 53, 60, 201, 210
psychology, 51
Persuasion, 41, 317
Pew Research Center, 16

Peytcheva, 16
Philippines, 175
Phone, 20, 21, 33, 48, 87, 122, 208, 300, 308
Photographs, 331
Physical activity, 59, 60
Physiological measures, 71, 194, 279
Poland, 118, 146–148, 153
Polarization, 250, 262, 271
Police officers, 308–310, 313, 332
 police-civilian interactions, 308–310, 312, 316
 police, confidence in, 309, 311, 312, 317, 318
 police, satisfaction with, 309, 310
Policing, 5, 9, 309–312, 316, 317
Policing-style, 310
Policy, immigration, 117, 144, 155–157
Policymaking, 332
Policy positions, 144, 155, 162, 163
Political affiliation, 242, 257, 260–263, 267, 268
Political orientation, 50, 327
Political parties, 258, 259, 311
Politicians, 50, 306
Politics, 50, 151, 152, 163, 259
Pollsters, 306
Poor, 53, 122, 123, 170, 279, 285, 314, 315
Population, immigrant size, 6, 120, 126, 143–164, 326
Portugal, 146
Postal, 18, 20, 25, 26, 37, 38, 254
Postcards, survey invitations, 254
Post-incentive, 16
Postmaterialism, 71
Power, 4, 7, 8, 52, 70, 87, 92, 93, 103, 143, 147, 169–184, 195, 271, 320, 325, 327, 331, 332
Power distance, 4, 69, 74–79, 173, 180–182
Pragmatic interpretations, 54
Pragmatism, 70
Precision, 202, 208, 212, 277, 282, 311
Prejudice, 120, 156, 163, 328
Prejudice-reduction, 156
Presser, S., 58, 61, 73, 117, 205
Prestige, 89, 92, 103
Pre-suasion theory, 32, 41
Pre-testing, 100
Priming, 9, 59, 205, 332
Privacy, 38, 46, 77, 241
Probing, 54, 196–197, 199, 202–203, 209, 213, 223, 228–229, 233, 235, 237, 241–242, 279
Process, 2, 4, 7, 22, 24, 27, 30, 32, 35, 39, 40, 46, 47, 49, 52, 54, 55, 59, 61, 67, 76, 88, 89, 92, 95, 99, 116, 117, 139, 146,

Index 343

161–163, 169, 193, 196, 199, 213, 215, 249, 251, 271, 277, 283, 288, 297, 298, 306, 308, 309, 319, 329, 332
Pronouns (they), 130
Protesters, 308–310, 317
Protests, 185, 223, 308–310, 317, 318
Psychology, 1–3, 51, 201
Public opinion, 1, 5, 9, 117, 119, 121, 305–319, 325
Push-to-web, 41
Putnam, R., 173

Q
Qualitative research, 278
Quasi-filters, 257
Queer, 7, 193, 197, 198, 200, 202, 203, 207, 209, 213, 214, 224
Queerness, 206, 207
Queer theory, 325, 332
Questionnaires, 5, 6, 21, 23, 26, 32, 48, 50, 60, 61, 79, 89, 151, 169, 170, 181, 183, 230, 241, 242, 251, 254, 257, 258, 260, 262, 268, 270, 286
Questions, close-ended, 53
Question testing, 297
Quota sampling, 285

R
Race, 2, 5, 50, 67, 87, 105, 120, 151, 171, 224, 251, 260, 297, 316, 329
Race/ethnicity, 5, 172, 260, 262, 263, 283, 300
Racism, 117, 153–155, 318
Random digit dial (RDD), 16–18, 227
Rapport, 22, 223, 229, 240
Rapport-building, 32, 223, 228, 229, 235, 238
Rating scales, 74, 205, 282
Rational choice theory, 332
Reasoned action and planned behavior theory, 3, 29
Recall, 46–47, 49, 60, 96, 99
Reciprocation, 30, 37
Reflected appraisals, 53–55
Refugees, 118
Refusals, survey, 33, 34, 36, 147
Reliability, 8, 99, 214, 231, 248, 251, 259, 261, 262, 264, 268, 269, 271, 297, 330, 332
Religion, 2, 50, 70, 71, 119, 139, 172, 173, 229, 233, 242
Religiosity, 46, 50, 58, 60, 120, 152, 154
Religious conservatives, 328

Repetition, requests for, 280, 289, 293
Reporting bias, 97
Representation, 18, 42, 72, 119, 148, 150, 182, 183, 226
Representativeness, 152, 227
Republicans, 312
Requests, survey, 15, 16, 19, 21, 23, 24, 28–30, 32, 33, 35, 39, 41
Research artifacts, 101, 104
Research ethics violations, 278
Respond, 15, 17–19, 21–23, 25, 27–35, 37, 38, 50, 51, 53, 72, 77, 78, 97, 106, 143, 147, 152, 160, 165, 280, 282, 298, 318
Respondents, 2, 15, 45, 67, 95, 120, 151, 170, 224, 251, 297, 315, 326
Responding, survey, 6, 29, 39, 47, 49, 50, 53, 58, 59, 99, 144, 153, 173, 203, 219, 241
Response rates, 26, 79, 146, 147, 149, 170, 219, 242, 251, 259, 270, 328
Response, survey, 2, 3, 15–41, 79, 306
Restraint, 4, 70
Restrictionism, immigration, 157, 160, 161
Retention, 38, 278
Rich, 2, 169, 226, 297
Ridgeway, C., 90, 91, 93, 102, 103, 105, 249
Ridolfo, H., 219, 220, 223–226, 240
Risk, 34, 120, 138, 143, 164, 171, 181, 182, 194, 205, 220, 248, 278, 279, 287, 299, 327
Risk behaviors, 195, 205
Roles, 30, 34, 51, 55, 56, 59, 61, 70, 71, 116, 118–121, 131, 133, 139, 174, 213, 222, 253, 309, 331
Romania, 145, 146
Roper, 103, 279
Rosenberg, M., 56

S
Salience, 4, 7, 57–59, 120, 170, 306, 330
Saliva samples, 286, 298
Same-sex marriage, 328
Samples, survey, 17, 23, 28, 38
Sampling, survey, 254
Satisfaction, 70, 152
Satisficing, 75, 151, 152, 155, 157, 163
Saving face, 47
Scale, bipolar, 205, 209
Scales, 74, 156, 197, 210, 250, 269–271, 315, 316
Scale, unipolar, 250
Scarcity, 31, 37, 48, 71

Schaeffer, N.C., 8, 50, 52, 99, 101, 199, 204, 223, 227, 228, 277, 281, 287, 290, 294, 295, 298–300
Schooling, 6, 116, 119, 121, 130, 131, 133, 136
Schooling status-based, 120
Schooling, skills-based, 119
Schoua-Glusberg, A., 225, 296
Schuman, H., 3, 73, 101, 307, 325
Schwartz, S.H., 68, 70, 75, 77, 80
Scope conditions, 87, 88, 93–95, 97, 99, 100, 104–106, 330
Screener, 79, 96
Scripted, question, 279
Secularism, 2
Secularization, 4
Secularization theory, 325
Secular-rational, 4, 71, 72
Security, 19, 70, 71
Selection, 116, 126, 147, 254, 260, 281
Self-administered surveys, 31, 50, 54, 60, 78, 170
Self-administration, 22–24, 31, 38–40
Self-appraisal, 52, 53
Self-awareness, 99
Self-classification, 175, 176
Self-completion, 177, 181
Self-concept, 56, 329
Self-deception, 49, 60, 76
Self-direction, 70
Self-enhancement, 69, 173
Self-expression, 4, 71, 72
Self-fulfillment, 71
Self-identification, 262
Self-monitoring, 47
Self-perception, 205, 250
Self-presentation, 47, 200, 201, 206
Self-ratings, 8
Self-reports, 58, 76, 285
Self-transcendence, 70
Self-views, 4, 46, 49, 53–55, 60, 329–331
Sell, J., 90, 94, 102
Semantic interpretation, 329
Sensitive questions, 223, 242, 329
Sensitivity, question, 51, 60, 61, 170, 219, 221–224, 227, 228, 232, 233, 237, 238
Sentiments, 5, 6, 46, 98, 116–122, 131, 132
Serpe, R.T., 56–58
Sex, 8, 50, 100, 127, 219, 247, 328
Sex-typed, 253
Sexual, 7, 8, 46, 100–102, 193–215
Sexual identity question (SIQ), 8, 219–242

Sexuality, 2, 5, 50, 102, 193, 197, 213, 214, 224, 230, 237, 238, 248, 252, 255–257, 264, 265, 267, 268
Sexual orientation, disapproval of, 221
Sexual orientation, disclosure, 194
Sexual orientation, dis-identification of, 225
Short-term orientation, 70
Singer, E., 21, 32, 34, 35, 38
Slovakia, 146
Slovenia, 147
Smartphone, 39
Smith-Lovin, L., 249
Smyth, J.D., 7, 8, 18, 20, 35, 97, 219–242, 253–255, 283, 327, 330
Social desirability, 3–5, 46–51, 76–78, 95, 98, 99, 115, 117, 120, 121, 128, 132, 136, 139, 328
Social desirability bias, 4, 95, 98, 117, 120, 128, 130, 132, 136, 210
Social determinants, 119, 120
Social exchange, 4, 32, 34–36, 40, 41, 332
Social exchange theory, 4, 32, 34, 35, 325, 332
Social norms, 4, 20, 45–50, 68–70, 76, 77, 115, 252
Social status, 70, 75, 169, 329
Social validation, 31, 37
Social/natural, 71, 72
Socialization, 71, 117, 121, 201, 207
Socially-advantaged, 314
Socially-disadvantaged, 171, 314
Sociodemographic, 130, 131, 293, 296
Sociological, 1, 51, 116, 169, 331
Sociologists, 1–3, 5, 9, 10, 51, 132, 247–250, 306, 326, 332
Sociology, 1–10, 71, 81, 117, 284, 325, 328
Software, 16
South Korea, 176
Spain, 146
Spanish-speaking, 225
Sponsorship, 19, 21, 26, 27, 36
Standardized measurement, 280, 297
Standardized survey interviewing, 279, 298
Status beliefs, 91, 104, 106
Status characteristics, 5, 6, 87–106, 329, 330
Status characteristics and expectation states theory (SC-EST), 5, 87–106, 325, 327, 329, 332
Status differences, 89, 93
Status dynamics, 104
Status generalization process, 89
Stereotypes, 91, 203, 208, 278

Stets, J., 52, 55
Stigma, 6, 115–132, 220, 221, 226, 328
Stigmatization, 117, 119, 132, 221, 224, 328, 331
Stigmatized, 221, 222, 327, 328
Stimson, J.A., 307, 310, 312, 317, 319
Stimuli, 307, 311, 317
Stop-and-frisk, 310
Stouffer, S., 1
Straight-lining, 315
Stratification, 69, 183, 195
Structural symbolic interactionism, 52, 56, 332
Stryker, S., 52, 56–58, 306
Subconscious, 306
Subjective states, 61
Suburban/suburbs, 152
Sudman, S., 72, 205, 251
Suicidality, 102
Suriname, 118, 174, 177
Survey, 1, 15, 45, 67, 95, 115, 143, 170, 225, 254, 298, 315, 326
   artifacts, 3, 9, 48
   design, 16–18, 24, 25, 27, 32, 33, 35, 37, 39, 41, 48, 96, 232, 260, 305, 307, 308, 319, 328
   error, 2–4, 6, 67–81, 305, 306, 327, 331
   interview, 10, 46, 47, 52, 54, 60, 77, 79, 223, 241, 277, 280, 326
   interviewer, 54, 331
   methodology, 1–10, 50, 51, 57–59, 87–89, 97, 99, 100, 104, 106, 116, 169, 205, 214, 284, 305, 325–333
   modes, 18, 19, 26, 27, 78, 270
   onerous, 20, 21, 26
   participation, barriers to, 7, 79
   questions, 2, 6, 7, 21, 37, 49, 50, 58, 61, 76, 99, 122, 124, 151, 153, 155, 157, 169–171, 173, 183, 193, 196, 197, 199, 201, 203, 209, 212, 213, 277, 279, 280, 282, 288, 296–298, 306, 311, 328, 330, 331
   reports, 59, 330
   research, 1–3, 9, 46, 74, 87, 103, 104, 143, 147, 162, 172, 195, 197, 214, 219, 247–249, 277, 298, 305, 308, 318–320, 325–331
   research, critiques of, 80, 332
   response, 2, 3, 15–41, 67, 72, 73, 79, 131, 151, 170, 283, 284, 306
   sponsors, 16, 19, 20, 22
Surveying, 19, 35, 40
Surveys, federal, 23, 220
Surveys, short, 21, 24

Survival, 4, 71, 72
Sweden, 146–148, 157, 174
Switzerland, 120, 147, 148
Symbolic interactionism, 3, 4, 51–57, 332

T
Tailoring, 33
Taiwan, 181
Target population, 174, 279
Task-orientation, 95
Taxation/taxes, 122, 123, 150, 188
Technology, 18, 20, 21, 40, 227, 308
Telephone, 7, 8, 15, 18–20, 22, 25, 33, 37, 38, 220, 221, 224, 225, 227, 232, 240–242, 270, 286, 300, 327
Telephone-administered survey, 78
Television, 148–150, 155, 157, 163
Termination, survey, 21
Thailand, 176
Theory, 2, 17, 46, 70, 87, 116, 151, 330
Thye, S., 90, 91, 102, 106
Timbrook, J., 7, 219–242, 257, 327, 329
Time diaries, 59, 61
Timing, survey, 23
Tissue samples, 286
Tokens, speech, 8, 209, 282, 287, 288
Tolerance, 6, 69, 70, 74, 116, 118, 120, 121, 124, 125, 128–131, 134, 139, 173, 182
Total survey error (TSE), 2, 4, 6, 67, 72, 73, 80, 305
Tourangeau, R., 2, 46, 47, 58, 76, 98, 170, 212, 214, 222, 224, 225, 227, 251, 305, 306
Traditional, 4, 70–72, 120, 242, 268
Traditionalism, 76
Trans, transgender, 90, 224, 226, 249, 312
Transatlantic Trends Studies (TATS), 144–146
Transcriptions, 286–288, 297
Transcripts, 8, 199, 203, 231, 287
Transition, gender, 224
Triandis, H.C., 77, 173
True Score Theory, 116
Trump, Donald, 317
Trust, 8, 9, 20, 32, 34, 35, 38, 183, 284, 286, 289, 290, 293, 299, 300, 309, 327, 330
Turkey, 118, 145, 146
Turns-of-talk, 287
Tuskegee Syphilis Study, 330

U
Uncertainty avoidance, 4, 69, 72, 74, 76–78, 173, 178, 181, 182

Uncodable answers, 231, 232, 280, 281, 293
Unconscious, 49, 76, 122, 206
Underestimate, 143, 153
Underestimating, 144, 163
Underestimation, 132, 152, 156
Underestimators, 153, 156
Underrepresentation, 278, 286
Unemployment, 152, 154, 188
Unethical, 278
United States, 19, 77, 90, 91, 93, 102, 281, 316, 332
Unit-of-talk, 282, 286
Universalism, 70
University, 3–9, 19, 127, 128, 130, 193, 325–331
Utilitarian theory, 332
Utterance, 53, 282, 289

V
Validation, 31, 37, 76
Validity, 8, 101, 145, 214, 248, 250–255, 257, 260, 264, 265, 268, 269, 271, 297, 311, 316, 330, 332
Value frameworks, 4, 70
Values, 3, 21, 48, 67, 90, 117, 150, 172, 230, 247, 312, 329
Vandalism, 308, 317
Variability, 72, 73, 78, 80, 172, 179, 183, 184, 197, 205, 250, 279, 306
Variable error, 277
Variables, 25, 60, 73, 102, 126, 143, 170, 228, 254, 298, 313, 327
Variance, 8, 178, 179, 181, 259, 261, 262, 266, 269, 279, 289, 291, 294, 306
Variation, 6, 47, 49–51, 67, 96, 117, 118, 121, 122, 128, 136, 144, 145, 147, 161, 171, 172, 179, 184, 195, 203, 210, 249, 250, 252–254, 259–261, 264, 271, 283, 284, 306, 314, 317

Vehicle, 277, 280, 297, 308, 310
Venezuela, 176
Veracity, 116, 122
Verification, 52, 55, 254, 259, 263
Vignettes, 96, 100, 250
Violence, 202, 308, 317
Voice, 22, 38, 46, 202, 279, 285, 331
Voting, 47, 50, 53, 54, 119

W
Wealth, 77, 314, 315
Web-push, 41
Webster, M., 90, 93, 94, 102, 103
Welfare, 70, 188
Well-being, 173, 182, 195
Whites, 171, 278, 283, 284, 293, 296, 316, 332
Wilders, G., 119
Women, 7, 8, 91, 93, 95, 96, 100, 101, 105, 134, 138, 155, 171, 177, 181, 193, 211, 213, 225, 248, 250–253, 259–263, 265–269, 271, 278, 289, 330
Work, 5, 6, 8–10, 29, 31–33, 40, 41, 47, 56, 58–61, 71, 72, 76, 79, 81, 89, 97, 100, 101, 106, 116, 117, 119–122, 126, 131–134, 148, 149, 152–154, 183, 227, 241, 249, 251, 253, 257, 266, 269, 270, 279, 286, 296, 299, 305, 307, 330, 332
World Values Survey, 75, 76
Wozniak, K.H., 9, 305–319, 330, 331

X
Xenophobia, 120, 151, 153, 163, 327

Y
Yugoslavia, 175